Gender Equality in a Global Perspective

Gender Equality in a Global Perspective looks to discuss whether gender equality can be adopted as it has been defined in international documents anywhere, or whether it needs to be adapted in a more local context; discuss which factors and perspectives need to be taken into account when adapting gender equality to specific contexts; suggest research approaches for studies on whether a universal (Western) concept of gender equality fits in certain specific contexts; and finally suggests challenges to the existing interpretation of gender equality (e.g., theory of intersectionality) and the development of legal and policy framework.

This book is situated within the tradition of comparative gender studies. While most other such books take up and compare various ways of implementing (or not implementing) gender equality, this book studies and compares whether or not (and to what extent) a specific definition of gender equality (GE) could be adopted by various nations. Thus, all chapter contributors will engage with the same definition of GE, which will be presented within the book, and discuss the possibilities and constraints related to applying such a definition in their particular national context.

Readers will learn about the problems of applying a universal concept of gender equality and the possible reasons for and modes of adapting gender equality to different contexts. *Gender Equality in a Global Perspective* looks to maintain a critical and reflexive stance towards the issues raised and will seek to present multiple perspectives and open-ended answers. As such it hopes to contribute to the international discussion of human rights more broadly and gender equality specifically.

The intended audience is not limited only to but will include policy makers, scholars and students with an interest in gender issues, organizational theory, political science, human development, policy analysis, globalization and other management sub-disciplines.

Anders Örtenblad is Professor of Organization and Leadership at Nord University, Norway.

Raili Marling is Associate Professor of American Studies at the University of Tartu, Estonia.

Snježana Vasiljević is Professor of European Law and Fundamental Rights, European Anti-discrimination Law, EU Law and Gender at the Zagreb University, Croatia.

Routledge Advances in Management and Business Studies

For a full list of titles in this series, please visit www.routledge.com/series/ SE0305

Gender Equality in a Global Perspective

Edited by Anders Örtenblad,
Raili Marling and Snježana Vasiljević

Routledge
Taylor & Francis Group
New York London

First published 2017
by Routledge

711 Third Avenue, New York, NY 10017
2 Park Square, Milton Park, Abingdon, Oxfordshire OX14 4RN

Routledge is an imprint of the Taylor & Francis Group, an informa business

First issued in paperback 2018

Library of Congress Cataloging in Publication Data
Names: Ortenblad, Anders, editor. | Marling, Raili, 1973– editor. | Vasiljevic, Snjezana, editor.
Title: Gender equality in a global perspective / edited by Anders Ortenblad, Raili Marling, and Snjezana Vasiljevic.
Description: 1 Edition. | New York : Routledge, 2017. | Series: Routledge advances in management and business studies ; 68 | Includes bibliographical references and index.
Identifiers: LCCN 2016038473 | ISBN 9781138193246 (hardback : alk. paper) | ISBN 9781315639505 (ebook)
Subjects: LCSH: Sex role. | Sex discrimination against women. | Feminism. | Human rights.
Classification: LCC HQ1075 .G463194 2017 | DDC 305.3—dc23
LC record available at https://lccn.loc.gov/2016038473

ISBN: 978-1-138-19324-6 (hbk)
ISBN: 978-0-367-02652-3 (pbk)

Typeset in Sabon
by Apex CoVantage, LLC

Contents

Figures and Tables

Figures

Tables

Contributor Presentations

Mohamed Arafa is Professor of Law at Alexandria University Law School (Egypt); Adjunct Professor of Law at Indiana University McKinney Law School (USA); Ph.D. from Indiana University McKinney Law School and LL.M. from University of Connecticut Law School. Now, he is a Visiting Professor at University of Brasilia Law School. His scholarship is about International and Comparative Law and Islamic Law.

Colleen E. Arendt is an Assistant Professor of Communication at Fairfield University. Her research interests within organizational communication include gender, specifically gendered careers and sport, and strategic communication, specifically critical approaches to crisis communication. She has published in the *International Journal of Communication, Communication Studies* and *Cases in Public Relations: Translating Ethics into Action*.

Kara Beavis (MA, Grad Cert, BA) is a gender and violence against women specialist in Sydney. She is a Ph.D. candidate at Sydney University and sessional lecturer in gender analysis of public policy at Flinders University. Kara has worked in women's policy management roles in Sydney, Brisbane, London and Johannesburg. She works at Australia's National Research Organisation for Women's Safety.

Aleksandar Bošković is Professor of Anthropology at the University of Belgrade, Serbia, and Director of Research at the Institute of Social Sciences in Belgrade, where he is also Head of the Centre for Political Studies and Public Opinion Research. His main research interests are history and theory of anthropology, rationality, myth and religion, and gender.

Patrice M. Buzzanell is a Distinguished Professor of Communication in the Brian Lamb School of Communication and in the School of Engineering Education by courtesy at Purdue University. She serves as the Chair and Director of the Susan Bulkeley Butler Center for Leadership Excellence. Her scholarly interests center on career, praxis and resilience.

Ahmed El-Ashry is Teaching Assistant at Alexandria University Faculty of Law (Egypt). He is currently enrolled in the Masters of Law Program at

Alexandria Law School. Also, he participated in the 2014 Vienna Moot Court Competition. Ahmad focuses his research in Islamic law, Economics, and Philosophy and History of Law.

Alma Espino is an economist. She is Professor of Gender and Economics at Faculty of Economics Sciences and Administration, University of the Republic, Uruguay. Her main research interests are gender, labor and income distribution. She is the author or coauthor of several journal articles in refereed and non-refereed publications, working papers and participated in the drafting of several book chapters.

Sonia M. Frías holds a Ph.D. in sociology. She is a researcher at the Regional Center for Multidisciplinary Research (National Autonomous University of Mexico). Her main research interests are violence against women and children, gender equality and victim's access to justice.

Suzana Ignjatović is Senior Research Associate at the Institute of Social Sciences in Belgrade. Her main research interests are public policy, gender, family, and sociological theory. She has done academic and policy-oriented research on gender-related topics. She was a member of the Council for Gender Equality of the Government of the Republic of Serbia.

Raili Marling is Associate Professor of American Studies at the University of Tartu, Estonia. Her research interests include gendered discourses in literature, gendered affects under neoliberalism, and gender in the post-socialist context. She is a managing editor of *Aspasia: International Yearbook of Central, Eastern and Southeastern European Women's and Gender History* and *Ariadne Lõng*, Estonian journal of gender studies.

Anuradha Mundkur, Associate Director Gender Consortium, Flinders University, has extensive practical experience in the fields of gender and development, which informs her research and teaching. She has worked on several gender projects funded by the Department of Foreign Affairs and Trade (Australia Aid) in the Indo-Pacific region focusing on gender mainstreaming, women's leadership and gender-based violence.

Anders Örtenblad is Professor of Organization and Leadership at Nord University, Norway. He is the editor-in-chief of *The Learning Organization* (Emerald) and has edited several books, published by Edward Elgar Publishing, Routledge and Sage. One of his many research interests is whether it is possible and preferable to adopt the same version of a particular concept in different contexts.

Funmi Josephine Para-Mallam is a professor of gender and development at the National Institute for Policy and Strategic Studies, Kuru, Nigeria. She is a social justice activist serving as National Coordinator of a women's NGO running a Safe Harbour Initiative for vulnerable women and girls. Her research interests include gender-based violence, peace and security, religion and development and governance.

Snježana Vasiljević, (M.Phil. Cantab; Ph.D.) is a professor of European Law and Fundamental Rights, European Anti-discrimination Law, EU Law and Gender (Jean Monnet Module) at the Zagreb University. She specialized in gender equality at the Cambridge University, LSE, Liverpool University, Columbia University NY and UCLA. She is an expert of the EU Fundamental Rights Agency and the Council of Europe.

Archana Preeti Voola is an Ewing Postdoctoral Research Scholar at The University of Sydney, Australia. Her primary research interests include poststructural feminist analyses, sociology of gender, social policy and poverty alleviation. Her teaching experience spans sociology, international development, social policy, social work and research methods. She co-chairs the international academic network, Academics Stand Against Poverty (ASAP), Oceania Chapter.

Yan Zhao holds a Ph.D. degree in sociology and is associate professor of social work at Nord University, Norway. Her research interests include migration studies, critical race and whiteness studies, gender studies and adoption studies. She has also theoretical interests in feminist methodology, transnational feminism, postcolonial theories, intersectionality and Actor Network Theories.

Preface

Another long journey has come to an end as we hand in the finalized manuscript for this edited book. It has been a very stimulating project, but sometimes also exhausting. Anders took the initiative in starting the book project a couple of years ago, and invited Raili and Snježana, both with much more professional experience in the area of gender equality than Anders had. Thereafter we have met quite often, mainly in emails but sometimes also via Skype. So far we have not met AFK (away from keyboard) but hope to do so as soon as possible, and celebrate that our project has been finalized.

Nor have we met many of the contributors to the book AFK, but we very much hope to meet you too in the near future. We believe that intercultural meetings are one way of making the world a better place, and hopefully the content of the book will also help in that ambition. Our authors are not just from all over the world, but they are also men and women. This, we hope, in a small way shows that gender equality can be achieved when men and women together undertake the difficult process of change.

We would like to first and foremost thank the authors who contributed to the book. We are grateful to you for your support and patience in the often stressful editing process, especially in the finalization stage. We also thank colleagues who helped us with finding contributors from such a wide range of countries.

We are also deeply indebted to the support of our editors at Routledge, especially Brianna Ascher and David Varley, without whom we would not have been able to finish the work as efficiently.

Raili Marling's work for this study was supported by the Estonian Research Council (PUT192) and by the European Union through the European Regional Development Fund (Centre of Excellence in Estonian Studies).

Anders Örtenblad, Stockholm, Sweden,
Raili Marling, Tartu, Estonia, and
Snježana Vasiljević, Rijeka, Croatia
August 2016

Part I
Background and Introduction

1 Introduction

Different Dimensions of Gender Equality in a Comparative Perspective

Snježana Vasiljević, Raili Marling and Anders Örtenblad

Introduction

This comparative book gathers ten case studies from different cultures to interrogate whether a universal (Western) concept of gender equality (GE), such as expressed in different international documents (in our case specifically in the UN Convention on the Elimination of all Forms of Discrimination Against Women [CEDAW]), can be applied in different specific contexts according to the same broad legal definition or whether local adaptations are needed. Primarily, we highlight the need to discuss factors and perspectives that need to be taken into account in such location-specific adaptations, especially in the application of laws and international norms. International norms may be added to national legislations but they need not be enforceable in exactly the same way. Slogans of universal human rights, including GE, need to be supplemented with localized discussions of adaptation and application. The book will also highlight challenges to the existing interpretation of GE in the context of intersectionality. We hope that the results of this comparative research can be used as a basis for further recommendations in the development of legal and policy frameworks in different countries and international organizations. The articles included in the volume also suggest avenues for further research.

To create a sound basis for the following volume, the present introduction will try to detect and critically assess crucial changes in concepts of equality on the doctrinal as well as the institutional, pragmatic level. The introduction will first describe the conceptual difficulties related to the notion of GE in different waves of feminist thought. Special attention is given to the concept of intersectionality and transnational feminist challenges to the previous universalist language of Western feminism. The introduction provides an overview of feminist legal theory and an in-depth look at the CEDAW definition of gender equality and the EU gender equality framework that have both had an immense role in shaping international GE discourses. Finally, we outline the starting point for the discussion in the subsequent chapters and explain the choice of countries analyzed.

Gender Equality

The feminist and legal questions of gender equality cannot be separated from broader social developments in the 20th century, such as changing patterns of labor force participation, technological innovations, changes in social ideologies, including gender ideologies. It is these changes that frequently guide interpretations of the concept of equality and equal rights. Gender is in this study treated as a social construct, the social meanings given to biological sexual difference. It is gender that defines the roles, rights, responsibilities and obligations of women and men. The role of women and men has always been interpreted in terms of social expectations about behaviors that are considered appropriate for both genders. The norms are not biologically but socially determined. In other words, one becomes a man or a woman fitting their society's expectations in the process of socialization. As famously posited by the French feminist philosopher Simone de Beauvoir (1972, p. 267), "one is not born but becomes a woman." According to Mikkola (2011, p. 68), "females become women through a process whereby they acquire feminine traits and learn feminine behaviour." The same applies to men as well. In other words, women and men are the "intended or unintended product[s] of a social practice" (Haslanger, 1995, p. 97). There are scholars who argue that biological difference is also socially constructed (e.g., Butler, 1990; Laqueur, 1990).

Men and women, however, are not just socialized into different roles, but their roles have a different social status, as noted already by de Beauvoir. Gender difference is also a hierarchy in which practices and behaviors associated with men have historically been valued higher than those linked to women, resulting in women's disadvantaged status in all spheres of society. Feminist authors have called attention to this for centuries, but most emphatically in the 20th century when different strands of feminist politics and philosophy have offered different explanations of gender imbalance and equally different visions for correcting it.

Feminism has been on the legal agenda for over a century already, and has gone through several phases, focusing first on sameness, then differences and finally diversity. The first and second phases are characterized by the discussion on differences between men and women, and the third phase by focusing on differences between women, multiple identities and multiple oppression. It seems that feminism has come to its fourth phase, which is characterized by thinking about goals, subjects and feminist strategies. The core question of today's debate in feminism is whether women are still the only object of feminism, whether the goal of feminism is achieving substantive equality for women and how to achieve it. In other words, feminists grapple with the question of whether the focus of feminism is the elimination of all forms of discrimination against women (like it is legally described in the CEDAW, the document we use extensively in the book) in order to avoid gender imperialism and the false universalism which produces distortion and marginalization of female experience in cases of minority women and strengthens the binary understanding of gender identities.[1]

Feminist legal theorists have produced numerous criticisms of existing laws but there is no one single interpretation of what the transformation of law and legal standards should look like. Therefore, it is not surprising that different countries in the world have different understandings of gender equality as well as different interpretations of national law and policy measures adopted within the general international gender equality framework (e.g., defined by the CEDAW). In general, in feminist theory, there is also no joint standpoint on how the internationally adopted policy measures should be interpreted and implemented. Different approaches have been offered by liberal, cultural, radical, postmodern and intersectional feminists.

The focus of liberal feminism was the removal of discriminatory practices in everyday life as well as from legal documents. Despite the fact that in the 1960s and 1970s, liberal feminists created some positive changes in the position of women, certain obstacles in achieving substantive equality also became obvious. Liberal feminism, also known as equality feminism, believes that men and women are born equal and thus deserve equal treatment without any hindrance. This is the type of feminism that has been most vocally associated with GE in the public sphere, from suffrage struggle to the fight against gender discrimination in the workplace. Liberal feminism does not seek to challenge the current social structures and practices, but to open them to women. As the Australian ecofeminist Val Plumwood (1993, p. 27) has suggested, this position "attempted to fit women uncritically into a masculine pattern of life and masculine model of humanity and culture which is presented as gender neutral." An additional challenge was the lack of attention to differences between women, especially race and sexuality, as critical race theorists, postcolonial and lesbian feminists pointed out. The mainstream liberal feminists were frequently blind to their own privilege (see e.g., Lorde, 1984).

While the liberal feminist strategy was very successful in questioning discriminatory laws and irrational classifications, that strategy was unsuccessful in challenging laws that provided justification for a different treatment of men and women on the grounds of biologically determined differences. For example, the principle of equal treatment is hardly applicable in a situation when there is no man as a point of comparison, such as in cases of pregnancy. To put it more plainly, liberal feminists insisted on gender neutrality. However, if the law mirrors mainly male experiences, women will not benefit from gender-neutral laws. In other words, equal treatment in such cases does not lead to a substantive equality; actually in most cases it results in more inequalities.

Legal concepts are imperfect, mostly subjective and partial. Feminist legal scholars believe that the subjectivity and partiality of legal concepts mirror male dominance. In other words, gender-neutral rules are created to maintain male dominance over women (MacKinnon, 1989, p. 114).[2] Sameness does not mean equality but male dominance and female subordination (MacKinnon, 1989, p. 33). The legal system that pretends to be gender-neutral does not necessarily serve the needs of both sexes equally well. This is reflected in women's distrust in the justice system and, for example, their reluctance to report sexual violence. Carol Smart (1989, p. 69) also claims that women should be careful in the application of law since it is not gender-neutral and advantages men. Therefore, she insists on feminism as a new form of knowledge which will offer a new reality for women, without the legal methods created by men.

Cultural feminism appeared in the late 1970s as a reaction to the failure of liberal feminism to achieve substantive equality. The idea of cultural feminism was not to assimilate women into a male-dominated society and adjust them to the male-oriented norms. Instead, the goal was to strengthen the institutional structures to support women's needs. However, cultural feminism was criticized because emphasizing differences as valuable sometimes may lead to discrimination (e.g., part-time work agreements or genuine occupational requirements justified by the protection of women's supposedly sensitive nature indirectly discriminate against women and perpetuate women's subordinate position).

For many contemporary feminists, even the definition of the concept of the woman is problematic. Although the concept of woman is a central point of departure for all feminists, different schools of feminist thought interpret it differently. Starting from the 1970s, there has been increasing discomfort with the universal definition of the woman and the "overdetermination of male supremacy" (Alcoff, 1988, p. 405).

A new approach is offered by postmodern feminists who do not place women in the center of feminist theory or political action. Postmodern feminism, as a reaction to previous feminisms, does not represent a single theory and does not believe that there is a unique solution for the oppression of women. Instead, postmodernists believe that individuals consist of multiple identities which "overlap, intersect and even contradict each other" (Bartlett, 1994, p. 14). "Postmodern feminism made its entry into the law by way of the critical legal studies movement (CLS), a loose coalition of left-leaning academic scholars who, beginning in the 1970s argued that law is intermediate, non-objective, hierarchical, self-legitimating, overly-individualistic and morally impoverished. . . . Feminist scholars have incorporated ideas of CLS and tried to transform them into the core of a constructive feminist practice" (Bartlett, 1994, p. 13). However, they also criticized the CLS movement for its failure to develop a positive program that could survive its own critique.

Intersectionality offers an alternative challenge to the universalist approaches to gender and thus invites us to look critically also at GE and whether and how its definition is adaptable to local contexts not just de jure but also de facto. This is extremely important from the standpoint of different experiences and different identities (e.g., black women, gay people of different ethnic origins, women with disabilities, etc.) who face multiple discrimination and whose position needs to be analyzed intersectionally (Crenshaw, 1991). In her work in critical legal theory and critical race theory, Crenshaw (1989, p. 149) argued that "because the intersectional experience is greater than the sum of racism and sexism, any analysis that does not take intersectionality into account cannot sufficiently address the particular manner in which Black women are subordinated." Crenshaw's (1994, p. 1244) utilization of intersectionality "highlights the need to account for multiple grounds of identity when considering how the social world is constructed." Courts are usually using the so-called single-axis approach, which makes the hierarchy of equality visible and actually shows that some groups enjoy preferential treatment while others remain marginalized or even invisible. Black feminists criticized existing feminist theory and critical legal studies for race essentialism in feminist theories and lack of gender awareness in critical race theories (Crenshaw, 1989; Harris, 1990). Black women have traditionally worked outside the home and their number had significantly exceeded the share of white women in the working class. The fact that black women must work is in conflict with the norms that women should not work, which often created personal and emotional relationship problems. Minority women who fail to adapt to "appropriate" gender roles and who do not fit social stereotypes are described as a threat to mainstream society's system of values. This is only one aspect of intersectionality which cannot be understood by analyzing the traditional patriarchal patterns rooted in the white experience.

The theory of intersectionality mostly criticized existing feminist theory for being founded on white women's experience. However, white women also have multiple intersecting identities and feminist theory recognized only the part of women's identity common to the majority of the female population. Previous feminist thought did not recognize the experiences of disabled, lesbian, ethnic or immigrant women. For example, focusing on two dimensions of male violence against women—battering and rape—proves intersectional discrimination on grounds of sex, race or ethnicity.[3] If we focus on the European context, the examples can be found in recent European history of Balkan wars (1991–1995). Frequent ethnic rape was proof of "superiority" of the army, which dominated over someone else's territory (Vasiljević, 2009, p. 175). Such rapes are never shown from the multidimensional experience of women's oppression, but only as sexual violence.

As can be seen from above, the meanings given to gender difference vary greatly even in feminist theories and the theories approach the fact of gender inequality differently. However, what hinders the political and legal attempts at securing GE is frequently the wide misinterpretation of the word "equality" itself. Many of the problems arise from the application of the principle borrowed from Aristotle according to which "justice consists in treating like cases alike and different cases differently" (Jaggar, 1990, p. 239). In the case of men and women the question of similarity and difference has been anything but solved, as can be seen from the brief introduction to divergent feminist views above. Gender difference exists, yet it can be equally perilous to overemphasize it or ignore it (Minow, 1990, p. 49).

The question is not an innocent academic disagreement but also plays an important role in politics. As Joan Scott (1990, p. 144) has argued:

> Placing equality and difference in an antithetical relationship has, then, a double effect. It denies the way in which difference has long figured in political notions of equality and it suggests that sameness is the only ground on which equality can be claimed. It thus puts feminists in an impossible position, for as long as we argue within terms of discourse set up by this opposition we grant the current conservative premise that since women cannot be identical to men in all respects, they cannot expect to be equal to them.

This has derailed many national efforts at creating gender equality legislation (e.g., famously in the case of the US Equal Rights Amendment). The only way we can overcome this bind is to deny the false opposition of equality and difference, and to remind the public that the antonym of equality is inequality.

Two (interrelated) conceptions of equality have been important in the legal context: one in which equality is defined in terms of equal formal rights to men and women; and the other in which equality has been related to equal access to welfare and equal opportunities. The first conception is formal and legal, the second mainly material and social. Other authors have differentiated between the equality of outcome and equality of opportunity. In the first it is assumed that women and men should have equal political representation and equal salaries; the second that they should be guaranteed equal opportunities to compete for political positions or jobs that would give them equal salaries. While GE policies initially sought to address the former, they have increasingly started to stress the latter (Kantola, 2010, p. 6). Johanna Kantola (2010, p. 6) also perceives a shift "from theories of distributive justice to theories of recognition as fundamental to equality." In other words, while the initial GE policies sought to ensure the just distribution of social resources between men and women, they have increasingly moved towards identity politics. Fraser (2010) suggests that both redistribution and recognition were crucial in addressing inequality. However, in her recent work, she believes that the change of emphasis towards recognition has left economic questions under-analyzed in today's feminism (see Fraser, 2013). Contemporary feminist theories believe that law cannot be interpreted as a scholarly field deprived of moral or political context, independent of social reality (Shukla et al., 2015, p. 45).

Today the universalist language of earlier feminist theorizing has been challenged by transnational feminism and by intersectional feminism. As postcolonial theorists have shown, many well-meaning feminist texts have been inherently Western-centered, that is, presenting West and its social norms as normative for all cultures. This has been critiqued famously by Chandra Talpade Mohanty (1984) who, in her analysis of feminist texts of the period, demonstrated the representation of non-Western women as monolithically traditional and victimized, as a convenient Other against which Western feminism can define its own superiority. This work often depends on "sanctioned ignorance" from the West (Spivak, 1988, p. 287) and helps to perpetuate the power difference between West and non-West. Perhaps even more crucially, the non-Western women are made into silent objects of Western feminist observation and knowledge-creation. Non-Western women are not allowed to speak for themselves, but are being interpreted by Westerners. This critique of unequal access to knowledge creation continues to be an important argument in transnational feminism today (see e.g., Suchland, 2011, p. 854). Our book is aware of this criticism and it is for this reason that we have sought out authors from different cultural locations to offer their perspective on their cultures, instead of imposing a uniform Western analytical framework on everybody. We want to escape the typical transhistorical Western approach that locks non-Western societies into an eternal process of catching up—but because they are trying to catch up to the Western model that need not fit them, they will always remain secondary to the West (Koobak & Marling, 2014; Sarkar, 2004).

Legal systems have thus been facing a great challenge in dealing with GE. Equal formal rights are based on the philosophical supposition that men and women are born equal. Equality in this sense is a fundamental condition: as a result, men and women should be equal before the law. Although this position has a long tradition, it was not totally taken for granted before the re-activation of feminist movements in the Western countries in the 1960s. Feminist legal theory has provided the most consistent work on how this is to be achieved.

The above discussion shows, however, that the understanding of GE has not been uniform within feminist theory and feminist legal theory and that past two decades have seen the vocal critique of both a simplified view of male-female difference and also of the possibility of devising universal legal remedies that would not perpetuate the power differential between the West and the rest. Different authors also caution about excessive optimism about the mere formal granting of rights that need not effect meaningful change (Smart, 1989, p. 144). Mitchell (1987, p. 26) also concurs, suggesting that "equal rights are an important tip of an iceberg that goes far deeper."

GE in International Law

GE has been defined as a central developmental goal by the United Nations (UN), World Bank, Organization for Economic Co-operation and Development (OECD), International Labor Organization (ILO) and many other international organizations. Usually, the term GE means women having the same opportunities in life as men. However, equal opportunities do not necessarily lead to equality of outcomes. Gender inequalities exist because of both outright discrimination in society and persistent gender stereotypes, difficulties with regulating the private sphere, the segregation of the labor market, etc. Primarily, gender inequalities start in families and spread through the institutional structures and in most cases they dominate in the labor market (e.g., because of the difficulty of balancing work and family life, which continues to be seen as the woman's responsibility in most countries). But inequalities do not stop at this point; they reach all aspects of education, practices and stereotypes, which leads to the disempowerment of women. Thus, equal rights are an important concept that needs to be established in international legal practice.

The international organization that first tackled GE as an international issue was the UN. According to the Convention to Eliminate All Forms of Discrimination Against Women (CEDAW), "equality is the cornerstone of every democratic society that aspires to social justice and human rights." To this day, the most universally accepted instrument for realizing GE and influencing cultural and traditional definition of gender roles and family relations is the CEDAW. CEDAW was adopted in 1979 by the UN General Assembly. CEDAW represents an international bill of rights for women. It introduced a duty for states to implement substantive equality for women. The critics argued that the existing UN human rights agreements were deficient regarding the protection and promotion of women's human rights and this resulted in the adoption of the Declaration on the Elimination of Discrimination against Women in 1967. However, the Commission on the Status of Women considered it necessary to adopt a legally binding instrument which would give a normative effect to the provisions of the Declaration. Therefore, CEDAW is a product of the growing need to deal with discrimination against women in a comprehensive way (UN Women, n.d.).

CEDAW consists of a preamble and 30 articles, and defines what constitutes discrimination against women and sets up an agenda for national action to end such discrimination. CEDAW defines discrimination against women as ". . . any distinction, exclusion or restriction made on the basis of sex which has the effect or purpose of impairing or nullifying the recognition, enjoyment or exercise by women, irrespective of their marital status, on a basis of equality of men and women, of human rights and fundamental freedoms in the political, economic, social, cultural, civil or any other field" (*Convention to Eliminate All Forms of Discrimination Against Women*). 187 countries (out of 194) have ratified the treaty. Six countries have not ratified CEDAW, including the United States, Iran, Somalia, Sudan and two small Pacific Island nations (Palau and Tonga).

CEDAW continues to be a major tool in international GE campaigns. However, when we look at legal literature, we see quite a number of challenges to the effectiveness of CEDAW as a tool of promoting equality of women and men de facto. There is a clash between the normative framework and social practice. Therefore, many feminists have criticized international law in general and CEDAW in particular, arguing that international law is blind to female experience (Charlesworth et al., 1991, p. 644). Mostly, criticisms are directed against the disinterest of international law in substantive equality issues, its normative structure and problem that some states are reluctant to ratify treaties or usually make reservations on them. This is highly problematic in terms of enforcement of human rights. Moreover, international law is focused on the public sphere in the area of political and social rights rather than the private sphere (Brooks, 2002, p. 345). This proves to be very problematic in the context of gender since women's roles in the domestic sphere frequently hinder their participation in the public sphere.

The central feminist argument in criticizing CEDAW is that it is assimilationist and it is framed according to the male model as the dominant norm (Brooks, 2002, p. 347). According to CEDAW, there is no need to change anything except stereotypes and formal barriers to access (Brooks, 2002, p. 351). Another argument comes from the theory of intersectionality, which criticizes feminism which cannot be adequately applied to women of different ethnicities, cultural or class identities (Crenshaw, 1989, p. 154). CEDAW observes and treats women as a homogenous group (Otto, 2010, p. 357). Essentially, CEDAW offers only de jure equality, and the implementation of equality is not assured. However, despite the criticisms it is also important to stress that "CEDAW provides a strong normative basis for overcoming the ideological barrier of traditionalist culture and religion to women's equality in all these contexts, predicating a hierarchy of values in which women's right to equality prevails over discriminatory traditionalist rules or practices" (Raday, 2012, p. 520).

CEDAW has not been the only international attempt to establish universal rules about GE. In Europe where the clash between traditions, societal trends and recently established legal concepts has meant that GE was sometimes implemented, sometimes not, there was a need to establish a clear GE concept. The general principle of equal treatment between men and women was established in the Treaty of Rome of 1957 (Article 119 of the 1957 European Economic Community (EEC) Treaty) and now this principle is prescribed in Article 157 of the Treaty on the Functioning of the European Union (TFEU), which is recognized as a fundamental norm of EU law (Treaty on the Functioning of the European Union, 2007). The principle of GE is prescribed by Article 23 EU Charter of Fundamental Rights, which establishes that the equality between men and women must be ensured in all areas, including employment, work and pay (Charter of Fundamental Rights of the European Union, 2000). The EU Charter of Fundamental Rights represents a comprehensive catalogue of fundamental rights and is legally binding since 2009. For four decades, EU actions in this field of discrimination were limited to sex discrimination in the workplace. With the entry into force of the Amsterdam Treaty, the EU obtained a clear legal basis for combating discrimination, which is currently enshrined in Article 19 of the TFEU on a number of grounds other than sex. The principle of non-discrimination is also established in Article 21 of the EU Charter of Fundamental Rights on the grounds of sex, race, color, ethnic or social origin, genetic features, language, religion or belief, political or any other opinion, membership of a national minority, property, birth, disability, age or sexual orientation. The general principle of equality between men and women was the legal basis for the adoption of numerous GE directives and case law of the Court of Justice of the European Union.

However, despite the EU's comprehensive equality framework, women are still discriminated against on the basis of their sex and underrepresented in decision-making. By comparing the international human rights law standards with EU law, it might be concluded that EU law does not offer the same level of protection as either the European Convention or UN standards (Vasiljević, 2015a, p. 61). Another issue is that in the EU there is the normative deficiency of anti-discrimination law. It is limited to the market mentality and does not go beyond the EU competences. "It is committed to a normative vision of market equality and unwittingly reflective of patterns of market exclusion by lumping disengaged individuals together in groups, which are in fact merely sets" (Somek, 2011, p. 157). Furthermore, the EU equality concept is founded on the prerequisite that a society is cleansed of prejudice and exclusion. There is a fear that "anti-discrimination law can become a very blunt tool of social protection in the hands of a business-friendly judiciary" (Somek, 2011, p. 158). Also, some scholars note that EU legislation may prove to be ineffective because it does not provide comprehensive legal protection based on a combination of multiple experiences (Vasiljević, 2015b, p. 186).

CEDAW, which is the source of international law, is the framework for mainstreaming women's rights in all structures of daily life. The CEDAW framework defines two critical principles: the principle of non-discrimination and the principle of equality. CEDAW provides the equality of opportunity and the equality of results. The equality of opportunity is a formal equality which requires all laws to have provisions on GE. But this formal equality is not enough for the achievement of equality in practice. States should provide conditions that actually enable women to exercise and enjoy their rights to equal opportunities.

Enforcement mechanisms provided by CEDAW are outlined in Article 29 and Article 18. The first mechanism is the interstate procedure, which outlines that all conflicts dealing with the interpretation of CEDAW have to be arbitrated. If the conflict cannot be resolved during arbitration, it is sent to the International Court of Justice, the decisions of which are binding for states. The problem is that usually a state is reluctant to bring a claim against another state. Another strong deterrent is a fear of retaliation acts. Furthermore, state parties can use a reservation to avoid having to answer to interstate claims.

The second mechanism is state reporting (Article 18). States who sign CEDAW are obliged to submit an initial report within the first year of ratifying CEDAW and must submit further reports every four years. The purpose of the reporting mechanism is to monitor what progress the government has made in implementing CEDAW into domestic law. State reports are reviewed by the Committee for the Elimination of All Forms of Discrimination against Women, which was established under Article 17. The Committee consists of 23 independent experts who are nominated and elected to CEDAW by states. The Committee issues general recommendations, but they do not have the authority to issue sanctions.

The relationship between international law and domestic law depends on the principles of dualism and monism. In a case of conflict between domestic and international law, in national legal orders that recognize the dualist approach, the domestic courts would apply international law. In contrast, monism invokes the supremacy of international law within the national legal system and describes the individual as a subject of international law.

In Europe there are two separate supranational levels of human rights protection. The first is the European Convention of Human Rights (ECHR), operating under the auspices of the Council of Europe (CoE), and with the European Court of Human Rights (ECtHR) as the final judicial body to hear and settle alleged violations of the Convention by the CoE's 47 member states. The second is the Treaty on the Functioning of the European Union (TFEU) and the Charter of Fundamental Rights of the European Union (EU Charter) that was promulgated by the 2009 Lisbon Treaty. However, the legal order of the EU, interpreted by the Court of Justice of the European Union (CJEU), creates a new arena for the further development of fundamental rights protection.

Given that all EU member states are also members of the Council of Europe, it would appear that there is no need for two sources of European human rights law enforced by two separate legal institutions. Both European courts represent enforcement mechanisms for the implementation of European non-discrimination and equal opportunities standards. Like CEDAW, the ECHR as a basic legal foundation for the ECtHR judgments is a source of international law, and its applicability in national legal orders differs from state to state. State parties of the ECHR are obliged to enforce ECtHR judgments of a financial nature. The ECtHR also examines domestic law and policies. For this reason, some consider the European Court of Human Rights to perform the function of a constitutional court for Europe. In the EU it is very important to emphasize the supreme character of EU law. This means that you cannot depart from the EU law by a subsequent national law. The CJEU has also been clear that EU law takes precedence over all other claims of international law and the decisions of other international tribunals. Due to this supreme character, EU law can be directly applicable. The principle of direct effect of EU law enables an individual of a member state to rely on, for example, the treaties before national tribunals and national courts. A European norm can have a direct effect when it meets three requirements: namely, the text has to be sufficiently clear, unconditional and not requiring other legal actions.

The Court of Justice has jurisdiction over cases brought by a member state against another member state for treaty infringement, by a European Community institution against a state and by individual citizens or organizations against European Community institutions. The Court of Justice does not have jurisdiction over the appeals of national court decisions. EU member states are obliged to enforce and implement CJEU judgments. The CJEU has developed a general principle of state responsibility for non-compliance with EU law. State liability derives from the fact that EU member states are responsible for the creation and above all for the implementation and enforcement of EU law.

Issues deriving from different definitions of GE, interpretations of international law, intersectionality and cultural differences will be observed through research analysis of GE in different countries included in this book. Feminist jurisprudence is deficient because it has not devoted enough attention to real-life experiences of women who do not speak along the lines of the "dominant discourse." According to Patricia Cain (1988, p. 165), "most female legal theorists, focusing on sameness and difference, have fallen into the assimilationist trap (all women are equal to men/all women are equal) or the essentialist trap (all women are different from men in an essential way/ all women are different, but what is important is their common essence)". The core difference between these two views lies in the fact that the former neglects the reality of differences, while the latter considers that differences are not important. These two ideas overlap in that they understand women as a group that consists of essentially equal individuals. While it is necessary to determine similarities among women, it is important not to ignore differences. A normative principle that respects only what we have in common does not respect women's individuality, ignores differences (experiences of women of color, migrant women, lesbians, women with disabilities, etc.), and sends out the message that the differences among women are not relevant. It does not suffice to identify the differences in race, class and sexuality. The differences need to be interpreted.

The readers will learn about the problems of applying a universal concept of GE and the possible reasons for and modes of adapting gender equality to different contexts. The book will maintain a critical and reflexive stance towards the issues raised and will seek to present multiple perspectives and open-ended answers. As such it hopes to contribute to the international discussion of human rights more broadly and GE specifically.

Aims of the Book

Our desire to provide case studies from within different societies dictates the choice of comparative methods for the research. As Inderpal Grewal and Caren Kaplan (1994, p. 17) suggest, meaningful transnational interventions require "comparative work rather than the relativistic linking of 'differences'." The chapters tackle different political and legal systems and their changes over time, historical transformations that the countries under discussion have undergone, and cultural factors and traditions that hinder or promote the adoption of GE. The development of GE requires good governments and political frameworks that give men and women equal voices in the gender debate on defining the relationship in the hierarchy of power.

The starting point for all chapters is the CEDAW definition of GE:

> According to the Universal Declaration of Human Rights all humans are born free and equal, and the Convention on the Elimination of All Forms of Discrimination against Women refers to this declaration in its second paragraph. CEDAW represents the most powerful international mechanism for promoting the "same rights" and the "same opportunities" which must be available to all men and women in various fields of human activity, including but not limited to education, marital legislation, and labour. In its preamble CEDAW is repeating the terms "equal rights of men and women" and "equality of rights of men and women" as well as reaching the "full equality of men and women" in the final opening paragraphs before Article 1. Therefore, the concept of gender equality may be taken to primarily refer to the full equality of men and women to enjoy the comprehensive list of political, economic, civil, social and cultural rights, with no one being denied access to these rights, or deprived of them, because of their sex.

All authors were asked to analyze, given the above definition:

- To what degree is there GE already in the country you study? What has the legal development been?
- Is GE only formally guaranteed in legislation or also embraced in everyday social life (implementation of international standards/European legislation, issues that have arisen in implementation, difficulties of interpreting (at the institutional and judicial level) and/or adapting international/European standards to the local context)?
- Would it be possible to fully (everywhere, always) adopt GE in practice in your country? How has the historical/traditional/political background of the country influenced the adoption and popular perception of GE?
- Which parts of GE would be impossible to adopt in practice? Why?
- What would need to be done (and how) to enable for GE to be fully adopted in practice?

The chapters illustrate their answers to the above questions with evidence derived from empirical data or literature reviews on different aspects of social life: political participation and access to political power, labor force participation, education, health. Authors were asked to be attentive to intersectional dimensions in addition to gender (race, ethnicity, class, sexuality, age, ability, etc.). We sought nuanced discussion and in-depth analysis of GE in the particular country, based on local knowledge that may be inaccessible to international observers.

The selection of countries covered in the volume includes states that are frequently considered having achieved a high degree of GE (Australia, the US, although we will show continued problems in both) as well as a range of countries where the application of GE has been facing challenges: postsocialist Central and Eastern Europe, Africa, Latin America and China. Our volume does not include analyses of the Nordic countries because there is already ample literature about their gender policies. For the same reason, we have tried to de-emphasize Western Europe and instead have zoomed in on Central and Eastern Europe (CEE), where post-socialist transition has created different obstacles to the acceptance of GE. Our three case studies from the region show how countries of CEE that are frequently lumped together as a single region have distinctive trajectories, depending on the history and religious composition of the countries. For the same reason, we also chose two case studies from the Americas and Africa. All chapters prove that challenges to the adoption of international gender equality norms are rooted in local histories and cultural traditions that should not be overlooked in policy making, international law or international development.

Our study is truly global in reach as we have covered all continents and countries with very different levels of development. The chapters are organized regionally, so that a reader who is interested in, for example, Africa, can find the chapters from that continent one after another. We have chosen to organize our chapters so as to break the traditional Western and Eurocentric thinking. Thus we start from the countries from Africa, to draw attention to the complexities related to the application of GE there. Our volume features a chapter from Nigeria by Funmi Josephine Para-Mallam and a chapter from Egypt by Mohamed Arafa and Ahmed El-Ashry. We then move on towards the East, to China (chapter written by Yan Zhao), a major global player but one under-discussed in GE literature. Australia is ranked high in international gender equality indices, but as Archana Preeti Voola, Kara Beavis and Anuradha Mundkur note in their contribution, the country faces a number of challenges. In the context of the Americas, we also move from South to North: Alma Espino analyzes GE in Uruguay, Sonia M. Frías in Mexico, and Colleen Arendt and Patrice M. Buzzanell in the US. In the case of Europe, we have opted to cover three Central and Eastern European countries to provide a more detailed analysis of the challenges of post-socialist transition. Suzana Ignjatovic and Aleksandar Boskovic discuss the situation in Serbia, Snježana Vasiljević in Croatia and Raili Marling in Estonia.

Our overall aim is twofold. First, we seek to show that GE, despite being a universal value touted internationally, remains just an abstract value if we do not analyze the interpretation and application of international GE laws and standards in different cultural and political locations. We call for local analyses written not by international observers often on the basis of English-language international reports, but by scholars and activists on the ground in different cultural locations. Second, we hope to encourage more comparative scholarly work on gender equality that could be used as a basis for substantive legal and political changes.

Notes

1 Both gender imperialism and false universalism are covered by the term essentialism (Bartlett, 1994, p. 1).
2 MacKinnon is responsible for making sexual harassment recognized as a legal category.
3 Unambiguous focus on rape as a manifestation of male power over women's sexuality blurs the use of rape as a weapon of racial terror. The white man's power was strengthened by the judicial system in which the successful conviction of white men of raping black women was virtually unthinkable.

References

Alcoff, L. (1988). Cultural feminism versus post-structuralism: The identity crisis in feminist theory. *Signs*, **13** (3), 405–436.

Bartlett, K.T. (1994). Gender law. *Duke Journal of Gender Law & Policy*, **1** (1), 1–18.

Beauvoir, S. de (1972). *The Second Sex*. Trans. H.M. Parshley. Harmondsworth: Penguin.

Brooks, R.E. (2002). Feminist justice, at home and abroad: Feminism and international law: An opportunity for transformation. *Yale Journal of Law and Feminism*, **14** (2), 345–361.

Butler, J. (1990). *Gender Trouble*. New York and London: Routledge.

Cain, P.A. (1988). Teaching feminist legal theory at Texas: Listening to difference and exploring connections. *Journal of Legal Education*, **38** (1–2), 165–181.

Charlesworth, H., Chinkin, C., & Wright, S. (1991). Feminist approaches to international law. *American Journal of International Law*, **85** (4), 613–644.

Charter of Fundamental Rights of the European Union. (2000). *Official Journal of the European Communities No. 364/1*. Retrieved from http://www.europarl. europa.eu/charter/pdf/text_en.pdf (accessed 14 August 2016).

Convention on the Elimination of All Forms of Discrimination against Women (CEDAW). (1979). New York: United Nations. Retrieved from http://www. un.org/womenwatch/daw/cedaw/cedaw.htm (accessed 18 June 2016).

Crenshaw, K. (1989). Demarginalizing the intersection of race and sex: A black feminist critique of antidiscrimination doctrine, feminist theory and antiracist politics. *The University of Chicago Legal Forum*, **1989** (1), 139–167.

Crenshaw, K. (1991). Race, gender and sexual harassment. *Southern California Law Review*, **65** (3), 1467–1476.

Crenshaw, K. (1994). Mapping the margins: Intersectionality, identity politics, and violence against women of color. In M. Albertson Fineman & R. Mykitiuk (Eds), *The Public Nature of Private Violence*, New York: Routledge, pp. 93–118.

Fraser, N. (2010). *Scales of Justice: Reimagining Political Space in a Globalizing World*. New York: Columbia University Press.

Fraser, N. (2013). *Fortunes of Feminism: From State-Managed Capitalism to Neoliberal Crisis*. London and New York: Verso.

Grewal, I., & Kaplan, C. (eds) (1994). *Scattered Hegemonies: Postmodernity and Transnational Feminist Practices*. Minneapolis, MN: Minnesota University Press.

Harris, A. (1990). Race and essentialism in feminist legal theory. *Stanford Law Review*, 42 (3), 581–616.

Haslanger, S. (1995). Ontology and social construction. *Philosophical Topics*, 23 (2), 95–125.

Jaggar, A.M. (1990). Sexual difference and sexual equality. In D.L. Rhode (Ed.), *Theoretical Perspectives on Sexual Difference*, New Haven and London: Yale University Press, pp. 239–256.

Kantola, J. (2010). *Gender and the European Union*. Basingstoke, UK: Palgrave Macmillan.

Koobak, R., & Marling, R. (2014). The decolonial challenge: Framing post-socialist central and Eastern Europe within transnational feminist studies. *European Journal of Women's Studies*, 21 (4), 330–343.

Laqueur, T.W. (1990). *Making Sex: Body and Gender from the Greeks to Freud*. Cambridge, MA: Harvard University Press.

Lorde, A. (1984). *Sister Outsider*. New York: Random House.

MacKinnon, K.A. (1989). *Toward a Feminist Theory of the State*. Cambridge, MA: Harvard University Press.

Mikkola, M. (2011). Ontological commitments, sex and gender. In C. Witt (Ed.), *Feminist Metaphysics*, Dordrecht, Netherlands: Springer, pp. 67–83.

Minow, M. (1990). *All the Difference: Inclusion, Exclusion and the American Law*. Ithaca, NY: Cornell University Press.

Mitchell, J. (1987). Women and equality. In A. Phillips (Ed.), *Feminism and Equality*, New York: New York University Press, pp. 24–43.

Mohanty, C.T. (1984). Under Western eyes: Feminist scholarship and colonial discourses. *Boundary 2*, 12 (3), 333–358.

Otto, D. (2010). Women's rights. In D. Moeckli, S. Shah & S. Sivakumaran (Eds), *International Human Rights Law*, Oxford: Oxford University Press, pp. 345–364.

Plumwood, V. (1993). *Feminism and the Mastery of Nature*. London: Routledge.

Raday, F. (2012). Gender and democratic citizenship: The impact of CEDAW. *International Journal of Constitutional Law*, 10 (2), 512–530.

Sarkar, M. (2004). Looking for feminism. *Gender and History*, 16 (2), 318–333.

Scott, J.W. (1990). Deconstructing equality-versus-difference: Or, the uses of poststructuralist theory for feminism. In M. Hirsch & E. Fox-Keller (Eds), *Conflicts in Feminism*, New York and London: Routledge, pp. 134–148.

Shukla, N., Pandey, M., & Singh, S. (2015). Service laws and working women: Filling inclusion gaps in national development. *Vidyabharati International Interdisciplinary Research Journal*, 4 (1), 43–46.

Smart, C. (1989). *Feminism and the Power of Law*. London and New York: Routledge.

Somek, A. (2011). *Engineering Equality: An Essay on European Anti-Discrimination Law*. Oxford: Oxford University Press.

Spivak, G.C. (1988). Can the subaltern speak? In C. Nelson & L. Grossberg (Eds), *Marxism and the Interpretation of Culture*, London: Macmillan, pp. 271–313.

Suchland, J. (2011). Is postsocialism transnational? *Signs*, 36 (4), 837–862.

Treaty on the Functioning of the European Union (TFEU). (2007). *Official Journal of the European Union No. C 326/47*. Retrieved from http://eur-lex.europa.eu/legal-content/EN/TXT/PDF/?uri=CELEX:12012E/TXT&from=EN (accessed 14 August 2016).

UN Women. (n.d.). *Short History of CEDAW Convention*. Retrieved from http://www.un.org/womenwatch/daw/cedaw/history.htm (accessed 18 June 2016).

Vasiljević, S. (2009). Intersectional discrimination: Difficulties in implementation of a European norm. In E. Prügl & M. Thiel (Eds), *Diversity in the European Union*, New York: Palgrave Macmillan, pp. 169–182.

Vasiljević, S. (2015a). New law and values: Anti-discrimination law in post-communist countries. In N. Bodiroga-Vukobrat, S. Rodin & S. Gerald (Eds), *Europeanization and Globalization, New Europe—Old Values? Reform and Perseverance*, Cham: Springer, pp. 55–76.

Vasiljević, S. (2015b). Equality, non-discrimination & fundamental rights: Old habits die hard! In M. Vinković (Ed.), *New Developments in EU Labour, Equality and Human Rights Law*, Osijek, Croatia: J.J. Strossmayer University of Osijek Faculty of Law, pp. 177–195.

Part II

Examining Gender Equality in a Global Perspective

2 Gender Equality in Nigeria

Funmi Josephine Para-Mallam

Introduction: Gender Matters

Human beings are essentially gendered beings shaped by biology, culture and environment to play roles that may or may not conform to personality type or other preferences. Postmodernists argue that gender is a mere product of human discursive processes and, therefore, not a firm source of identity or inequality. But in social contexts like Nigeria where traditional and religious values are dominant in shaping the attitudes and behavior of its 178.5 million people (*UNDP*, 2015), gender does matter—a whole lot. The Federal Republic of Nigeria, the most populous African nation, is a country of rich cultural diversity where the combined legacies of indigenous traditional, Islamic and colonial patriarchy are evident in the way the various ethnic groupings interpret being male or female (Nweze & Takaya, 2001). Such interpretations serve as determinant factors in shaping gender identity, roles and relations by rendering "biological sex" a type of "master status" for allocating rights, resources, opportunities and privileges as well as affecting life chances. A Gender in Nigeria Report (*British Council of Nigeria*, 2012, p. iii) showed that, owing to systematic gender inequality "Nigeria's 80.2 million women and girls have significantly worse life chances than men and also their sisters in comparable societies. . . ."

Makama (2013) demonstrates that gender inequality in Nigeria is both a cause and product of poverty and underdevelopment. Inequality has short- and long-term repercussions on human capital development and for overall national socioeconomic development (Todaro & Smith, 2012). It is manifested in female social exclusion or, more accurately, their disproportionate inclusion into the social, political and economic system through the denial of opportunities, rights and entitlements (Sen, 1990). According to the former UN Secretary General Kofi Annan (2006), persistent gender inequality is a major reason for stunted progress in achieving development and sustainable peace.

Nigeria is Africa's most populous country as well as its largest economy and market. In real terms, however, Nigeria lags behind most low human development countries in and outside the African continent with respect to overall human development and gender parity indicators of health and educational status, and political and economic empowerment (UNDP, 2015). Nigeria's 2015 Gender Development Index of 0.514 is even below the Sub-Saharan African average (0.518)! During the period of the Millennium Development Goals agenda (2000–2015) Nigeria made slow progress towards their attainment. The Federal Ministry of Women Affairs and Social Development has declared its intention to ensure better outcomes under the current Sustainable Development Goals (SDGs) 2030 with emphasis on achieving gender equality and female empowerment (Goal #5) as a key strategy.

However, Nigeria is a society caught in the tension between old ways and modern pressures. Nigerian men and women find themselves having to renegotiate hardcore gender ideologies in the context of a developing country adjusting to the growing influence of globalized Western culture. Tradition and religion are being challenged and contested, sometimes subtly, at times overtly by the emerging realities brought about by urbanization, modern technology and the expanding reach of digital media (Para-Mallam 2010). Thus, the pull and push of traditional and modernizing forces hold gender in a constant tension lived out in private and public domains. This gendered bifurcation of daily life varies noticeably across the ethno-religiously and geopolitically diverse groups that make up the Nigerian state. It also has distinct implications for men and women of different socioeconomic status and backgrounds. In this chapter I explore the causes and dimensions of gender equality in Nigeria in view of its culturally and geopolitically diverse makeup. To do this it is important to provide a roadmap for applying gender equality terminology to the Nigerian social context and discuss regulatory frameworks put in place to empower women as well as highlight difficulties that confront state and non-state actors in implementing them. In light of the combustible nature of contestations around gender equality agendas, particularly since the country's return to democratic governance in 1999, I suggest an incremental approach to edging the nation toward a more equitable environment for women.

A Conceptual Roadmap: Root Causes of Gender Inequality in Nigeria

It is important to clarify what I do and do not mean by gender equality. This is because in Nigeria, gender equality is actually a contentious issue as many people, including importantly law and policy makers, often interpret demands for it as women's desire to become men! Kabeer (2003) offers a useful clarification of the meaning of equality by breaking it down into three essential elements: *formal, substantive* and *agential* equality. By formal equality she refers to equal treatment under the law and equal opportunity. Substantive equality implies that the peculiar circumstances of individuals and groups (e.g., women and men) need to be taken into account to avoid disadvantage or unfair outcomes in development programming or policy formulation and implementation. Bustelo (2001, p. 10) correctly points out that substantive equality "implies equity, i.e. proportionality in the degree of access to the benefits and costs of development, and also redistributive justice, grounded in collective solidarity." By agential equality Kabeer implies ensuring that both women and men have the ability to make strategic choices for themselves taking account of the circumstances under which such choices are made.

This threefold definition is relevant in light of the identified root causes of gender inequality as "the continuous interaction of indigenous and inherited patriarchy from the colonial administration, the strong inhibiting effects of traditionalism and capitalist ideologies" (Item 1.1 of National Policy on Women (Federal Ministry of Women Affairs and Social Development, 2000)). This implies that social, cultural, political and economic processes and organizations are imbued with a patriarchal undercurrent that undercuts gender equality agendas. As I will show using examples from the Nigerian context, patriarchy works to forestall resistance to systematic gender discrimination. It does this by erecting ideological and formal structures to curtail the range of choices through which females may exercise agency to fulfill their human potential and contribute maximally to societal development.

Beteille (2003) points out quite correctly that, very often, social inequality is justified or explained as emanating from "natural" or "divine" origins. If one were to conduct an opinion poll among Nigerians about why inequalities exist between males and females in society, they are likely to come up with reasons like: "God or the Bible/Koran said it," or "It is natural because men and women are made that way." It is clear then that culture-based and religiously supported ideologies regarding gender identity and roles entrench a conventional "woman the gatherer" (homemaker) and "man the hunter" (breadwinner) mentality. As in other parts of the world, Nigerian women's experience of inequality is fractured and multi-layered based on other identities and social categories (ethnicity, class, religion, etc.) that intersect across multiple time-spaces. Hence, not all Nigerian women experience gender inequality in the same way or to the same extent.

In *Nigerian Women Speak: A Gender Analysis of Government Policy on Women* (Para-Mallam, 2007), I present empirical data from interviews and focus group discussions with Nigerian women from all walks of life. All of them agreed that female subordination was a personal reality to varying degrees and that it normally impacts negatively on women's lives. Female farmers, traders, students, professionals and top-level public officers described various forms of discrimination and injustice they had suffered simply for being women. They ascribed negative experiences related to being female primarily to customary and/or religious norms, laws and practices. I will elaborate more specifically on the role of culture and religion later. In the next section I examine major formal mechanisms that shape gender identity, roles and relations, including those explicitly established to promote gender equality. There are also numerous non-codified customary and religious norms that impact on the lives of men and women. I shall discuss these later in relation to cultural and religious dimensions of gender inequality.

Regulatory Frameworks for Gender Equality in Nigeria

Successive government administrations in Nigeria have demonstrated keenness in signing and ratifying international conventions aimed at promoting equality. Notable among these is the 1979 Convention on the Elimination of all Forms of Discrimination Against Women (CEDAW), which Nigeria ratified in 1985. This section briefly outlines formal mechanisms for promoting gender equality in the Federal Republic of Nigeria where the legal system consists of three divergent and concurrent legal regimes (Statutory Law, Customary Law and Sharia Law). At the same time, it highlights some of the complexities and contradictions inherent in a tripartite legal system shaped by the historical interaction of African tradition, colonialism and religious belief systems.

Under the injunction of major international, regional and sub-regional treaties, conventions and declarations, Nigeria set up public agencies, laws and policies to address women's needs and promote gender equality. In 1995, momentum from the Beijing Platform for Action Conference led to the establishment of the Ministry of Women Affairs and Social Development at Federal and State levels with local government representation in the form of Social Welfare Departments. The Beijing Platform of Action (BPfA) and CEDAW call for the establishment of a Gender Management System to serve as a national machinery for the promotion of women's rights and gender equality. The Federal Ministry of Women Affairs and Social Development is the lead agency of Nigeria's Gender Management System (GMS) responsible for monitoring the mainstreaming of gender perspectives in national policy formulation and implementation processes. The GMS was designed to consist of focal desk officers in all line ministries and other government agencies, a National Team of Technical Experts, a National Gender Committee and gender equality structures at state and committee levels. Due to poor funding most of these structures are not functioning as originally intended.

Constitutional Grounding for Gender Equality

The 1999 Constitution is considered to be the grand norm establishing non-discrimination on the basis of sex and other biosocial distinctions, notably ethnicity and geopolitical origin. To protect the multi-ethnic and multi-religious character (referred to as Federal Character) of the Federal Republic of Nigeria, the Constitution prohibits the preponderance of any section or group of persons in government positions. To institutionalize the concept and practice of Federal Character, a Federal Character Commission was set up under the 1970 Federal Character Act to promote fair representation of all ethnic groups is public agencies. Yet, despite the fact that women comprise approximately 51% of the population, little has been done to guarantee equitable gender representation to promote what MarkOdu (2000) refers to a the "Gender Character" of the country.

The Constitution establishes the entitlement of all citizens to fundamental human rights. Yet, Chapter II of the 1999 Constitution where such rights are set out is non-justiciable, implying they cannot be invoked in a court of law. Furthermore, the document restricts its interpretation of discrimination on the basis of sex to the liberal conceptualization of equal treatment before the law. Even then, there are certain contradictory provisions that function to negate formal legal equality. Sections 26 and 29 (4)(b) of the 1999 Constitution are examples; the former permits only men to transfer nationality/ residency rights to foreign spouses and the latter promotes girl-child marriage. Thus, the legal status of foreign wives of Nigerian men remains quite precarious as they are treated as aliens without recourse to the same legal rights as their husbands. For example, a Nigerian-born woman from the Republic of Benin was threatened by child welfare services with the loss of her children if she did not agree to go back to her husband though she had endured over a decade of domestic violence. In relation to girl-child marriage the double-standard approach of the law and law operators to women and girls' issues is apparent. In 2015, the National Assembly surreptitiously passed a law legalizing girl-child marriage citing Section 29 (4) (b). Yet, in 2016 the National Assembly threw out a bill proposing women's empowerment and gender equality.

Lawmakers continue to resist repeated calls from women's and human rights groups to amend the 1999 Constitution. As a result of political horse-trading, a provision upholding the legality of Sharia law in civil matters was introduced into the Constitution since 1976, which further undermines the equal rights of Muslim women. But non-Muslim women are also affected by this because many who live in predominantly Muslim states find it difficult to access rights guaranteed under statutory law owing to the prevalent value system that shapes the thinking and professional conduct of supposedly secular law enforcement agents. In light of the cultural diversity in Nigeria's wide array of customary norms and practices, the current Constitution also sanctions the role of customary laws and courts in the judgment of civil matters such as marriage, divorce and custodial rights. The majority of such laws privilege the rights of husbands/fathers over those of wives/mothers. Under both Sharia and Customary Law children are deemed to belong to their father, who usually gets custodial rights in the event of separation or divorce. This is one of the reasons women's rights groups have agitated for constitutional and legislative amendment.

Furthermore, Section 12 of the 1999 Constitution poses a strong barrier to the incorporation of international standards of women's rights into Nigerian municipal law. It stipulates that ratified international treaties can only be invoked before Nigerian courts after being passed into law through a two-stage process at federal and state level. Nigeria has signed and ratified major international and regional conventions and treaties dealing with the rights and well-being of women and girls. Most notable among them are: Convention on the Elimination of all Forms of Discrimination Against Women (CEDAW), African Charter on Human and Peoples' Rights and its Protocol to the Banjul Charter on Women's Rights, Convention on the Rights of the Child (CRC) and International Protocol on Trafficking in Human Persons. It was as a result of advocacy efforts of civil society groups, including women activists, that the National Assembly domesticated international child rights and anti-trafficking legislation by enacting two separate acts to protect children's rights, and prohibit and prosecute sex trafficking, respectively, in 2003. Nigerian governments also participated actively in articulating, declaring or supporting a number of important non-treaty agreements committed to female empowerment such as the New Economic Partnership for Africa's Development (NEPAD), the Millennium Development Goals (MDGs) and now the SDGs.

Ordinarily, such international/regional agreements should impose obligations on the state and its agencies, as duty-bearers of human rights. However, owing to the constitutional requirement in Section 12, the Nigerian judiciary is not automatically obliged to comply with international treaties. The male-dominated political establishment has not been as forthcoming in fulfilling the constitutional requirement to incorporate ratified international agreements into domestic legislation through enactments by the national and state houses of assembly. Accordingly, NGO coalitions monitoring the implementation of CEDAW in Nigeria have consistently presented reports to the UN Committee on the Status of Women citing statistical and descriptive evidence of discrimination against women and girls perpetrated by the state, its institutions and society at large arising from its non-domestication and non-implementation (Nigerian NGO Coalition, 1999, 2008). Even the Child Rights Act and the Human Trafficking Prohibition Act were only passed after several years and rounds of contentious lobbying.

Still, the Child Rights Act (CRA) is yet to be domesticated by all states of the federation, particularly those in the predominantly Muslim far north. Some of such states that have domesticated it amended provisions they felt contradict Sharia Law and Islamic values. For example, there was substantial controversy in the National Assembly over the marriageable age for girls, stipulated under the CRA to be 18 years. In Kano State, this was reduced to 14 years in contravention of the internationally agreed standard (Sabo, 2015). Another bottleneck in the legal system slowing down gender equality legislation relates to the gazetting of new laws. After parliamentary enactment laws are required to be gazetted before they can be used in a court of law, which in the Nigerian context often takes several years. For example, Plateau State was the first to domesticate CEDAW in the form of a Gender and Equal Opportunities Act in 2015. The Act is yet to be gazetted and is therefore still not available for use in any court in the absence of a duly signed copy of the law. Even the Child's Right Act is not yet gazetted in most states where it is domesticated, including Plateau, which was the first to do so 11 years ago. Nevertheless, Atsenuwa (2008) contends that international treaties may still be cited as part of case law, without gazetting, in municipal courts as was upheld in the case of *Muoje-kwu vs. Ejikeme*.[1]

In some southern states women activist groups worked to circumvent the non-domestication of CEDAW at the national level by introducing excerpts of the document in various bills at the level of state houses of assembly. Anambra, Bayelsa, Cross Rivers, Delta, Edo, Enugu, Ekiti, Oyo and Rivers States enacted various laws against harmful widowhood rights, female genital mutilation and for safe motherhood. A case study of the 2005 *Anambra State Malpractices against Widows and Widowers (Prohibition) Law* (Adamu et al., 2010) revealed a number of challenges surrounding the implementation of such laws. This is due to the lack of political will occasioned by the prevailing patriarchal mindset of policy/law enforcement agents, traditional institutions and the wider society.

Nigeria's Triple Legal System

The tripartite character of the Nigerian legal system further complicates female access to justice and gender equality. This is because there exist three, often conflicting, law regimes that govern civil and criminal offences: Statutory Law, Sharia Law and Customary Law (Odinkalu, 2008). Statutory law derives from English Common Law and the 1999 Constitution is the grand norm on which all other laws are based. Certain civil aspects of Sharia Law are also enshrined in the Constitution. Customary laws in Nigeria vary between ethnic backgrounds and are yet to be codified into a coherent body of law. Their application is left to the discretion of courts established to adjudicate on customary matters. Women tend to have fewer rights under customary and Sharia laws, yet much of the grassroots population finds them more relevant and accessible.

Imam's (2009) meta-analysis of the works of legal scholars and activists discussed implications of the country's triple legal system for the enforcement of women's rights. The major challenge is that very divergent customary and religious belief systems—Roman/Judeo-Christian, Islamic and African traditional religion—with non-egalitarian value judgments about women and their place in society undergird the three legal regimes. For example, the Northern penal code (which derives from Sharia Law and is applicable only in Northern Nigeria) permits a husband to chastize his wife, although any injury sustained must not lead to a stay in hospital exceeding 20 days! In parts of Southern Nigeria, traditional widowhood rites impose severe ordeals on women such as having to drink the bathwater from a husband's corpse as a ceremonial ritual to prove innocence of his death. Such practices are prohibited under the Statutory Law Criminal Code. This is not to suggest that women only have human rights protection under Statutory Law, as there are provisions that protect women under the Penal Code and customary laws. However, they are not as far-reaching.

On the other hand, Madaki (2014) has pointed out that there are still numerous gaps under the Criminal Code, which serve to undermine women's human rights. For example, marital rape is not acknowledged as a crime under the Criminal Code, but is under the Sharia Law. On these contrasting cultural and religious premises embodied in the three legal systems, the National Assembly has persistently thrown out bills presented to it to advance women's rights through the domestication of CEDAW provisions— the most comprehensive legal document on women's human rights, or aspects of it. So far, the National Assembly has rejected four bills: on anti-violence in 2001, reproductive health in 2005, and gender and equal opportunities in 2006 and 2016.

After years of intense lobbying, women's groups recorded a landmark victory when, on May 25, 2015, the anti-violence bill finally passed into law as the Violence Against Persons Prohibition Act (VAPP). Nevertheless, in February 2016, the tacit constitutional approval of Sharia Law in the Constitution was used as a justification by lawmakers from the core Muslim North of the country to throw out the "Women Empowerment and Equal Gender Opportunities Bill" sponsored Senator Funme Olujimi, a female legislator.

The National Gender Policy

Based on recommendations made in the 1985 Nairobi Forward Looking Strategies, Nigeria set up national machinery to look after women's interests. The military government, under General Ibrahim Babangida, established the National Commission on Women in 1986, which the administration of General Sani Abacha converted to a fully-fledged Federal Ministry of Women Affairs in 1993. In 2000 the democratically elected government of Chief Olusegun Obasanjo approved a National Policy on Women (NPW) to redress gender imbalances in the Nigerian polity (Federal Ministry of Women Affairs and Social Development, 2000). The NPW was reviewed and replaced by the 2006 National Gender Policy (NGP). The policy stipulates 35% affirmative action to increase female representation in all appointive and elective posts. This provision is yet to be given legal backing or to be implemented, and thus remains a mere statement of intent. Item 1.2 of the NGP emphasizes the patriarchal root causes of gender inequality in the Nigerian social context. It argues that over the years Nigerian governments adopted "gender-blind" and "gender-biased" policies predicated on a patriarchal interpretation of appropriate gender roles, rights and entitlements (Federal Ministry of Women Affairs and Social Development, 2006, p. 2).

The Policy justifies its existence on the premise of persistent gender disparities in key human and socioeconomic development indicators in education, health, labor force participation, politics and decision-making and overall resource management and utilization (Items 1.1 and 1.2 of the NGP) (Federal Ministry of Women Affairs and Social Development, 2006). It outlines the development implications of gender misconceptions and persistent policy inequalities (Item 1.3) and underscores a more holistic approach to development planning and to gender policy that integrates the unique needs and peculiarities of women and men into national development (Federal Ministry of Women Affairs and Social Development, 2006). Part 2 of the policy document sets out the policy framework, guiding principles, policy objectives and priority areas of action within a graphic conceptual framework (Federal Ministry of Women Affairs and Social Development, 2006). The NGP seeks to promote gender equality through the establishment of a framework for gender-responsiveness in public and private spheres using gender mainstreaming as a core value and practice in all development programming and budgeting processes. Time-bound priority targets are set out as areas of action within the context of these objectives. An overview of these is presented in Table 2.1. Part 3 elaborates the policy delivery strategies and institutional framework designed to achieve the stated objectives and targets along with their expected outcomes. The implementation strategies consist of seven overarching focal areas cutting across policy and economic reform, Information, Communications and Technology (ICT) for value reorientation, capacity building, human rights legislation, evidenced-based planning and Monitoring and Evaluation (M&E).

It is important to note that the lofty ideals of gender equality for accelerated national development espoused in the NGP have not been realized because the necessary conditions required within the wider policy and institutional environment at micro and macro levels are yet to be created. These include gender parity in access to educational and economic opportunities and outcomes, a level political playing field and, most of all, the erosion of patriarchal ideologies that sustain harmful traditional practices against women and girls. I turn to this issue in the final section. First, it is important to examine the nature and extent to which gender inequality remains

Table 2.1 Education Indicators for Nigeria by Sex

	Literacy Rate (Adult) (2011)	Literacy Rate (Youth) (2011)	Primary Enrollment Rate (2010)	Primary Completion Rate (2010)	Primary Enrollment Rate (2013)	Secondary Completion Rate (2013)
Male	74%	78%	54.3%	53.3%	62.1%	53.2%
Female	48%	66%	45.7%	46.7% (fell to 46.6% in 2013)	47.9%	46.8% (fell from 47.1% in 2010)

Source: 2010–11 World Bank Indicator Tables (World Bank, 2013); *Demographic Statistics Report* (National Bureau of Statistics, 2013)

evident in the daily reality of women in 21st-century Nigeria. The next section looks at the various dimensions and effects of gender inequality on
women and girls living in Nigeria today.

Gendered Reality of Everyday Life: Are Formal Mechanisms Enough?

The *Nigeria 2006 Millennium Development Goals Report* (Federal Government of Nigeria, 2006) and the *Gender in Nigeria Report* (British Council
of Nigeria, 2012) demonstrate the comparatively low status of women and
girls in every part of the country. They present evidence that stark gender disparities persist despite the emplacement of formal institutions and regulatory
mechanisms to promote women's rights and gender equality. Both reports
highlight the fact that gender inequality is profoundly ingrained in the social
mores, norms and institutions of Nigeria. Thus, it is still considered by the
majority of the populace to be "normal" or "natural" for women and men to
have significantly differentiated access to and control over societal resources
and entitlements. It is safe to say that most Nigerians do not believe that men
and women were created equal or should be considered equal.

Poverty and inequality are generally widespread among both Nigerian
men and women due to income, ethnic, social, religious and occupational
differences, as well as the general climate of a low-income developing country. However, in addition to these more general causes of inequality, Nigerian women and girls experience discrimination and inequality in virtually all
fields of endeavor purely on the basis of their sex. It could be argued that men
also confront gender discrimination in the form of marginalization within
predominantly female career paths or by being excluded from typical female
roles. However, male gender roles—father, husband, breadwinner, leader,
warrior, hunter, etc.—are more heavily weighted and carry greater economic,
political and social advantage. As such, the outcomes of male gender discrimination tend to carry far less social costs and produce far less suffering.

In seeking to understand the nature and dimensions of gender inequality,
three interconnected domains are particularly relevant for a gender analysis
of their ideological content, internal functioning and gendered outcomes.
These are: culture and religion, socioeconomic organization and the political system. It is essential that we recognize the ways and extent to which
these domains embody and sustain gender discrimination. More specifically,
they depict how being a woman in Nigeria impacts on both private and
public life.

Cultural and Religious Manifestations and Dimensions of Gender Inequality

Adamu et al. (2010, p. 9) refer to the work of Aina (1992) to highlight
the historical and cultural roots of gender inequality, stating that, "gender

domination and oppression are inherent in African culture and also imbibed through the African women's unique experiences under slavery, colonialism, and imperialism." As noted in the introduction, traditional custom and religion play a dominant role in shaping private and public life in Nigeria. Nigeria is reputed to be one of the most religious countries on earth, comprising 60% Christians and 40% Muslims.[2] Traditional customs and religious beliefs help to construct the status of men and women in both practical and psychological ways. Research carried out under a Department for International Development (DFID)-sponsored Religions and Development Program between 2007 and 2011 found that customary and religious arguments were the major justifications put forward by Nigerian legislators for their rejection of bills to promote women's rights and gender equality (Adamu et al., 2010; Adamu & Para-Mallam, 2012).

According to a 1999 baseline survey on harmful traditional practices against women, discriminatory traditional customs sanctioned and/or reinforced in the doctrines and teachings of religious texts and leaders are a major root cause of anti-female discrimination and gender-based violence (Federal Ministry of Women Affairs and Social Development, 1999). Nweze and Takaya (2000, p. 1) describe Nigerian cultures as a graduated synthesis of Eastern (Arab Islamic), Western (Judeo-Christian) and African customs and traditions and contend that

> If there is any trait on which all Nigerian sub-cultures appear to be totally united, it is in the anti-female gender discrimination, culminating in the unfair subjugation and abridgement of the rights of women. Clearly, it is in our character.

Correspondingly, the values Nigerian society places on females and males, their work and socially ascribed roles are prescribed and embodied in customary and/or religious provisions. Most of these provisions engender a strict sex segregation of social roles, which results in a triple burden for women who are accorded primary responsibility for reproductive labor (housekeeping, child rearing and caregiving of children, the sick and the elderly). In addition, society generally expects women to carry out productive and community duties as "subordinate . . . adjuncts" to men (Okome, 2000, p. 9). Numerous traditional norms comprise the written and unwritten body of customary laws legalized under the 1999 Constitution and adjudicated in Customary Courts. Such norms vary substantially from one ethnic group and geopolitical zone to the other. Under them women generally have fewer and different rights than men do. For example, in the event of the dissolution of a marriage, fathers are entitled to custody of children because traditionally the father owns the child whose name he/she also bears. In the case of very young children the mother may retain custody until the child is of age. Customary as well as religious (i.e., Sharia) laws also prescribe discriminatory inheritance and property rights in favor of men.

At a more fundamental level, textual, language, mythic and physical symbols enshrined in customary norms and religious beliefs shape the psychological constitution of individuals and groups of people. First, they affect how people identify themselves and perceive their identity and roles in relation to others. In this way, they facilitate the acculturation of women and men to gender-coded social scripts (Chirkov et al., 2005) and map out the possible range of choices, capabilities and opportunities available to each. Therefore, the Nigerian woman is socialized to embrace a conventional "God-given" primary support role of wife, mother and caregiver. While in most cases she is not totally excluded from the public sphere, except women in seclusion, her public role is circumscribed by the time constraints imposed by the sex segregation of domestic and public roles. Akande's 1981 study on rural women in four states in the South West and South South geopolitical zones of Nigeria showed that, unlike men, women experience time constraints imposed by unpaid subsistence work and reproductive labor. Her study can be compared with participatory rural appraisal (PRA) findings drawn from my doctoral research with rural women and low-income urban women in Kaduna and Plateau States in North Central Nigeria (2007). They showed that rural men spend approximately two hours per day less than women doing work (productive and reproductive) and have one hour per day more than women for rest and recreation. Although men spend 40 minutes per day more than women on productive labor, the study found that most of women's work, which takes up between 13 and a half to 13 hours, 40 minutes per day, consisted of unpaid subsistence labor.

This indicates that choice, as a critical development resource, is especially restricted for women living in rural areas where the status quo of female subordination is enforced and entrenched through taboos and the threat of harsh socio-cultural censorship. Among almost all ethnic groups, a married woman who commits adultery risks the wrath of the gods, ancestors or other "powers that be" whose duty is to impose severe penalties such as childlessness, madness, exile, etc. The gender-biased interpretation of religious texts, whether in rural or urban milieus, reinforces traditional custom by implying that it is God's will for the female to be subordinate and subservient. Cultural anthropologists Divale and Harris (1979, p. 328) make the point powerfully:

> In order to rear passive and submissive women, males enlist aid of the supernatural. Hence women are intimidated by bull-roarers, masked male dancers, and male religious specialists.

All these exert intense psychological pressure on females to internalize religio-cultural norms that devalue and relegate them to the background, particularly in public life. For, in a social context where custom and religion serve as markers of identity and community belonging, women do not want to go against the will of God. This also applies in the domain of reproductive rights where women and girls are precluded by the dictates of tradition and religion from exercising primary rights over their bodies in terms of when to get married, have sex or how many children to bear. Men still exercise greater decision-making power in such matters, particularly among low-income and rural populations.

For their part, Nigerian males are socialized to a hegemonic form of masculinity that portrays the ideal man as strong, autonomous, dominant, unapologetic, belonging to the public sphere and sexually laissez-faire. Alemika (2001) and Ogunyemi (1996) explain how for the Nigerian male, the resultant imbalanced overly masculinized persona breeds male hegemony and predisposes men towards aggression and violence. Reports, such as the 2008 UN Women survey on gender-based violence in Nigeria, demonstrate a high level of violence against women and girls perpetuated by individuals, groups and the state (CWEENS (forthcoming); Effah-Chukwuma et al., 2001, 2002; UN Women, 2013). Women, on the other hand, are socialized to be the "weaker" sex, dependent, passive, self-effacing, belonging to the private domain and sexually repressed. Acculturation to these gender modes is sustained through the combined influences of traditional and religious ideologies, rituals, rites of passage and language. In particular,

> The potency of ideology and culture lies in their ability to sustain resistance to change and insist on traditional ideas and methods. This is partly why constitutional, legislative and policy reforms are not enough to guarantee attitudinal changes from firmly entrenched cultural practices and patterns.
>
> (Para-Mallam, 1997, p. 12)

Culture and religion have proved tenaciously impervious to the efforts of women's pressure groups, not to mention the self-improvement efforts of individual women, to change or reverse established gender hierarchies. Yet, Western education, modernization and globalization are shifting the goalposts of gender identity, roles and relationships in urban Nigeria. Increasingly, educationally and economically empowered women are able to break free from traditionalism and gender bigotry through greater access to human capital and productive assets (Ishola & Alani, 2011; Para-Mallam, 2013). I will go into more detail on this in the next section.

Socioeconomic Manifestations and Dimensions of Gender Inequality

The *Poverty Profile for Nigeria* (National Bureau of Statistics, 2006) was the first gender-aware government document to provide statistical evidence of the feminization of poverty as a national phenomenon across rural and urban areas. The trend is confirmed in the *2014 Statistical Report on Women and Men in Nigeria* (National Bureau of Statistics, 2014). Economic gender inequality in Nigeria has most tangible manifestations in terms of access to disposable income, land, education, gender-specific health care services/

facilities as well as in time use and female labor force participation. Gender disparities in these areas show glaring patterns of inequality. Women face severe constraints to owning land due to discriminatory customary and religious inheritance and property rights laws (Centre on Housing Rights and Evictions, 2004). Right from pre-colonial times in Nigeria, as in most of Africa, polygamy served the functional purpose of producing more farm laborers as well as instituting men as landowners. Today, approximately 49% of the Nigerian populace is engaged in agricultural production and 70% of the rural labor force (Ajani, 2008).

In most parts of the country, women constitute the majority of the agricultural labor force. Although the nature and level of female participation is poorly documented in national statistics and accounting systems, Ajani's meta-analysis (2008) points to micro-level empirical studies that prove this is the case in many states. As she argues, most women possess only user rights over the land they work on and do not always exercise full control over the income deriving from their labor. A materialist argument partly explains economic inequality between men and women in this area. Agrarian economic organization from pre-colonial times still characterizes much of Nigeria, with about 60% of the populace living in rural areas where entitlement to land is predicated on strong patrilineal kinship ties and inheritance patterns. In the absence of deliberate land reform of the 1976 Land Reform Act not much has changed. According to the British Council of Nigeria's *Gender in Nigeria* report (British Council of Nigeria, 2012, pp. iv, 1), in the agricultural sector of the economy,

> The UNDP (2009) estimates that women in Nigeria produce 60%–80% of food, with important implications for national food security. Yet, on average, they own only 7.2% of land—4% in the North East and just over 10% in the South East and South South geopolitical zones.

It is easier for women to obtain land in their own names in urban areas. However, urban dwellers retain strong social, political and economic ties to their village communities, where women are still disenfranchised. In urban cities where land ownership is, at least in principle, open to those who can afford it, women are less likely to have sufficient personal capital or collateral to obtain loans.

Nigerian males also outstrip females in educational status. Table 2.1 portrays an overview of some key sex disaggregated educational statistics for 2010 and 2013. It shows adult and youth female literacy rates lag considerably behind those of males at 48%/74% (adults) and 66%/78% (youth). Girls had 4.9 mean years of schooling in 2014 compared to boys at 7.1 years. These figures mask variations across geopolitical zones, given that gender disparities are worse in the north, particularly the core Muslim north (Federal Ministry of Education, 2010). In 2006 and 2011 two ActionAid-led studies, consisting of a baseline and endline survey on girl-child education in

Northern Nigeria showed persistent gender gaps in female gross enrollment, retention and transition rates at primary and secondary levels. Stark gender disparities in education statistics are strongly correlated with high rates of poverty, girl-child marriage, fertility, and maternal and infant mortality (NBS, 2013, 2014). Several empirical studies reveal that low female human capital formation (education and health) contributes to the disproportionate prevalence of female poverty, particularly among rural dwellers and the urban poor (Ajani, 2008; Lawanson, 2008; Para-Mallam, 2013; Umoru & Yakoub, 2013).

In fact, human and gender development index scores for Nigeria are generally lower than four other major African economies with comparable sub-regional socioeconomic indices (Ghana, Kenya, Rwanda and South Africa), and the Sub-Sahara African average as shown in Table 2.1. Nigeria's Gender Development Indicator (GDI) score (0.841) classifies it under Group 5 along with Ghana (0.885), rated as low gender inequality countries. This compares unfavorably with countries like Kenya (0.913—Group 4: medium to low gender equality), South Africa (0.948—Group 3: medium gender equality) and Rwanda (0.957—Group 2: medium to high gender equality).

Low gender equality is brought into sharp relief in the area of female health. As noted in the introduction, the 2015 *Human Development Report* (UNDP, 2015) gives Nigeria a 2014 HDI score of 0.514 with a ranking of 152 out of 188 countries! On the Human Development Indicator (HDI), male and female life expectancy rates in Nigeria depict a marginal differential of 1.3 years at 53.1 years and 52.4 years, respectively. Similarly, the male/female sex ratio (102:100) for 2013 remained consistent across all age groupings including 60+. Although this marked a drop from 103:100 sex ratio in 2010, it suggests higher patterns of morbidity and mortality for females as also data from the 2013 *Demographic Statistics Report* clearly affirms (National Bureau of Statistics, 2013). Similarly, Table 2.2 shows that the 2011 HIV/AIDS prevalence rate for males was 1.1% compared to 2.9% for females. After 15 years aimed at improving maternal health, among other Millennium Development Goals, Nigeria's Maternal Mortality Ratio (MMR) of 560/100,000 live births remains higher than the Sub-Saharan average of 506/100,000.

Other statistics attest to female disadvantage in relation to earned income and labor force participation. Nigerian women only have a 38.1% share of the gross national income compared to men's 61.9%. Women do not always have full control over the income they earn. Married women, in particular, sometimes feel compelled by cultural expectations or other coercive means, including physical violence, to surrender their income to husbands or other male relatives. As in many countries, Nigerian women are disproportionately underrepresented in paid work and over-represented in unpaid domestic and subsistence work. Formal labor force participation is skewed in favor of males at 64.5% and 35.5% for females, as revealed in Table 2.2. Female representation in senior management stands at 34% at the state level and 26% at federal level.

Table 2.2 Earned Income, Labor Force Participation, Maternal Mortality Ratio and HIV Prevalence by Sex
The table shows significantly worse economic and health indicators for women than men in terms of earned income, labour force participation, vulnerability to HIV as well as the added risk of high maternal mortality rates in Nigeria.

ECONOMIC INDICATORS			HEALTH INDICATORS	
	Share of GNI (Gross National Income) PPP (Purchasing Power Parity) US$	*Labor Force Partici- pation*	*HIV Prevalence Rate*	*Maternal Mortality Rate (MMR)*
Male	6,585 (61.9%)	64.5%	1.1%	NA
Female	4,052 (38.1%)	35.5%	2.9%	560/100,000

Source: 2015 *Human Development Report* (UNDP, 2015)

The report notes that there are several states, especially in the south, where women dominate the labor market. Nevertheless, recent studies show that women still tend to be at the lower end of low-paying pink-collar jobs in the service sector as well as in the informal economy (Nwakeze, 2012; Para-Mallam, 2013). These data all highlight the relatively poor health and economic status of Nigerian women and girls. But to get a proper picture of the situation of Nigerian women in the world of work, one must consider unpaid subsistence and domestic labor. After their regular day jobs, women work an invisible double shift in the form of sex-segregated reproductive labor doing housework and caring for children, the sick and the elderly. Studies examining the time use of Nigerian women reveal that men, on the other hand, have more spare time for social, political and leisure activities (Akande, 1981; Para-Mallam, 2007, 2013).

There is a strong positive association between the triple development burden Nigerian women carry (through involvement in reproductive, productive and community development work) and their capacity to participate in community/public decision-making. These data drawn from various indicators measuring human well-being all highlight the relatively low health, social and economic status of Nigerian women and girls.

Political Dimensions of Gender Inequality

Nigeria's poorest gender equality performance is in political representation, especially in relation to elective positions. Men overwhelmingly dominate all arms of government at federal, state and local government level. Beteille (2003) defines social (or political) inequality as the unequal distribution of authority, esteem and advantage in society as opposed to those inequalities that arise from the unequal distribution of natural endowments, such as physical and mental abilities or aptitudes. Kwame Nkrumah believed that the political kingdom is the gateway to all forms of power and influence in society. Gunew and Yeatman (1993) assert that political participation and representation is the means by which individuals and groups ensure their peculiar needs and interests are placed on the public policy agenda. Since Nigeria's return to democratic rule in 1999, women have not recorded sufficient success in becoming equally visible or making their voice heard in the political space to induce meaningful change for the majority of the country's women.

According to the most recent data contained in a *Research and Ranking Report* (Winihin Jemide Series, 2016) the proportion of women elected into the National Assembly doubled from 3.3% (1999–2003) to 6.85% (2003–2007). However, it then declined from 7.8% (2007–11) to 7% (2011–15) and is currently 5.2% (2015–19). The data in Figure 2.1 indicates that despite some progress, Nigeria still lags far behind the Sub-Saharan Africa average of 20.6% female representation in parliament (UNDP, 2015). Between 2011 and 2015, under the Transformation Agenda Mid-Term Development Plan, President Goodluck Jonathan's Administration awarded the highest number of ministerial appointments to women in Nigerian history comprising almost 32% of total ministerial slots (Federal Government of Nigeria, 2011). The Buhari Administration, which took over in May 2015, did not build on this momentum as the number of female ministerial appointees fell from 11 (31.4%) to 6 (19.4%). This suggests that without the special measures instituted by forward-looking African countries like Rwanda, Sudan, South Africa, Tanzania and Uganda, equal gender representation in politics is not assured.

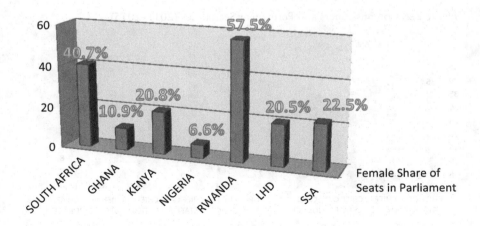

Figure 2.1 Female Representation in Parliament in Some African Countries (2014)

On the other hand, while female representation in top-level public office nationwide remains below 10%, women are making greater inroads into executive positions in the Civil Service and the Judiciary. Figures 2.2 and 2.3 display the distribution of commissioners and permanent secretaries, and chiefs of staff and chief justices, respectively, at state level by sex. Figure 2.2 shows that, as of April 2015, 17.7% and 24.3% of commissioners and state permanent secretaries, respectively, were female.

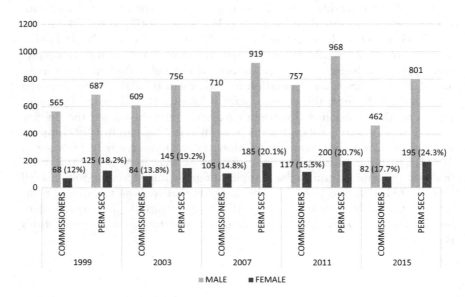

Figure 2.2 Commissioners and Permanent Secretaries (2011–2015)

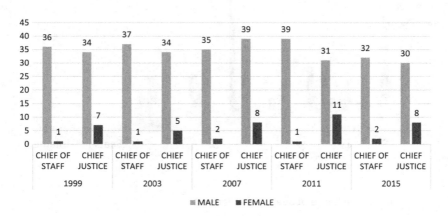

Figure 2.3 State Chiefs of Staff and Chief Justices (2011–2015)

The situation was somewhat better in Plateau State, which is atypical for Northern Nigeria. Between 2007 and 2011 there were five women (22.7%), including the Deputy-Governor, in the 22-member state executive council. However, the state house of assembly consisted of only three women (12%) and 22 men. Ten (27.8%) of the 36 chief executives of state boards and parastatals are female (Winihin Jemide Series, 2016). These figures are substantially higher than in most states and the national average. However, they still fall short of the 35% minimum stipulated in the 2006 National Gender Policy, and even the 30% previously stipulated in the 2000 National Policy on Women, which the NGP superseded. Lovenduski (2001) argues that a one-third (33%) representation is required for any group to form a critical mass to sway public policy in its favor.

To the extent that men wield political power almost exclusively in Nigeria the entire political, administrative and legislative framework encapsulates male preferences and promotes male privilege. In this context gender bias and discrimination become "normal," routinized or institutitionalized to the extent of being invisible, and thus largely incontestable. Within this context of political exclusion and marginalization women are often granted tokenist representation in public office at the benevolence of male authority figures or through their filial associations, as wives with powerful women spearhead women-centered pet projects in the spirit of "femocracy" (Mama, 1997). Neither tokenism nor femocracy have succeeded in expanding female political space to any significant degree (Mama, 1997).

For years, gender analysts, human rights activists and development practitioners in Nigeria have argued for a restructuring of the political space to promote more genuinely inclusive democratic practice. In 2007, the Justice Uwais Electoral Reform Committee recommended, albeit unsuccessfully, a change from the current winner-takes-all system to one of proportional representation as a tested strategy for promoting inclusion and national integration. Although the Nigerian political elite deemed it fit to enshrine proportional ethnic representation in the Constitution, and to implement affirmative action policies to redress geopolitical disadvantage, it has been averse to similar approaches to remove structural and systemic obstacles to gender empowerment and gender-inclusive democracy. As noted earlier these obstacles arise from deep-seated cultural and religious bias, which infuses the public policy space and undermines the capacity of the policy/legal framework to bring about gender equality.

Political power also affords those who wield it the opportunity to fashion laws and policies that promote the ideologies and interests of dominant groups. These ideologies generate social norms and customs that become firmly entrenched in the moral and structural fabric of society. They become accepted as the standard for measuring and judging right and wrong and for allocating punishment and rewards. The resultant gender bias is reflected in the nature and impacts of Nigeria's tripartite legal system of Customary, Sharia and Statutory laws, which create a multi-layered gender-differentiated citizenship experience with direct implications for women's participation in decision-making. For example, certain religious and customary laws prohibit women from holding executive positions in faith-based and traditional institutions. According to an opinion survey on attitudes to leadership conducted by Agbaje et al. (2003), the mindset of female exclusion from decision-making carries over to the modern sphere of formal politics. The study proved that hidden culture-based gender bias predisposes the electorate, both male and female, towards selecting and electing male leaders.

The home is another vital level of decision-making in which the political becomes personal and vice versa. Gender power dynamics in Nigerian families are built primarily on the notion of male headship and male guardianship among Christians and Muslims, respectively (Adamu & Para-Mallam, 2012). By popular interpretation of sacred texts this generally implies that the man is the household decision-maker and women have to submit to male authority. The home is, in principle, a non-negotiable space for the exercise of male leadership. The gender coding of leadership takes place within households as men, as divinely ordained heads of homes, model hegemonic masculinity to boys, and girls learn to defer "naturally" to male direction (Awe, 1992; Ogundipe-Leslie, 1994; Para-Mallam, 2011). Intra-household and community socialization to gender hierarchy is another critical factor negating formal mechanisms for gender equality.

Putting Gender on the Agenda: Difficulties, Dilemmas and Political Doublespeak

Since the International Year of the Woman in 1975, women's groups, scholars and professionals have worked hard to create a space for women's gender interests on the Nigerian policy agenda. The current Gender Management System moderated by the Federal Ministry of Women Affairs and Social Development (FMWASD) represents the culmination of years of feminist struggle to increase women's share of national resources through female capacity building for enhanced engagement in development. Despite efforts by national and state governments to enact gender-sensitive policies and laws, state orientation is yet to fully transit from a women-in-development perspective that treats women's issues in isolation of the broad picture of unequal gender power relations. State policy is caught between tradition and change in female social roles. Pittin (1991, pp. 38–39) clarifies further:

> In relation to women, state policy at the level of federal text and tenor appears supportive and benign [. . .] This, however, must be related to other aspects of law, statute, and policy, associated with control over production and reproduction [. . .] The overall direction of these policies is the maintenance of ideological assertion of women as mothers, housewives, helpmates to men, and peripheral workers. This justifies women's continuing to undertake the entire burden of domestic labour withdraws women from competition for wage labour and justifies

unequal access to education, information, technology, credit, training, and productive resources including land and landed property.

Consequently, government rhetoric on gender equality falls short of far-reaching policy action required for promoting women's strategic gender interests towards long-term structural change. In every budget line since its inception the FMWASD has been the least-funded ministry with a litany of projects it cannot implement. Besides official doublespeak, there are difficulties arising from the false consciousness and resistance of Nigerian women and men, respectively.

Do Nigerian Women Really Want Equality?

Empirical evidence from *Nigerian Women Speak: An Analysis of Government Policy* (Para-Mallam, 2007) indicated that, to a great extent, Nigerian women have internalized the identity and roles prescribed by a patriarchal worldview and become so acculturated as to find change inconceivable (Chirkov et al., 2005). They are not yet psychologically ready for the full implications of what gender equality and gender mainstreaming in public policy entail. Most of the study participants made it clear that most women are not ready to leave the "comfort zone" of cultural and economic dependency on the socially ascribed male protector and provider role. Costs associated with fighting for and achieving equality, such as loss of marital status, income and public recognition, appeared far too high. An interviewee cited in Adamu et al. (2010, p. 16) puts it succinctly:

> Women's desire and dependency on relationships prevents them from committing to a women's movement. I learnt this from the women themselves. In women's groups they talk and shout but at home they are like mice and they would rather protect that relationship and be totally subordinate [. . .] even if she has a PhD. Being married is more important to Nigerian women than the fight for women's rights; even if the marriage is a farce, a pretence and shadow; even if she's not being treated properly as a wife. She is concerned about the public image of being married.

In addition, analyses of the nature of Nigerian women's organizing portray fragmented and discordant social change agendas marked by a disconnect between elitist feminist goals for gender equality and grassroots "womanist" efforts for incremental improvements in women's material conditions (Adamu et al., 2010; Mama, 1997; Para-Mallam, 2007). To resolve the tension between what is widely perceived as Western feminist propaganda and homegrown womanist empowerment agendas, some activists and development practitioners find it more appropriate to speak of gender equity. Equity is seen as allowing for functional gender role distinctions, including traditional male hegemony, while providing a case for justice and right to development for women (Para-Mallam, 2011).

Male Resistance to Gender Equality

According to a former top-ranking government official interviewed and cited in Para-Mallam (2007), Nigerian men fear the loss of status that women's empowerment and gender equality would bring about. Because gender equality fundamentally entails an equitable distribution of power, privilege and resources between men and women, it hits at the core of male identity and male privilege created and reinforced by deeply embedded traditional and religious ideologies that permeate institutions. Pittin (1991, p. 38) explains how this applies to the Nigerian policy environment:

> In Nigeria the state, or sections of the state, pursue parallel yet often contradictory policies, differentially verbalised or operationalised depending on the underlying and immediate interests to be served.

This shows clearly that a pervasive patriarchal ideology provides the justification for gender inequality, and it is intrinsically tied to the way both men and women perceive of themselves and each other in terms of roles, rights and responsibilities. Herein lies the key difficulty in seeking to narrow the gap between men and women in Nigerian society. It appears to be the missing link in the strategies spelled out in most women's empowerment and gender equality agendas by both governmental and non-governmental organizations, which tend to focus on measures external to the psychological makeup of socio-political actors. Although gender awareness strategies are employed, they are usually aimed at appealing to the sense of morality of opinion molders and stakeholders and convincing them of the practical utility of women's empowerment for all. They do not sufficiently address the need for a wholesale re-evaluation of the values, practices and institutional avenues (especially family, religious and traditional institutions) through which gender identities and relations become conditioned and ultimately distorted to circumscribe human potential.

To bridge the lacuna, there is an urgent need to stimulate informed gender dialogue from the grassroots up to the policy-making level with a view to generating popular commitment to implement action plans that can induce enduring societal transformation. Rather than rehash the commonly accepted strategies for promoting gender equality, the next sub-section takes a closer look the content of gender dialogues and how they may engender social change.

Towards Gender Equality in Nigeria

In *Gender, Citizenship and Democratic Governance in Nigeria* (Para-Mallam, forthcoming) I discuss practical and strategic steps towards increasing women's democratic space as a means of promoting gender equality. Owing to the heterogeneity of women's identities and experience, I propose a combination of incremental and structural changes to address women's diverse social locations and realities. Strong contestations around the idea of gender equality imply that an effective change agenda needs to be far-reaching yet feasible. At the practical level, grassroots women living in rural areas and low-income urban centers are desperately in need of increased access to social security, basic needs and skills to even raise them to a place where they can begin to pursue more strategic gender interests and goals. Development schemes that have strong educational and economic empowerment content are vital for strengthening women's human capabilities (Nussbaum, 2001). This would reposition them to take advantage of opportunities that would enhance livelihoods, build self-esteem and leverage in intra-household and public decision-making.

The Federal Ministry of Women Affairs and donor agencies know this and are organizing more of such capacity building schemes at the grassroots level. However, there is a risk of market saturation of the same products and services related to petty trading and single-commodity cottage industries. The effect is that rural and low-income women are unable to acquire sufficient comparative advantage to rise substantially above the level of subsistence living. In this regards, countries like Sierra Leone and Ghana present good practices in using new, but easy-to-use solar agro-based technologies to promote value-chain addition for female rural dwellers and agriculturalists. The resultant additional income has often served the strategic end of enhancing women's social prestige and decision-making power within their communities.

At the level of women's strategic gender interests, Molyneux (1985) and Moser (1993) advocate for an intentional approach to dismantling underlying structures of oppression. In the Nigerian context, this would mean pushing for legislative and electoral reform to give legal teeth to the National Gender Policy 35% baseline for female political representation to promote a critical mass of women in governance at all levels. There is also a need for nationwide public dialogues geared towards interrogating patriarchal ideologies that generate and sustain inequality. I elaborate further on these below.

Gender Dialogues for Social Change

There is a considerable amount of ignorance, misconception and fear about women's empowerment and the agenda for gender equality. Some believe it entails helping women get their fair share of the national cake. Others, particularly but not exclusively men, are afraid that the women want to take over power and dominate their male counterparts. This reasoning arises from the conventional political science understanding of power as a zero-sum winner-take-all game where to hold power means to exercise control over others, frequently in the interest of the power holder. Although within this model all people, including the seemingly powerless, may bear residual power and influence to a lesser or greater degree, generally the top echelons of the political hierarchy carry greater authority and prestige. Conversely, Rowlands (1998) enunciates a feminist model of power that conceptualizes alternative modes of exercising authority in a way that promotes inclusiveness, collaboration, mutuality and respect for others. She discusses how in contrast to the exclusive "power over" model, power could also be cooperative ("power with"), enabling and motivational ("power to") and psychospiritually generative ("power from within").

Findings from my doctoral fieldwork conducted among men and women between 2003 and 2004 indicate that the fear of the loss of power poses a severe threat to male identity and therefore lies at the heart of male resistance to gender equality agendas (Para-Mallam, 2007). Indeed, where men try to adopt egalitarian behavior in domestic and public spaces they are often regarded as instigators of "class suicide" and encounter ridicule and social pressure to "conform to the norm." Women also fear censorship and/or the loss of community belonging and acceptance that attends social conformity to prescribed gender roles. Gender dialogues could increase the social space for alternative femininities and masculinities. Such dialogues may take place as women-to-women, women-to-men and men-to-men interactive sessions. Important issue-areas for discussion are outlined below.

Women-to-Women Dialogue

Women-to-women dialogues provide opportunities for women to share, negotiate and strategize in concert across ethnic, racial, religious, class and political divides. Critical issues for discussion include patriarchy and strategies for long-term transformation and the implementation of CEDAW:

1   Women's relationship with patriarchy: Should women continue to bargain with it or work towards a systematic dismantling of patriarchal ideologies and structures as the NPW/NGP suggest? A proper understanding of patriarchy reveals an inherent incompatibility with gender equality; the two are mutually exclusive. This implies that women must work to do away with an exclusively male-centric worldview that informs and interprets religious discourse and institutions. In private life they must also work to do away with those marital regulations and practices that put women at a disadvantage. In politics they must work to overhaul rather than adapt to the political culture by working to do away with the zero-sum winner-take-all approach that excludes the poor, and overwhelmingly women. Nigerian women need the foresight and the courage to dialogue and work together to forge people-oriented, women-friendly political systems where power is construed as a sacred trust to enable others rather than a passport to dominance, control and largesse.

2 Collaboration for long-term strategic transformation: Women commonly adopt a persecution complex that claims that because women have been oppressed, they deserve concessions without necessarily working for them. Affirmative action is a case in point. While affirmative action and quotas are important and justifiable tools for redressing gender imbalances, they have often been used to advance mediocrity and promote tokenism, particularly in the public sector (Mama, 1997). A few hand-picked women are granted access to economic or political power while the vast majority remain "un-reached." More often than not, such women are either not gender-aware or they are too few to form a critical mass required to engender change. It is critical that women resist tokenist representation and social engagement by "femocratic" fiat spearheaded mainly by first ladies. Women need to dialogue and strategize together to promote competence and merit as well as insist on representation that will advance gender interests. A note of caution is in order here. Gender interests are under constant threat of a divide-and-rule tactic (Molyneux, 1985). They risk being compromised by competing ethnic, religious, class identities and interests or co-opted (as opposed to mainstreamed) by the prevailing political system. Cooptation robs gender of its political content and thrust to bring about structural transformation. It is important that women confront the "handout syndrome" with action plans aimed at bridging other divides between and among them in order to organize effectively around strategic gender interests.

3 Women need to talk about CEDAW and the African Women's Protocol! The point has been made that legislative reform is not a cure-all for women's problems. The provisions of CEDAW and the Protocol are now assimilated into the Gender and Equal Opportunities Bill (GEOB), which is to be re-presented to the National Assembly. It provides a powerful locus upon which women can make justiciable gender-based claims to enforce their human and civil rights. It is imperative that all Nigerian women are made aware of the GEOB and mobilized to adapt its provisions to local needs and lobby governments to enshrine them in domestic law. Once this is done, women must be active in monitoring their enforcement at all levels.

Women's and Men's Dialogue

Women alone cannot accomplish social transformation. They need to work in partnership with men who have been made gender-aware in the context of non-confrontational, constructive dialogue. Men need to listen to women articulate the silence that veils their pain and be persuaded that ultimately female empowerment has payoffs for all members of society. While it may be impractical to expect a change in the attitudes and behaviors of all or even most men in the short term, gender dialogues will provide a forum for men and women to understand each other's fears and engage constructively with the issues, thereby paving way for future change.

Men-to-Men Dialogue

Men-to-men dialogues are underway in many parts of the world in response to feminist advocacy. Development workers and analysts are discovering the strategic importance of involving men in gender and development projects as peer educators as well as target beneficiaries (Chant & Gutmann, 2000; Sampath, 1997). In Latin America indigenous men's groups are working with men and boys against gender-based violence. Men come to realize that "gender" is not synonymous with "women," it concerns the holistic well-being of both, and that gender-sensitivity does not imply weakness. Through participation and dialogue men have a chance to take the initiative and make change happen in ways only they can do. Men-to-men open dialogue is an urgent prerequisite for women's empowerment in Nigeria. Such dialogues explore male identity formation, competing masculinities and their complicity, or otherwise, in gender oppression. They give men the rare opportunity to examine deep-seated psychological attachments to standard expectations of male behavior and the fear of deviating from it. The aim is for men to engage in transparent and frank discussion on how stereotypical expectations of masculinity adversely affect all members of society—male and female—and to encourage alternative male identities that precipitate equitable and harmonious social relations.

Conclusion

This chapter reviewed structural root causes and dimensions of gender inequality in Nigerian society. In spite of numerous efforts to reduce gender inequality at government and civil society levels, gender disparities across all sectors of the Nigerian economy persist. Progress in redressing the low socioeconomic status of women is slow but steady, yet intense resistance from important individual and institutional stakeholders, including women themselves, hamper change efforts. Despite the various institutional frameworks and strategies put in place to promote gender equality, deep-seated psychological, ideological and material factors prevent female access to non gender-differentiated citizenship. An important step towards change in the context of weak policy action is the organization of gender dialogues around sensitive and controversial issues relating to identity, roles and relations. There is need for nationwide dialogues to address critical issues and themes that uncover and confront misconceptions, fears and ignorance about the meaning and implications of gender equality. The impetus for gender equality is premised on the indisputable fact that it is a critical factor in national productivity and holistic development.

Table 2.3 Overview of NGP Objectives and Priority Targets

OBJECTIVES	PRIORITY TARGETS	TIME FRAME
1 Establish the framework for gender-responsiveness in all public and private spheres	Launch National Gender Strategic Framework (NGSF)	June 2007
	Develop/operate gender sensitive sectoral policies	2010
	Establish/operationalize the national GMS	NA
	Strengthen capacity of State Ministries of Women Affairs	2008
	Build effective public/private sector/civil society partnerships	2008
	Prioritize gender equality principles in international partnerships	2008
2 Develop and apply gender mainstreaming approaches tools and instruments towards national development	Establish and strengthen appropriate educational, training, institutional and operational frameworks	2010
	Remove gender-based barriers to agricultural production	2010
3 Adopt gender mainstreaming as a core value and practice in social transformation	Entrench a culture of gender sensitivity and equality principles	2010
	Eliminate harmful cultural, religious and social gender-based practices	2020
	Institute and enforce laws to penalize discriminatory practices	2008
4 Incorporate the principles of CEDAW and other global and regional frameworks for women's empowerment	Achieve equity and equality in employment opportunities	2015
	Build capacity of the legislature, the judiciary and other law enforcement agencies	2010
	Institute a culture of respect for the human rights of women and men	2010
5 Achieve a minimum threshold of public representation for women	Provide equal opportunities for women and men to enjoy and attain an acceptable minimum threshold of universal access to social amenities (potable water, sanitation, electricity, etc.)	2015
	Adopt special measures, quotas and mechanisms for achieving equal political representation	2015
6 Undertake women and men-specific projects as a means for developing the capabilities of both	Ensure equal access of women and men to critical resources	2012
	Address gender dimensions to HIV/AIDS infection rates	2010
	Reduce maternal mortality rates by at least 35%	2015
7 Educate and sensitize all stakeholders on the centrality of gender equality to the attainment of national development	Guarantee equal access to education and skills	2015
	Improve demand and supply factors that hamper retention and completion of secondary school	2010
		2008

Source: *National Gender Policy* (Federal Ministry of Women Affairs and Social Development, 2006)

Notes

1 Emeka Muojekwu v Okechukwu Ejikeme (2000) 5 NWLR 403, cited in Atsenuwa (2008).
2 Nigeria's 2006 Census Data did not contain information on religious affiliation.

References

Adamu, F.L., & Para-Mallam, O.J. (2012). The role of religion in women's campaigns for legal reform in Nigeria. *Development in Practice*, 22 (5–6), 803–818. DOI: http://dx.doi.org/10.1080/09614524.2012.685875
Adamu, F.L., Para-Mallam, O.J., Lawal, A., & Lanre-Abass, B. (2010). A review of literature on the role of religion in women's movements for social change. Working Paper Series 46, Religion and Development Programme, Birmingham, UK: University of Birmingham. Retrieved from http://www.birmingham.ac.uk/Documents/college-social-sciences/government-society/rad/working-papers/wp-46.pdf (accessed 15 August 2016).
Agbaje, A., Okunola, R., & Alarape, A. (2003). *Perspectives on Leadership in Nigeria: Report of a National Survey October–December 2002*. Lagos: Macmillan.
Aina, O. (1992). African women at the grassroots: The silent partners of the women's movement. Paper presented at the Conference on Women in Africa and the African Diaspora (WAAD), Nsukka, Nigeria, July 1992. In O. Nnaemeka (Ed.), *Sisterhood: Feminisms and Power, from Africa to the Diaspora*, Trenton, NJ: Africa World Press, pp. 65–88.
Ajani, O.I.Y. (2008). Gender dimensions of agriculture, poverty, nutrition and food security in Nigeria. Nigeria Strategy Support Program (NSSP) Background Paper No. NSSP 005.
Akande, J. (1981). Participation of women in rural development (Nigeria). Paper prepared for the International Labour Office, Tripartite African Regional Seminar, Rural Development and Women, Dakar, Senegal, 15–19 June 1981.
Alemika, E.E.O. (2001). Pattern of gender violence and gender discrimination in the North Central States of Nigeria. Paper presented at the workshop on Gender Violence and Poverty organized by the Office of the Special Adviser to the President on Women Affairs, Jos, Nigeria, 11 July 2001.
Anambra State Malpractices against Widows and Widowers (Prohibition) Law. (2005). Awka, Nigeria: Anambra State Government.
Annan, K. (2006). *Ending Violence against Women: From Words to Action*. New York: United Nations.
Atsenuwa, A. (2008). Study of national legislations, policies and practices congruent and incompatible with the provisions of the Convention on Elimination of All Forms of Discrimination (CEDAW) and the protocol to the African charter on human and people's rights on the rights of women in Africa. Unpublished report, funded by CIDA. Lagos: Legal Research and Resource Development Centre.
Awe, B. (1992). *Nigerian Women in Historical Perspective*. Lagos and Ibadan: Sankore.
Beteille, A. (2003). Poverty and inequality. *Economic and Political Weekly*, 38 (42), 4455–4463.
British Council of Nigeria. (2012). *Gender in Nigeria Report 2012: Improving the Lives of Girls and Women in Nigeria: Issues, Policy and Action*. UK: DFID.

Bustelo, E.S. (2001). Expansion of citizenship and democratic construction. In W. van Genugten & C. Perez-Bustillo (Eds), *The Poverty of Rights: Human Rights and the Eradication of Poverty*, London: Zed Books, pp. 3–28.

Centre on Housing Rights and Evictions. (2004). *Bringing Equality Home: Promoting and Protecting the Inheritance Rights of Women: A Survey of Law and Practice in Sub-Saharan Africa*. Geneva: COHRE.

Chant, S., & Gutmann, M. (2000). *Mainstreaming Men into Gender and Development: Debates, Reflections and Experiences*. Oxford: Oxfam.

Chirkov, V., Ryan, R., & Willness, C. (2005). Cultural context and psychological needs in Canada and Brazil: Testing a self-determination approach to the internalization of cultural practices, identity, and well-being. *Journal of Cross-Cultural Psychology*, 36 (4), 423–443.

Constitution of the Federal Republic of Nigeria (Promulgation) Decree 1999. (1999). Official Gazette No. 27/86. Government notice no. 66. Lagos: Official Gazette.

CWEENS. (forthcoming). *An Overview of Violence Affecting Women and Girls in Nigeria: Challenges and Change Strategies*. Nigeria: CWEENS.

Divale, W., & Harris, M. (1979). Population, warfare, and the male supremacist complex. In D. McCurdy & J. Spradley (Eds), *Issues in Cultural Anthropology: Selected Readings*, Boston: Little Brown and Co, pp. 240–322.

Effah-Chukwuma, J., Osakwe, B., & Ekpeyong, U. (2001). *Beyond Boundaries: Violence against Women in Nigeria*. Lagos: Project Alert on Violence against Women.

Effah-Chukwuma, J., Osakwe, B., & Ekpeyong, U. (2002). *No Safe Haven: Report of Attacks on Women in Nigeria December 2000–November 2002*. Lagos: Project Alert on Violence against Women.

Federal Government of Nigeria. (2006). *Nigeria 2006 Millennium Development Goals Report*. Abuja: FGN Press.

Federal Government of Nigeria. (2011). *Final Report on Transformation Agenda 2011–2015*. Abuja: FGN Press.

Federal Ministry of Education. (2010). *NIGERIA: Digest of Education Statistics 2006–2010*. Abuja, Nigeria: FME.

Federal Ministry of Women Affairs and Social Development. (1999). National Baseline Survey on the harmful and positive traditional practices affecting women and girls in Nigeria. Centre for Gender and Social Policy Studies, Obafemi Awolowo University, Ile-Ife, Nigeria.

Federal Ministry of Women Affairs and Social Development. (2000). *The National Policy on Women*. Abuja, Nigeria: Government Press.

Federal Ministry of Women Affairs and Social Development. (2006). *National Gender Policy*. Abuja, Nigeria: Federal Secretariat.

Gunew, S., & Yeatman, A. (eds) (1993). *Feminism and the Politics of Difference*. Boulder, CO: Westview Press.

Imam, A. (2009). Adopting women's human rights legislation in Nigeria. Study funded by DFID Nigeria's Security, Justice and Growth (SJG) Program in collaboration with UNIFEM, DFID, CIDA, OSIWA, Oxfam.

Ishola, W., & Alani, R. (2011). Human capital development and socio-economic growth: Empirical evidence from Nigeria. *Asian Economic and Financial Review*, 2 (7), 813–827.

Kabeer, N. (2003). *Gender Mainstreaming in Poverty Eradication and the Millennium Development Goals: A Handbook for Policy-makers and Other*

Stakeholders. Ottawa: International Development Research Centre, Commonwealth Secretariat.

Lawanson, O. (2008). Female labour productivity in Nigeria: Determinants and trends. Paper presented for Oxford Business and Economics Conference.

Lovenduski, J. (2001). Women and politics: Minority representation or critical mass. *Parliamentary Affairs*, **54** (4), 743–758.

Madaki, L. (2014). Women and child rights protection from gender-based violence: An overview of Nigerian law. Paper presented at Capacity-Building Workshop for CWEENS at CRUDAN, Plateau State, Nigeria, 5 August 2014.

Makama, G. (2013). Patriarchy and gender inequality in Nigeria. *European Scientific Journal*, **9** (17), 115–144.

Mama, A. (1997). Feminism or femocracy? State feminism and democratization in Nigeria. In J. Ibrahim (Ed.), *Expanding Democratic Space in Nigeria*, Dakar: CODESRIA, pp. 77–96.

Mark-Odu, P. (2000). Political affirmative action for Nigeria. Paper presented at a one-day pre-conference seminar of the National Association of Women Academics (NAWACS), National Centre for Women Development, Abuja, 31 March 2000.

Molyneux, M. (1985). Mobilization without emancipation? Women's interests, state, and revolution in Nicaragua. *Feminist Studies*, **11** (2), 227–254.

Moser, C. (1993). *Gender Planning and Development: Theory, Practice and Training*. London: Routledge.

National Bureau of Statistics. (2006). *Poverty Profile for Nigeria*. Abuja, Nigeria: National Bureau of Statistics.

National Bureau of Statistics. (2013). *Demographic Statistics Bulletin*. Abuja, Nigeria: Demographic Statistics Division.

National Bureau of Statistics. (2014). The 2014 statistical report on men and women in Nigeria. Retrieved from http://www.nigerianstat.gov.ng/pdfuploads/2014%20Statistical%20Report%20on%20Women%20and%20Men%20in%20Nigeria_.pdf (accessed 17 May 2016).

Nigerian NGO CEDAW Coalition. (2008). CEDAW and commitment to gender equality in Nigeria: A shadow report. Submitted to the 41st Session of the Committee on the Elimination of All Forms of Discrimination Against Women. Lagos: BAOBAB.

Nigerian NGO Coalition. (1999). NGOs CEDAW report for Nigeria: NGOs report on the implementation of the Convention on the Elimination of All forms of Discrimination against Women. Lagos: Nigerian NGO Coalition.

Nussbaum, M. (2001). Women and equality: The capabilities approach. In M.F. Loutfi (Ed.), *Women, Gender and Work: What Is Equality and How Do We Get There*, Geneva: ILO, pp. 45–68.

Nwakeze, N. (2012). Gender and labour force participation in Nigeria. Unpublished Conference Proceedings. Lagos: University of Lagos.

Nweze, A., & Takaya, B.J. (2001). Relative deprivation of the Nigerian female personality as gender violence: A Nigerian overview. Paper presented at the workshop on Gender Violence and Poverty organized by the Office of the Special Adviser to the President on Women Affairs, Jos, Nigeria, 11–13 July, 2001.

Odinkalu, C.A. (2008). *Domesticating CEDAW in Nigeria: A Stakeholder Analysis and Report*. Abuja, Nigeria: UNIFEM.

Ogundipe-Leslie, M. (1994). *Recreating Ourselves: African Women & Critical Transformations*. Trenton, NJ: Africa World Press.

Ogunyemi, C.O. (1996). *African Wo/man Palava: The Nigerian Novel by Women*. Chicago: University of Chicago Press.

Okome, M.O. (2000). Women, the State and the travails of decentralising the Nigerian federation. *West Africa Review*, 2 (1). Retrieved from http://www.westafricareview.com/vol2.1/okome.html (accessed 17 May 2016).

Para-Mallam, O.J. (2007). *Nigerian Women Speak: A Gender Analysis of Government Policy on Women*. Saarbrücken, Germany: Verlag Dr. Müller.

Para-Mallam, O.J. (2010). Promoting gender equality in the context of Nigerian cultural and religious expression: Beyond increasing female access to education. *Compare: A Journal of Comparative and International Education*, 40 (4), 459–477.

Para-Mallam, O.J. (2011). No woman wrapper in a husband's house: The cultural production of hegemonic masculinity in Nigeria. In O. Obafemi & A. Yerima (Eds), *Cultural Studies: Concepts, Theories and Practice*, Kuru and Ilorin, Nigeria: National Institute Press & Haytee, Press and Publishing Company, pp. 1–27.

Para-Mallam, O.J. (2013). Human capital for socio-economic development and the transformation agenda: A study of female labour productivity in Nigeria. Long Essay submitted on Senior Executive Course 35, National Institute for Policy and Strategic Studies, Kuru.

Para-Mallam, O.J. (forthcoming). Gender, citizenship and democratic governance in Nigeria. In F. Soetan & B. Akanji (Eds), *A Centenary of Nationhood: A Gender Balance Sheet of Nigeria's Development Pathways*, Lagos: Springer Publishers.

Pittin, R. (1991). Women, work and ideology in Nigeria. *Review of African Political Economy*, 18 (52), 38–52.

Rowlands, J. (1998). A word of the times, but what does it mean? Empowerment in the discourse and practice of development. In H. Afshar (Ed.), *Women and Empowerment: Illustrations from the Third World*, London: Macmillan, pp. 11–34.

Sabo, M. (2015). Violence against children: A study of legislation in Kano State. Long Essay submitted on Senior Executive Course 37, National Institute for Policy and Strategic Studies, Kuru.

Sampath, N. (1997). Crabs in a bucket: Reforming male identities in Trinidad. *Gender & Development*, 5 (2), 47–54.

Sen, A. (1990). Gender and cooperative conflicts. In I. Tinker (Ed.), *Persistent Inequalities: Women and World Development*, New York: Oxford University Press, pp. 123–149.

Todaro, M.P., & Smith, S.C. (2012). *Economic Development* (revised edition). Boston: Pearson.

Umoru, D., & Yakoub, J.O. (2013). Labour productivity and human capital in Nigeria: The empirical evidence. *International Journal of Humanities and Social Sciences*, 3 (4), 199–221.

UNDP. (2015). *Human Development Report 2015: Work for Human Development*. New York: UNDP.

UN Women. (2013). *A Baseline Survey on Violence against Women: An Analysis of the 2008 Demographic Health Survey in Nigeria*. Abuja, Nigeria: UN Women.

Winihin Jemide Series. (2016). *Research and Ranking Report*. Lagos: Winihin Jemide Series.

World Bank. (2013). *World Development Indicators*. Washington, DC: The World Bank.

3 Gender Equality in the Arab and Muslim World

Whither Post-Revolutionary Egypt?

Mohamed Arafa and Ahmed El-Ashry

Introduction

Gender equality is a natural right, for all human beings are born free and equal. However, this has not always been recognized in laws and social practice. Power has often superseded inherent rights. Modern civilizations are still trying to recover from the resulting injustice and to restore natural inherent rights. However, each community is distinctive, imprinted by factors which affect restoring those rights.

Egypt has striven to restore gender equality as a natural right since the emergence of the feminist movement in the 1919 revolution (Al-Ali, 2002, p. 5). Gender equality has survived, managing to advance within a relatively close community. Historical factors have contributed to shape the emerging concept of gender equality, its legal regulation and its impact in practice.

Equality in essence does not always indicate justice. Justice, in this respect, is a much broader concept which moves beyond equality as "sameness of rights" to accommodate not only objective elements, but also personal elements.[1] As a result, justice does not always entail sameness of rights.

The term "gender justice" would be more adequate, particularly in Egypt where equality in the sense of "sameness of rights" would not be agreed upon under the Islamic *Shari'a*.[2] It acknowledges differences between men and women in some matters and, accordingly does not provide the same rights to men and women (Abo-Zeid, 2004; El-Helw, 2014). In other words, the Islamic *Shari'a* assigns different rights to men and women in some matters of personal status, specifically marriage, divorce and inheritance. Such provisions only apply to Muslims of the state where Christians and Jews are governed by the principles of their religions (*Constitution of the Arab Republic of Egypt*, 2014, Article 3). *Shari'a* principles apply only to those who believe in Islam and they are not mandatory to non-Muslims. Thus, the Muslim majority do not perceive the substantive provisions that assign different rights to men and women to be unjust. However, it is important to stress that the Islamic *Shari'a* laid down a great deal of flexibility for its provisions to befit the conditions of every community and every time (Abo-Zeid, 2004). This allows women to have just rights under *Shari'a* in personal status matters. For example, men's right to divorce is immediate, whereas women's right to divorce requires different procedures. She has to prove the harm in the case of fault divorce and to forgo her financial rights in the case of no-fault divorce (*Khul'*). However, the decreased respect for Islamic provisions (refusing to divorce wives who seek divorce) in the modern era should make it easier for women to get a divorce.

Gender inequality in various aspects of life was a strong motive leading women to actively participate in the January 25, 2011 revolution (Moruzzi, 2013). A broad concept of social justice was an essential demand of the massive protests in the revolution. Social injustices, inefficient policies, lack of freedom and democracy, and deteriorating conditions have been barring a great nation, two-thirds of which are youth, from development and progress. Unfortunately, the uprising could not achieve what people aspired to. Rather, political instability has dominated the situation in Egypt since 2011, which has negatively impacted the society in various fields, including the empowerment of women (The United Nations Development Program, 2015).

To give a more elaborate analysis of gender equality in Egypt, part one of this chapter will briefly review the legal development of gender equality since its modern emergence in the context of the surrounding environment. It will also highlight the impact of international programs operating for the promotion of gender equality. Finally, it will discuss the factors characterizing the Egyptian society and how they influence shaping the advancement of the equality principle. Part two will give a clear view of the legal framework of gender equality in various fields of politics, economics, employment, health, education and personal status. It additionally will examine the efficacy of the legal regulation of gender equity and governmental policies in practice within statistical evidence. Finally, a conclusion will present the key findings summing up practical implications, implementation issues, and to what degree the nature of Egyptian society would accommodate gender equality. It also will provide recommendations on further promotion of gender justice and empowerment of women.

Overview: Development and the Influencing Factors

Egypt is a trans-continental country positioned in Northeast Africa at the crossroads of Asia and Europe. It is at the center of the Arab world and has always been a considerable power in the region. With a population that recently exceeded 90 million (two-thirds of whom are below 29 years), it is the most populous country in the Arab world and the third in Africa (The United Nations Development Program, 2015). Women are almost half of the population, which poses a challenge to development in a country where gender justice has seen a shackling setback. The population is composed of 90% Muslims and 10% Christians. Islam is the religion of the state and principles of Islamic *Shari'a* are the primary source of legislation (*Constitution of the Arab Republic of Egypt*, 2014, Article 2). The country has for decades been enduring a lack of democracy, political freedom and inefficient economic strategies, causing an unfair distribution of wealth and increased cost of living led eventually to inflation (Arafa, 2011). Additionally, the diminishing quality of education, poor health services, lack of respect for human rights and dignities, and widespread corruption of government officials were all factors leading to the January 25th outburst (Arafa, 2011).

Gender equality as a basic human right, as defined in international treaties to which Egypt is a state party, has not progressed much; rather, it has remained associated with the prevalent political, economic, social and cultural conditions. Such a connection has always been obvious throughout Egyptian legal development since the emergence of the feminist movement. This will be illustrated with a brief overview of the legal development of gender equality in the context of the surrounding factors in modern Egypt.

The Legal and Ideological Development of Gender Justice

The Egyptian women's movement emerged with women's participation in the 1919 revolution against the British colonizers and the subsequent rise of the Egyptian Feminist Union [EFU] (Bayoumi, 1987). The EFU called for political rights for women, equal secondary and university education, employment opportunities and changes in personal status law governing matters of marriage, divorce, child custody and inheritance. Despite women's active participation in the 1919 revolution, which was welcomed by the nationalists, the EFU's claims were neglected in the 1923 constitution. In 1948, a new Egyptian feminist movement, *Bint El-Nil* (Daughter of the Nile) was created as an initiative whose primary purpose was to claim full political rights for women (Bayoumi, 1987). However, their efforts shifted towards issues of independence and class struggle that surfaced at that time.

It was under the rule of Gamal Abd El-Nasser (1954–1970)[3] that feminist activism retreated as a result of the state's strict monitoring of political activism and the banning of any kind of autonomous organization. However, this restriction was paralleled by the appropriation of women's issues. Women's rights were increased, although within the limits set by the government (Al-Ali, 2002). The 1956 constitution adopted the principle of equality, declaring all Egyptians equal, regardless of gender. Moreover, women were granted political rights to voting and running for political positions (Ahmed, 1982). The educational system was reformed, providing equal opportunities for women to increase their enrollment in both primary and secondary education. The outcome of that reform in practice was the increase in female participation in higher education (Hatem, 1993). The labor law was also amended to guarantee state jobs for all holders of high school diplomas and college degrees, irrespective of gender. This period of the state's legal or ideological commitment to women's rights was labeled "state feminism" (Hatem, 1993).

Despite the wide-scale popularity of Nasser's regime owing to the reform policies it provided, the state policy changed at the beginning of the rule of

Anwar Al-Sadat (1970–1981), who succeeded Abd El-Nasser.[4] The state's role in economic and social affairs was diminishing for the *Infitah* (open door) policies, including the support for women's rights (Hatem, 1993). The *Infitah* policies included the shift from Nasser's socialism to capitalism's free market. For that purpose, El-Sadat adopted privatization policies (selling national economic projects that Nasser founded), diminishing the state's intervention in the economic activities. This negatively affected economic performance, leading eventually to inflation. This policy resulted in labor migration, especially to Gulf countries, leaving many women with no choice but to take over the household tasks which had previously been assigned to men. Nonetheless, the situation was characterized by high rates of women's unemployment and inequality in the workplace (Hatem, 1993). The period also lacked independent feminist organizations. It was only the United Nations Decade for Women (1975) and the state's increasing ties with new allies, particularly the US, that drove the state to consider gender issues. That was exemplified by the reform of the Personal Status Law (1979) granting women legal rights in marriage, polygamy, divorce and child custody. Furthermore, another law was introduced which changed women's representation in the parliament (Hatem, 1993). The Personal Status Law provided a quota (for the first time) of 30 seats for women's representation in the parliament. Although the state encouraged a secular coalition of men and women for the sake of an internationally improved image, this was not in conflict with the Islamic *Shari'a*. The Islamic *Shari'a* has been the primary source of legislation since 1971. Women's representation in the parliament and the rights granted to women in personal status matters were all compatible with the *Shari'a*. Requiring the consent of the wife for polygamy and granting her access to fault divorce were among the amendments.

What needs to be stressed is that the Egyptian feminist movement has often provoked debates and questions. Egyptian feminist activists have been discredited and labeled by different constituencies as agents of Western colonization and a tool of their destructive schemes (Al-Ali, 2002). Such contempt is nowadays complemented with allegations of adopting "Western thought" versus "indigenous culture" (Al-Ali, 2002). Nevertheless, such tendency has been diminishing due to wide-scale promotion of education and recently the support of the media.

The feminist movement re-emerged with the Mubarak regime (1981–2011), yet it became a tool compromised by the government to achieve stability. The personal status law amended by El-Sadat was the center of the debate, opposed by the conservative Islamists who perceived it to be liberal and also by the leftist nationalists who opposed Sadat's policies of *Infitah* and reconciliation with Israel (Al-Ali, 2002). In 1985, the law was constitutionally challenged and repealed on procedural grounds. Yet the government was under pressure to adhere to the UN conventions concerning women's rights. Economic dependence on aid from the US and international organizations (the International Monetary Fund and the World Bank) compelled the regime to present itself as committed to human rights and women's rights (Al-Ali, 2002). Therefore, a new law was passed restoring some benefits of the repealed law only after two months of its cancellation. In addition, the government earlier in 1981 had signed and ratified the UN Convention on the Elimination of All Forms of Discrimination against Women (CEDAW), still with reservations on the grounds of contradicting with the *Shari'a*. Confrontations with the Islamists over the implementation of *Shari'a* pressured Mubarak's regime, resulting in the state's legislation of more conservative laws and policies toward women. Among its manifestations are Islamic schools and Islamic banks. Hence, feminist organizations re-emerged, but remained isolated from each other, which led to no prominent advancements.[5]

The stimulus for combining the efforts of women's rights organizations was the preparations for the UN International Conference on Population and Development (ICPD) in Cairo 1994 (Al-Ali, 2002). It provided space for many women activists and organizations to meet and discuss issues of common interest and focus joint efforts on project-oriented work (Al-Ali, 2002). Discussions addressed previously taboo topics of abortion, violence and reproductive rights, among other issues of equality before the law, political participation and discriminatory laws. During the conference, state officials proclaimed their commitment to banning female genital mutilation (FGM) by law. However, opposition of the conservative Islamists backed by *Al-Azhar*[6] succeeded in pressuring the Ministry of Health to retreat and, again, misinterpretation of religion and deep-rooted traditions prevailed (Al-Ali, 2002).

The Mubarak regime largely depended on the restriction of public-sphere activities where independent associations were prohibited from carrying out political activities (Al-Ali, 2002). Forbidding political activities has been a means for controlling Egypt's civil society and restricting regional and international activities. The law no. 153 of 1999 governing associations and civil institutions (the law of associations and civil institutions) enabled the government to further restrict the formation of independent associations, such as political parties, unions, associations or NGOs (Al-Ali, 2002).

The situation continued at this pace, where the promotion of women's rights was often subjected to political restrictions. Gains in the field were the result of continued pressure by peaceful protest in Egypt and by the international community. The government often compromised for the sake of economic aid and so did some feminist associations. The government even had to compromise with the civil society organizations through different methods of courtship and threats, especially after the widespread use of the Internet and the openness to the international community. Moreover, the general decline in economic and social affairs in addition to the restriction of freedoms and non-respect for human rights all contributed to the widespread outrage that manifested itself in the January 25, 2011 revolution (Rage Revolution) (Arafa, 2011).

A spirit of freedom prevailed for some time after Mubarak was deposed, where a large sector of the society (especially youth) were involved in initiatives and activities of reform and development, including gender justice. Such involvement soon diminished with the re-embracing of the fallen regime's policies in some respects. As for gender equality, it declined when the Muslim Brotherhood (in coalition with the Salafists who are considered more conservative), who had all along been against the feminist movement and the promotion of women's rights, assumed power. Yet, even the Muslim Brotherhood involved women of their belief spectrum in public affairs and in the parliament to present itself as civilized and supporting women's rights to maintain stability for their regime by gaining the support of secular forces and the international community.

In conclusion of this development, gender equality in Egypt has always been captive to several factors including the prevalent misconception of Islamic norms in addition to the outdated misleading indigenous beliefs and traditions widely spread in the 20th century due to illiteracy and ignorance. More importantly, it has been dependent on the political will of the state and a part of its policy. Furthermore, it has been evident that the state policy is largely affected by the economic conditions and compromises between opposing internal forces.

The Factors Influencing the Development of Gender Justice

Observing the previous development of women's rights and its relation to the surrounding environment, we find it influenced by some factors more than others. It is therefore important to explain these factors to clarify the extent to which gender justice is prevalent in the Egyptian society and in what areas of social activities. Besides, recognizing the nature of the community and these factors helps to direct the focus to the issues that do not constitute a stumbling block, which provide more room for advancement.

Gender equality and the promotion of women's rights as a pressing social issue has largely been attached to state policy. In other words, the state is the qualified entity that, with its vast resources, is capable of shaping gender equality and enforcing it in everyday social life (Al-Ali, 2002). Political will determines whether the state is concerned or not with the promotion of human rights in general and gender justice in this context. In Egypt, the regime has always been an authoritarian one that depended on survival dynamics and disregard of human rights. Survival dynamics often imposed flexibility. Mere political and economic gains and pressure by the feminist associations and international organizations have often been the main reasons for addressing gender justice. The only time gender issues were addressed as a part of the state's policy was under Nasser's nationalism, which included women as a pillar for modernization and national development (Al-Ali, 2002). As a consequence, disregard of the issue has caused its aggravation, where it now poses a challenge to development.

On the other hand, a misconception of Islamic norms and outdated beliefs and traditions have all contributed to a misunderstanding that has been prevalent for decades. Low rates of education and wide-scale illiteracy have helped a male-dominated society to lay down the impression that women are inferior to men. In our analysis, this is a core problem. The increased rates of education have not affected the dilemma. The implications in practice are far uglier. For example, sexual harassment and violence against women have plagued the country in recent years (Social Institutions and Gender Index, 2014). The media and the material it presents has played its role in the decline in morality and ethics (The National Council for Women, 2014).[7] Instead of providing problematic representations of gender relations, the media should play a central role in spreading awareness and developing educational cultural content. However, it has been controlled by the ruling authoritarian regime, which benefits from the wide-spread ignorance, constantly undermining all opposing voices and enlightenment advocates.[8] All these elements together helped to formulate the prevalent misguided beliefs and traditions.

On the side of religion, it is also misconceived that the Islamic *Shari'a* does not provide gender justice. In the correct interpretation, the Islamic *Shari'a* has laid down a comprehensive set of norms that regulates individual relations and the relations between man and woman, in all its aspects (Bassiouni & Badr, 2002). In some cases (specifically within personal status matters including marriage, divorce, custody and inheritance), both sides of the relationship are granted distinct rights. However, such a distinction or "the non-sameness of rights" does not necessarily entail injustice (Al-Shronbasy, 2013).

An illustration of this perspective is provided through a brief analysis of the controversial matter of inheritance. Inheritance in Islamic Law is governed by a set of detailed provisions under which inheritors are divided into two layers or ranks. The first, *Ashab Al-Frood*, are ten "defined persons," six of which are women, who are entitled to a "defined share" of the estate.[9] The second layer, *Al-'Asabat*, consists of those who are entitled to what remains after distributing the shares of the first layer. In this second rank, when a man and a woman are of the same kinship (like a brother and sister), a man is entitled to a share equal to that of two women. The reason for such a distinction is that the man in this case is responsible for providing household expenses after the father's death and providing his sister with the expanses she bears in her marriage (which is quite a considerable amount of money in Egypt) and he remains similarly responsible for other expenses (Al-Shronbasy, 2013). Besides, he has to provide for his own family as the head of the household, while his sister will be provided for by her husband. What needs to be highlighted here is that the law endorses the Islamic distribution system, but there is no specific law to compel the man, the brother in the previous instance, to fulfill his obligations. These have been known as moral obligations "that are not endorsed by legal provisions," which has reduced the sense that they are compulsory in nature (Saad, 2012). However, they can be enforced under civil law on the ground that they are a civil obligation rather than a natural one in light of the Islamic *Shari'a*.

Debates about the fairness of the different allocation of rights in some personal status matters would not be of such importance if it were acknowledged that the Islamic community refuses to change the substantive compulsory provisions provided by the *Qur'an*.[10] The more pressing issue to address is the enforceability of these rights in practice. In other words, even those contested rights face complications when it comes to implementation in practice. A large percentage of women are denied their inheritance owing to the long set of procedures required before the courts which could extend to years.[11] This is a common obstruction to women obtaining their rights since they might not be able to afford the court expenses or have the necessary time. The same argument can be made concerning divorce where both sides have access to divorce, but women's access is subject to similar obstructions.

To conclude this point, misconceiving the Islamic religion through highlighting men's rights and neglecting women's is a main impediment to achieving gender equity, even from an Islamic perspective. This misconception, in light of the wide-spread ignorance, has deepened and led to resistance to gender equity and equality in other matters. A considerable percentage of the population often misconceive the rule of inheritance (concerning the case of brother and sister) for application in cases other than inheritance which constitutes grave injustice. Islam has also been used as a ground for the conservatives to oppose women's rights movements. In the same vein, outdated beliefs and traditions play the same role though they are not compatible with the modern age where injustices and inequalities inflicted upon women constitute a challenge to development and serious social consequences. The prominent example here is female genital mutilation (FGM), which has taken hold of the society only on the basis of indigenous traditions. Islam has also been used as a pretext to fight the calls for banning FGM, although it is backed by no provision in the Islamic *Shari'a*.

Legal Regulation versus Practice

Gender equality has been endorsed by the 2014 constitution in more than one position. The constitution establishes equal opportunities for all citizens without discrimination. The state commits itself to achieving equality between women and men in all civil, political, economic, social and cultural rights (*Constitution of the Arab Republic of Egypt*, 2014, Articles 9 & 11). The constitution also forbids discrimination based on religion, belief, sex, origin, race, color, language, disability, social class, social or political affiliations (*Constitution of the Arab Republic of Egypt*, 2014, Article 53). Clearly the new constitution has adopted gender equality and banned any sort of discrimination; however, many constitutional guarantees were undermined through clawback clauses (such as "to be regulated by law"). These loopholes opened the door for repressive legislations, decrees and wide-scale administrative violations. For instance, employers could discriminate in employment on grounds of discretionary power given by the law. The new constitution does little in this respect. It provides, in Article 92, that no law should restrict human rights in a way that "infringes upon their essence or foundation" (Social Institutions and Gender Index, 2014).

Such guarantees have little effect in practice where legislation continues to contain gender inequality. The Egyptian penal code, for example, continues to discriminate against women in that the penalty for committing adultery is harsher for women (up to two years) than men (limited to a six-month sentence). Evidentiary standards also differ in that a man must commit adultery at the marital house while women's act is punishable anywhere (*Law Promulgating the Penal Code*, 1937; Articles 274 & 277). It is worth noting that such discrimination has no basis in Islamic *Shari'a* where the distinction is mainly limited to personal status matters (Abo-Zeid, 2004).

Additionally, a constitutional foundation was established for the National Council for Women (NCW) and the constitution insured its independence and access to resources for consultation with regards to draft laws and regulations pertaining to women's affairs and fields of work (*Constitution of the Arab Republic of Egypt*, 2014, Article 214). It was established in 2000 as an independent body subordinate to the president. Its main purpose is empowering women in different fields nationwide. It also has the right to report to the president and public authorities any violations pertaining to its field of work. Yet, it provides advisory opinions which have little effect in practice and it is occasionally influenced by the authorities to which it reports. There are no other formal equality mechanisms.

Moreover, although Egypt is a state party to the CEDAW, it maintains reservations to Article 16 concerning personal status matters on the ground of it colliding with the Islamic *Shari'a* as the basic source of legislation.[12] The reservation extends to Articles 2 and 29 (2) concerning policy measures and submitting to arbitration in case of a dispute. It also is established under Article 93 that treaties to which Egypt is a state party have the force of law, which ensures its application and effectiveness in practice. However, CEDAW is not effective to the point of amending the discriminatory provisions, such as the penal code.

Furthermore, statistics indicate that gender equality in Egypt has been improving, though on a minor scale. This is an outcome of national NGOs' efforts, pressure by the international community and the cooperation of the current regime. Their efforts within Egypt through women's empowerment campaigns have been increasingly affecting the community in a positive way, especially after the recent revolution where hope for change was motivating a large number of individuals to get involved. However, they have been for a time, after the revolution, operating in ambiguous conditions.

According to the UN Human Development Report of 2014, Egypt ranks 130th on the gender equality index among 187 countries (The United Nations Development Program, 2015). This indicates a marginal increase in gender equality. The persistent gap continues to challenge development, which requires more urgent measures to overcome the issue; hopefully the current regime will take the necessary steps. More elaboration on the situation of gender equality in different areas of social activity is to follow. The analysis highlights the issues and obstacles that hinder gender equality in those domains. This will be done through observing the legal provisions and their impact in practice, supported by empirical data and statistics.

Political Empowerment

The 2014 constitution establishes that the state shall take the necessary measures to ensure the appropriate representation of women in the houses of representatives, as specified by Law on parliamentary elections from 2015 (No. 92). It also mandates the state guarantee women's right to hold public and senior management posts, in addition to their appointment in judicial bodies without discrimination (*Constitution of the Arab Republic of Egypt*, 2014, Article 11).

It is evident that a male-dominated political structure has done very little regarding gender equality. A better representation of women in Egypt (who constitute half the population) is a pressing demand, as women bring an important perspective to the decision-making process (Nagy, 2014). Thus, the constitutional foundation for equal rights to public posts is an important guarantee to better involvement of women in higher management posts that has already happened in practice. This is proven by the increased percentage of women holding senior management posts and diplomatic and consular posts (The National Council for Women, 2014).[13] However, women are still denied the right to hold the judge's post without discrimination, constituting an infringement of the constitution and the Rule of Law (the enforcement of the law). They are entitled the right to appointment in only two branches of the judiciary (the Administrative Prosecution and the State Counselors) which do not involve the judgment function. Such a violation is maintained by the State Council (the administrative judiciary) and the Public Prosecutor's Office on the ground that it is not fitting for women to be judges (Deif, 2004). Although it has been confirmed by *Al-Azhar*, the chief center for Islamic affairs, in 2013 that women assuming judicial posts is not in conflict with the Islamic *Shari'a*, the situation has not changed (Fayed, 2014).

On the other hand, the 2014 constitution ensured better representation of women in the local councils where it establishes that one-quarter of the local council seats must be allocated to women (*Constitution of the Arab Republic of Egypt*, 2014, Article 180). It, however, did not dedicate the quota system regarding the houses of representatives or mandate the state to take the necessary measures to ensure the appropriate representation of women in both houses as specified by the law (*Constitution of the Arab Republic of Egypt*, 2014, Article 11). The new electoral law allocated 12% of seats to women, which could reach up to 70 seats of the parliament. The authors argue that such a percentage is far from the adequate representation of half the Egyptian population. In the past years, a considerable number of women actively engaged in public affairs, especially after the revolutionary uprising. Women have intensively gone to the streets, proclaiming their rights and freedoms despite extreme suppression measures taken against the mass protests in 2011. In the same vein, the parliamentary elections of 2015 showed that women won 89 seats (15%), 75 of which are elected and the other 14 are appointed, proving the need for more adequate representation (The National Council for Women, 2014). Such important advancement was a result of the amendment to the parliamentary election law in 2014 ensured by the current regime, which reflects the desire for greater gender equality promotion. This percentage was the highest in Egypt's history, where the first prominent representation of women was a quota of 12% in the 2010 parliament, which declined severely to 2% during the rule of Muslim Brotherhood (The National Council for Women, 2014). It reflects the greater involvement of women in public affairs and political sphere, promising more extensive representation in the political structure in the near future.

To conclude this point, political empowerment of women is the most pressing of all aspects of activity. It means the inclusion of women, who represent almost half the population, in the political structure, where more consideration would be assigned to gender equity. It thus will help to promote women's rights in other areas of activity where they are represented within the decision-making process. Political empowerment has been advancing, especially after the revolution, although still on a marginal scale due to the current restricted environment. According to *The Global Gender Gap Report* (2015), Egypt scores 0.048, where 1.00 means equality and 0.00 means inequality (World Economic Forum, 2015). This score was the highest in the last decade. This only reflects the fact that the political environment is relatively unstable in Egypt. Dramatic change is attached to other conditions where the government is focused on recovering economic performance to manage and promote other sectors. Thus, development will be achieved as a result of pressure on the national and international levels until that happens.

Economic Participation

There is a strong correlation between gender equality and the economic participation of women. Whereas economic prosperity is a result of the empowerment of women, gender inequality is a challenge that hinders economic growth. According to *The Global Gender Gap Report* (2015), the gap of gender equality in economic aspects is the highest among other activities (World Economic Forum, 2015). This has been the result of limited opportunities for women to actively participate in the economic development. Besides, the severe deterioration of economic conditions after the revolution, where inflation has reached 14%, could lead to even more ruinous outcomes (*The Economist*, 2016).

As for labor force participation, discrimination on the basis of gender is constitutionally banned under Articles 9 and 11, which ensure equal opportunities and the right to appointment without discrimination. The labor law (law no. 12 of 2003) also includes a chapter on the employment of women, intended to enable women to carry out their duties towards their families and children without suffering prejudice or deprivation of rights in work. It prohibits any gender discrimination in employment and secures women's right to work without discrimination between men and women performing the same job.

This should have ensured at least a close range of employment rate; however, statistics indicate that women represent 24% of the labor force, while men represent 76% (Khairy, 2014). It is also noticeable that the increased educational attainment of women in the past decade has not translated into favorable employment conditions (El-Ashmawy, 2016). This is all explained by the poor economic conditions, the major decrease in public-sector employment opportunities in general and the limited opportunities in the private sector (El-Ashmawy, 2016). This has created a rough environment for married women in particular, who prefer public-sector employment. Moreover, the deterioration of job quality and lower wages, in light of the increasing inflation rate, affect both men and women. Still, women are more affected and have found it hard to accommodate to the worsening conditions (which has required that some have to have a second job or work overtime) because of their household duties and reproductive role (El-Ashmawy, 2016). In other words, it is hard to set a life-work balance in light of the harsh socioeconomic conditions.

Additionally, though the legal provisions governing both public and private sectors mandate equal pay for men and women, the gender pay gap has reached 25% in the public sector and 23% in the private sector. This proves the inefficacy of the systems governing the labor market, which impose considerable injustice as 15% of women (more than half of the women working force) are heads of a household (The National Council for Women, 2014).

Furthermore, despite the fact that the labor law ensures more favorable working conditions for women, it may actually lead to discrimination against them. It over-burdens the employer with obligations towards women, such as maternity leave, setting up a nearby nursery when the number of female employees exceeds 100, and providing transportation for those working at night (European Training Foundation, 2010). This has made employers operate outside the legal system and has meant that female workers suffer violations of their legal rights—but there is no specific law to address the issue. Given the circumstances, women find no choice but to accept such work: 47% of working women undertake jobs in the informal sector (The National Council for Women, 2014).

An unfriendly perception of working women is a problem, as is horizontal segregation, with 42% of working women employed in education and health sectors, and 39% working in agriculture (The National Council for Women, 2014). It comes as no surprise that this contributes to increasing poverty. Some 26% of the population are below the poverty line, which in turn causes socioeconomic difficulties that hamper economic recovery, especially after the downfall of the tourism sector, which constituted a basic element of Egyptian economy, in addition to a lack of investments. There has been no governmental strategy to address the issues in question until the moment of writing (*The Economist*, 2016). Rather, analysts predict even greater deterioration of the Egyptian economy (*The Economist*, 2016).

Educational Attainment

Education is an essential element of women's empowerment. In fact, the authors see it as the reason behind the feminist movement in Egypt. It is an essential factor for empowering women in all other dimensions. Thus, it was established with Article 19 of the 2014 constitution that education is not only a right of every citizen, but is obligatory until the end of the secondary stage or its equivalent. The state grants free education in different stages in state educational institutions. It additionally is committed to uphold its aims in education curricula and methods, and to provide education in accordance with the global quality criteria, and to allocating no less than 4% of the GDP for education along with a gradual increase until it reaches the global rates. Besides, the state is committed to developing technical education and professional training (*Constitution of the Arab Republic of Egypt*, 2014, Article 19).

The Egyptian state has committed itself to a free and obligatory education since Nasser's nationalism. Discrimination was widely exercised before Nasser's reign when education was expensive and more available to the elite few. Since then, education rates have kept growing, however with gender discrimination. This is the explanation of the current disparity in the literacy rate (65% of women to 82% of men) (World Economic Forum, 2015). The prevalent traditions that discouraged women's education created this discrimination (European Training Foundation, 2010). The obligatory education system paid off, elevating the enrollment ratio in primary and secondary education with a slight disparity between males and females. The enrollment ratio in primary education was 96% for females and 98% for males in 2015, whereas in secondary education it was 85% for females and 86% for males (European Training Foundation, 2010). The tertiary education enrollment ratio is much lower, at 31% for females and 35% for males (European Training Foundation, 2010).

The general reasons behind such disparities, especially in higher education, often pertain to the socioeconomic background and geographical distance to the educational institution (The World Bank, 2012). Access to education remains lower for those living in rural areas than urban areas because transportation can be a problem. It is often affected by the educational level of the parents who accordingly would be supportive or not. The rising unemployment rate, especially among university graduates, and the methods and quality of education also have a role in school-to-work transition. Nevertheless, the general gender equality rate in education is high: according to the *Gender Gap Report* it reached 93% in 2015.

The more important issue to address is the quality of education, which affects gender equality positively or negatively in an indirect way. The authors argue that traditions and beliefs have been a setback for Egypt that prevent it from easily advancing in the promotion of women's rights and equality. This problem can only be eliminated through high-quality education and awareness. The increase in education rate has had a basic role in promoting gender equality and women's rights. The past decade proves this argument as the gender equality rate has risen and women are engaged in most domains of activity (World Economic Forum, 2015).

Health Integrity

The health sector in Egypt has experienced major improvements over the last decades. Such improvements have led to better health care services, which are reflected in the large decline in maternal mortality rate, infant mortality rate and improvements in other services (World Economic Forum, 2015). It is proven by the fact that gender equality in health care has reached up to 97% in 2015 (World Economic Forum, 2015). Such equality is established by the constitution in Article 18, which ensures that "every citizen is entitled to health and comprehensive health care with equality criteria" (*Constitution of the Arab Republic of Egypt*, 2014).

On the other hand, gender-based violence has been a wide-spread phenomenon that surged in the streets, particularly after the revolution. Women have constantly been subject to violence in its different forms, including sexual harassment, sexual violence, domestic violence, rape and female genital mutilation (FGM) (Fidh et al., 2014). The constitution and several human rights treaties commit the state to the protection of women against all forms of violence (*Constitution of the Arab Republic of Egypt*, 2014, Article 11). However, acts of sexual harassment and sexual assault continued unabated from 2011 to 2014 with no specific law to criminalize them or count its forms. It was not until 2014, after four years of pressure, that the sexual harassment law was issued. It mainly incorporated sexual harassment as part of public indecency and elevated its penalty to a minimum of six months imprisonment in general (Fidh et al., 2014).

However, a wide range of forms of sexual assault have not yet been covered by the law (Fidh et al., 2014). Rape is a criminal offense in the Egyptian law, but not spousal rape (*Social Institutions and Gender Index*, 2014). This has implications in practice where rape and sexual violence remain taboo topics, which makes it difficult for victims to speak out or file charges. Police attitudes are another barrier as they lack sensitivity in dealing with victims (for example, questioning victims in front of others present).

Human rights activists contend that the regime has amplified the problem. This is backed by empirical data suggesting that violence inflicted upon women has been systematic and constant in the streets during the 2011 revolution and continued for some years since then (Fidh et al., 2014). A surge of violent sexual assaults has been reported since the beginning of the revolution. Cases include sexual harassment and rape in the public sphere, specifically Tahrir Square. Many cases occurred with the police present and without any intervention (Fidh et al., 2014). Thus it can be argued that sexual harassment and sexual assault have been used systematically as a method to scare away female protesters and it has indeed been effective. It is even reported that police did not respond to interrupt such actions of harassment. It is no surprise that these constant violent acts have turned into a trend that increases during holidays and national occasions.

It is also important to mention that domestic violence is an extremely widespread phenomenon in Egypt and is addressed by no specific law to this moment. Statistics indicate that domestic violence is more common among wives, with 36% of married women having been subject to violence in its different forms. Beating is a prominent form of domestic violence, as 29.5% of reported violence. However, the authors argue that the accurate percentage is far higher, because of the social restrictions to speaking out, as most women depend on those inflicting harm, regardless of whether it is the husband, father, son or brother. Some of these practices are so severe that they constitute dangerous crimes. This grave phenomenon affects women and children and is a direct cause of the increase of violence among youth. Domestic violence is closely related to social attitudes and conditions, and the economic situation in practice. This phenomenon requires not only legal confrontation, but also social remedy and economic improvements.

Furthermore, female genital mutilation (FGM) was formally criminalized in 2008 after long arguments for its banning since the 1990s. The penalty for the violation of the law for performing such an act extends from three months to two years in prison and a fine of LE 1,000–5,000 [Egyptian pounds] (Fidh et al., 2014). However, doctors are allowed to perform FGM only in cases of "medical necessity" (Fidh et al., 2014). This loophole has rendered the law ineffective in practice as FGM has continued under the name of medical necessity. Statistics show that in 2008 90% of women have undergone FGM. It also indicates that such practices remain active, particularly in rural areas where it is carried out in private clinics. However, national and international organizations have initiated several nationwide campaigns that reached rural areas and made people question such practices and in the authors' opinion have been quite effective.

Moreover, the penal code criminalizes abortion except in cases of medical necessity. This provision is compatible with the Islamic *Shari'a*, which cares for preserving human life and forbids taking a life, especially in pregnancy.

Early marriage is, however, a controversial issue in Egypt. Raising the age of marriage to 18 years old by amendment to the law no. 143 of 1994 in 2008 encountered social debates. The provision has been largely ineffective to this moment, especially in rural areas. In fact, the media has been investigating several cases of child marriage in the past couple of years. During the rule of the Muslim Brotherhood there were calls to challenge the amendment. It should be noted that the age of marriage has nothing to do with the Islamic *Shari'a*, though religion was used to advocate the challenge. Another violation of women's reproductive rights is the forced virginity examination. Forced virginity examination has been a common practice by the police during and after the January 25, 2011 revolution, directed against female protesters. Reports have indicated that such practices continued to severely harm female protesters alongside sexual harassment and sexual violence to scare them away, which indeed has proved effective.

Key Findings and Recommendations

This paper is a brief review of gender equality in Egypt, its conception, influencing factors and its effectiveness in practice. Its purpose is to identify the extent of gender equality in everyday social life and the implications that arise. An approach of practical viability was adopted in identifying the conclusions to follow.

In view of the legal and ideological development of gender equality in Egypt, it is apparent that it has been closely associated with the approach of the state. If the state endorses the concept by incorporating it in the legal system, it starts to take hold, even if it encounters controversy in practice. Women's rights advanced a lot when Nasser included them as partner in his national development policy.

When the political will does not exist for reform or development, other pressures take the lead role for achieving gains. The progress of gender equality after Nasser was achieved through pressure by international organizations concerning economic aid. However, the achievements were often compromised for the sake political stability on the internal front under the pressure of the conservatives.

On the other hand, the nature of the society, its firm beliefs and indigenous traditions have a strong say in embracing new attitudes in practice. The Egyptian environment has been hampered by misconceived beliefs and outdated traditions. This context constitutes a restrictive framework for gender equality. It is apparent through the time and efforts it has taken for the issuance of a law banning FGM, which has no origin in Islam or Christianity but is an indigenous practice that stretches back before both. Though it has been a criminal offence, it is still being practiced.

In the same vein, maintaining misconstrued beliefs and traditions has been imprinted with religious overtones. It has been used for holding onto these manifestations, preserving a conservative conception of the Islamic *Shari'a*. It has developed into a wide-scale misconception in light of a lack of necessary knowledge for addressing Islamic provisions or interpreting them. This has established a society in which it is difficult to embrace gender equality in every field.

Within the legal regulation, Egypt is a state party of the CEDAW and other human rights treaties, which all constitute an integrated part of the constitution. It is then committed, under the international law and the relevant ratified treaties, to embedding gender equality in the legal framework and to excluding any discriminating provisions. It is also committed to the same goal under several constitutional articles. However, discriminating and inadequate provisions entailing injustice continue to exist within some laws.

Gender injustice is more prominent in political empowerment and economic participation. The equality percentage in the political field is only 4.8%, whereas in the economic sector it has reached 44%. The near-exclusion of women from the decision-making process indicates less consideration of their issues, and denying their right to be a member of the judiciary is a severe example of discrimination. The economic participation of women suggests eminent injustices. Social attitudes towards working women, poor quality of education and deteriorating economic conditions are more likely to harm women, given the state's lack of attention to women's vulnerabilities.

On the other hand, gender equality in educational attainment and health integrity has basically advanced to the extent that the gap is almost closed. The percentage of gender equality in education reached 93.5% and in health care 97%. It is only affected by general conditions inflicted on both sexes, however, impacting women more as residue of social attitudes that prevailed for a long time.

In this study, attention was given to identifying the nature of the Egyptian environment and the factors impacting the growth of gender equality. Recommendations in this respect will address the issue in general and the discussed dimensions.

The promotion of gender equality in general is hampered by two main obstacles: the political lack of attention, which is starting to diminish, and the social impediments. The political disregard of the issue can be influenced by pressure on the national and international levels.

On the internal front, opposing forces and civil society organizations can jointly negotiate with the regime and press for further reforms and developments. Alliances with parliamentary representatives and using wide-scale media campaigns can assist to strengthen the effect. Wide-scale awareness campaigns also help mobilize individuals to support the claim. However, the current limitation on the independence of voices seeking reforms renders these efforts limited in effect.

However, pressure could be more effective from the international perspective. Severely deteriorating economic performance is a powerful tool for pressure in a country where urgent aid is needed. Subsequently, the powerful forces of the international community, such as international donor organizations and powerful states, could effectively pressure the regime for more development, to which it would adhere for building alliances.

The social impediment can be remedied through improvements in the quality of education. The state should allocate more resources to the educational attainment and upgrade the educational system. The media should have a more effective role in enhancing knowledge of women's rights and issues. Wide-scale campaigns can also assist in improving knowledge and correcting prevalent misconceptions. Religious institutions should also contribute to the spreading of the correct understanding of religious norms.

Specific recommendations for achieving gender justice include:

- The state should repeal reservations to Articles 2 and 29 (2) of the CEDAW and abide by the provisions of human rights law, treaties to which it adheres and the provisions of the constitution concerning the promotion of gender equality. In the same vein, it should also commit itself in the first place to enforcing the provisions of the law concerning gender equality. Furthermore, it must review and amend the discriminatory provisions in different legislations. Exception can be made to those that collide in essence with the Islamic *Shari'a* such as the allocation of shares in inheritance. Rather, women's rights in these matters currently suffer as a result of the lack of enforcement in practice. This means that a review of enforcement methods is necessary.
- On the other hand, the state shall review enforcement and implementation mechanisms in relation to women's rights to ensure effectiveness in practice. It also shall lift the restrictions on and provide a supportive environment for the feminist activist organizations to freely operate. It should combine efforts with them for the promotion of gender equality. Besides, it must activate the role of the National Council of Women to receive complaints of gender discrimination and provide it the competence to communicate with relevant authorities regarding such reports.

Political Empowerment

The state shall involve women in the judiciary including the State Council and the Public Prosecutor Office. It also must increase the representation of women in political posts in the government, bringing a long-marginalized perspective to the decision-making sphere. This includes particularly a better representation of women in the parliament where 15% is far from adequate. In addition, state and civil society organizations shall raise community awareness of successful women in high management posts and political posts as role models to encourage women's involvement in the political sphere.

Economic Participation

The state shall eliminate all governmental obstacles that hinder investment. Such obstacles include the large number of permits and bribes needed for the operation of an enterprise. It likewise must increase public investments, creating more opportunities for women and youth in general, which also will assist in boosting economic performance. It could further create a strategy to subject the informal labor sector to the relevant laws to combat discrimination against women and violations of their rights.

Moreover, it must provide companies with fiscal incentives to employ more women or partly fund the costs of maternity leave, nurseries and transport. The state shall as well raise community awareness of various fields of work and the qualifications it requires, examples of successful women, and examples of companies promoting gender equality to correct the unfriendly perception of working women in different sectors and reduce segregation. It likewise must activate the role of the Ministry of Manpower as an oversight authority to receive reports on gender discrimination such as unequal pay complaints.

Educational Attainment

The state shall provide transportation to the residents of remote geographical areas where higher education institutions are far away, especially in rural areas. It also must raise community awareness through campaigns that reach families with low socioeconomic backgrounds, especially in rural regions, to encourage the enrollment and completion of education. Likewise, it shall increase public and private investments in areas of high poverty to remedy the school-to-work transition and combat poverty to provide for education.

Furthermore, the state shall allocate an adequate amount of resources for the upgrade of educational quality, review of educational curricula, practical training and teaching methods. It also could include awareness of gender and impediments in social life within the tasks of the social counselor at every educational institution for raising a future generation with correct gender equality perception.

Health Integrity

The state, including all of its authorities, shall commit to the protection of women against all crimes, and the police shall take all necessary measures to ensure a rapid and effective response in preventing these crimes. The police or any other agency shall in no circumstances use women as pawns in pursuit of suspects, or inflict any physical or mental harm on women in violation of the relevant legal provisions. Additionally, it could establish a distinct body with the competence to receive complaints of police violations against women and take the legal steps in prosecuting perpetrators. It shall also provide protection for victims of sexual violence as well as suitable setting for trial.

Moreover, it shall enact new, detailed legislation that unambiguously defines sexual assault in all its forms and imposes severe penalties to ensure public deterrence. It could as well establish a distinct unit within the Ministry of Interior and qualifying its personnel with the necessary training to receive complaints and investigate sexual violence crimes in a non-hostile attitude. The state must also raise community awareness of the legal provisions governing these crimes and their penalties, reporting methods and strategies to assist victims.

Last but not least, the state shall provide health care units and its personnel with the necessary resources and training to better attend to victims and in a friendly attitude that encourages addressing such acts. It likewise shall raise community awareness of the harms of FGM, correcting the prevalent misconception of its origin as a religious practice particularly within educational and religious institutions.

Finally, the Egyptian environment has always been complicated in nature. Political disregard, social misbeliefs and deep-rooted traditions, misconceptions of religion and deteriorating economic conditions have all contributed to the slow promotion of gender equality. However, it has managed to advance despite the harsh conditions. Endorsing gender equality in the legal framework and committing the state to its enforcement is a must, and hopefully soon. More interest in boosting the quality of education and awareness campaigns on gender issues will help eliminate the deep-rooted social obstructions. Egyptian society, after recent developments in the political sphere, is more ready to embrace values of social justice including gender equality. Thus, there has never been a better time to continue the struggle.

Notes

1 Such conception of equality entailing "sameness of rights" is clearly adopted by the CEDAW and repeated within its preamble and the articles of the convention.
2 Islam is the official religion of the state (Article 2 of the constitution) and the principles of Islamic *Shari'a* are the main source of legislation.
3 Gamal Abdel-Nasser was the second president after monarchy as a result of the military coup, supported by the vast majority of Egyptians, in 1952. He was the leader of the militant group (The Free Officers) who executed the coup and assumed power after deposing the first president, Mohamed Naguib, who wished for democracy and for the army to leave power. For his rule to take hold, Abel-Nasser performed wide-scale reforms and adopted the Arab Nationalism Movement to liberate the Arab world and Africa from colonization. However, he monopolized power, restricted political activism and changed the economic system from capitalism to socialism, which all resulted in deterioration in the long term.
4 President Anwar Al-Sadat assumed power after Nasser's death. At the beginning of his rule, a part of the state's territory (Sinai) was occupied by the Israeli forces with the help of Great Britain and France in the 1967 Six-Day War. The state's focus, at that time, was exclusively directed to the retrieval of the occupied land.
5 Examples include the Arab Women's Solidarity Association (ASWA) and the Progressive Women's Union, which were the prominent feminist organizations at that time.
6 *Al-Azhar* is one of the first universities in Egypt, founded to spread Islamic learning, which now also oversees a large national network of schools. It has been considered as the chief center of Arabic literature and Islamic learning in the world.

7 Statistics prove that hours dedicated to educational attainment and women's empowerment severely declined from 2007 to 2012 (roughly from 3,000 hours in the radio to 1,500 and from about 6,000 hours in television to 1,100 hours).

8 This has included complete ignorance among a large percentage of people who did not know about their rights; even a vast number have opposed the recent revolution that claimed rights and freedoms out of ignorance. The case was the same among the people who are literate but only nominally because of poor education policies.

9 These specified shares are 1/2, 1/4, 1/8, 2/3, 1/3 or 1/6 of the inheritance and those who are entitled to a defined share are the husband, the wife, the father, the mother, the grandfather, the grandmother, the daughter, the son's daughter, the half-sisters and the mother's children. Their share is determined in accordance with the case in question.

10 The *Qur'an*, the holy book of Muslims, is the first and the main source of Islamic law in which the word of God was revealed to the Prophet Muhammad verbally through the Angel Gabriel over a period of 22 years (610–632 CE) (Bassiouni & Badr, 2002, pp. 135–150).

11 There is an uncountable number of such cases where this happens among kinship and in secrecy where women concede as a consequence of the inefficient implementation policies.

12 It is worth noting that Egypt is not a signatory to the optional protocol to the CEDAW (1999) (UN Office of the High Commissioner, 2016).

13 According to the National Council for Women's 2014 statistics, the number of women holding senior management posts has increased by 5% to 36% in 2013, while it increased by 3% in diplomatic and consular sector at the same time.

References

Abo-Zeid, M. (2004). *Al-Musawah Bayn Al-Gensein [Gender Equality]*. Cairo, Egypt: Al-Nesr Al-Zahabi Le-Elteba'a.

Ahmed, L. (1982). *Women and Gender and Islam: Historical Root of a Modern Debate*. New Haven, CT and London, UK: Yale University Press.

Al-Ali, N. (2002). The women's movement in Egypt, with selected references to Turkey. UN Research Institute for Social Development, Civil Society and Social Movements Program. Paper No. 5. Retrieved from http://www.unrisd.org/80256B3C005BCCF9/search/9969203536F64607C1256C08004BB140?OpenDocument (accessed 13 August 2016).

Al-Shronbasy, R. (2013). *Provisions of Inheritance in Islamic Jurisprudence*. Alexandria, Egypt: Dar Al-matbo'at Al-gam'eya.

Arafa, M. (2011). Towards a culture of accountability: A new dawn for Egypt. *Phoenix Law Review*, 5 (1), 12–15.

Bassiouni, M., & Badr, G. (2002). The Shari'ah: Sources, interpretation, and rule-making. *UCLA Journal of Islamic & Near Eastern Law*, 1 (2), 135–150.

Bayoumi, A. (1987). *Al-Haraka Al-Nissa.iyah fi Misr Bayn Al-Thawratayn 1919.1953 [The Women's Movement in Egypt between the Two Revolutions 1919.1953]*. Cairo: Hay'at al-Kitab al-Amaa.

Constitution of the Arab Republic of Egypt. (2014). Official Gazette No. 1/3. Cairo: Al-Amiria Printing House. Retrieved from https://www.constituteproject.org/constitution/Egypt_2014.pdf (English translation) (accessed 13 August 2016).

Deif, F. (2004). Divorced from justice. *Human Rights Watch*, 16 (8), 15–16. Retrieved from https://www.hrw.org/reports/2004/egypt1204/egypt1204.pdf (accessed 13 August 2016).

The Economist. (2016, August 6). After the Arab Spring: The ruining of Egypt. Retrieved from http://www.economist.com/news/leaders/21703374-repression-and-incompetence-abdel-fattah-al-sisi-are-stoking-next-uprising (accessed 13 August 2016).

El-Ashmawy, K. (2016). The social and economic empowerment of women in Egypt: Towards a new development paradigm. Egypt Network for Integrated Development. Policy brief 036, January 2016. Retrieved from http://www.enid. org.eg/Uploads/PDF/PB36_socioeconomic_empowerment.pdf (accessed 13 August 2016).

El-Helw, M. (2014). *Dostoriat Al-Qur'an [Constitutional Principles of Quar'an].* Alexandria, Egypt: Dar Al-Gam'a Al-Gadida.

European Training Foundation. (2010). Women and work in Egypt: Tourism and ICT sectors as a case study. Retrieved from http://www.etf.europa.eu/pubmgmt. nsf/(getAttachment)/D3E0FA7D21DC7D7EC1257610005A2381/$File/NOTE 7UUM9B.pdf (accessed 13 August 2016).

Fayed, H. (2014). *Women Endeavor to Assume Judicial Position at Resisting State Council.* Retrieved from http://thecairopost.youm7.com/news/80699/inside_ egypt/legal-battle-for-female-judges-in-state-council (accessed 13 August 2016).

Fidh, Nazra, New Women Foundation, and the Uprising of Women in the Arab World. (2014). *Egypt Keeping Women out.* Retrieved from https://www.fidh.org/ IMG/pdf/egypt_women_final_english.pdf (accessed 13 August 2016).

Hatem, M. (1993). Toward the development of post-Islamist and post-nationalist feminist discourses in the Middle East. In Judith E. Tucker (Ed.), *Arab Women: Old Boundaries, New Frontiers*, Bloomington, IN: Indiana University Press, pp. 29–48.

Khairy, A. (2014). *An Analysis of the Gender Pay Gap in the Egyptian Labor Market.* Egypt: Central Agency for Public Mobilization and Statistics (CAP-MAS). Retrieved from http://iariw.org/egypt2015/amalkhairy.pdf (accessed 13 August 2016).

Moruzzi, N. (2013). *Gender and the Revolutions.* Middle East Research and Information Project [MERIP], 268. Retrieved from http://www.merip.org/mer/ mer268/gender-revolutions (accessed 13 August 2016).

Nagy, T. (2014). *Egyptian Women Deserve Better from Their Political System.* Retrieved from http://muftah.org/egyptian-women-deserve-better-political-system/#. V6YW0NJ97IV (accessed 13 August 2016).

The National Council for Women. (2014). Statistics of women in Egypt 2014. Retrieved from http://ncwegypt.com/index.php/en/download (accessed 13 August 2016).

Promulgating the Penal Code. (1937). Official Gazette No. 58/1937. Retrieved from http://sub.eastlaws.com/GeneralSearch/Home/ArticlesTDetails?MasterID=4015 (accessed 13 August 2016).

Saad, N. (2012). *Masader Al-Eltizam [Sources of Obligation].* Alexandria, Egypt: Dar Al-matbo'at Al-gam'eya.

Social Institutions and Gender Index. (2014). Analysis and statistics about gender equality in Egypt. Retrieved from http://www.genderindex.org/country/egypt-arab-rep (accessed 13 August 2016).

The United Nations Development Program. (2015). Human development report: Citing Egyptian Central Agency for public mobilization and statistics. Retrieved from http://www.eg.undp.org/content/egypt/en/home/countryinfo/ (accessed 13 August 2016).

UN Office of the High Commissioner. (2016). Ratification status. Retrieved from http://indicators.ohchr.org/ (accessed 13 August 2016).

The World Bank. (2012). Inequality of opportunity in educational achievement. Retrieved from https://blogs.worldbank.org/files/arabvoices/inequality_of_opportunity_in_educational_outcomes-_report_no_70300.pdf (accessed 13 August 2016).

World Economic Forum. (2015). The global gender gap report. Retrieved from http://reports.weforum.org/global-gender-gap-report-2015/economies/#economy=EGY (accessed 13 August 2016).

4 (Un)doing Gender Equality in China

Yan Zhao

Introduction

This chapter addresses the implementation of gender equality (GE), as defined by the Convention on the Elimination of All Forms of Discrimination against Women (CEDAW), in the People's Republic of China. China ratified CEDAW in 1980, soon after its adoption that year. In acceding to CEDAW, the Chinese government is obliged to implement its various articles as well as to promote gender equality as outlined in the Convention. Now, after more than 30 years have passed, to what degree does GE exist in China? Is GE only formally guaranteed in legislation, or is it also embraced in everyday life? Addressing these questions can help illuminate whether or not a universal understanding of GE is feasible worldwide.

GE was not a new concept in China and was not introduced by CEDAW. In China, the promulgation of women's rights and GE is widely considered to have started in the late Qing Dynasty (Fan, 2012; Huang, 2004), and the principle of equality between men and women had also been considered to be the mainstream ideology under the socialist Mao era (Wang, 2005). Therefore, it is necessary to discuss China's implementation of GE in relation to the historical process of women's emancipation and development. Moreover, 1980, the year China ratified CEDAW, was also the beginning of the new political era of Deng Xiaoping, who enacted economic reforms and the policy of opening the country up. This era began in 1979 and brought fundamental and far-reaching changes to all aspects of Chinese society (Saich, 2004). The socialist market economy and the new form of governance in what Hoffman (2010) calls "late socialist neoliberalism" (p. 17) have certainly influenced the politics of GE. Therefore, discussions in this chapter will pay particular attention to these historical, economic and political contexts.

In other words, this chapter illuminates whether and how a universal understanding of GE as expressed in CEDAW can be fully adopted in a politically communist yet economically market-oriented Chinese context. How has the country's historical, traditional, political and economic background influenced its adoption and implementation of CEDAW? The chapter starts with a brief historical overview of the women's movements and developments from the late Qing Dynasty to China's ratification of CEDAW. I then detail how China has implemented its GE obligations in the new economic and political era from the late 1970s and up to the present. The focus in this part of the chapter is on what has been done and achieved through political and legal processes. In the next section, I provide a general picture of how gender equality works today, with a focus on women's education and labor force participation. Descriptions and discussions in this section build upon statistics and findings from relevant empirical studies. Combined, these sections illustrate the gap between *de jure* GE and *de facto* GE: despite the legal and institutional progress made, gender inequality and discrimination still exist.

I then move on to explore this gap by (1) discussing why laws are insufficient to protect women's rights, and (2) questioning the state's willingness to pursue GE under a market economy. In particular, I argue that the government's inclusion of GE in economic and social development plans in practice means that GE is subordinated to the goal of economic development. Given that historically GE and women's development in China was subsumed under the National Salvation Movement, Communist Revolution and socialist construction, I also argue that there has never been an independent women's movement and GE politics in China. This is an important factor in explaining the gap between *de jure* GE and *de facto* GE.

Women's Movements in China—A Historical Overview from the Late Qing Dynasty to the Late 1970s

Within feminist scholarship, traditional Chinese society is often described as a patriarchal system in which men are privileged and women are marginalized (Li, 1995; Wolf & Wikte, 1975). The patriarchal repression of Chinese women can be exemplified by the Confucian doctrines of "Three Obediences and Four Virtues."[1] Central to this tradition is the idea that "men should be respectable and women humble," and that "lack of learning in women is a virtue" (Li, 1995, p. 413).

The promulgation of women's rights appeared first in the women's emancipation movements, starting in the late Qing Dynasty at the end of the 19th century, and reaching its apex in the New Culture Movement[2] in the May Fourth Era from 1915 to 1921 (Li, 2012; Wang, 1997). Women's movements in this period can be described as *male feminism* (Q. Wang, 2014), as these movements were initiated by male intellectuals who found Western liberal feminism to be a weapon with which to revolt against the dominant Confucian culture (Wang, 1997). Women and progressive youth, with the support of male intellectuals, began to attack the patriarchal family system and called for equal rights between men and women, with particular focus on women's rights to education, social participation and freedom of marriage. Another important feature of the women's movement in this period is that it was one part of and subsumed under an anti-imperialist and anti-colonial National Salvation Movement (Fan, 2012).

On its establishment in 1921, the Chinese Communist Party (CCP) launched its own women's movements as part of its revolution towards a communist regime in China. The Chinese gender scholar Song Shaopeng (2013) divides the communist women's movements into two stages, the early stage before 1927 and the stage of the Mao era, especially the period after 1949. According to Song, the early women's movements launched by CCP had absorbed the liberalist ideas from the feminist movements in the May Fourth Era. It further developed these ideas by incorporating women's emancipation and demand for equal rights into a larger project about the overall transformation of Chinese society (Song, 2013). However, exactly because they had always been subsumed under the National Salvation Movements, women's movements at this stage were gradually submerged by nationalism and communism. In this context, women had to restrain their fight for equal rights and ally with men to fight for the country's independence (Li, 2015).

Women's emancipation movements in the Mao era, and especially in the period between 1949 to 1978, are a form of *state feminism* (Wang, 2005). Adopting Marxist theories on women and gender relations, the CCP considered women's oppression to be part of the class conflict and oppression. Therefore, to achieve emancipation, women needed to participate equally in the socialist and communist revolution and to eradicate the private property rights in the capitalist system. In socialist China, the equality between men and women thus became the mainstream ideology, which was written into the People's Republic of China's first constitution in 1954 (*Constitution of P. R. China*, 1954, Ch. 3):

> Citizens of the People's Republic of China are equal before the law.
>
> (Article 85)
>
> Citizens of the People's Republic of China who have reached the age of eighteen have the right to vote and stand for election, whatever their nationality, race, sex, occupation, social origin, religious belief, education, property status, or length of residence, except insane persons and persons deprived by law of the right to vote and stand for election. Women have equal rights with men to vote and stand for election.
>
> (Article 86)
>
> Women in the People's Republic of China enjoy equal rights with men in all spheres of political, economic, cultural, social and domestic life. The state protects marriage, the family, and the mother and child.
>
> (Article 96)

These articles have remained in the current constitution (*Constitution of P. R. China*, 2004), though the wording is slightly different and the article numbers have changed to Articles 33, 34 and 48 in Chapter 2. In addition, the new constitution adds a general statement in Article 33: "The state respects and protects human rights." It also adds in Article 48: "The state protects the rights and interests of women, applies the principle of equal pay for equal work to men and women alike and trains and selects cadres from among women."

The state feminism in the Mao era had four key features. Firstly, the Western feminist ideas introduced to the women's movements under the May Fourth Era were abandoned as the communist government regarded them as one part of Western capitalist ideology. Secondly, in order to rebuild the country's economy after years of wars, the CCP government pushed the women's movements forward through top-down political mobilizations with slogans like "It is a new era—men and women are the same!",[3] "Women, out of the home!",[4] "Whatever men can do, women can do!",[5] "Women are turning over a new leaf and are emancipated!"[6] and "Women hold up half the sky!"[7] The result of the political mobilizations, together with a direct deployment of the labor force under the command economy, was that a large number of women came out of the family and participated in the labor force, including in heavy industries. For example, there were fewer than 600,000 female workers in enterprises under the ownership of the entire people in 1952. By 1957, this figure had reached 3,286,000 and by 1960 it had reached 10,087,000 (Jin, 2009). Thirdly, by emphasizing equal rights in the public sphere (in contrast to the private sphere), women were looked upon as equal social actors in the socialist construction. Furthermore, GE was understood as "men and women are the same," an understanding which ignored sex differences between men and women (Dong, 2013; Jin, 2009). Finally, equal rights were granted to "women" as a collective identity, which means that to enjoy equal rights, women had to subject to this collective identity and ignore their individual differences (Dai, 2004). Therefore, state feminism, though it promoted women's rights and social status, was accompanied by de-gendering and de-individualization processes.

Implementing GE in the Era of Economic Reform after CEDAW

As I mentioned in the introduction, when China ratified CEDAW in 1980, the country was also at the start of a new political and economic era. The strict command economy with the ownership of entire people, the total egalitarianism and the "closed-door policy" under the Mao era were abandoned completely. With the economic reform, the new leadership headed by Deng Xiaoping gradually developed a socialist market economy, with market-based supply and demand as the main principle for allocating resources and "pay according the contribution"[8] as the main principle for distribution of income. Meanwhile, the policy of opening the country up was launched, including for foreign investments, with the state actively participating in foreign trade as well as expanding foreign relations more broadly. China's ratification of CEDAW must be understood in the context of the "opening up" policy.

Earlier I explained that GE or the "emancipation of women" had been on the country's political agenda since 1949 under state feminism. What is new after the ratification of CEDAW is that China has to carry out the politics of GE in relation to international standards. GE has also become a part of China's international politics. China has a special relationship to CEDAW and the UN Entity for Gender Equality and Empowerment of Women, having been the host country for the Fourth World Conference on Women in 1995. The outcome of the conference, *The Beijing Declaration and Platform for Action*, is considered an important milestone in the UN's work for gender equality and empowerment of women worldwide. The Chinese government highlights this special connection in all of its white papers on gender and women's development and in its reports to the Committee on the Elimination of Discrimination against Women, claiming it as one of the contributions China has made to enhance gender equality and women's development worldwide. Interestingly, in its internal annual government reports in 1995 and 1996, the UN conference in Beijing and its outcome were addressed as a foreign relations and international cooperation achievement.

China's implementation of GE in the recent two to three decades has also centered on the UN conference in Beijing. In total, the Chinese government has issued three white papers on gender equality and women's development, in 1994, 2005 and 2015. The foreword to the 1994 report, issued one year before the conference, states that the purpose of the white paper is "to welcome the conference," as well as "to help the international society know more about women's situation in the host country." The following two white papers were issued at the 10th and 20th anniversaries of the conference. In these white papers, the government systematically lists the achievements as well as the problems related to its obligations under CEDAW. The latest white paper (2015), includes the following prologue:

> China has always upheld the **constitutional principle of equality between men and women**, which is also a basic state policy for promoting progress in the country and in society. Over the years, China has progressively improved its laws and regulations, developed public policies, worked out development plans and pressed forward steadily with gender equality and women's development.
>
> (The State Council Information Office, 2015, the original emphasis)

Firstly, we can see that GE is understood as *equality between men and women*, which is in line with GE as defined in CEDAW (see Chapter 2, this volume). Secondly, the first sentence also demonstrates GE's central place in both China's legislation and its state politics—it is a *constitutional principle* as well as *a basic state policy*.[9] Thirdly, when introducing what China has directly done in its implementation of GE, the document focuses on the legislative ("laws and regulations"), the political ("public policies") and the administrative ("development plans") means to achieve GE. I provide a brief summary of these areas below.

Public Policies

In terms of policy making, one of the milestones highlighted in the white paper is that GE is now clearly formulated as one of the seven basic state policies in China. Its significance, according to the government, lies in that it "transforms GE from being a concept and awareness into the will of the state" (*The State of P. R. China*, 2015). This achievement has a clear connection to the international climate and agenda on GE, as the formulation of GE as one basic state policy was first introduced by then-President Jiang Zemin at the opening ceremony of the Fourth World Conference on Women in 1995. However, the legal status of this state policy was not established until 10 years later, when it was written into the amended law on Protection of Rights and Interests of Women in 2005. Meanwhile, some scholars and critics have pointed out that GE does not have the same status or the same effects as other basic state policies, such as the one-child policy (Lü, 2012, p. 7). In line with this criticism, I will also question the state's willingness to implement GE in its politics.

Development Plans

"Development plans" mainly mean the three national plans for promoting women's development: *Program for Chinese women's development 1995–2000*, *Program for Chinese women's development 2001–2010* and *Program for Chinese women's development 2011–2020*. In these plans, the government has defined the overall goals, key areas, and policies and measures for women's development. Without going into details, I would point out two main aspects of these plans. *First*, the key areas identified in the plans coincide well with the prioritized areas outlined in UN documents, such CEDAW and the *Beijing Declaration and Platform for Action*, including poverty, economy, education, health, power and decision-making, social insurance, laws and rights, the media and the environment. *Second*, these plans are included into China's 10th, 11th and 12th five-year plans for economic and social development (The State Council Information Office, 2015). But what does this inclusion mean? How does the government deal with the relationship between women's development and economic and social development? I will address this question later.

Another important plan is China's *Action Plan against Human Trafficking* (2013–2020), issued in 2013. As a direct result of this action plan, 25,852 rape cases and 4,537 cases of women being abducted and trafficked were uncovered in 2013 (The State Council Information Office, 2015).

Legislation

Besides the constitution, another important law which is at the core of China's legal system for protecting women's rights and interests is the *Law of P. R. China on the Protection of Rights and Interests of Women* (1992), which was amended in 2005. This law clearly stipulates that women enjoy equal rights with men in these six aspects:

1   Political rights: Women and men have equal rights to vote and stand for election. An appropriate number of women should be represented in the People's Congress at all levels, and the proportion should gradually be increased. Gender equality is an important principle in appointing leadership candidates. It is important to train and select women for leadership positions.

2   Cultural and educational rights, including enrollment, graduation, jobs upon graduation, the opportunity to be sent abroad for education, engagement in scientific and technological research, and literary and artistic creation. Government, society, schools and families share responsibility for ensuring that girls receive compulsory education.

3   Labor rights, including equal rights to employment, equal pay, promotion, rights to rest, health and special protection, and rights to social insurance. Discrimination against women in any aspect of working life is illegal. Women enjoy special protection during menstruation, pregnancy, maternity leave and breast-feeding, and dismissing female employees during these periods is prohibited. Placing women in jobs that are "inappropriate for women" is also prohibited.

4   Property rights. Women and men in rural areas have equal rights to land; women and men have equal rights to property ownership and inheritance in their family of origin and after marriage, and widowed women have rights to dispose of inherited property without interference.

5   Rights relating to the person, including the right to life and health, individual freedom, the right to their image, reputation, right to kinship, guardianship, fame and status as a producer and other rights relating to the person. The law prohibits the abandonment and drowning of female infants and other forms of infanticide and bans discrimination against and maltreatment of women who give birth to female infants and women who are sterile. The law bans any forms of violence, maltreatment and abandonment of aged women. Abduction of and trafficking in or kidnapping of women are prohibited.

6   Rights in marriage and within the family, including the right to self-determination in marriage, right to child-bearing in accordance with relevant state regulations, and the freedom not to bear any child. Women and men have equal right in marriage and the family and women enjoy special legal protections with regard to divorce. (The State Council Information Office, 1994, Ch. 2)

These rights are also addressed in other state laws and regulations, including: Marriage Law of P. R. China of 1980 (2001), Law of P. R. China on Maternal and Infant Health Care (1994), Compulsory Education Law of P. R. China of 1986 (2015), Labor Contract Law of P.R. China (2008), Law of P. R. China on Promotion of Employment of 2008 (2015), Organic Law of the Villagers Committees of P. R. China of 1998 (2010), Social Insurance Law of P. R. China (2011), and Special Rules on the Labor Protection of Female Employees (2012). Very recently, China has passed its first Anti-Domestic Violence Law of P. R. China (2016), a result of a long campaign by Chinese civil society to combat the high number of domestic violence cases.[10] The law took effect on March 1, 2016.

As we can see, women's rights are comprehensively covered in Chinese law. At the same time, the government claims to have constantly improved the legislation to strengthen the protection of women. For example, the Amendment IX to the Criminal Law of P. R. *China* (2015) specified harsher punishments for the crimes of raping girls under 14 and abducting and trafficking women, and the courts have established *special collegial panels* for safeguarding women's rights and interests (The State Council Information Office, 2015). However, this does not tell us whether and how there is a gap between *de jure* and *de facto* GE. I address this question in the next section.

Gender (In)Equality in China

De facto GE concerns the question of how GE works in social life. According to UN's Human Development Report 2015 (United Nations Development Program, 2015), China ranks number 90 on the Gender Inequality Index (GII). The dimensions that are measured in this index include women's reproductive health, political participation, education and labor force participation. In Table 4.1, I list the statistics for China compared to Norway, which ranks as number 1 on the GII, and Singapore, which ranks as number 11 internationally and number 1 among Asian countries/regions. Through the comparison, we can get a brief idea of where China is in terms of GE internationally and in which dimensions China lags according to the GII.

When we read these statistics, we must bear in mind that China is a large country with great internal inequalities between urban and rural areas, different regions, different social classes and so on. For example, for the maternal mortality rate, in 2000 the number for the western undeveloped areas was 5.4 times higher than the number for the eastern developed area, and the number was 2.6 times higher in 2014. Such internal inequalities exist not only in women's health, but also in other social aspects, such as women's education, labor force participation, economic income, political participation and so on. At the same time, the state has also put some effort into reducing the internal differences, in particular the difference between urban and rural areas. One successful field is women's health. During the past 10 years, the state has increased funding for maternal health care in

Table 4.1 Gender Inequality Index (GII) for China, Norway and Singapore

Country (rank)	Maternal Mortality Ratio (deaths per 100,000 live births)	Adolescent birth rate (births per 1,000, age 15–19)	Women's share of seats in parliament (%)	Population with at least some secondary education, (%, age 25 and older)	Labor force participation rate (%, age 15 and older)
China (No. 90)	32[11]	8.6	23.6	Female: 58.7 Male: 71.9	Female: 63.9 Male: 78.3
Norway (No. 1)	4	7.8	39.6	Female: 97.4 Male: 96.7	Female: 61.2 Male: 68.7
Singapore (No. 11)	6	6	25.3	Female: 74.1 Male: 81	Female: 58.8 Male: 77.2

(Resource: UN Development Program, 2015)

rural areas. With the implementation of major projects to improve public health in rural areas and to subsidize hospital childbirths for rural pregnant and lying-in women, the national hospital birth rate had reached 99.6% in 2014. Consequently, the gap in maternal mortality rates between urban and rural areas was reduced from a factor of 2.4 in 2000 to 1.08 in 2015 (The State Council Information Office, 2015). However, rural/urban differences are still significant in other areas. Compared with areas like education and labor force participation, public health is an area that the state can more easily intervene in to promote gender equality. The reason is that the implementation of state policies to improve women's maternal health will not meet the same resistance from traditional gender norms and market mechanisms as those concerning women's education and labor force participation. In my discussion below, I therefore focus on gender (in)equality in education and labor force participation.

Rural Girls Are Most Vulnerable with Regard to Education

As shown in Table 4.1, only 58.7% of Chinese women have secondary or higher education in comparison with 71.9% of Chinese men. Since the mid-2000s, the state has implemented a special policy to ensure that school-aged girls enjoy equal access to and complete nine-year compulsory education,[12] particularly in western rural areas (The State Council Information Office, 2015). Consequently, the official statistics shows that in 2014, the net primary school enrollment rates of boys and girls were both 99.8%, "meaning that China has achieved the UN's Millennium Development Goals ahead of time" (The State Council Information Office, 2015). However, several national surveys reveal the continued differences in girls' education rates between urban and rural areas. For example, the *Third Survey on Chinese*

Women's Social Status in 2013 (He, 2013a) shows that while 97.8% of girls from urban areas were attending school at the time of the survey, the number for the rural areas was 92.2%. This difference expanded significantly for age groups over 14: while the proportion of girls attending school at age of 14 in rural areas was 97.2% (98.3% in urban areas), the number was 63% at age 17 (90.4% for urban areas). Meanwhile, China's Sixth National Population Census in 2010 showed that the completion ratio for compulsory education was lower in rural areas than in urban areas. The ratios for girls and boys in rural areas were 70.6% and 72.1%, whereas the numbers in urban areas were 93.2% for girls and 92.1% for boys (He, 2013b). This means that for basic education, the rural/urban difference is even more striking than the gender difference.

Despite the rural/urban differences, children in rural and urban areas enjoy the same rights to education, and compulsory education is free for all children. However, poverty is the most significant factor that can explain the high drop-out rate in rural areas. For instance, in 2013, the disposable income for urban residents was 26,955 Yuan per capita, whereas the annual net income for rural residents was 8,896 Yuan per capita (Cao & Zhang, 2015). As I have already shown, the difference in graduation rates from compulsory education for boys and girls in rural areas is small, at 72.1% for boys and 70.6% for girls. However, according to an investigation conducted jointly by China Children and Teenagers' Fund (CCTF), China Philanthropy Research Institute (CPRI) and Women's Studies Institute of China (WSIC), gendered differences exist in terms of when and why children drop out of school (CCTF, CPRI & WSIC, 2015). Figure 4.1 illustrates the age difference between boys and girls in rural areas at the time they drop out of school.

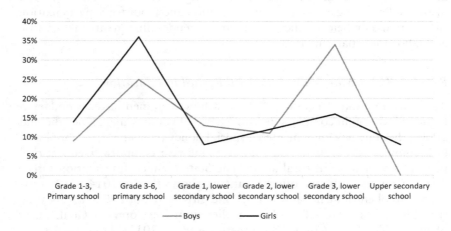

Figure 4.1 Drop-out School Percentage by Gender in Rural Areas
(Resource: CCTF, CPRI & WSIC, 2015, p. 17)

The statistics in Figure 4.1 show that in rural areas, girls generally dropped out of school much earlier than boys, which means that among those who have not completed compulsory school, boys tend to have more education than girls. The investigation has also revealed that the reasons for dropping out of school are different for boys and girls. While the most common reason for girls' dropping out of school is poverty—38.9% in contrast to 29% for boys—the most common reason for boys is a lack of interest—38.1% in contrast to 20% for girls (CCTF, CPRI & WSIC, 2015). Therefore, though poverty is one of the key obstacles preventing students from graduating from compulsory education in rural areas, it affects girls' education more profoundly than it does boys' education. With limited resources, parents often prioritize boys' education due to the traditional gender roles.

Meanwhile, the one-child policy has had a different impact on girls' education in rural and urban areas. In urban areas, the policy has changed parents' attitude towards investing in girls' education. Since a couple can only have one child, girls' and boys' education are likely to be invested in equally. However, things are different in rural areas. Despite the one-child policy, many rural couples choose to give birth to several children and pay the large fine. The financial penalty exacerbates poverty, which again has a negative impact on girls' education in rural areas.

The other important factor that influences rural children's education negatively is the segregated rural/urban household registration system, or *Hukou* in Chinese. Under this system, even if a rural resident has migrated to and works in a city, their household would remain registered as rural. Therefore, their children can only enjoy free schooling in their home village. In practice, this means that many rural children are left behind in their parents' village with grandparents or other relatives. The separation from parents, and in particular the lack of parental emotional support, influences not only these children's upbringing, but also their schooling. According to the *Third Social Survey of Chinese Women* conducted by National Bureau of Statistics of P. R. China (2011), 10% more of the girls who are left behind in villages experience emotional and school-related differences than boys who are left behind. In addition, the girls are more likely to be exposed to sexual abuse than the boys (CCTF, CPRI & WSIC, 2015, pp. 35, 37). Therefore, with the intersection of gender and rural/urban segregation, girls in rural areas are the most vulnerable and disadvantaged group with regard to basic education.

Labor Force Participation

With 63.9% participation in the labor force, women in China participate more in the labor force than women in Norway and Singapore (Table 4.1). However, this does not mean that Chinese women enjoy more equality in the labor market. First, the inclusion of the entire population above the age of 15 can likely explain China's comparatively high rate for women's labor force participation. As discussed above, the percentage of women in China who have higher educations is quite low. Second, the high participation rate does not say anything about women's position. Several surveys reveal that women are not positioned equally to men in the labor market (National Bureau of Statistics of P. R. China, 2001; Qiu, 2014; Wang, 2002; Zhang, 2010). The expanding wage gap between men and women strongly indicates that there is gender inequality in the labor market. According to the UN Women China Office, in 1990, the average wage of women in urban areas was 77% that of men, while rural women's wage was 79% that of men. These numbers had further decreased to 67.3% and 56%, respectively, in 2012 (Broussard, 2012). The wage gap can be explained by women's unequal position in the labor market, both horizontally and vertically.

Table 4.2 illustrates that women are underrepresented in many of the sectors and industries, in particular high-income and high-prestige sectors such as state/government/party organs, business management agencies, real estate, research and technological services, and business and trade.

Despite the legal prohibition on gender discrimination, both direct and indirect gender discrimination exists and is even widespread in the labor market (Zhang, 2010). For example, some employers clearly state that they prefer men. When hiring women, some employers require female employees to not give birth within a certain period or even for the whole contract period (Zhang, 2010). Sometimes, these requirements appear in contract

Table 4.2 Gender Composition of Employees in Urban Units

Branches	Male (%)	Female (%)
Agriculture, forestry, husbandry, fishery	62.89	37.11
Wholesale/retail and catering	55.14	44.86
Building industry	82.92	17.08
Extractive industries	74.71	25.29
Metallurgical industry	56.96	43.04
Enterprises	62.91	37.09
Geological survey and water management	73.01	26.99
Public institutions	55.33	44.67
Education, culture, arts and media	54.45	45.55
State/government/party organs and social groups	74.76	25.24
Health, sports and social welfare	42.01	57.99
Enterprise management agencies	64.61	35.39
Real estate	65.84	34.16
Transport, storage, post and telecommunications	71.73	28.27
Finance and insurance	54.12	45.88
Research and technological services	66.54	33.46
Business and trade	60.14	39.86

(Resource: *The Second Social Survey of Chinese Women* by the National Bureau of Statistics of P.R. China, 2001, see also Zhang, 2010, pp. 20–21)

provisions but are disguised by other state policies. For example, a labor contract for a teacher's position from an education center in Shenyang reads, "In response to the state's call to late childbearing, Part B [refers to the female employee] voluntarily commits to no childbearing in the contract period." (Zhang, 2010, p. 34).

A case study on the employment processes of graduates from Nankai University, Tianjin in 2002 reveals that many female graduates experienced gender discrimination in their employment processes (Wang, 2002). For example, the study shows that to get employment, female graduates on average had submitted more CVs than male graduates, and male graduates were more likely to get interviews than female graduates. Consequently, it took longer for female graduates to be employed than for male graduates (Wang, 2002). A 2003 survey on employers' needs and expectations in employing university graduates also uncovered significant gender bias in the labor market (Tang, 2003). When asked, "With the same wage, would you like to employ a male or a female graduate?" 94.23% of survey respondents chose male graduates. While 82.2% thought that marriage would have a negative impact on a female employee's work performance, only 5.7% considered this to be the case for male employees. Female employees are thus more likely to be laid off. In particular, women above age 45 tend to be targeted for layoffs (National Bureau of Statistics of P. R. China, 2011; Zhang, 2015).

With regard to vertical discrimination, highly educated women in China also hit the "glass ceiling" in their careers. For example, a survey on senior talent in companies in Shanghai revealed that women occupy 42.1% of middle-management positions. However, when it comes to top management positions, the number falls to 16.6% (Zhang, 2010, p. 39). Table 4.3 and Table 4.4 illustrate the distribution of highly qualified female employees in

Table 4.3 Distribution of Female Managers and their Wage Levels in Companies in Guangzhou

	Female (%)	*Monthly Wage (Yuan)*
HR manager/director	80	8,000–20,000
Finance and accounting manager/director	60	8,000–25,000
Administrative manager	90	5,000–15,000
Sales manager/director	40	≥ 10,000
Technical manager/director	2	≥ 15,000
Other department manager	40	≥ 8,000
Factory director	0	≥ 30,000
Production manager	10	≥ 8,000
Purchase manager	30	≥ 8,000
Logistics manager	20	≥ 8,000
General manager	0	≥ 30,000

(Resource: 51Job[13] (Guangzhou), in Zhang, 2010, p. 40)

Table 4.4 Distribution of Female Managers and their Wage Levels in Companies in Beijing

	Female (%)	Monthly Wages (Yuan)
HR manager/director	60	8,000–30,000
Finance and accounting manager/director	30	8,000–40,000
Marketing manager/director	22	10,000–50,000
COO (Chief Operating Officer)	20	10,000–25,000
CTO (Chief Technology Officer)	2	12,000–30,000
PR manager	50	6,000–15,000
Chief engineer or chief architect	15	15,000–30,000
Production director	10	10,000–20,000
Finance and investment manager	15	12,000–40,000
CEO (Chief Executive Officer)	10	20,000–60,000

(Resource: Beijing Talent Consulting Agency, in Zhang, 2010, p. 40)

management positions in Guangzhou and Beijing. Again, the statistics confirm that female managers are not preferred in top management positions even though they are overrepresented in certain middle-management positions, such as positions in finance and accounting, human resources (HR), public relations, sales and administration.

The employers often justify their discrimination against female managers by referring to certain stereotypical, naturalized gendered differences between men and women, for instance that women are hardworking and patient, yet not good at leading a team and that women are empathetic and keen, but lack the ability to do macro analyses (Liu, 1995). These gendered stereotypes thus result in a shared sense that women are less qualified for top management positions than men.

Based on his study of several key headhunting agencies in Beijing and Guangzhou (Table 4.3 and Table 4.4), Zhang Kangsi concludes that the biggest obstacle for women to achieve top positions is age. According to Zhang, a male manager can often reach his career pinnacle after turning 40, while for a female manager, the golden career period is approximately from 35–40 (Zhang, 2010). In other words, a female manager has a shorter and more intense period to develop her career. Zhang's conclusion coincides with findings from my pilot study on the work/life balance of white-collar middle-class women in Chongqing (Zhao, 2013), which demonstrates how the career paths of highly educated middle-class women also rely on an intergenerational contract about mutual care that is based on the gendered and collectivist Chinese traditional ideology about responsibilities of care within the family. The informants who were in their late 30s, married, had a child and held upper-middle-management positions told me that their work/life balance was temporarily not a big problem for them, because they had relatively young parents (mostly mothers or mothers-in-law) who were taking care of the home and the children. However, they all expressed concern for their work/life balance and career stagnation later on, when the elder generation would no longer be able to take care of the home and the child, at which time the women would also need to "pay back" the care the elder generation had provided (Zhao, 2013). Both Zhang's study and my own point to the intersection of gender and age as crucial in constituting middle-aged female managers as disadvantaged subjects for career advancement. Moreover, the one-child policy that started in the late 1970s exacerbates women's difficult position, because it means that many couples born after the late 1970s will be responsible for the care of four seniors.

Exploring the Gap

Thus far, we can conclude that though there has been legal and institutional progress, GE is far from being a reality in China. With regard to education, girls in rural undeveloped areas are marginalized and constitute the most vulnerable group in terms of their graduation rates. Their vulnerable position in the education system is a result of their families' low socioeconomic status in intersection with traditional gender norms. With regard to labor force participation, although the government claims to have constantly improved laws to strengthen the protection of women, the laws are clearly insufficient to protect women's rights. Despite the legal prohibition on gender discrimination, both direct and indirect as well as horizontal and vertical discrimination persist in the labor market. In this section, I explore the gap between *de jure* and *de facto* GE. I focus on women's labor participation because the gap here is most obvious.

Legal Systems Lagging Behind

To explain the gap between *de jure* and *de facto* GE, Zhang Kangsi points out that the Chinese legal system for women's labor rights is still lagging behind, and that problems exist in both legislation and enforcement (Zhang, 2015). In terms of *legislation*, the biggest problem is the vague definitions of discriminating behaviors. In other words, the laws are unclear and unspecific in defining what behaviors constitute discrimination. Furthermore, despite the increasing number of legal provisions to protect women's rights, the laws do not provide concrete instructions on how to operationalize the provisions. According to Zhang, the wordings of laws related to gender equality thus sound more like slogans than feasible legal provisions (Zhang, 2015). In terms of the *enforcement of laws*, Zhang points out that the legal system lacks targeted and valid punishments. For example, the usual punishments for discriminating against women's rights include an "order to correct,"[14] "administrative penalty,"[15] and a "fine and economic compensations." However, given that an "order to correct" and "administrative penalty" are means of punishment under the old state-planned economy and labor system, they are only applicable to government agencies, state-owned enterprises and other labor units with authorized state staff systems. Many employers are thus excluded from the actual punishments. With regard to fines and compensation, there is no specific provision on the standard for imposing this or for the calculation of economic loss caused by gender discrimination. Finally, Zhang points out that to effectively enforce the laws, there is a need for a specialized functional legal body, such as the Equal Employment Opportunity Commission (EEOC) in the US, to deal with gender discrimination and to promote GE in the employment (Zhang, 2015).

In addition to what Zhang has pointed out, weak legal awareness among women, especially those with little education, is another possible explanation for the gap between *de jure* and *de facto* GE in the labor market. On the one hand, many of the gender biases are based upon deep-rooted traditional gender roles, which some women would in fact identify with. In these cases, women who have experienced gender discrimination may not recognize it as a form of discrimination. On the other hand, it can be argued that the female victims are fully aware of the discriminating behaviors, but choose not to resort to the law because of the high cost of legal proceedings and the well-known fact that the role of the court in labor disputes resolution is limited (Peerenboom & He, 2009).

It is also important to bear in mind that historically, there is little tradition in China for the rule of law. While traditional Confucianism emphasizes the importance of political leaders' virtues in regulating human behavior, under the communist regime, administrative and political measures are very often more effective means of regulating behavior than legal strategies. Sometimes, local administrative rules may also conflict with the laws. In such cases, the local authorities are more likely to follow the administrative rules than the laws. A 2003 legal case on the discrimination of a married woman in Liangping County, Chongqing related to the lease of land[16] is such an example. The plaintiff was not permitted to continue leasing land in her home village after her marriage to a man from another village. The local authority justified this decision by referring to the local land administration rule that after marriage, women ought to move their household registration to their husband's family. According to this rule, the woman is no longer a resident of her home village, and thus has no right to lease the land. However, legally, women enjoy the same rights to land as men. In addition, married women can choose to maintain their household registration in their home village, and they enjoy the same rights as other villagers. Obviously, the local authorities did not rely on law in their handling of the case, and the local land administration rules are themselves discriminatory to women. Eventually, this legal case ended with the local court dismissing the plaintiff's claim. This case illustrates how difficult it can be for individuals to turn to the law and legal processes to defend their legal rights.

The State's Willingness to Implement GE under the Socialist Market Economy

If administrative and political measures are more effective, then why does the government not apply such measures to promote GE in labor force participation as it did in the Mao era? One question is how much the state *can* regulate the labor market under the socialist market economy. With the marketization of labor, the state has limited room for intervening in the labor market. Lisa Hoffman also points out that the economic reform has led to a new form of governing that she calls "late-socialist neoliberalism," which considers the planned system and strong state intervention in the labor market to be a problem (Hoffman, 2010). In other words, the real question is how much the state *is willing* to regulate the labor market to achieve GE.

As noted earlier, the Chinese government claims that GE, being a basic state policy, is the will of the Chinese state. Furthermore, the government has included GE in its national plans for economic and social development. However, what does this inclusion mean? I question the state's willingness to implement GE by examining how the government deals with the relationship between GE and the central goal of sustaining economic development. Based on my analysis of official documents on gender and gender development, I argue that the inclusion of GE into national plans for economic development in practice means that the goal of GE is subordinated to economic development, or even sacrificed for the sake of economic growth.

When addressing gender inequality as a problem, the government has adopted a Marxist approach, according to which gender relations belong to the "superstructure," which is determined by the development of the "economic base"[17] (Marx, 1977). For example, in the first national plan on gender and women's development for the period 1995–2000, the government accounts for gender-related problems in this way:

[A]s China is a developing country, restricted by the level of economic and social development and affected by old ideas, the level of women's education and their participation in social development is still not high enough: the laws stipulating gender equality have not yet been fully implemented, social discrimination against women still exists, and the living conditions of women in poverty areas are to be improved.[18]

(The State Council, 1995)

Similarly, in the latest national plan on gender equality and women's development,

Restricted and impacted by the developmental level of the productive forces and civilization at the early stage of socialism, women's development still faces many problems and challenges. Sex discrimination in employment has not been eliminated: there is still a gap between women and men in terms of their possession of resources and income, women's participation in decision-making and management is still at a low level, women's level of education is still lower than men, women's health requirements must be better met, the social environment for women's development needs to be further optimized, and the social security for women needs to be further improved. The interests and needs of women in different strata are increasingly diversified, and the uneven development between urban and rural women has not been fully solved.[19]

(The State Council, 2011)

In both quotes, the problem of gender inequality is represented as an issue related to a low level of development—and in particular the low level of economic development—as well as the "old ideas," or in other words the patriarchal ethics from China's long feudal history. The underlying understanding is that as long as the economy is developed, women's development will be promoted and GE will be achieved. Another implicit message is that gender inequality is a historical problem, which the government attempts to solve through economic and social development. However, in the second quote, the government has also admitted that the ongoing economic development at the early stage of socialism has produced new forms of inequality at the intersection of gender, social stratification and rural/urban segregations. Therefore, the relationship between GE and economic development is paradoxical: economic development is both the solution and the source of gender inequality.

To further the argument, we can look at how the Chinese state legitimizes the social inequalities produced by the socialist market economy. Deng Xiaoping, the architect of China's economic reform, legitimized the uneven development and social inequalities with the following statement:

Under the principle of common prosperity, we must let some people and some regions get rich first. Regions with rapid development can drive the development of other regions. This is a shortcut to accelerate the development and to achieve common prosperity.

(Deng, 1995, p. 155; see also E. Wang, 2014)

The important message is that the inequalities are an inevitable outcome of the development of a market economy, and to meet the need for economic development, we have to accept the inequalities, which according to Deng are short-term and temporary. Though Deng did not mention gender inequality, the inequalities he addressed clearly have a gendered dimension. Therefore, I argue that GE in practice is not included in, but rather is subordinated to, economic development. This also suggests that the state has a certain tolerance for gender inequalities at the early stage of socialism, and that it is prepared to sacrifice GE for the purpose of short-term economic growth. Similarly, by examining the major schools of political thought that have emerged in post-Mao China and analyzing how these ideas treat the question of GE, Q. Wang (2014) argues that the current reform politics are built upon a political consensus that national modernization for this time no longer needs to center around women's status and gender equality. With regard to women's labor force participation, it is therefore not difficult to understand why gender discrimination exists in the labor market even though the state has declared that it would solve this problem in all its national plans for women's development. This discrimination persists precisely because it is fueled by economic incentives (Zhang, 2010). I would also like point out that this neoliberalist prioritization of economic incentives exists in not only the official discourse but also in everyday discourse. Therefore, gender issues are often trivialized in the labor market.

Conclusion

In this chapter, I have discussed the implementation of GE in the Chinese context after China's ratification of CEDAW in 1980. This question is discussed in relation to China's ongoing process of developing the socialist market economy and the political process of what Hoffman (2010) calls "late socialist neoliberalism." I also embed this discussion in the historical, political and social contexts in China, from "male feminism" in the late Qing Dynasty and the May Fourth Era (from the late 19th century to the early 1920s), to the women's movement under the communist revolution (from 1921 to 1949), and to "state feminism" after the establishment of the People's Republic of China. The main conclusion is that even though the Chinese government has improved the legal framework and developed policies and plans for GE, GE is far from being a social reality. For instance, in terms of women's labor force participation, even though laws stipulate that women have equal rights and prohibit gender discrimination, these are insufficient to protect women's rights in practice and gender discrimination is common in the labor market. To explain the gap between *de jure* and *de facto* GE, I have critically examined the legal system and the state's willingness to implement GE policy.

Though the government has improved the legal framework, the legal system is, in general, still lagging behind (Zhang, 2015). By analyzing how the government deals with the relationship between gender equality development and economic development, I have also questioned the willingness of the state to implement GE. Though the government has included GE in China's economic and social development plan, I argue that this inclusion in practice means that GE is subordinated to the goal of economic development. The relationship between GE and economic development is also paradoxical, as the communist government considers economic development to be both the solution to and the source of gender inequality. As the development of the socialist market economy also produces other forms of social inequalities between regions and rural/urban areas which intersect with gender inequality, it will be more difficult to treat women as one and the same underprivileged group in China. In particular, the urban/rural segregation and inequality are important dimensions that intersect with gender in producing new forms of social inequalities. Girls' education in rural areas is an example of this.

Given that historically GE and women's developments in China have successively been subsumed under the anti-imperialist and anti-colonial National Salvation Movement, Communist Revolution, socialist construction and now economic development under the market economy, I also argue that there has never been an independent women's movement and GE politics that have really uprooted the deep gender bias and norms in China. This is an important factor underlying the gap between *de jure* and *de facto* GE.

Notes

1 "Three Obediences" means that a woman were to obey her father as a daughter, her husband as a wife and her son as a widow, while "Four Virtues" refers to the virtues of loyalty, proper speech, modest demeanor and diligent work.
2 The New Culture Movement (simplified Chinese: 新文化运动) sprang from the disillusionment with traditional Chinese culture following the failure of the Chinese Republic, founded in 1912 to address China's problems. Many famous scholars with classical educations, such as Chen Duxiu, Cai Yuanpei, Li Dazhao, Lu Xun, Zhou Zuoren and Hu Shih began to lead a revolt against Confucianism and called for the creation of a new Chinese culture based on global and Western standards, especially democracy and science. Influenced by these scholars, younger followers called for vernacular literature; an end to the patriarchal family in favor of individual freedom and women's liberation; a view of China as a nation among nations, not as a uniquely Confucian culture; a reexamination of Confucian texts and ancient classics using modern textual and critical methods; democratic and egalitarian values; and an orientation to the future rather than the past.
3 In Chinese, 时代不同了，男女都一样。
4 In Chinese, 走出家门。
5 In Chinese, 男同志能办到的事情，女同志也能办到。
6 In Chinese, 妇女翻身解放
7 In Chinese, 妇女能顶半边天。
8 In Chinese, 按劳分配.
9 There are seven basic state policies: one-child policy, gender equality, reform and opening up, protection of farmland, conservation of soil and water, conservation of resources and environmental protection.
10 According to the statistics by the All-China Women's Federation, domestic violence exists in nearly 30% of 270 million families in China. In 90% of the cases, victims are female (Chen, 2005).
11 The number is 21.7 according to China's official statistics (The State Council Information Office, 2015).
12 Compulsory education in China includes six years of education in primary schools and three years of education in lower secondary schools.
13 51job is a leading human resource solutions provider in China, offering a broad array of services in the areas of recruitment solutions, training and assessment, and HR outsourcing and consulting services.

14 In Chinese, 责令改正
15 In Chinese, 行政处罚
16 The case was published by several local and national media outlets, including *People's Daily* (2003).
17 The Chinese government has also used the formulations "material civilization" (物质文明*Wuzhi Wenming*), which refers to economic performance, and "spiritual civilization" (精神文明 *jingshen wenming*), which refers to development of other social aspects, including gender. For example, in the government annual reports for 2000, 2002 and 2003, gender development is mentioned under the achievement of spiritual civilization.
18 The author's own translation.
19 The author's own translation.

References

Amendment IX to the Criminal Law of P.R. China (中华人民共和国刑法修正案[九]). (2015). Retrieved from http://en.pkulaw.cn/display.aspx?cgid=256286&lib=law (accessed 14 August 2016).

Anti-domestic Violence Law of P.R. China (中华人民共和国反家庭暴力法). (2016). Retrieved from http://www.lawinfochina.com/display.aspx?lib=law&id=20841 &EncodingName=big5 (accessed 14 August 2016).

Broussard, J. (2012). Empowering woman. Speech given at the Third Female Leadership Forum, Shanghai, 28 March.

CCTF 中国儿童少年基金会, CPRI 北京师范大学中国公益研究院, & WSIC. 全国妇联妇女研究所 (2015). Research report of Chinese girls' education and development needs 2015 中国女童教育与发展需求研究报告2015. Retrieved from http://www. cctf.org.cn/files/%E5%A5%B3%E7%AB%A5%E6%95%99%E8%82%B2%E4 %B8%8E%E5%8F%91%E5%B1%95%E9%9C%80%E6%B1%82%E7%A0 %94%E7%A9%B6%E6%8A%A5%E5%91%8A.pdf. (accessed 11 July 2016).

Chen, Y. 陈裕亮 (2005). *Violence Exists in 30% of 270 Million Chinese Families*中国2.7亿家庭30%存在暴力 严惩施暴者须立法: *Legislation Required for Strict Punishment*. Retrieved from http://legal.people.com.cn/GB/42732/3950479.html (accessed 11 July 2016).

Compulsory Education Law of P.R. China (中华人民共和国义务教育法). (1986). Retrieved from http://www.china.org.cn/government/laws/2007–04/17/content_1207402.htm (accessed 14 August 2016).

Constitution of P.R. China (中华人民共和国宪法). (1954). Peking: Foreign Language Press.

Constitution of P.R. China (中华人民共和国宪法). (2004). Retrieved from http://www.npc.gov.cn/englishnpc/Constitution/node_2825.htm (accessed 14 August 2016).

Dai, J. 戴锦华 (2004). Introduction II: Dillema or breakthrough? 导言二， 两难之间或突围可能? In S. Chen 陈顺馨& J. Dai 戴锦华 (Eds), *Women, Nation and Feminism*《妇女，民族和女性主义》, Beijing: Central Compilation & Translation Press中央编译出版社, pp. 27–38.

Deng, X. 邓小平 (1995). *The Selected Works of Dang Xiaoping* (Vol. 3) 《邓小平文选》第三卷. Beijing: People's Publishing House 人民出版社.

Dong, L. 董丽敏 (2013). The production of gender and its political crisis: A reflection on women's studies in the new era 性别的生产及政治危机——对新时期中国妇女研究的反思. *Open Times* 《开放时代 》, (2). Retrieved from http://www. opentimes.cn/bencandy.php?fid=368&aid=1710 (accessed 8 July 2016).

Fan, H. 范红霞 (2012). Women, family and nation state 妇女，家庭与民族国家. In L. Tan 谭琳 & X. Jiang 姜秀花 (Eds), *Women's Development and Gender Equality in China: History, Reality and Challenges*中国妇女发展与性别平等：历史，现实，挑战, Beijing: Social Sciences Academic Press 社会科学文献出版社, pp. 62–71.

He, J. 和建花 (2013a). Girls' survival and development, and women's status 女童生存发展与妇女地位. In X. Song 宋秀岩 (Ed.), *Investigation of Chinese Women's Social Status in the New Era* 《新时期中国妇女社会地位调查研究》, Beijing: China Women Publishing House 中国妇女出版社, pp. 733–796.

He, J. 和建花 (2013b). The situation of girls' survival and development in China 中国女童生存发展状况. In L. Tan 谭琳 (Ed.), *Annual Report on Gender Equality and Women's Development in China (2008–2012)* 《2008—2012年：中国性别平等和妇女发展报告》, Beijing: Social Science Academic Press社会科学文献出版社, pp. 112–129.

Hoffman, L. (2010). *Patriotic Professionalism in Urban China: Fostering Talent.* Philadelphia: Temple University Press.

Huang, L. 荒林 (2004). *Feminism in China*中国女性主义. Guilin, China: Guangxi Normal University Press 广西师范大学出版社.

Jin, Y. 金一虹 (2009). Rethinking "iron girl": Gender and labour during the Chinse cultural revolution "铁姑娘"再思考——中国"文化大革命"期间的社会性别与劳动. In Y. Li 李银河(Ed.), *Family and Gender Review* 家庭与性别评论 (Vol. 2), Beijing: Social Sciences Academic Press 社会科学文献出版社, pp. 27–55.

Labor Contract Law of P. R. China (中华人民共和国劳动合同法). (2008). Retrieved from http://english.gov.cn/archive/laws_regulations/2014/08/23/content_281474983042501.htm (accessed 14 August 2016).

Law of P. R. China on Maternal and Infant Health Care (中华人民共和国母婴保健法). (1994). Retrieved from http://www.npc.gov.cn/englishnpc/Law/2007–12/12/content_1383796.htm (accessed 14 August 2016).

Law of P. R. China on Promotion of Employment (中华人民共和国就业促进法). (2008). Retrieved from http://www.for68.com/new/2009/6/wa327201951192690021180–0.htm (accessed 14 August 2016).

Law of P. R. China on the Protection of Rights and Interests of Women (中华人民共和国妇女权益保障法). (1992). NPC Gazette No. 58/192. Retrieved from http://www.china.org.cn/english/government/207405.htm (accessed 14 August 2016).

Li, X. (1995). Gender inequality in China and cultural relativism. In M.C. Nussbaum & J. Glover (Eds), *Women, Culture, and Development*, New York: Oxford University Press, pp. 407–425.

Li, X. 李晓蓉 (2012). Analysis of the characteristics of the Chinese contemporary feminism, from late Qing-Dynasty to the May fourth 中国近代女权特色之分析（晚清至五四）. *Journal of National Kaohsiung Normal University* 高雄师大学报, **33** (1), 43–59.

Li, Z. 立早 (2015). *A Brief History of Chinese Feminist Movements* 一个简略的中国女权运动史. Retrieved from https://site.douban.com/211878/widget/notes/13513823/note/496116880/ (accessed 7 July 2016).

Liu, B. 刘伯红 (1995). Women's employment condition in China 中国女性就业状况. *Sociological Studies* 《社会学研究》, (2), 39–48.

Lü, M. 吕美颐 (2012). The tracks: Retrospect and prospect of women's and gender studies in mainland China 春华秋实的足迹——大陆"女性/性别"研究的回顾与展望. In S. Tan 谭少薇, H. Ye叶汉明, H. Huang 黄慧贞& J. Lu 卢家咏 (Eds),

Gender Awakening, Gender Studies in Mainland China, Hongkong and Tai-wan《性别觉醒，两岸三地社会性别研究》, Hongkong: Commercial Press 商务印书馆, pp. 2–13.

Marriage Law of P.R. China (中华人民共和国婚姻法). (1980). Retrieved from http://www.china.org.cn/china/LegislationsForm2001–2010/2011–02/11/content_21897930.htm (accessed 14 August 2016).

Marx, K. (1977). *A Contribution to the Critique of Political Economy*. Moscow: Progress Publishers. Notes by R. Rojas.

National Bureau of Statistics of P.R.China (中华人民共和国国家统计局). (2001). Report of main data from the second social survey of Chinese women 第二期中国妇女社会地位抽样调查主要数据报告. Retrieved from http://www.stats.gov.cn/tjsj/tjgb/qttjgb/qgqttjgb/200203/t20020331_30606.html (accessed 16 July 2016).

National Bureau of Statistics of P.R.China(中华人民共和国国家统计局). (2011). Report of the main data from the third social survey of Chinese women 第三期中国妇女社会地位抽样调查主要数据报告. Retrieved from http://www.wsic.ac.cn/staticdata/84760.htm (accessed 16 July 2016).

Organic Law of the Villagers Committees of P.R. China (中华人民共和国村委会组织法). (1998). Retrieved from http://www.china.org.cn/english/government/207279.htm (accessed 14 August 2016).

Peerenboom, R., & He, X. (2009). Dispute resolution in China: Patterns, causes and prognosis. *East Asia Law Review*, 4 (1). Retrieved from https://www.law.upenn.edu/journals/ealr/articles/Volume4/issue1/PeerenboomHe4E.AsiaL.Rev.1%282009%29.pdf (accessed 11 July 2016).

People's Daily (人民日报). (2003). The first legal case of discriminating against women's right to land in Chongqing har started in court 重庆首例"土地歧视妇女"案开庭. People's Daily Online, 21 March 人民网. Retrieved from http://www.people.com.cn/GB/shehui/44/20030321/949023.html (accessed 5 July 2016).

Qiu, Y. 邱玥 (2014). Concern: How female graduates deal with labour discrimination 关注：女大学生如何过"就业歧视"这道坎儿. *Guangming Daily* 光明日报, 5 May. Retrieved from http://theory.people.com.cn/n/2014/0505/c40531–24974220.html (accessed 7 June 2016).

Saich, T. (2004). *Governance and Politics of China*. New York: Palgrave Macmillan.

Social Insurance Law of P.R. China (中华人民共和国社会保险法). (2011). Retrieved from http://www.lawinfochina.com/display.aspx?lib=law&id=8328 (accessed 14 August 2016).

Song, S. 宋少鹏 (2013). Socialist feminism and liberal feminism: The internal consensus and divergence within the Chinese women's movement in 1920s 社会主义女权与自由主义女权：二十世纪二十年代中国妇女运动内部的共识与分歧. *Research of Chinese Communist Party History* 《中共党史研究》, **179** (5), 76–88.

Special Rules on the Labor Protection of Female Employees (女职工劳动保护特别规定). (2012). Retrieved from http://en.acftu.org/28616/201408/26/140826131330762.shtml (accessed 14 August 2016).

The State Council (国务院). (1995). Program for Chinese women's development 1995–2000 《中国妇女发展纲要 (1995–2000年)》. Retrieved from http://news.xinhuanet.com/ziliao/2003–09/08/content_1068085.htm (accessed 15 February 2016).

The State Council (国务院). (2011). Program for Chinese women's development 2011–2020 《中国妇女发展纲要 (2011–2020年)》. Retrieved from http://www.china.com.cn/policy/txt/2011–08/08/content_23160230.htm (accessed 16 July 2016).

The State Council Information Office (国务院新闻办公室). (1994). White paper: The situation of Chinese women 《中国妇女的状况》白皮书. Retrieved from http://www.scio.gov.cn/zfbps/ndhf/1994/Document/307996/307996.htm (accessed 16 July 2016).

The State Council Information Office (国务院新闻办公室). (2015). White paper: Gender equality and women's development in China《中国性别平等与妇女发展》白皮书. Retrieved from http://www.scio.gov.cn/zfbps/ndhf/2015/Document/1449896/1449896.htm (accessed 16 July 2016).

The State of P. R. China (中国政府). (2015). P. R.China's report on implementation of The Beijing Declaration and Platform for Action and Resolutions adopted at the 23rd UN General Assembly Special Session 中华人民共和国执行《北京宣言和行动纲领》（1995年）及第23届联大特别会议成果文件（2000年）情况报告. Retrieved from http://www.unwomen.org/en/csw/csw59-2015/preparations (accessed 16 July 2016).

Tang, K. 唐矿 (2003). Value deviations between employers and university graduates, graduates shall pay attention to change of needs in labour market 用人单位和毕业生存在观念偏差，毕业生择业要注意需求变化. *China Education Daily*, 8 October.

United Nations Development Program. (2015). Human development report 2015: Work for human development. Retrieved from http://hdr.undp.org/en/2015-report (accessed 30 May 2016).

Wang, E. (2014). Deng's reform, theory and practice. In X. Li & X. Tian (Eds), *Evolution of Power, China's Struggle, Survival and Success*, Lanham, MD: Lexington Books, pp. 101–122.

Wang, Q. (2014). Collective male feminism, feminism, and feminist politics in transitional China. Paper represented at the 8th Annual Nordic NIAS Council Conference, "A Multitude of Encounters with Asia: Gender Perspectives", Reykjavík, Iceland, 13–17 October.

Wang, X. 王小波 (2002). Gender difference and discrimination in university graduates' entry to labour market: An empirical analysis of female graduates' employment difficulties 大学生劳动力市场入口的性别差异与性别歧视——关于"女大学生就业难"的一个实证分析. *Youth Research* 《青年研究》, (9). Retrieved from http://www.lqq5.com/5933197925/ (accessed 11 July 2016).

Wang, Z. (1997). Maoism, feminism, and the UN Conference on women: Women's studies research in contemporary China. *Journal of Women's History*, 8 (4), 126–152.

Wang, Z. (2005). "State feminism"? Gender and socialist state formation in Maoist China. *Feminist Studies*, **31** (3), 519–551.

Wolf, M., & Wikte, R. (1975). *Women in Chinese Society*. Stanford: Stanford University Press.

Zhang, K. 张抗私 (2010). *Gender Discrimination in Labour Market and Social Gender Exclusion* 《劳动力市场性别歧视与社会性别排斥》. Beijing: Science Press. 科学出版社.

Zhang, K. 张抗私 (2015). Gender discrimination in labour market and protection of female human rights 劳动力市场歧视与女性人权保护. *Human Rights*《人权》, (4). Retrieved from http://www.humanrights.cn/html/2015/zxyq_1105/11498.html (accessed 11 July 2016).

Zhao, Y. (2013). Gender_GenderEquality@Feminism.China: The challenges of balancing work and family among the emerging middle class women in China. Paper represented at the 7th Annual Nordic NIAS Council Conference "The power of knowledge, Asia and the World". Sønderborg, Denmark, 4–6 November, 2013.

5 A "Fair Go" in the Lucky Country? Gender Equality and the Australian Case

Archana Preeti Voola, Kara Beavis and Anuradha Mundkur

> *In the spirit of respect, the authors acknowledge the Traditional Owners of the land across Australia on which we work and live. We pay our respects to Aboriginal and Torres Strait Islander elders past, present and future and we value Aboriginal and Torres Strait Islander history, culture and knowledge.*

Introduction

It is easy to assume that Australia is making great strides in meeting its international commitments to gender equality. The Global Gender Gap Index ranked Australia 36 out of 145 countries (World Economic Forum, 2015). Within the Asia-Pacific region, Australia ranks third (out of 24 countries) in closing 73% of the gender gap in economic participation and opportunity, educational attainment, health and political participation, although in varying degrees for each category (World Economic Forum, 2015, pp. 15–26). Such rankings fuel the belief that Australia is a world leader in achieving gender equality (Inglehart & Norris, 2003; Plibersek, 2008; Scott, 2008). However, while Australia is discursively constructed as a "fair" and "lucky" country, we find that Australian egalitarianism is mediated by race, ethnicity, postcode, migration status, sexual orientation, gender identity and whether a person lives with a disability, among other factors.

In addition, although Australia was an early adopter of the United Nations Convention on the Elimination of all Forms of Discrimination Against Women (CEDAW), gender equality is a contested space occupied by differing definitions and varying levels of commitment to its adoption. This contestation, we argue, is because the pursuit of gender equality has been and remains dependent on the government of the day and their priorities; support for governance mechanisms including the presence of feminists or "femocrats" within women's policy units; and the mobilization of vocal and visible non-government actors. As a result, gender equality in Australia is neither evenly distributed throughout the population, nor is it a story of incremental gains.

The definition of gender equality, as articulated in this book, embodies the three principles of equality enshrined in CEDAW, namely non-discrimination, state obligations and substantive equality. The first two principles reflect formal equality. The third refers to lived experience of access to rights. In this chapter we argue that, in Australia, there is a tension in the translation of formal equality into substantive equality. There are significant regional variations causing a disjointed uptake of laws, policies and programs. For instance, accessing abortion remains unlawful (with variations in when it is performed) in most states, but is decriminalized in the states of South Australia, Victoria and the Australian Capital Territory (Costa & Douglas, 2015). This is in part due to the federated system of governance dividing legislative powers between federal (also called Commonwealth), state and territory governments. The federal government legislates on matters of national interest (such as trade, foreign affairs, defense, immigration, taxation, marriage and divorce), while a state's legislative powers extend over sectors like health, education, policing, infrastructure and so forth.

Another layer of complexity in the regional variations can be attributed to the ruling political party, which can vary based on the federal and state levels. At the time of writing this chapter, the more conservative coalition (comprising the Liberal Party of Australia, National Party of Australia, Liberal National Party and Country Liberal Party) was returned to power during the 2016 federal election. In the states of Victoria, Queensland, South Australia and the Australian Capital Territory, the more progressive Australian Labor Party (ALP) is in power. These challenges and their impacts on the gender equality agenda are highlighted in the Concluding Observations of the CEDAW Committee's on Australia's Combined 6th and 7th CEDAW report (CEDAW, 2010).

As in the rest of the world, women are not a homogenous group. Aboriginal and Torres Strait Islander women are 35 times more likely to be hospitalized as a result of intimate partner violence as compared with non-Aboriginal and Torres Strait Islander women (UPRA, 2015, p. 2). Women born overseas are more likely to be unemployed, compared with women born in Australia; unemployment rates for Aboriginal and Torres Strait Islander women stood at 14.5%; and rates of disability for Aboriginal and Torres Strait Islander people was just under 51% for both male and female Aboriginal and Torres Strait Islanders (ABS, 2016). Women with disabilities are more likely to live in poverty, less likely to be accessing sexual and reproductive health rights and more likely to be affected by the lack of affordable housing (UPRA, 2015). Australia's Human Rights Commissioner Gillian Triggs (2013b) underscores that, rather than any single attribute, it is a combination of race, gender, migration status and disability that results in multiple and intersecting forms of discrimination faced by some Australian women.

Against such a sobering reality, this chapter will discuss Australia's progress towards achieving gender equality. A brief recounting of Australia's engagement with CEDAW is followed by a critical review of a few significant legal and policy frameworks and formal institutional mechanisms established to advance gender equality. We then focus on the unique challenges of intersectional inequality faced by Aboriginal and Torres Strait Islander women and conclude with a summary of where Australia stands in terms of CEDAW's definition of gender equality and what is required to achieve substantive equality.

Australia's Engagement with CEDAW

Australia's engagement with CEDAW is founded on a long history of the women's movement dating back to 1827 when female convicts at the Parramatta Female Factory rioted over conditions and food deprivation. The Victorian Women's Suffrage Society was founded in 1884 and in March 1895 South Australia became the first state to grant women the right to vote and to stand for elections. Eight years later, in 1902, the Commonwealth Franchise Act (1902) granted women the right to vote and stand for election for the Australian parliament on the same basis as men. However, it would take 60 years for Aboriginal and Torres Strait Islander peoples to access the same rights (AEC, 2006). It took some 40 years before the first woman, Dame Enid Lyons, was elected to House of Representatives. The Australian Labor Party's Dorothy Tangney became the first female member of the Senate and 108 years later, Julia Gillard, in 2010–2013, became the first female Prime Minister (Australian Women's History Forum, n.d.). It took until 2016 for the first Aboriginal woman, Linda Burney from the ALP, to be elected to the House of Representatives.

The decade prior to the signing of CEDAW in 1983 was characterized by significant shifts in social, economic and political rights for women and other groups such as working people, single mothers, Aboriginal and Torres Strait Islander peoples, lesbian, gay, bisexual, trans, intersex and queer (LGBTIQ) communities. In 1969, the Arbitration Commission committed to incremental increases in women's wages, with the intention that pay parity would be achieved in 1972 (Australian Women's History Forum, n.d.). At the time of writing this chapter, Australian women are still waiting for this to be realized, with the current gender wage gap unmoving at 17.9% (WGEA, 2016, para. 1). The appointment of Australia's first advisor of women's affairs, Elizabeth Reid AO, by the former Prime Minister Gough Whitlam in 1973, and later, "femocrats" who joined the Australian Public Service in the 1970s, played a pivotal role in the advancement of the political, economic and social status of women. Femocrats, i.e., feminists who joined women's policy units, were part of a strategy devised by a visible and active women's movement to achieve social justice through the implementation of progressive social and economic policy (Sharp & Broomhill, 2012). Under the ALP, in 1983, femocrats were instrumental in initiating the world's first Women's Budget Statement, which systematically analyzed the different flow-on effects for men and women of the federal budget and in doing so consolidated Australia's position as a women's rights leader on the global stage during this period (Sharp & Broomhill, 2012).

However, in Australia international treaties are not self-executing—that is, formal acceptance does not mean that treaty provisions become part of domestic law. Nevertheless, because of the strong presence of femocrats in the public machinery and the influence of non-state actors such as women's and union movements, women's rights were codified in Australia's law. Starting with the enactment of the Sex Discrimination Act (1984), significant legislations since signing the CEDAW include the Fair Work Act (2009), the Paid Parental Leave Act (2010) and Workplace Gender Equality Act (2012). In addition, the National Plan to Reduce Violence against Women and their Children 2010–2022 (DSS, n.d.) is a significant initiative, in keeping with CEDAW commitments, to address the endemic levels of violence against women in Australia.

It is noteworthy that Australia committed to CEDAW with two reservations—one relating to paid parental leave and the second to the employment of women in combat/combat-related positions in the defense force. It is unclear why Australia is yet to revoke these reservations given that the Paid Parental Leave Act (2010) provides 18 weeks of paid parental leave and in 2011 the federal government announced the removal of gender restrictions from Australian Defence Force combat roles with implementation scheduled for 2016 (Department of Defence, n.d.; Thompson, 2011). Recent federal developments in ensuring accountability to human rights (including women's rights) include the Human Rights (Parliamentary Scrutiny) Act (2011) and Australia's third National Human Rights Action Plan (released in 2012). The Human Rights (Parliamentary Scrutiny) Act (2011) ensures that any proposed laws comply with Australia's human rights obligations with respect to the seven main treaties to which Australia is a signatory (Triggs, 2013a). The third National Human Rights Action Plan outlines a number of measures to improve the protection and promotion of human rights, including women's rights (Broderick, 2014).

A Critical Review of Key Legislative/Policy Frameworks

While Australia does not have a Bill of Rights to guarantee protection of human rights, some protections are contained in federal and state legislations. In this section, we critically analyze the extent to which some legislations have advanced gender equality in Australia.

Sex Discrimination Act (SDA) 1984

The SDA, making discrimination based on sex unlawful, was one of the first pieces of legislation passed after Australia signed CEDAW. The Act does not provide a definition of gender equality, but its provisions are aligned with principles of non-discrimination articulated in CEDAW. The Act prohibits discrimination on the basis of sex, marital status, pregnancy or potential pregnancy, breastfeeding and family responsibilities in public life. It also makes it unlawful to sexually harass another person. The most recent amendment to the Act, The Sex Discrimination Amendment (Sexual Orientation, Gender Identity and Intersex Status) Act 2013 makes it unlawful to discriminate against a person on the basis of sexual orientation, gender identity and intersex status.

Cusack (2009) succinctly summarizes the key limitations of the SDA, beginning with its focus on public life and limited grounds for discrimination, as opposed to CEDAW's call for prohibiting all forms discrimination in all spheres of life. Pointing to the 2008 report of the Senate Committee on the Effectiveness of the Sex Discrimination Act, Cusack (2009) further highlights SDA's limitations in addressing multiple and intersecting forms of discrimination on the grounds that women are treated as a homogenous group. For example, the lack of an overarching framework that would consolidate all of the anti-discrimination laws (Age Discrimination Act, 2004; Disability Discrimination Act, 1992; Racial Discrimination Act, 1975; Sex Discrimination Act, 1984) results in a fragmented scheme which is difficult to utilize. The Gillard government drafted the Human Rights and Anti-Discrimination Bill 2012, which among other reforms sought to consolidate all the anti-discrimination laws, along the lines of the United Kingdom's Equality Act 2010, which combines previous sex, race and disability anti-discrimination laws under a single act. However, in 2013 a decision was made not to proceed with this bill on the grounds of the need for "appropriate balance between the right to freedom of speech and the right to be protected from discrimination" (as cited in Rout, 2013, para. 12), business groups' displeasure over the ALP's proposal to create new grounds for discrimination (e.g., political opinion, industrial activity and nationality) and shifting the onus away from the complainant. States like Victoria, New South Wales and Queensland also raised concerns that the new law could potentially conflict with state anti-discrimination laws.

The mechanism of filing individual complaints also restricts the ability of SDA to addresses systemic discrimination for two reasons. First, "individual relief is limited in its ability to prevent future acts of discrimination before they occur . . . [and] is also dependent on a woman asserting her rights, which may often prove difficult in circumstances where there are obstacles that impede access to justice" (Cusack, 2009, p. 88). These obstacles include resources to pursue legal action and access adequate legal representation. Thus supporting women's organizations such as Working Women's Centers, Women and Community Legal Services and Legal Aid Services are vital in order to ensure access to justice. Unfortunately, this access has received a significant setback in the wake of the 2014 budget, where the coalition government has cut $6 million from community legal centers, $15 million from legal aid commissions and $43 million from advocacy services (Doran, 2016, para. 3).

Fair Work Act (2009), Paid Parental Leave Act (2010) and Workplace Gender Equality Act (2012)

Australia has significant legal provisions in the sphere of labor market, such as the Fair Work Act (2009), Paid Parental Leave Act (2010) and Workplace Gender Equality Act (2012), all of which appear to conform to the CEDAW definition of gender equality. Nevertheless, a critical evaluation of these legal provisions reveals several constraints related to applying the CEDAW definition of gender equality in practice. The latest census data reveals that 65.1% women and 78.3% men (aged 20–74) made up the Australian labor force (ABS, 2016). However, for every dollar that men earned in the labor market, women earned only 87 cents (ABS, 2015) even with similar or higher educational background (for instance, 57% of higher education students in 2011 were women, AHRC, 2014, p. 15). In addition, the labor market is highly segregated into female- and male-dominated occupations. For instance, occupations in the health care and social assistance industries have 79% female employees whereas the construction industry has 88% male employees (Huppatz & Goodwin, 2013, p. 292). Within the sex-segregated labor market, employed Australian women face discrimination through suboptimal working conditions such as uncertainty about wage rates and pay rises, lack of holiday or leave entitlements, job insecurity, restricted promotional opportunities, limited access to education and training and so on.

Both the Fair Work Act (2009) and the Workplace Gender Equality Act (2012) provide useful illustrations in understanding how CEDAW's definition is adopted with regard to wage discrimination. The Fair Work Act contains mechanisms to intervene in minimum wage determination, equal remuneration and to safeguard minimum safety net of terms and conditions of employment (Charlesworth & Macdonald, 2015). The principle of equality for men and women seems evident in these mechanisms as they seek to protect people in part-time and casual employment (primarily women, for instance 43.8% of employed women worked part time relative to 14.6% of employed men, ABS, 2016) through the quest for higher minimum wage, gender-equal wage and equal terms and conditions of employment. Nevertheless, enforcement of these regulations and provisions are contingent upon political will and civil society support. For example, the female-dominated social and community service (SACS) industry was the first sector to test Fair Work Act in 2010 with a favorable outcome leading to a pay increase from 19–41% (Charlesworth & Macdonald, 2015, p. 433). Cortis and Meagher (2012) note that this case won because of unprecedented support from federal and state governments (the employers) and employee unions. Without the key stakeholder support, the case may not have succeeded (FWA, 2012), which calls into question the equality-enhancing feature of the law if stakeholder support is not guaranteed.

The Workplace Gender Equality Act, which evolved from the original Affirmative Action Act (1986) and the Equal Opportunity for Women in the Workplace Act (1999), sets its first principal outcome as "to promote and improve gender equality (including equal remuneration between women and men) in employment and in the workplace" (Workplace Gender Equality Act, 2012, p. 5). Compared to previous iterations of the Act, it represents a shift in focus from procedural measures to substantive outcomes (Thornton, 2012) in gender equality, such as requiring employer reporting on gender equality indicators in the workplace. However, these standards are not set by legislation; rather they are determined by the relevant minister in office. Therefore, the onus of reporting is on the employer, with no requirement to address discrimination or legal recourse for employees if benchmarks are not met (Abetz & Cash, 2014; WGEA, 2013).

Another significant area of discrimination for Australian women in the labor market is the gender gap in unpaid work and life/work balance. Australian men on average spend twice as long as women on paid work, leaving the bulk of unpaid work to women (ABS, 2008). Interestingly, even when couples work similar hours, women end up doing significantly more unpaid domestic work relative to men (Daley et al., 2012, p. 40). The astounding gap is seen in childcare provision, where working mothers spend more time on childcare than non-working fathers (Miranda, 2011, p. 19). The gendered nature of unpaid work is a structural impediment to achieving equality between men and women. Consequently, time spent in unpaid work has a direct impact on time available for paid work, and given the above statistics, women are forced into false options of part-time, flexible and casual work. In 2014–15, 62.2% women with a child under five worked part time as compared to 7.7% for men (ABS, 2016).

These trends also have detrimental effects on superannuation benefits for men and women. Given the tight linking of superannuation to paid work, men are likely to accumulate higher average superannuation compared to women. In 2013–14, men had a superannuation balance of $321,993, while women had a balance of $180,013 in the age group 55–64 (ABS, 2015). Due to the efforts of non-state actors, worker's unions, media and support from general public, the Paid Parental Leave Act came into existence in 2010. Under this Act, the Paid Parental Leave scheme came into force with the stated objective to assist mothers to stay at home with their infants, increase female workforce participation by linking leave payments to employment and recognize the caring role of both parents (Baird & Whitehouse, 2012). The Paid Parental Leave scheme pays national minimum wage of approximately $543.78 per week for a period of 18 weeks to new mothers or primary carers if a child is adopted (Pocock et al., 2013). Findings from evaluation reports of the scheme highlight that 99.4% of the recipients were women (ISSR, 2013, p. xvi). When augmented by the Dad and Partner Pay scheme (specifically for men), about 36% of fathers chose to use the benefit (ISSR, 2014, p. 11). In other words, there is little take-up of parental leave by fathers. Even if they intended to, the options provided are limited.

Gender stereotypes of males as breadwinners and females as caregivers are institutionalized in Australian social policy, exacerbating structural inequalities in everyday life. The concept of family wage is one such example. The family wage was calculated based on the minimum income needed to support a wife and three children. The widespread assumption that women are not the primary breadwinners and should be paid less as they do not have dependents has become institutionalized even though the family wage model does not exist in Australia anymore (Sayer et al., 2009). Recent statistics suggest that only 51.5% and 41.4% of Aboriginal and Torres Strait Islander men and women, respectively, are employed in the labor market (ABS, 2012). Interestingly, while the proportion of Aboriginal and Torres Strait Islander women who worked part time was similar to that of non-Aboriginal employed women (45%), the proportion of Aboriginal and Torres Strait Islander men who worked part time (23%) was more than the same percentage for non-Aboriginal men (18%) (ABS, 2013a).

Substantive changes that can lead to a genuine adoption of the CEDAW concept of gender equality in Australia require a shift in the gender division of roles and gender hierarchy of activities, practices and relations. Just as reforms aimed at facilitating women's entry into paid work have gained ground, so too should reforms aimed at encouraging men into care and domestic work. There are useful policy examples from universal welfare policies of Nordic countries that Australia can emulate. For instance, a comparison study of fathers' uptake of paternity and paid leave in Sweden, Finland, Norway, Denmark and Iceland concluded that fathers are more likely to use parental leave options if there is a generous period of leave, universal coverage, substantial compensation, work flexibility and incentives to share/transfer leave (Baird & Whitehouse, 2012; Haas & Rostgaard, 2011). As recommended by the Australian Human Rights Commission (AHRC, 2010), Australian families would benefit from 12 months of paid parental leave that can be shared by the parents, a minimum of four weeks paid to fathers and supporting carers, leave paid at the rate of two-thirds of income and superannuation on paid leave (p. 4).

National Plan to Reduce Violence Against Women and their Children (2010–2022)

If the pervasiveness of gender-based violence is a key indicator of gender equality, Australia has not yet achieved substantive equality. While some legislative protections exist, men's violence towards women and children in the home persists with deadly consequences. Australian women are overrepresented in intimate partner homicide statistics. Their partners or ex-partners kill one Australian woman each week (AIC, 2013). Domestic and family violence is the greatest preventable cause of death, disability and illness for Australian women aged 15–44 years (VicHealth, 2004). According to the National Council to Reduce Violence against Women and their Children, unless appropriate action is taken "three-quarters of a million Australian women will experience and report violence in the period of 2021–22, costing the Australian economy an estimated $15.6 billion" (FaHCSIA, 2009, p. 4). The cost to the nation of violence against Aboriginal and Torres Strait women is estimated to be $2.2 billion by 2021 (NCRVWC and KPMG Consulting, 2012). But more importantly, the economic cost does not capture the detrimental impact of violence on lives and communities.

As a result of profound transformation in public awareness, elected politi-cal leaders have made commitments to addressing violence against women. Prior to signing CEDAW, the Family Law Act (1975) was introduced. Each state has legislation intended to protect a person from intimate partner violence (Bartels, 2010). Other relevant developments at the federal level include the ratification of the Convention on the Rights of Persons with Dis-abilities and its Optional Protocol (2008); the National Partnership Agree-ment on Homelessness (2009) and the National Plan to Reduce Violence against Women and their Children (the National Plan). While not legally binding, the National Plan is an unprecedented 12-year bipartisan strategy to end violence against women in Australia (Dunkley & Phillips, 2015). At the state level, progress was achieved through the Criminal Justice Legisla-tion Amendment Act (2011), Domestic and Family Violence Protection Act (2012), the Special Taskforce on Domestic and Family Violence Protection Act (2016) and the Royal Commission into Family Violence (Victorian Gov-ernment, 2016) in Victoria.

However, while legal and policy infrastructure exists, it has not yet pro-duced equality of outcomes. In the case of family courts, for example, arbi-trations typically happen when women and children are at considerable risk of escalating violence and negotiating state-issued court orders (Braaf & Meyering, 2011). Women frequently describe feeling "re-victimized" by having to relive experiences of abuse and defend their competency as par-ents (Bancroft et al., 2012). Part of the problem is that contested definitions of violence against women appear across policy and legislation in Austra-lia (Campo et al., 2014). Not all legislation describes domestic and family violence as a pattern of masculinist assertion of power and control over women and children. Instead, some state-based laws, such as the Domes-tic and Family Violence Protection Act (2012) refer to the mostly female victims as "applicants," "aggrieved" and "persons applying for an order." Even the National Plan, which enjoys bipartisan support, uses a gender-neutral definition of "acts of violence that occur between people who have, or were, an intimate relationship" (Dunkley & Phillips, 2015, p. 1). Domes-tic violence restraining orders, which are state-based, use diverse defini-tions of domestic and family violence. Gender-neutral legislation places the onus on magistrates to understand the gendered dynamics of violence and impacts of abuse.

In July 2010, the CEDAW Committee requested information within two years on how effectively the National Plan was implemented with a rec-ommendation "to implement specific strategies within the National Plan to address violence against Aboriginal and Torres Straits Islander women including funding culturally-appropriate Indigenous women's legal ser-vices in urban, rural and remote areas of Australia" (CEDAW, 2010, p. 8). An egalitarian society requires recognition of Aboriginal and Torres Strait Islander people, their sovereignty and the profound pain caused by coloni-zation. While family violence is not part of Aboriginal culture, the on-going impacts of European colonization include vulnerability to victimization and perpetration of violence by Aboriginal and Torres Strait Islander peoples (Al-Yaman et al., 2006). Despite bringing unique insights and knowledge, Aboriginal women's voices are conspicuously absent in domestic and family violence discourse (Smallacombe, 2004). If Aboriginal and Torres Strait Islander women were leading the solution, there would likely be a focus on healing, restoration of family and community, culturally appropriate courts and services, and restorative justice for perpetrators (Olsen & Lovett, 2016). Aboriginal women use domestic violence refuges differently from non-Aboriginal women (Gordon et al., 2002) and value opportunities to come together with other Aboriginal women (Karahasan, 2014).

The National Plan's efficacy will rely on the presence of vocal and visible non-government actors. In particular, specialist women's services are central to a coordinated, national response to violence against women. Specialist services use feminist principles to comprehensively guide women and children through high-risk situations to long-term recovery from trauma. They include women's refuges, women's court support, women's legal, rape crisis centers and Aboriginal women's services. Many evolved due to demand for gender-specific, empowering and holistic support for women. The history of the women's movement in Australia is instructive in this space. Because women needed safe accommodation when fleeing violence at home, Australia's first women's refuge began in 1974 in Sydney by young women (Power, 1995). Since then, specialist women's organizations have led prevention and response efforts, advocated for survivors, changed negative public attitudes to women, described barriers to services, supported women and children through complex legal systems, and created behavior change programs for men who use violence (Australian Women Against Violence Alliance, 2016). In contrast to this feminist approach was the rise of neoliberalism in Australia since the late 1980s. The austerity cuts to public services are part of the neoliberal agenda, with serious implications for women and children. The most recent example of this trend is a $34 million cut to community legal services announced in the May 2016 federal budget.

The political leadership in Australia is fraught with contradictions. For instance, the political posturing of the need for a cultural shift and to "stop disrespecting women" (Ireland, 2015) by the current Australian Prime Minister Malcolm Turnbull is not substantiated by befitting, consistent action. On International Women's Day in March 2016, domestic and family violence leave provisions for Commonwealth public servants, who work for the Commonwealth Minister for Women Senator Michaela Cash, were stripped. Specified leave entitlements for victims of family violence were said to be an enhancement to workplace entitlements (Towell, 2016). But the removal of these rights is at odds with government rhetoric about addressing the national crisis of violence against women. Even with a national strategy for ending gender-based violence, if structural and non-government support are not increased, women and children will face barriers to escaping violent relationships.

Institutional Mechanisms, Political Participation and Access to Political Power

The legislative and policy frameworks discussed previously enjoy federal support through institutional mechanisms such as the Office for Women. Located within the Department of Prime Minister and Cabinet, the Office for Women provides strategic policy advice to the Prime Minister and the Minister for Women. This office works across government agencies to support domestic gender-inclusive policies and programs as well as international engagements in relation to gender equality issues (such as Commission on the Status of Women and periodic CEDAW reports). The Office for Women also provides monetary support to three issue-based and two sector-based National Women's Alliances, which are peak bodies for civil society and women's organizations, providing policy inputs and reports. The three issues-based alliances are economic Security4Women (eS4W), Equality Rights Alliance (ERA) and Australian Women Against Violence Alliance (AWAVA), and the two sector-based alliances are National Rural Women's Coalition (NRWC) and National Aboriginal and Torres Strait Islander Women's Alliance (NATSIWA).

Intergovernmental work on gender issues is supported by the Council of Australian Governments (COAG), whose members include the Prime Minister (as chair), State and Territory Premiers and Chief Ministers and the President of the Australian Local Government Association. The COAG promotes policy reforms that are of national significance, specifically when coordinated action is required by federal and state governments. Two other institutional mechanisms, which specifically moderate the legislative and policy frameworks aimed at achieving gender equality are the Workplace Gender Equality Agency (WGEA) and the Sex Discrimination Commissioner. WGEA is a statutory agency created by the WGE Act and tasked with ensuring that the private and public sector comply with the provisions of the act. The Sex Discrimination Commissioner is one of seven Commissioners of Australian Human Rights Commission. The Commissioner's statutory responsibilities include human rights education, resolving discrimination and human rights complaints, ensuring human rights compliance and policy and legislative development.

However, the power of this machinery, particularly the Office of Women and COAG, to push for a transformational gender agenda was significantly diminished over the last decade. Maddison and Partridge (2007) suggest that the women's machinery was the strongest during the Hawke Government (ALP, 1983–1991) due to its location within the Department of Prime Minister and Cabinet. With the backing of a cabinet-level minister, this women's portfolio established requirements for gender auditing of cabinet submissions, undertook gender budget analyses and sought the presence of feminists at senior levels in public service (Eisenstein, 1996). Equally important, as Sawer (2007) argues, is that the women's movement saw the women's machinery "as an avenue to promote social justice and the election of governments with a reform agenda" (as cited in Sharp & Broomhill, 2013, p. 8).

Sawer and Rimmer (2014) neatly summarize the waxing and waning of the powers of this machinery under the conservative coalition leadership of John Howard (1996–2007), the Labor governments of Rudd-Gillard and subsequent coalition governments under Tony Abbott (2013–2015) and now Malcolm Turnbull (2015-onwards). An overall disinclination to discuss women's policy during election campaigns and the decommissioning of key intergovernmental bodies—such as the Ministerial Conference on the Status of Women (1991–2011), COAG's Select Council on Women's Issues (2011–2013) and the Standing Committee on Women's Advisers—indicates a lack of national consensus on progressing a gender agenda (Sawer & Rimmer, 2014). Without the Select Council on Women's Issues, which had oversight over implementation of the National Plan, it is unclear how this nationwide effort will be coordinated. The COAG Advisory Panel on Reducing Violence against Women and their Children, which was set up in 2015, has a restricted remit with no focus on implementation. Its role is to develop a model law framework for Domestic Violence Orders, informing a national information sharing system to support the proposed model law framework, developing national perpetrator accountability standards, and creating a national campaign to change community attitudes to violence.

The spectacular weakening of the once-strong public service is a consequence of deliberate strategies to silence the voices of feminists within the public service and shrink the women's non-government sector. Under the Howard coalition government, the Public Service Act 1999 required all public servants to be apolitical, actively discouraging the expression of independent political views or critical comments on government policy. Feminism, seen as a political ideology by many, was thus effectively silenced and with it ceased the use of gender analysis tools such as the Women's Budget Statements, which were often critical of government policies. The women's non-government sector was not spared either. The coalition government of Howard often withheld and refused funding to women's organizations that engaged in advocacy, thereby curtailing the remit of their activities to service delivery (Sawer & Rimmer, 2014). In fact, in a reversal of sorts, the government provided selective funding to organizations such as the Lone Fathers Association, which aligned with the coalition's conservative views on women at the cost of supporting more progressive women's organizations like the National Council for Single Mothers and their Children (Sawer, 2002). While the Gillard Labor government legislated the Not-For-Profit Sector Freedom to Advocate Act (2013) to prevent future restrictions on the advocacy functions of civil society organizations, the subsequent coalition government's closure of the government's Charities and Non-For-Profit Commission in the name of reducing red tape makes it "unclear whether the advocacy functions of organizations, in receipt of government funding will continue to be protected" (Sawer & Rimmer, 2014, p. 14).

The weakness of institutional mechanisms is exacerbated by the glacial pace of change in the proportion of female elected parliamentarians. For instance, there was a paltry 16% increase in the proportion of female elected parliamentarians in 20 years from 13% in 1993 to 29% in 2014 (McCann & Wilson, 2014). The situation is no better in the most recent 2016 elections, as the winning coalition government will have only 13 women MPs out a total of 76 in the House of Representatives (Lower House; total seats 150). As a result of 27 women from the opposition party (67 seats, ALP) being elected to the parliament, the overall women's representation in the new parliament now stands at 26.6%, albeit still below the recommended 33% international benchmark (Bongiorno, 2016). For the winning coalition this represents a 3% drop in women's representation from the 2013 election, and for the opposition a 4% gain since the last election (Bongiorno, 2016). It is hardly surprising that the Inter-Parliamentary Union, which ranks 193 countries on the basis of number of women in the lower house, places Australia 56th (Inter-Parliamentary Union, 2016).

In addition to low parliamentary representation, women are more likely to hold parliamentary secretary positions than lead ministries. In 115 years only one woman was appointed as the Governor General, only one elected as Prime Minister and only two have served as Speaker in the House of Representatives (McCann & Wilson, 2014). Under Prime Minister Julia Gillard (ALP 2010–2013) a record nine women held ministerial positions, with five of them in the cabinet. There was a dramatic drop to just one woman in cabinet and four women in the outer ministry when the coalition took control with Tony Abbott as Prime Minister (2013–2015). Prime Minister Malcolm Turnbull's cabinet reshuffle in 2015 saw numbers of women in cabinet jump up to six, including Australia's first female defense minister, Marise Payne.

The ALP's record with female representation in parliament is attributed to quotas introduced in 1994 ensuring that women would be preselected for 35% of winnable seats at all parliamentary elections by 2002. The commitment to increasing female ALP parliamentarians was reiterated at the 2015 ALP National Conference, where a unanimous resolution was adopted, committing the ALP to having women comprise 50% of Labor parliamentarians by 2025 (Sawer, 2015). The role played by civil society organizations like EMILY's List Australia, established in 1996 by women ALP members, cannot be ignored. With the slogan "When women support women, women win," its sole purpose is to ensure that more progressive ALP women are elected. Since its establishment, 164 ALP women Members of Parliament have received financial, political and personal support to win their elections (Arnold & Kovac, 2014). In contrast, the coalition has not articulated an affirmative action policy, leaving it up to local branches to nominate more women candidates (Owens, 2016).

Aboriginal and Torres Strait Islander peoples' representation in the Australian parliament is abysmal. Only three Aboriginal and Torres Strait Islander people have ever been elected and only one of them in the House of Representatives. The 2016 Federal election set a record of sorts with 13 Aboriginal and Torres Strait Islander candidates contesting the elections, eight of whom were women (Liddle, 2016), and for the first time Linda Burney (ALP), an Aboriginal woman, was elected to the House of Representatives. Poor representation can be attributed to both the lack of temporary special measures like quotas (for women and Aboriginal and Torres Strait Islander peoples) as well as deeply entrenched sexism and racism. The resistance to temporary special measures like quotas stems from a misconceived notion that such measures go against a merit-based system—the Australian cultural motif of a "fair go" for all Australians. Arguments that a meritocracy assumes a level playing field and does not recognize structural barriers to equality, have failed to register on the national psyche.

Such views, Sawer argues, reflect "sexist misrepresentation of women in public life" (2013, p. 106). Nowhere is this more evident than in the comments made against Julia Gillard prior to and during her time as Prime Minister. For instance, former Liberal senator, Bill Heffernan openly questioned her ability to lead a country, given that she was "deliberately barren" (cited in Harrison, 2007, para. 1). He is not alone in his view that "one of the great understandings in a community is family and the relationship between mum, dad and a bucket of nappies" (cited in McGuirk, 2007, para. 4). This stereotyping of women as carers worked against Julia Gillard. An unnamed ALP member of parliament, explaining the issue of her leadership challenge against former Prime Minister Kevin Rudd, had this to say: "Change is never pretty. There is always blood on the floor, but having a woman do it—that offends the natural order of things. There is the idea that women should not seize power" (cited in Summers, 2012, para. 9). A female cabinet minister succinctly captures the double standards women leaders face: "You literally cannot win. You are criticized if you dedicate yourself to your career and don't have children. Or if you do have them, you're told you are neglecting your family. Or, when you spend time with them, that you are not doing your job properly" (cited in Summers, 2012, para. 20).

The experience of discrimination at the intersection of race and gender has serious impacts on access to political power. The vitriolic hate mail that Nova Peris (the first Aboriginal and Torres Strait Islander woman to be elected to the Senate) received during her term is a clear illustration of this. A letter received by Senator Peris reads "she needed to be 'put back where you rightfully belong, crawling on all fours out in the deserts of central Australia, pissed out of your mind and scavenging for food'" (cited in Obrien, 2016, para. 16). When Senator Peris was nominated to contest for the Senate on an ALP ticket, it was perceived as a tokenistic gesture, despite her credentials as a treaty ambassador for the former Aboriginal and Torres Strait Islander Commission and her personal foundation work supporting young women in the Northern Territory's Aboriginal communities. These deeply entrenched racist and sexist constructions of women's supposed roles directly impact the achievement of substantive equality in the political sphere.

The arguments for expanding diverse women's equal political participation are premised on the notion of greater gender-inclusive policies and
therefore positive outcomes for women (Schwindt-Bayer & William, 2005).
However, some scholars assert that even a small number of women representatives are able to significantly influence legislative agendas since it is not
the quantity but rather quality, i.e., substantive gender equality, that matters
(Ayata & Tiitiincii, 2008). A case in point is the election of independent
candidate Pauline Hanson to the Senate in the 2016 Federal elections. She
is known for her disparaging comments on Aboriginal and Torres Strait
Islander communities, same-sex marriage and Islam—how her interactions
with the first Muslim woman elected to parliament, Dr. Anne Aly, plays
out remains to be seen. Pauline Hanson is also supportive of men's rights
groups, which are specifically seeking to dismantle the family courts in favor
of peer-based tribunals in joint-custody decisions (Borrello, 2016). The slim
majority with which the coalition has returned to power would necessitate
negotiations with independents such as Hanson, which at best would stall or
at worst reverse the progress towards gender (and other types of) equality.

To achieve substantive equality, Australia needs a significant cultural shift
that affords greater value to representation from Aboriginal and Torres
Strait Islander women, women with disabilities, women from culturally and
linguistically diverse backgrounds and lesbian, gay, bisexual, transgender,
intersex and queer peoples. Seismic change is needed in how women leaders
and women in general are perceived. Family-friendly parliaments can serve
as an incentive for women to consider entering politics. The recent changes
to parliament rules, following an incident where a sitting MP was asked
to express more breast milk so that it would not interfere with her parliamentary duties (Ireland, 2016), are welcome reforms that point to a greater
acknowledgement of women's diverse roles. Campaigns like Our Watch,
which challenge common sexist beliefs, are a step in the right direction and
need to infiltrate mainstream media and attitudes. The broad-based support for quotas from both conservative and progressive women politicians
suggests that such mechanisms are essential if women are to access political
power. The challenge to address Aboriginal and Torres Strait Islander representation requires not just a system of reserved seats but reforms to the
electoral system along the lines of what was established in New Zealand.
Since 1993, laws in New Zealand have changed to proportionate representation. That is, the number of Maori voters on the electoral roll determines
the number of Maori seats.

Aboriginal and Torres Strait Islander Women

The chapter thus far has laid out legal/policy frameworks and institutional
mechanisms available in Australia and their remit in achieving substantive
gender equality. An important part of the discussion, which needs special
attention, is related to the concerns of Aboriginal and Torres Strait Islander
peoples, especially women. While other women (refugee and asylum seekers,

culturally and linguistically diverse women and women with disabilities) require similar focus, it is beyond the scope of this chapter to tackle them in detail. The discrimination faced by Aboriginal and Torres Strait Islander peoples is a function of violent colonization by the British, leaving them enslaved, disposed of sacred lands and separated from families and communities (Buxton-Namisnyk, 2014). This discrimination has continued from 1788, to the Northern Territory Emergency Response (also known as NT Intervention) in 2007 and the most recent abhorrent treatment of Aboriginal and Torres Strait Islanders children in juvenile detention which made the news headlines in 2016. During the NT Intervention, for example, the coalition-led government suspended the Race Discrimination Act of 1975 in order to wield its power to enforce particular bans on a group of people (73 Aboriginal communities) based solely on race (Coghlan, 2012, p. 123). The ongoing disempowerment of Aboriginal and Torres Strait Islander peoples is linked to entrenched disadvantages—unemployment, poverty, welfare dependency, mental and physical health concerns and powerlessness (Coram, 2008; Cripps, 2010).

Willfully ignored in all the discussions surrounding race discrimination in Australia are Aboriginal and Torres Strait Islander women. The legal, policy and institutional frameworks operate in silos prioritizing particular dimensions of identity—race, gender, disability, sexuality and religion. Lost in the gaps are those with multiple and intersecting identities and their specific experiences of discrimination. A case in point is the intersectional experience of discrimination faced by Aboriginal and Torres Strait Islander women in the judicial system. Over the last decade aboriginal women's incarceration rates have shown a sharp increase. Approximately 2% of the Australian female population identify as being Aboriginal or Torres Strait Islander but they comprise one-third of the female prison population (ABS, 2013b). The entrenched racist stereotype of all Aboriginal and Torres Strait Islanders as violent has resulted in women being placed in maximum security prisons for crimes such as non-payment of fines, shoplifting and welfare fraud, most of which do not warrant imprisonment (Baldry, 2013). Many Aboriginal and Torres Strait Islander women in prison are themselves victims of physical and sexual abuse (Baldry & Sotiri, 2009).

During her term as Rapporteur of the United Nations Permanent Forum on Indigenous Issues, Professor Megan Davis highlighted significant issues faced by Aboriginal and Torres Strait Islander women in accessing justice. Of significance are the lack of knowledge about civics, law, government services and programs, insufficient services such as legal aid to deal with civil matters and inadequate access to legal representation. These individual and institutional level issues are compounded by cultural barriers such as accusations of "disloyalty" when Aboriginal and Torres Strait Islander women speak about the violence they face at the hands of Aboriginal and Torres Strait Islander men (Davis, 2012, p. 2). The lack of economic independence results in many Aboriginal and Torres Strait Islander women being reluctant to report crimes committed against them for fear of becoming destitute. Commenting on women's vulnerability, Professor Davis notes the "impunity of perpetrators on the basis of this 'breadwinner' argument—that perpetrators should avoid punishment because they are the primary income earner or subsistence provider in a family or community—an argument that is embedded in both formal and informal justice mechanisms" (Davis, 2012, p. 2).

The Rosie Anne Fulton case of 2012 is an example of how the pursuit of intersectional equality based on gender, race and disability is being derailed. This case involves the holding of a young Aboriginal woman in a Northern Territory prison without trial or conviction for 22 months after being charged with a minor driving offence. She was found unfit to plea, has fetal alcohol syndrome, a background of life-threatening neglect and the cognitive development of a child. Judicial practices that deny a fair trial based on disability undermine women's access to justice, liberty, security, equality and non-discrimination (Minkowitz, 2014). The Aboriginal Disability Justice Campaign suggests that at least 38 Aboriginal and Torres Strait Islander people with cognitive impairment are in indefinite detention in the Northern Territory alone (Aboriginal Disability Justice Campaign, 2016). The case highlights that the current legal, institutional and policy frameworks in Australia are ill equipped to address inequality in its intersectional dimensions and the need for therapeutic alternatives for and by Aboriginal and Torres Strait Islander women.

Conclusion

In this chapter, we have considered the extent to which the CEDAW definition of gender equality exists in Australia through an examination of legal, policy and institutional frameworks using illustrations from domains of social life, specifically, labor force participation, protection from gendered violence and political participation. We find that gender equality has remained a formal concept with limited impact on the gendering that occurs between women and men in everyday interactions. Our analysis, particularly drawing on the experience of Aboriginal and Torres Strait Islander women, highlights the woeful inadequacy of mechanisms to address multiple and intersecting forms of discrimination faced by Australian women. We argue that the pursuit of gender equality is dependent on the government of the day and its priorities, the presence of "femocrats" within women's policy units, and vocal and visible non-government actors.

We contend that equity goals will not have effect unless the mechanisms to achieve these goals are properly resourced, inclusive, meaningful, long-term and community-led. For instance, to counter the disproportionate burden of paid and unpaid work on women, structural and cultural shifts in work and care arrangements are required, specifically those that encourage men in unpaid roles and diminish the gender-based wage gap across industries and occupations. To increase protection from gendered violence, instead of austerity cuts, increased funding of specialist women's organizations that advocate and undertake prevention and response efforts is required. We conclude that achievement of gender equality is intertwined with how as a nation Australia addresses the negative social attitudes towards different classes, disabilities, cultures and sexualities. Without a properly funded eco-system, Australia will move further from, rather closer to, the attainment of gender equality.

References

Abetz, E., & Cash, M. (2014). *Minimum Standard for Gender Equality.* Joint media release, 25 March 2014. Retrieved from https://abetz.com.au/news/minimum-standard-for-gender-equality (accessed 10 July 2016).

Aboriginal Disability Justice Campaign. (2016). Home: Aboriginal disability justice campaign. Retrieved from http://aboriginaldisabilityjusticecampaign.org/home (accessed 9 August 2016).ABS (Australian Bureau of Statistics). (2008). How Australians use their time, 2006: Category No. 4153.0. Canberra: Australian Government. Retrieved from http://www.abs.gov.au/ausstats/abs@.nsf/mf/4153.0 (accessed 14 August 2016).

ABS (Australian Bureau of Statistics). (2012). Labour Force characteristics of Aboriginal and Torres Strait Islanders Australians: Category No. 6287.0. Canberra: Australian Government. Retrieved from http://www.abs.gov.au/ausstats/abs@.nsf/mf/6287.0?OpenDocument (accessed 14 August 2016).

ABS (Australian Bureau of Statistics). (2013a). Australian social trends, November 2013: Category No. 4102.0. Canberra: Australian Government. Retrieved from http://www.abs.gov.au/AUSSTATS/abs@.nsf/allprimarymainfeatures/5849F48 3A2C5646ECA257C9E00177D59?opendocument (accessed 14 August 2016).

ABS (Australian Bureau of Statistics). (2013b). Prisoners in Australia, December 2013: Category No. 4517.0. Canberra: Australian Government. Retrieved from http://www.abs.gov.au/ausstats/abs@.nsf/Lookup/by%20 Subject/4517.0~2013~Media%20Release~Australian%20prisoner%20num bers%20reach%2030,000%20for%20the%20first%20time%20(Media%20 Release)~10001 (accessed 14 August 2016).

ABS (Australian Bureau of Statistics). (2015). Survey of income and housing, Australia, 2013- 14: Category No. 6523.0. Canberra: Australian Government. Retrieved from http://www.abs.gov.au/ausstats/abs@.nsf/Lookup/6553.0main+f eatures12013–14 (accessed 14 August 2016).

ABS (Australian Bureau of Statistics). (2016). Gender indicators, Australia, February 2016. Category No. 4125.0. Canberra: Australian Government. Retrieved from http://www.abs.gov.au/ausstats/abs@.nsf/mf/4125.0 (accessed 14 August 2016).

AEC (Australian Electoral Commission). (2006). *History of the Indigenous Vote.* Canberra: Australian Government. Retrieved from http://www.aec.gov.au/indig enous/files/history_indigenous_vote.pdf (accessed 8 August 2016).

Affirmative Action Act. (1986). Federal Register of Legislation No. 91/1986. Canberra: Australian Government. Retrieved from https://www.legislation.gov.au/ Details/C2004A03332 (accessed 14 August 2016).

Age Discrimination Act. (2004). Federal Register of Legislation No. 68/2004. Canberra: Australian Government. Retrieved from https://www.legislation.gov.au/ Series/C2004A01302 (accessed 14 August 2016).

AHRC (Australian Human Rights Commission). (2010). *Gender Equity Blue Print*. Canberra: Australian Government. Retrieved from https://www.humanrights. gov.au/sites/default/files/document/publication/Gender_Equality_Blueprint.pdf (accessed 1 July 2016).

AHRC (Australian Human Rights Commission). (2014). Supporting working parents: Pregnancy and return to work national review report. Retrieved from https://www.humanrights.gov.au/sites/default/files/document/publication/SWP_ Report_2014.pdf (accessed 6 August 2016).

AIC (Australian Institute of Criminology). (2013). *Homicide in Australia: 2008–09 to 2009–10 National Homicide Monitoring Program Annual Report*. Canberra: Australian Government.

Al-Yaman, F., Van Doeland, M., & Wallis, M. (2006). *Family Violence among Aboriginal Peoples*. Canberra: Australian Institute of Health and Welfare.

Arnold, S., & Kovac, T. (2014). HERstory—the EMILY's List Australia success story. *Australasian Parliamentary Review*, 29 (2), 13–30.

Australian Government. (2009). National Partnership Agreement on homelessness. Retrieved from www.coag.gov.au/sites/default/files/20081129_homelessness-factsheet.rtf (accessed 14 August 2016).

Australian Government. (2016). *Special Taskforce on Domestic and Family Violence*. Brisbane: Queensland Government. Retrieved from www.qld.gov.au/dfv-taskforce/ (accessed 14 August 2016).

Australian Women against Violence Alliance. (2016). *The Role of Specialist Women's Services in Australia's Response to Violence against Women and Their Children*. Canberra: AWAVA. Retrieved from http://awava.org.au/wp-content/uploads/2016/05/AWAVASpecialistWomensServicesPolicyBrief2016.pdf (accessed 9 August 2016).

Australian Women's History Forum. (n.d.). *Timeline*. Retrieved from https://women-shistory.net.au/timeline/ (accessed 16 July 2016).

Ayata, A.G., & Tiitiincii, F. (2008). Critical acts without a critical mass: The substantive representation of women in the Turkish Parliament. *Parliamentary Affairs*, 61 (3), 461–475.

Baird, M., & Whitehouse, G. (2012). Paid parental leave: First birthday policy review. *Australian Bulletin of Labour*, 38 (3), 184–198.

Baldry, E. (2013). Continuing systemic discrimination: Indigenous Australian women exiting prison. In B. Carlton & M. Segrave (Eds), *Women Exiting Prison: Critical Essays on Gender, Post-Release Support and Survival*, New York: Routledge, pp. 98–116.

Baldry, E., & Sotiri, M. (2009). Social work in corrections. In P. Swain & S. Rice (Eds), *In the Shadow of the Law* (3rd edition), Melbourne: Federation Press, pp. 360–375.

Bancroft, L., Silverman, J.G., & Ritchie, D. (2012). *The Batterer as Parent: Addressing the Impact of Domestic Violence on Family Dynamics*. Thousand Oaks, CA: SAGE.

Bartels, L. (2010). *Emerging Issues in Domestic/Family Violence Research: Research in Practice No. 10*. Canberra: Australian Institute of Criminology. Retrieved from http://www.aic.gov.au/publications/current%20series/rip/1–10/10.html (accessed 9 August 2016).

Bongiorno, R. (2016, July 12). Coalition's lost ground on women MPs shows we need to tackle new gender biases. *The Conversation*. Retrieved from http://the-conversation.com/coalitions-lost-ground-on-women-mps-shows-we-need-to-tackle-new-gender-biases-62220 (accessed 31 July 2016).

Borrello, E. (2016, July 16). Nationals could help Pauline Hanson put Family Court back in the spotlight. *ABC News*. Retrieved from http://www.abc.net. au/news/2016–07–16/nationals-could-help-pauline-hanson-reform-family-court/7634202 (accessed 31 July 2016).

Braaf, R., & Barrett Meyering, I. (2011). *Seeking Security: Promoting Women's Economic Well-being Following Domestic Violence*. Sydney: Australian Domestic and Family Violence Clearinghouse.

Broderick, E. (2014). How to promote gender equality in laws and policies in Australia? All China Women's Federation Workshop, Beijing, China. Retrieved from https://www.humanrights.gov.au/news/speeches/how-promote-gender-equality-laws-and-policies-australia (accessed 31 July 2016).

Buxton-Namisnyk, E. (2014). Does an intersectional understating of international human rights law represent the way forward in the prevention and redress of domestic violence against indigenous women in Australia? *Australian Indigenous Law Review*, **18** (1), 119–137.

Campo, M., Kaspiew, R., Moore, S., & Tayton, S. (2014). *Children Affected by Domestic and Family Violence: A Review of Domestic and Family Violence Prevention, Early Intervention and Response Services*. Melbourne: Australian Institute of Family Studies.

CEDAW (UN Committee on the Elimination of Discrimination against Women). (2010). Concluding observations of the Committee on the Elimination of Discrimination against Women. CEDAW/C/AUL/CO/7. Retrieved from http://www2.ohchr.org/english/bodies/cedaw/docs/co/CEDAW-C-AUS-CO-7.pdf (accessed 17 July 2016).

Charlesworth, S., & Macdonald, F. (2015). Australia's gender pay equity legislation: How new, how different, what prospects? *Cambridge Journal of Economics*, **39** (2), 421–440.

Coghlan, J. (2012). Indigenous rights: NT Intervention and income quarantining. *Alternative Law Journal*, **37** (2), 123–125.

Commonwealth Franchise Act. (1902). Federal Register of Legislation No. 8/1902. Canberra: Australian Government. Retrieved from http://www.foundingdocs. gov.au/item-sdid-88.html (accessed 14 August 2016).

Coram, S. (2008). "Mainstreaming" indigenous inequality as disadvantage and the silencing of "race" in Australian social, educational and vocational training policy. *ACRAWSA e-journal*, **4** (1), 1–13. Retrieved from http://www.acrawsa.org. au/files/ejournalfiles/58StellaCoram.pdf (accessed 2 August 2016).

Cortis, N., & Meagher, G. (2012). Recognition at last: Care work and the equal remuneration case. *Journal of Industrial Relations*, **54** (3), 377–385.

Costa, C. de, & Douglas, H. (2015). Abortion law in Australia: It's time for national consistency and decriminalisation. *The Medical Journal of Australia*, **203** (9), 349–350.

Criminal Justice Legislation Amendment Act. (2011). Federal Register of Legislation No. 32/2011. Darwin: Northern Territory Government. Retrieved from www.austlii.edu.au/au/legis/nt/num_act/cjlaa201132o2011410/ (accessed 14 August 2016).

Cripps, K. (2010). Indigenous family violence: Pathways forward. In N. Purdie, P. Dudgeon & R. Walker (Eds), *Working Together: Aboriginal and Torres Strait Islander Mental Health and Wellbeing Principles and Practice*, Canberra: Australian Institute of Health and Welfare, pp. 145–154.

Cusack, S. (2009). Discrimination against women: Combating its compounded and systemic forms. *Alternative Law Journal*, 34 (2), 86–92.

Daley, J., McGannon, C., & Ginnivan, L. (2012). *Game-Changers: Economic Reform Priorities for Australia*. Melbourne: Grattan Institute. Retrieved from http://grattan.edu.au/wp-content/uploads/2014/04/Game_Changers_Web.pdf (accessed 4 July 2016).

Davis, M. (2012). Access to justice. Speech, United Nations Human Rights Council, Geneva. Retrieved from http://www.law.unsw.edu.au/sites/law.unsw.edu.au/files/docs/access_to_justice_un_davis.pdf (accessed 7 August 2016).

Department of Defence. (n.d.). Women in defense. Retrieved from http://www.defence.gov.au/women/ (accessed 1 August 2016).

Disability Discrimination Act. (1992). Federal Register of Legislation No. 135/1992. Canberra: Australian Government. Retrieved from https://www.legislation.gov.au/Series/C2004A04426 (accessed 14 August 2016).

Domestic and Family Violence Protection Act. (2012). Federal Register of Legislation No. 5/2012. Brisbane: Queensland Government. Retrieved from https://www.legislation.qld.gov.au/LEGISLTN/ACTS/2012/12AC005.pdf (accessed 14 August 2016).

Doran, M. (2016, February 23). Government cuts to community legal services and advocates undermining democracy, Human Rights Law Centre says. *ABC News*. Retrieved from http://www.abc.net.au/news/2016–02–23/government-cuts-to-legal-services-'undermining-democracy'/7191022 (accessed 10 July 2016).

DSS (Department of Social Services). (n.d.). *The National Plan to Reduce Violence against Women and Their Children 2010–2022*. Canberra: Australian Government. Retrieved from https://www.dss.gov.au/our-responsibilities/women/programs-services/reducing-violence/the-national-plan-to-reduce-violence-against-women-and-their-children-2010–2022 (accessed 3 August 2016).

Dunkley, A., & Phillips, J. (2015). *Domestic Violence in Australia: A Quick Guide to the Issues*. Canberra: Parliament of Australia: Parliamentary Library. Retrieved from http://www.aph.gov.au/About_Parliament/Parliamentary_Departments/Parliamentary_Library/pubs/rp/rp1415/Quick_Guides/DVinAust (accessed 9 August 2016).

Eisenstein, H. (1996). *Inside Agitators: Australian Femocrats and the State*. St. Leonards, New South Wales: Allen & Unwin.

Equal Opportunity for Women in the Workplace Act. (1999). Federal Register of Legislation No. 91/1986. Retrieved from https://www.legislation.gov.au/Details/C2009C00329 (accessed 14 August 2016).

FaHCSIA (Department of Families, Housing, Community Services and Indigenous Affairs). (2009). *The Cost of Violence against Women and Their Children*. Canberra: Australian Government. Retrieved from https://www.dss.gov.au/sites/default/files/documents/05_2012/vawc_economic_report.pdf (accessed 2 August 2016).

Fair Work Act. (2009). Federal Register of Legislation No. 28/2009. Canberra: Australian Government. Retrieved from https://www.legislation.gov.au/Series/C2009A00028 (accessed 14 August 2016).

Family Law Act. (1975). Federal Register of Legislation No. 53/1975. Canberra: Australian Government. Retrieved from www.legislation.gov.au/Series/C2004A00275 (accessed 14 August 2016).

FWA (Fair Work Australia). (2012). *Equal Remuneration Decision 2015 (C2013/5139 and C2013/6333)*. Melbourne: Fair Work Australia. Retrieved from https://www.

fwc.gov.au/documents/sites/caeremuneration/decisions/2015fwcfb8200.pdf (accessed 5 July 2016).

Gordon, S., Hallahan, K., & Henry, D. (2002). *Putting the Pieces Together: Inquiry into Response by Government Agencies to Complaints of Child Abuse and Family Violence in Aboriginal Communities*. Perth: Department of Prime Minister and Cabinet.

Haas, L., & Rostgaard, T. (2011). Fathers' rights to paid parental leave in the Nordic countries: Consequences for the gendered division of leave. *Community, Work & Family*, 14 (2), 177–195.

Harrison, D. (2007, May 2). I'm sorry, Heffernan tells Gillard. *The Sydney Morning Herald*. Retrieved from http://www.smh.com.au/news/national/im-sorry-heffernan-tells-gillard/2007/05/02/1177788206008.html (accessed 1 July 106).

Human Rights (Parliamentary Scrutiny) Act. (2011). Federal Register of Legislation No. 86/2011. Canberra: Australian Government. Retrieved from https://www.legislation.gov.au/Details/C2011A00186 (accessed 14 August 2016).

Huppatz, K., & Goodwin, S. (2013). Masculinised jobs, feminised jobs and men's "gender capital" experiences: Understanding occupational segregation in Australia. *Journal of Sociology*, 49 (2–3), 291–308.

Inglehart, R., & Norris, P. (2003). *Rising Tide: Gender Equality and Cultural Change around the World*. New York: Cambridge University Press.

Inter-Parliamentary Union. (2016). Women in National Parliament. Retrieved from http://www.ipu.org/wmn-e/classif.htm (accessed 31 July 2016).

Ireland, J. (2015, September 23). Malcolm Turnbull's scathing attack on men who commit domestic violence. *The Sydney Morning Herald*. Retrieved from http://www.smh.com.au/federal-politics/political-news/malcolm-turnbulls-scathing-attack-on-men-who-commit-domestic-violence-20150923-gjtpqt.html (accessed 5 August 2016).

Ireland, J. (2016, February 5). Australian Parliament changes rules for babies but working parents still face discrimination. *The Sydney Morning Herald*. Retrieved from http://www.smh.com.au/federal-politics/political-opinion/australian-parliament-changes-rules-for-babies-but-working-parents-still-face-discrimination-20160203-gmksd4.html (accessed 10 July 2016).

ISSR (Institute for Social Science Research). (2013). Paid Parental Leave evaluation phase 2 report. The University of Queensland. Retrieved from https://www.dss.gov.au/sites/default/files/documents/12_2013/paid_parental_leave_evaluation.pdf (accessed 10 July 2016).

ISSR (Institute for Social Science Research). (2014). PPL evaluation: Final report. The University of Queensland. Retrieved from https://www.dss.gov.au/sites/default/files/documents/03_2015/finalphase4_report_6_march_2015_0.pdf (accessed 10 July 2016).Karahasan, B. (2014). *Evaluation Report of the Aboriginal Family Violence Prevention and Legal Service Victoria's Early Intervention and Prevention Program*. Melbourne: Aboriginal Family Violence Prevention and Legal Service Victoria.

Liddle, C. (2016, June 27). Federal election 2016: The indigenous women giving me cause to hope. *The Daily Life*. Retrieved from http://www.dailylife.com.au/news-and-views/federal-election-2016-the-indigenous-women-giving-me-cause-to-hope-20160626-gps9x2.html (accessed 31 July 2016).

Maddison, S., & Partridge, E. (2007). *How Well Does Australian Democracy Serve Australian Women? Democratic Audit of Australia Report 8*. Canberra: School of Social Sciences, Australian National University.

McCann, J., & Wilson, J. (2014). Representation of women in Australian parliaments 2014: Parliament of Australia, politics and public administration section. Retrieved from http://www.aph.gov.au/About_Parliament/Parliamentary_Departments/Parliamentary_Library/pubs/rp/rp1415/WomanAustParl (accessed 31 July 2016).

McGuirk, R. (2007, May 2). Lawmaker's comments on women create stir. *The Washington Post*. Retrieved from http://www.washingtonpost.com/wp-dyn/content/article/2007/05/02/AR2007050200464.html (accessed 10 July 2016).

Minkowitz, T. (2014). Rethinking criminal responsibility from a critical disability perspective: The abolition of insanity/incapacity acquittals and unfitness to plead, and beyond. *Griffith Law Review*, 23 (3), 434–466.

Miranda, V. (2011). Cooking, caring and volunteering: Unpaid work around the world: OECD Social, Employment and Migration Working Papers, No. 116, OECD Publishing. Retrieved from http://dx.doi.org/10.1787/5kghrjm8s142-en (accessed 14 July 2016).

NCRVWC and KPMG Consulting. (2012). *The Cost of Violence against Women and Their Children*. Canberra: The Department of Families, Housing, Community Services and Indigenous Affairs (FaHCSIA). Retrieved from https://www.dss.gov.au/sites/default/files/documents/05_2012/vawc_economic_report.pdf (accessed 10 July 2016).

Not-for-profit Sector Freedom to Advocate Act. (2013). Federal Register of Legislation C2013A00056. Canberra: Australian Government. Retrieved from https://www.legislation.gov.au/Details/C2013A00056 (accessed 14 August 2016).

Obrien, S. (2016, May 27). Racism, not race, ended political career of Northern Territory Senator Nova Peris. *The Herald Sun*. Retrieved from http://www.heraldsun.com.au/news/opinion/susie-obrien/racism-not-race-ended-political-career-of-northern-territory-senator-nova-perris/news-story/b8d69e350f477832575de9176734c562 (accessed 10 July 2016).

Olsen, A., & Lovett, R. (2016). *Existing Knowledge, Practice and Responses to Violence against Women in Australian Indigenous Communities*. Sydney: Australia's National Research Organisation for Women's Safety. Retrieved from http://www.healthinfonet.ecu.edu.au/uploads/resources/30832_30832.pdf (accessed 9 August 2016).

Owens, J. (2016, April 18). Local branches should drive change on women says Malcolm Turnbull. *The Australian*. Retrieved from http://www.theaustralian.com.au/national-affairs/local-branches-should-drive-change-on-women-says-malcolm-turnbull/news-story/b5f3cbe7b527473919ef896a6d4c28b0 (accessed 31 July 2016).

Paid Parental Leave Act. (2010). Federal Register of Legislation No. 104/2010. Canberra: Australia Government. Retrieved from https://www.legislation.gov.au/Details/C2010A00104 (accessed 14 August 2016).

Plibersek, T. (2008). Women and men: A new conversation about equality. *The Sydney Papers*, 20 (4), 114–123.

Pocock, B., Charlesworth, S., & Chapman, J. (2013). Work-family and work-life pressures in Australia: Advancing gender equality in "good times"? *International Journal of Sociology and Social Policy*, 33 (9–10), 594–612.

Power, M. (1995). 21 years of political economy of women. *Australian Feminist Studies*, 10 (21), 177–185.

Racial Discrimination Act. (1975). Federal Register of Legislation No. 52/1975. Canberra: Australian Government. Retrieved from https://www.legislation.gov.au/Series/C2004A00274 (accessed 14 August 2016).

Rout, M. (2013, March 20). Discrimination reforms dumped. *The Australian*. Retrieved from http://www.theaustralian.com.au/national-affairs/discrimination-reforms-dumped/story-fn59niix-1226601065130 (accessed 10 July 2016).

Sawer, M. (2002). Governing for the Mainstream: Implications for community representation. *Australian Journal of Public Administration*, **61** (1), 39–49.

Sawer, M. (2007). Australia: The fall of the femocrat. In J. Outshoorn & J. Kantola (Eds), *Changing State Feminism*, New York: Palgrave Macmillan, pp. 20–40.

Sawer, M. (2013). Misogyny and misrepresentation: Women in Australian parliaments. *Political Science*, **65** (1), 105–117.

Sawer, M. (2015, July 30). The case for quotas in politics: The absence of women isn't merit-based. *The Conversation*. Retrieved from https://theconversation.com/the-case-for-quotas-in-politics-the-absence-of-women-isnt-merit-based-45297 (accessed 10 July 2016).

Sawer, M., & Rimmer, S.H. (2014). Knocking at the door? The women's portfolio from Labor to Coalition. Canberra: Australian Political Studies Association. Retrieved from http://apo.org.au/resource/knocking-door-womens-portfolio-labor-coalition (accessed 31 July 2016).

Sayer, L.C., England, P., Bittman, M., & Bianchi, S.M. (2009). How long is the second (plus first) shift? Gender differences in paid, unpaid, and total work time in Australia and the United States. *Journal of Comparative Family Studies*, **40** (4), 523–545.

Schwindt-Bayer, L., & William, M. (2005). An integrated model of women's representation. *Journal of Politics*, **67** (2), 407–428.

Scott, J. (2008). Changing gender role attitudes. In J. Scott, S. Dex & H. Joshi (Eds), *Women and Employment: Changing Lives and New Challenges*, Cheltenham, UK: Edward Elgar, pp. 156–176.

Sex Discrimination Act. (1984). Federal Register of Legislation No. 4/1984. Canberra: Australian Government. Retrieved from https://www.legislation.gov.au/Series/C2004A02868 (accessed 14 August 2016).

Sharp, R., & Broomhill, R. (2013). A case study of Gender Responsive Budgeting in Australia. The Commonwealth Secretariat, UK. Retrieved from https://consultations.worldbank.org/Data/hub/files/grb_papers_australia_updf_final.pdf (accessed 1 August 2016).

Smallacombe, S. (2004). Speaking positions on indigenous violence. *Hecate*, **30** (1), 47–55.

Summers, A. (2012, February 26). The gender agenda: Gillard and the politics of sexism. *The Age*. Retrieved from http://www.theage.com.au/federal-politics/political-news/the-gender-agenda-gillard-and-the-politics-of-sexism-20120225-1tv7n.html (accessed 10 July 2016).

Thompson, J. (2011, September 27). Women cleared to serve in combat. *ABC News*. Retrieved from http://www.abc.net.au/news/2011-09-27/women-on-the-frontline/2946258 (accessed 1 August 2016).

Thornton, M. (2012). Proactive or reactive? The Senate report on the equal opportunity for women in the workplace amendment bill 2012. *Australian Journal of Labour Law*, **25** (3), 284–291.

Towell, N. (2016, May 19). Fresh domestic violence dispute breaks out in public service. *The Canberra Times*. Retrieved from http://www.canberratimes.com.au/national/public-service/fresh-domestic-violence-dispute-breaks-out-in-public-service-20160519-goz33m.html (accessed 7 August 2016).

Triggs, G. (2013a). Using international human rights instruments to advocate for women's rights in Australia. Speech given at the Women's Legal Services NSW. Retrieved from https://www.humanrights.gov.au/news/speeches/using-interna-tional-human-rights-instruments-advocate-women-s-rights-australia (accessed 31 July 2016).

Triggs, G. (2013b). The economic rights of migrant and refugee women. Retrieved from https://www.humanrights.gov.au/news/speeches/economic-rights-migrant-and-refugee-women#_ftnref33 (accessed 31 July 2016).

UPRA (Universal Periodic Review of Australia). (2015). Australia's 2015 UPR—NGO coalition fact sheet 9. Retrieved from http://hrlc.org.au/wp-content/uplo ads/2015/07/9+Final+Gender+Equality+Fact+Sheet.pdf (accessed 31 July 2016).

VicHealth. (2004). *The Health Costs of Violence: Measuring the Burden of Disease Caused by Intimate Partner Violence.* Melbourne: Victorian Health Promotion Foundation.

Victorian Government. (2016). *Royal Commission into Family Violence: (2015).* Melbourne: Victorian Government. Retrieved from https://www.rcfv.com.au/ (accessed 14 August 2016).

WGEA (Workplace Gender Equality Agency). (2013). *Equal Remuneration between Women and Men: Gender Equality Indicator Three.* Sydney: WEGA. Retrieved from https://www.wgea.gov.au/sites/default/files/GEI3_equal_remuneration_tag. pdf (accessed 10 July 2016).

WGEA (Workplace Gender Equality Agency). (2016). *What Is the Gender Pay Gap?* Sydney: WEGA. Retrieved from https://www.wgea.gov.au/addressing-pay-equity/ what-gender-pay-gap (accessed 31 July 2016).

Workplace Gender Equality Act. (2012). Federal Register of Legislation No. 91/1986. Canberra: Australian Government. Retrieved from https://www.legislation.gov. au/Details/C2015C00088 (accessed 14 August 2016).

World Economic Forum. (2015). The global gender gap report. Geneva: World Economic Forum. Retrieved from http://www3.weforum.org/docs/GGGR2015/ cover.pdf (accessed 5 July 2016).

6   Gender Equality in Uruguay

Alma Espino

Introduction

Uruguay is recognized as having low levels of social inequality and in reference to this issue it is close to the welfare states of industrial economies in contrast with the majority of countries in Latin America. In fact, the country has economic, demographic and socio-cultural features that allow for broad comparisons with developed economies. Culturally, Uruguay does not exhibit strong tendencies against gender equality; however, we need to take into account all specific dimensions in order to analyze the situation as a whole. Progress in certain dimensions of women's well-being—education, health, income—has not been totally accompanied by cultural and ideological changes, since women's participation in deliberative bodies and entities that make rules and policies is still facing deep constraints. Even though a law was designed to invigorate women's participation during the 2015 elections, the political involvement of women remains low in the country. On the other hand, the country has institutionally moved forward in reference to sexual and reproductive rights of women and aims at doing this by introducing caring policies.

What kind of inequality is tolerated in Uruguay? Or to what extent do we tolerate it? This is difficult to determine because there are contradictions between rights and daily life, practices and speeches, and between speeches, rights and practices which allow the acceptance of inequity to have "constantly changing thresholds" (Álvarez Rivadulla, 2014, p. 115). Is gender inequality the most tolerated one when compared to ethnic, racial, social and economic inequalities? In which dimensions? What kind of economic and socio-cultural transformation is accepted and promoted in order to eliminate gender inequality? Based on these questions this article analyzes the degree of gender equality (GE) in Uruguay and its legal development in terms of labor force participation, use of time, political participation, reproductive and civil rights, and its legal development.

With this purpose the historical and political background of the country is reviewed to know how the adoption and popular perception of GE has been influenced; recent legislation is also reviewed as well as certain features of everyday social life. Finally, recommendations are provided for GE to be fully adopted in practice.

Social Inequality, Human Development and Gender

As mentioned in the introduction of this chapter, in Uruguay social inequality has never had as much importance as in other countries in the region and, in addition, it has tended to strongly decrease in the last two decades.[1] Income inequality is reflected in the Gini Index value (38.1 in 2014), which is considerably lower than the regional average (49.7 circa 2014) (CEPAL-STAT, 2016). When other dimensions of well-being are considered apart from income levels, the Human Development Index (HDI) elaborated by the United Nations Development Program (UNDP) may be taken into account. Its value is 0.793, positioning the country in the high human development category and ranking it 52nd out of 188 countries and territories. In respect of gender inequalities the Gender Development Index (GDI), which is based on the sex-disaggregated HDI, is defined as a ratio of the female to the male HDI. It measures gender inequalities regarding the achievement of three basic aspects of human development: health,[2] education and command over economic resources. The 2014 female HDI value for Uruguay is 0.797 in contrast with 0.783 for males, resulting in a GDI value of 1.018.

The Gender Inequality Index (GII) reflects gender-based inequalities in three dimensions—reproductive health (maternal mortality and adolescent birth rates), empowerment (the share of parliamentary seats held by women and attainment in secondary and higher education by each gender) and economic activity (labor market participation rate for each sex) (UNDP, 2015). The GII can be interpreted as a loss in human development due to inequality between female and male achievements in the three GII dimensions. Uruguay has a GII value of 0.313, ranking it 61st out of 155 countries in the 2014 index (UNDP, 2015). While reproductive health and economic activity have high values in the regional comparison, empowerment has a low value; it is not due to education levels but to the fact that 11.5% of parliamentary seats are held by women, while the average in Latin America is 27%. Until the 2014 elections Uruguay figured constantly among the last four countries in the region in respect of its female parliamentary representation rates. In this sense Uruguay can be seen as a clear case of a "gender paradox" (Bjarnegård, 2009).

In respect of reproductive health, maternal mortality rate (per 100,000 live births) shows that 14 women die from pregnancy-related causes; and the adolescent birth rate is 58.3 births per 1,000 women aged 15 to 19 (UNDP, 2015)[3]. Afro-descendant population has a demographic profile different from the rest of the population: higher proportion of youths, higher fecundity and lower life expectancy at birth.

Regarding education as part of empowerment, 54.4% of adult women have reached at least a secondary level of education compared to 50.3% of their male counterparts. Women have higher education levels than men among people over 24 years old; there is a higher percentage of men (32.5%) than women (22.7%) who have primary school as the highest level of education and the proportion of people reaching college or postgraduate degrees is the double for women than for men (Batthyány et al., 2014; INE, 2014).[4] As it will be further explained below, historically in Uruguay the gender gap in the population's average educational achievements has favored women.

In respect of economic activity, the number of women in the Uruguayan labor market has risen steadily since the mid 1980s; by 2015 it had increased to 55.4%.[5] In contrast, over the same period men's participation rate remained relatively stable and declined slightly, from 73.7% to 73.0%. In fact, a high level of women's participation is correlated to their increased levels of education, the low birth rate[6] and the rising trend in the divorce rate.

Historical Background

To analyze the evolution of women's status and gender equality in the country it is necessary to go back to the beginning of the 20th century. During the early years of modern Uruguayan economic history, the political system known as *Batllismo* (1903–1930) was responsible for the creation of the first welfare state on the continent.[7] The role of the state in this period involving political, economic and ideological issues probably still influences the current period.

In reference to the status of women, in this period politicians expressed, through social laws, their commitment to remove what they considered to be the "irritating injustice" against women. In accordance with a *Batllista* ideology, the emphasis was placed on the achievement of civil and political equality for women. In this regard it is possible to point out certain legal initiatives: the first divorce law was passed in 1907 (Divorce Law, 1907); in 1917 the country's constitution paved the way for granting voting rights to women, which was finally passed into law in 1932 (Civil Rights of Women Law, 1932). Women had started receiving formal education on a massive scale in the late 19th century,[8] and in order to overcome social resistance against further education for women (social norms, values and beliefs which ascribe women different roles and responsibilities), the so-called Women's University was set up in 1912 as a female institution for secondary studies (Espino & Azar, 2008).

Regarding access to secondary education, gender gaps were narrow by the early 1950s and from then on, they tended to favor women. In the 1960s the majority of students in tertiary education were men (60%), but by the 1980s this proportion was reversed (Filgueira, 1990). It is possible to affirm that over time, widespread social perceptions about women have been the biggest obstacle for their access to higher education levels. Favorable political conditions gave women access to education: it was and still is secular, public and free; and specific female institutions were created. If a woman did not study, it was due to deep-rooted cultural prejudices towards the role of women, which was very much confined to life at home (raising children and being housewives).

While the state played a crucial role in promoting certain gains for women in the early 20th century, demands for action had been made by women's organizations—charity groups, liberal intellectuals, women Freemasons, feminists, labor activists and anarchists, suffragists (National Council of Women), socialists (Socialist Women's Committee in the framework of the International Workers Association)—that denounced the living conditions and social status of women. They fought for the same education curricula regardless of sex, equal treatment in the public sector and equal opportunities in employment (Rodríguez Villamil & Sapriza, 1984).

The decade of the 1930s was characterized at a global level by a strong economic crisis that also affected Uruguay. A military coup in 1933 initiated a conservative period and a law focused on the "protection" of maternity and female workers in general was passed. In this period, for example, it was forbidden for women to work night shifts and for employers to hire them if they were pregnant. After 1942 economic and labor conditions improved and union activities were reinstated. However, there was also a strong gender division of work based on the "male provider/female caregiver" model. In 1950 legislation (Pensions and Retirement Benefits Law, 1950) allowed mothers to draw retirement pensions, provided they had worked for 10 years (Espino & Pedetti, 2012).

During the first half of the 20th century, gender relations were mainly determined by the traditional sexual division of labor. The recognition of women's civil rights and the progress in the area of labor legislation were oriented to safeguard their role in the households. Advances in education, health and social legislation mostly sought to ensure the reproduction of the labor force by reducing maternal and infant mortality and increasing life expectancy.

Since the economic stagnation of the mid-1960s, the female activity rate really went up as it was necessary to offset falling household incomes. In the early 1970s the Uruguayan economy experienced an acceleration of inflation, important trade imbalances and the inability to comply with external debt payments. In 1973 a coup brought a civic-military dictatorship to power, a period characterized by financial and international trade liberalization. From 1973 to 1985 one of the most remarkable effects of the economic policy regime was the massive entry of women into the labor market. This was caused by an increase in labor demand, which was expanding due to the non-traditional export-led growth[9] (textiles, garments, footwear, fish canning industry) and by the added worker effect associated with the declining real household income.

During the 1990s, economic openness favored the creation of jobs for women. Education played an important role in ensuring employment for highly qualified women (e.g., modern services). Labor segregation implied that although women were an important share of the best-qualified labor force, they were still cheaper to employ than men. On the one hand, female opportunities in the labor market have expanded so they could generate income and this would gradually influence their ability to make decisions at the household level. On the other hand, labor market segregation by gender has persisted and women have tended to remain excluded from bodies and entities that make rules and policies. Public policies did not put into practice programs to support childcare that would have been adjusted to the new requirements.

In the late 1970s, second-wave feminism and women's movements demanded respect for differences and right to equality. These ideas were part of a popular, progressive or left-wing ideology based on Marxism. The issue of discrimination against women has been the subject of public debate within the struggle for restoring democracy. On March 8, 1985, the first International Women's Day celebrated during democracy, a slogan referred to the political project of women's movement: "Women not only want to give life, but we also want to change it." Although female participation in Parliament was limited, since 1985 different women's groups have started to spread and feminist media has been introduced, the Women's Trade Union Committee has been created and women's commissions within political parties have been strengthened. In 1987, according to an Executive Decree, the Women's Institute was established under the Ministry of Education and Culture, but with the participation of different ministries and women's organizations aimed at creating government policies to tackle women's subordination. In 1988, by Executive Decree and under the Interior Ministry, the first Women's Precinct was created in Montevideo as a pilot program to deal with specific cases of violence against women.

An Overall Analysis of Women and the Labor Market

Gender inequalities in the division of labor between paid and unpaid work, women's primary responsibility for unpaid care work within the home, and the associated inequalities in the control of and access[10] to valued resources are at the core of women's subordinate status in society and have greatly affected women's participation in the labor market. Between 1908 and 1963,[11] women aged 20 to 24 had the highest activity rate. Women's labor-force participation declined steadily as cohorts aged, reflecting the traditional sexual division of labor in household following childbirth.

As previously mentioned, a massive entry of women into labor market took place in the 1970s.[12] Later, in the 1990s out of three jobs created, two were assigned to women. Modern services increased job opportunities for better qualified members of the labor force, particularly women, who enjoyed higher education levels. At the other end of the scale, the new private-care services (especially for the elderly and the sick) offered numerous jobs to the less qualified labor force, even to women with no previous experience in paid work. The commodification of the care economy was fostered by an increasing demand from middle- and upper-class women and by the unsatisfactory performance of the health care system, which forced households to find individual solutions to care for the sick.

Labor Institutions

In the early part of the 20th century, public policies sought to preserve women's presence in their households to the greatest extent possible. Legislation presumed that women who were in the labor force were "victims" who were "forced" to enter the labor market. Consequently, the first obligation of public institutions was to help women to raise their children properly and to carry out housework by shortening their working hours and protecting their health, especially with regard to maternity. Progressive labor legislation[13] typical of these years tended to patronize women, not foster gender equality[14] (Rodríguez Villamil & Sapriza, 1984).

Since the 1940s social dialogue regarding private-sector workers has taken place through collective bargaining in Salary Councils (excluding, until recently, rural and domestic workers).[15] Until 1985 there were no measures to guarantee equal remuneration, and even the Salary Councils' Law (1943) did not contain any specific reference to equal pay. In fact, the government ratified wage agreements between firms and trade unions, accepting differences of more than 20% between men's and women's remuneration. In 1985 when democracy was restored[16] Salary Councils were obliged to exclude any gender wage discrimination in agreements signed between firms and trade unions. In 1989 Uruguayan Congress passed a law (Ratification of ILO Conventions Law, 1989) ratifying International Labor Organization (ILO) Conventions, which refer to equal pay between working women and men (No. 100), equal access to employment (No. 111) and occupation and equal opportunities for workers with families (No. 156). In the same year the Parliament passed the Labor Activity Law (1989), which prohibits any discrimination that violates the principle of equal treatment and opportunities for both sexes in any sector of activity. Nevertheless, different studies confirm the persistence of considerable levels of occupational gender segregation (disproportionate concentration of women in certain occupations) and employment discrimination (Amarante & Espino, 2001; Espino, 2012; Katzkowicz & Querejeta, 2012).

Gender Segregation in Labor

Labor segregation and gender wage gaps are structural characteristics of the labor market of Uruguay and they are closely related. The first is determined by a strong feminization of certain occupations (e.g., nurses, teachers, psychologists, cooks and domestic workers) and masculinization of others (e.g., surgeons, workers, welders, chefs). Segregation results in the concentration of women in a limited number of occupations associated with tasks considered appropriate for them. Meanwhile, men are distributed in a wider range of occupations.[17] Horizontal labor segregation and the vertical one caused by the effect known as the "glass ceiling" are considered to be a significant explanation of the wage gaps. Between 1986 and 1999, 20 to 21 out of a total of 75 occupations could be considered female-dominated (where the share of women exceeded the average female employment). These female occupations represented almost 49% of total employment and accounted for about 80% of employed women. In this period the increase in occupational gender segregation developed among unqualified female workers but it diminished among the qualified ones, suggesting that better qualifications gave more employment opportunities for the female labor force (Amarante & Espino, 2001).[18] In the following decade (2001 to 2011) the Duncan Index for public and private employees shows that the segregation is generally lower for those who have completed tertiary studies and is lower for the public sector, with a strong tendency to decrease further. The main reason for this is that public employment has different rules of access to job positions, which guarantee, to some extent, that both men and women compete on equal terms. This result is compatible with the decline observed in the gender wage gap over the period.

Discrimination

Employed women have higher education levels than men; the percentage of employed women with primary school as the highest level of education is lower compared to that of men. It can be argued that the improvement in the education level of Uruguay's labor force responds mainly to the growth of women's participation. Despite the increase in women's labor force participation and improvements in their education, there are still very pronounced gender asymmetries in the labor market. Women's unemployment rate was 8.9% higher than that men's (6.4%) in 2015.[19] Although the trend aims at narrowing the wage gap, women's average hourly wage is 92.8% of the male hourly wage. This gap is wider among people with higher education levels. Broken down by education level, women who have graduated from the university earn only 70% of their male counterparts' earnings (INE, 2010).[20]

The gender wage gap used to be larger in the private sector, while in the public sector there was virtually no gender difference in wages, sometimes even favoring women. In the public sector the female-to-male hourly earnings ratio was 93.7% in 2000 and in 2014, with the female average hourly wage being 8.3% higher than the male wage. In the private sector the ratio was 87.7% and 87.0% in 2000 and 2014, respectively. On average, the gender wage gaps tended to become narrower as a result of the gradual decline in male wages during the 1990s and the improvements in women's education in the last decade (in 2000 the gender gap was 9.4% and in 2014 7.2%). In general terms, the persistent wage gap is explained mainly by the negative effect of women's concentration in female occupations with lower wages and, in contrast to the results in other countries, male wages are not affected by their insertion in female occupations (Amarante & Espino, 2002).

In the decade of 2000s, through the Oaxaca-Blinder decomposition, Katzkowicz and Querejeta (2012) found that the decrease in the wage gap during that period can be explained by education and experience, although women's wages are still being adversely affected by the participation in highly feminized occupations. More than 90% of personal care workers, cleaners and helpers are women and the wage is nearly one-half of the market average; among associate health professionals, the wage is lower than the average and more than 70% of the workers are women. In contrast, in masculinized occupations—for example, chief executives, public administration managers, executive members and legislators (72% are men), administration managers (71% are men), production and specialized services managers (66%), information and communications technology professionals (93%)—the wage is about two or two-and-a-half times higher than the average wages.

Espino (2013) analyzes the wage differences by gender by considering the effect of labor market segregation and mismatches in labor qualifications (sub- and over-education in relation to the required years for the occupied position) through an estimation incorporating these explanatory variables. The results of this work show that women have lower returns on education than men, even when they have the years required for the position they hold. The higher female schooling is thus counterbalanced by the fact that the years of required education for a position have lower efficiency for women. Even if women have invested the same or more than men in education, their wages are diminished because the returns for women are lower than for men and because they get lower-paid jobs than men at the same education level. Labor market segregation is a key aspect to understanding the persistence of wage gaps between male and female employees.

Improvements in women's education are not completely reflected in job opportunities or in the results achieved by women in the labor market.[21] It is possible that this is influenced by horizontal segregation in education, which may explain the range of sectors and activities in which female employees are positioned; by the barriers faced by women in accessing upper-echelon positions ("glass ceiling") (even when they match or exceed the required level of education) and by socially-assigned caring responsibilities, which means that during their life cycle, women will devote less time than men to paid work. This is how men are able to absorb the economic benefits of education to a greater extent than women.

Although women with higher qualifications have greater rates of activity and employment than the rest and are less affected by labor segregation, in 2011, 13 occupations had 75% of female employees with tertiary education and only 47% of men; in many of those occupations the wage gap oscillated from 20% to 30%. These gaps are significantly higher than the market average (Espino et al., 2014).

The factors that allow us to explain these gaps are the sex of the individual, the segregation of the occupation (in 2001 and 2011) and the economic sector. Changes throughout time show that the influence of the "sex" variable increases, as does the influence of the "segregation by occupation" variable, while the "segregation by type of activity" decreases in influence. These results suggest the existence of different types of labor force discrimination against women and a lower recognition of highly feminized activities.

The Caring System

Women are much more involved and spend more time in the care of children, people with disabilities and seniors. This is a clear example of the sexual division of labor that clearly leads to gender inequality. The Time Use Surveys carried out in 2003 in Montevideo and in 2007 and 2013 in Uruguay provide information about the hours men and women spend doing unpaid activities at home, including caring activities (INE, 2013). These surveys illustrate the differences in the total work volume of men and women. In 2013, women on average devoted 37.5 hours per week to unpaid work, compared to 19.5 hours by men. Therefore, the total working time, which is the sum of paid and unpaid work, is 50.2 and 55.8 hours per week for men and women, respectively. The provision of care has been gradually and increasingly moving from the household to the market, the state and non-profit institutions. The supply of unpaid female work is dramatically decreasing because of women's growing labor market participation, not only because they have improved their education level but also because their aspirations and expectations towards the life they want to live have changed (Espino & Salvador, 2013). At the same time, the proportion of nuclear households with children, where the man is the only breadwinner and the woman is a full-time housewife, is decreasing. There is a growing need for caring services due to the aging of the population as the number of children has decreased and life expectancy has increased due to improved health conditions (Batthyány et al., 2014).

Care services (for example residential care services) or support systems at home have not been developed to care for seniors. Instead, there is a wide range of retirement and pension funds in addition to some facilities which give socially vulnerable seniors access to housing and health plans (Salvador, 2010).

Public policies are starting to respond to these situations, trying to encourage the joint responsibility between women and men, state, society and the market. Recent initiatives include parental leave (for mothers and fathers) and the National Caring System. The parental leave was passed recently and guarantees 14 weeks for mothers and 10 days for fathers. It also enables parents, either the mother or the father, to reduce their working hours by half for the first six months of the life of their baby. The National Caring System (SNC) aims at promoting the co-responsibility between different institutional agents, market regulations and promotes the redistribution of caring services among men and women within the households. It is considered necessary to ensure equal conditions for men and women in the use of time and the volume of work and also, to respond to the aging of the population and the following increase in the rate of non-self-reliant people in contrast with the decrease of the number of people with time available for caring activities. Finally, it is important to mention the role of a consolidated Caring System as a condition for sustaining the development of and growth towards welfare in the long term. The SNC defines three priority groups: children from 0 to 3, dependent seniors (aged 65 and more) and dependents with disabilities. The introduction of this system implies a deep cultural change with respect to the "*familist*" regime in which the main welfare responsibility belongs to the family and to women within the kinship system, widespread in Latin America and Mediterranean countries (Aguirre, 2008). The change focuses on the belief that care is not an individual and private problem that each person has to deal with as s/he can and depending on the resources s/he has; instead, it is a collective problem which requires collective social responses (Batthyány Dighiero, 2015).

Women and Politics: A Path Towards Empowerment[22]

Since 1985 women's parliamentary representation rates have remained consistently low. In the following 25 years women held less than 12% of seats in the parliament. What explains this? Some institutional peculiarities of the Uruguayan system—small electoral districts and the double simultaneous vote (DSV), which allow a very high fractionalization within parties—together with continued resistance from male elites explain this lack of women in parliament. In relation to the first-mentioned aspect, the candidate selection process in small districts generally ends up being an informal procedure controlled by the local political elites, and leaders of party lists (who are mostly men) tend to be powerful local politicians with long political careers. Furthermore, the combination of the double simultaneous vote (in Spanish known as *Ley de Lemas*) and the closed-list proportional representation system allows political parties to present several blocked and closed *party faction* lists in each district, leading to an intense intra-party competition and fractionalization.

In addition, supply-side explanations suggest that the low female representation reflects the limited supply of applicants aspiring to a political career, women being less likely to run for an office than men. This line of argument is frequently used by political parties, claiming that they would like to select more women but that only a small number are coming forward. For different reasons, currently women do not belong to the parties' power structures and do not participate in the candidate selection process or in other relevant decision-making activities.

At the lower and even intermediate levels, the participation of men and women has almost reached the same proportion.[23] Then, at subsequent levels, different factors hinder the progress of women—for example, the principal barrier to the promotion of women is the fact that men comprise the overwhelming majority of political leaders. In addition, there are obstacles related to the role of women within households and to the fulfillment of care responsibilities. The exercise of politics is still dominated by men, has a male structure and is designed for men. When political parties were created, women's role was limited to support (not to act); they generally followed men but could not stand as candidates. Women have had to conform to the male-designed system controlled by an overwhelming majority of men and based on sexist practices and relationships, and this has been unattractive to women.

Public opinion surveys about Uruguayans' attitudes towards women in politics show that the population is generally in favor of women's involvement and activity in top political posts. A survey carried out in 2007, which contained a series of questions exploring citizens' attitudes and perceptions of women in politics, revealed that the majority of respondents were in favor of an increased presence of women in the parliament (60%), cabinet posts (55%) and presidential formulas (74%), and considered that women ministers performed as well as or even better than their male counterparts (80%) (Johnson & Josefsson, 2015).

The underrepresentation of women in politics led women's rights campaigners, both within political parties and within the women's/feminist movement, to espouse the cause of electoral gender quotas. Uruguay is among the countries where citizens are more favorable to positive action measures such as the Gender Quota Law (2009), which has an average support of 76.1 on a scale of 0 to 100 where 100 denotes the greatest support (Queirolo & Boidi, 2013, p. 71).

In October 2008 Uruguay received an official rebuke from the CEDAW's (Convention on the Elimination of All Forms of Discrimination against Women) Committee of Experts in its observations on Uruguay's latest implementation reports. The CEDAW Committee expressed concern because women are still insufficiently represented in political and public life and explicitly exhorted Uruguay to "to speed up adoption of draft laws on quotas and on political parties." (CEDAW/C/URY/CO/7, 2008, p. 5). In 2009 after a considerable effort and as one of the last countries in Latin America to do so, the Uruguayan Parliament passed a law on gender quotas. The Uruguayan quota law requires parties to include candidates of both sexes every three places on their electoral lists and establishes that the lists that do not comply will not be registered by the electoral authorities. This quota law only prescribed a one-off application in the 2014/2015 electoral cycle. The law disregards the "temporary" nature of such measures (CEDAW, 2004). The limitation of the quota period of application was necessary for obtaining the special majority required for the law to be passed and reflected the persistence of strong resistance among Uruguay's male elite to women's political participation.

Gender quotas are formal institutional reforms created to challenge existing gender norms and gendered power hierarchies. They can be a potent tool that adds to and interacts with formal and informal candidate selection procedures of political parties; it forces men to be replaced by women and changes the composition of the legislature even when there is a lack of political will. Therefore, the quota itself and/or the increasing number of women in positions of power may be an effective tool to redistribute gender in the political arena.

After the parliamentary elections in 2014 the quota law had the following results: women made up 26.7%[24] of the Senate and 18.2%[25] of the lower house. The number of women in the new Parliament as a whole is a record high for Uruguay. The three principal parties were represented by at least one female for the first time in the post-dictatorship era.

A combination of many small electoral districts and a highly fractionalized party system limit from the outset the potential impact of the law. Added to this, male control over candidate selection and gatekeepers' informal strategies that take advantage of the loopholes caused by institutional layering, along with continued resistance among male power monopolies have negatively impacted the law's effectiveness (Johnson & Josefsson, 2015, p. 17).

Women and Reproductive and Sexual Rights: Law Permitting Abortion

The Voluntary Interruption of Pregnancy Bill was submitted by the Senate to the Chamber of Deputies, the lower house of Uruguay's legislature, in September 2012. The lower house made significant changes to the bill proposed by the Senate, adding procedural requirements to be met for women to access abortions. The bill was passed in October 2012 by a margin of just one vote, with 50 deputies in favor and 49 against. In October, Uruguay's Senate ratified the Chamber of Deputies' version of the bill, clearing the way for the president's signature. The final version retains abortion as a crime under the criminal code, but waives penalties (Voluntary Interruption of Pregnancy Law, 2012).[26] The Bill requires women seeking abortions inform a doctor about the circumstances of conception and the economic, social or family hardships that would prevent her from continuing the pregnancy. The same or next day, the doctor is required to consult an interdisciplinary team of at least three professionals, including at least one gynecologist, one mental health professional and one specialist in social support. The interdisciplinary team must meet with the woman to inform her about the law, the process of abortion and any inherent risk of the procedure. It will also inform her of alternatives to abortion (economic support, provision of information and even the possibility of placing the child for adoption) and offer psycho-social support and information.

After this meeting between the woman and the team, the law requires a five-day reflection period before she can reassert her choice to continue with the abortion. Upon her informed consent, a doctor may perform the procedure. The decision to have the abortion remains solely with the woman.[27] The United Nations Special Rapporteur on the Right to Health has found that legal restrictions can make legal abortions inaccessible. Examples of abortion restrictions include: "requirements of counseling and mandatory waiting periods for women seeking to terminate a pregnancy" and "requirements that abortions be approved by more than one health-care provider" (Cavallo, 2015).

At the end of August 2015, a Uruguayan court ruled in favor of a group of gynecologists who claimed that the law violates their right to conscientious objection[28] to refuse to perform abortions (an objection on moral or religious grounds). This decision will only make it harder for women to access safe abortion services in Uruguay. The ruling prioritizes the rights of doctors over those of women and applies to all Uruguayan gynecologists—the only medical professionals permitted to provide abortions—and allow them to abstain from all stages of the process. Originally, gynecologists expressing conscientious objection were only permitted to abstain from specific steps in the process that involved them directly—namely writing a prescription for medical abortion or performing an abortion. They were originally obligated to see patients for the initial consultation, as well as various preliminary and subsequent steps in the process. But now these doctors can choose to withdraw from any step of the process. Abortion is only permitted in the first trimester of pregnancy and thus, not having a local gynecologist could have significant ramifications for women's health; longer wait times and inconveniences may force some women to seek clandestine, and often unsafe, abortions.

Uruguay reported that there was not a single death due to unsafe abortion in 2014 and it currently has one of the lowest maternal mortality rates (*Presidencia*, 2014) in the region. But this could change if this new ruling stands, gynecologists continue to cite conscientious objection and other barriers remain in place limiting women's access to safe services (Cavallo, 2015).

Women and Violence: Aiming at Physical Autonomy

Several policies have been implemented in order to tackle gender-based violence, in particular domestic violence (by a spouse or former partner); however, women still face various difficulties.

Legal regulation introduced a set of cross-sectoral rules and mechanisms aimed at the prevention and assessment of violence. For instance, the National Advisory Council against Domestic Violence (in Spanish CNCLVD) includes representatives of executive and judicial bodies as well as civil society organizations in the organization and articulation of sectoral and territorial policies. Many of the member bodies have protocols for action but they have been introduced without proper cross-sectoral planning.

The First National Plan against Domestic Violence was put into action between 2004 and 2010. The assessment of this plan indicates that many of its objectives were not achieved in spite of the mechanisms created to enable its implementation. Particularly, the enforcement of Domestic Violence Law (2002) gave rise to restrictions which interfere with its proper implementation in courts (specialized in violence) due to issues of location (e.g., inappropriate waiting areas for both the complainant and defendant), insufficient human resources to build professional teams to assist in each specific case, delays in hearings, work overload, shortage of defense attorneys, among others. It is important to consider the judicial system because a quarter of murdered women had already filed their complaints (Calce et al., 2015).

An alternative report for CEDAW (prepared by Meza Tananta, F., Lima, A. & Percovich, M., 2016) about Uruguay's compliance with the obligations established in the Convention on the Elimination of all Forms of Discrimination Against Women (CEDAW) outlines some of the problems that explain why we are not succeeding in the fight against domestic violence and offers recommendations to overcome them. Even though the Uruguayan state has made a serious effort and has provided resources to eradicate domestic violence (DV) since 2007, this is still the most reported crime after robbery. The increase in reports and the introduction of new governmental programs have not reduced the number of women who die because of DV and have not improved the living conditions of the surviving ones. Many of the women who seek protection in the justice system are eventually killed. This may be caused by deficiencies in the investigation of crimes: criminal judges generally regard violent acts (reported by the victim) as having low relevance and so they are not properly investigated. For instance, the report states that 310 rape cases are reported per year, including attempted and committed rapes, of which only seven perpetrators were indicted for rape and 35 for indecent assault. In most of the cases, violence persists after the report has been filed. This means that the report does not necessarily bring an end to the harassment suffered by women after a separation or divorce: breach of protection orders, manipulation of parent-child relationships or concealment or disappearance of assets as a way of failing to comply with alimony payment requirements (González et al., 2013).

When the judiciary fails to penalize the breach of a protection order decreed through civil proceedings, it results in a lack of trust in the justice system (Calce et al., 2015). Apart from the existence of values and prejudices in the society which also affect the judicial system, the report warns that judges are not properly trained regarding women's rights and gender issues and this may affect their decisions. There are few judges who decide to specialize in this subject and they have to do it voluntarily and at their own expense. This situation is reflected in the persistence of stereotypes and prejudices within the judicial system towards the victims of violence and is implied in the courts' decisions in which the behavior of the victims is open to doubt and the responsibility frequently shifts from the defendant to the complainant.[29]

It should be noted that although the Judiciary approved the creation of a Specialized Section in Gender and Human Rights as one of its plans for the period 2015–2024, the Executive Power did not approve the five-year budget (2015–2019) required for this purpose.

The number of police reports, legal proceedings, care services or phone calls to report DV (free telephone number 08004141) is far from reaching the data provided in the National Prevalence Survey carried out by the National Institute of Statistics. The quantity of care services for women victims of violence, assistance services and monitoring of the victims who are under protection orders to avoid new violent episodes and preventable deaths seems to be not enough. There is not enough information about protection orders and their grade of compliance.

In relation to the perpetrators, the report shows that the law is not being fully applied, given that the judicial practice does not embrace regional and international remedies that are ratified by the state. In the case of domestic violence, the acting judges just order the perpetrator to stay at a specified distance from the victim. In 2012, the judiciary published information based on more than 70% of the protection orders issued. It indicated that the orders containing measures such as provision of financial assistance to the victim and/or temporarily determination of children's custody or alimony are practically nonexistent. In addition, in 2012 under the Domestic Violence Law (2002) it is established that the judge is authorized to demand the perpetrator's "compulsory assistance to rehabilitation programs." However, the state has not introduced public services of rehabilitation for this purpose.

Despite numerous attempts by different administrations, domestic violence has remained a pervasive issue in Uruguayan society. One woman dies at the hands of a current or former partner every 15 days. In a country with a population of 3.2 million, 26 people have died in 2015 as a result of domestic violence. This figure is even higher than the 25 deaths reported for ECLAC 2015 (UNFPA-MIDES INMUJERES, 2013).[30]

In 1995 Uruguay officially recognized domestic violence within its penal code and ratified the Inter-American Convention on the Prevention, Punishment and Eradication of Violence Against Women in 1996. Later, in 2002, Uruguay passed the Domestic Violence Law No 17.514, which implements measures to prevent, detect, treat and eradicate domestic violence. The government complemented these efforts in 2004 with the National Action Plan Against Domestic Violence (INMUJERES, n.d.).

Recently, in April 2016, Uruguay's Council of Ministers put forward a government bill that aims "to guarantee women a life free of gender-based violence." The bill, which will now go to the Senate, not only defines gender violence and how it is manifested but also changes the current criminal law and creates an institutional response system as well as specialized courts. This comprehensive government bill received the input of all of Uruguayan ministries involved in the drafting of specific provisions on education, work, public security and the public prosecutor's office, among others. It also includes special provisions focused on children and adolescents, the elderly and disabled women. The bill also seeks to create a watchdog committee to monitor the problem (UN Women, 2016).

Domestic violence in Uruguay shows us that aggregate indicators do not always give us a full picture of the situation in a country. Even a country perceived to be seemingly stable must tackle important issues that affect the everyday safety of its population.

Machinery for Gender Equality

The National Institute of Women (INAMU) is located at the Ministry of Social Development (MIDES) as one of its 14 departments. In March of 2007 it was commissioned by Equal Rights and Opportunities among Men and Women in the Republic Law No. 18.104 (2007) to design the National Plan of Equal Opportunities and Rights with the objective of fulfilling the commitments made by the country at the international level (United Nations, Organization of American States and the Southern Common Market) concerning non-discrimination based on gender. In terms of hierarchical organization, INAMU is a low-ranking institution[31] considered to be incompatible with the international guidelines and demands of the women's movement in the sense that it should be regarded as a top-echelon institution addressing gender institutionalization. It is even quite far from the formal situation of other similar regional entities.

The main purpose of the Plan is to lead and promote gender mainstreaming; it can be seen as a process of organizational change[32] and it must be institutionalized through concrete steps, mechanisms and processes in all parts of the organization. This change involves policy processes and mechanisms, which means the adoption of horizontal cooperation on gender issues across all policy areas, levels and departments, and also policy actors,[33] who should know how to incorporate a gender perspective. Of course all of this has to be complemented with appropriate policy tools and techniques to integrate the gender variable in all public policies and to monitor and evaluate all policies from a gender perspective.[34]

In Uruguay progress on this issue has depended on the actions taken by the state primarily through the interaction between INAMU and the ministries on the basis of Commitments to Gender Equality by ministerial cabinets. These are unprecedented in Uruguay and, at least symbolically, show the commitment of public authorities to gender equality. Nevertheless, these commitments are mostly limited to the expression of political will and, to a lower extent, to the concrete planning of actions. Changes of government or changes in the political orientation may jeopardize the proper fulfillment of the proposed mission. This is to say that two aspects are called into question: the extent to which INAMU may impose its regulations to higher bodies of public administration, and the capacity of INAMU to commit resources of other public entities given the lack of an assigned budget for the execution of the Plan of Equal Opportunities and Rights.

The achievements of the National Coordinator Council of Public Policies[35] about Gender Equality regarding this subject are still insufficient: as Bianchi (2015, p. 49) suggested, "it is essential to move from formal political will (recognition of gender inequalities, development agencies that monitor compliance of international agreements and national legislation in favor of gender equality, discourses of political correctness)[36] to real political will." The latter involves considering gender equality as a priority and a goal in itself that may be achieved through the economic empowerment of women, the development of planned policies, the implementation and evaluation from the perspective of gender and, especially, through the allocation of necessary financial resources to meet that goal. For instance, even though many programs within the labor sector may be contributing somehow to the economic empowerment of women, they generally do not contemplate the gender dimension, its objectives and results. These positive actions—and the results they achieve—are the aspects which remind us that gender inequalities are not immutable, that they can be transformed and that we can learn a great deal from the work done or the work we have been doing on the ground.

Women still have domestic duties and care as a primary responsibility and this is consequently reflected in the persistence of labor gaps (wages, unemployment) caused by a lack of policies regarding social co-responsibility and reconciliation of paid labor, personal and family life. In this sense, the introduction of a National Care System will not overcome these gaps by itself if we do not consider labor, economic production and social policies in an articulate way so they can become a unique system concurrently attending to paid labor and the family life of men and women.

Final Reflections and Policy Recommendations

Gender-specific constraints are translated, in turn, into *gender inequalities* in the distribution of valued political and economic resources among others. The state, trade unions, organizations of civil society and mainly women's and feminist organizations have taken actions that challenge traditional inequalities and contribute to positive transformations in the lives of women as well as men. At the beginning of the chapter we proposed to answer several questions in regard to the degree of gender equality in Uruguay, both from an informal and formal point of view, with the purpose of reflecting about the extent to which gender equality exists and what it depends on. It is a difficult challenge to answer briefly and cogently as it may be appreciated in the previous pages. It shall be affirmed that society has the conditions to move forward along that way. Formal equality is very important; it is a legitimate basis and a support for cultural changes. However, it has proved to be insufficient if we do not work directly on concrete practices.

Overall, in Uruguay GE is formally guaranteed in legislation and in some aspects it is also embraced in everyday social life, as can be concluded from the review of different dimensions of well-being. But, in general terms, gender equality is an issue of power. Gender inequality means differences in the status, power and prestige that women and men have in societies. It is mainly caused by the fact that women have less power than men; in general, gender is a function of power relations and social organization of inequality. The driving force behind gender inequalities is a redistribution of power and interests that has come about as a result of modern economic and political organization interacting with women's aspirations, demands and resistance to subordination (Jackson, 2006). Gender configures power inequalities based on divisions such as class and ethnicity, and vice versa. The unequal power dynamics between women and men intersect, mirror and reinforce other power dynamics embedded in institutions and relationships such as the unequal power relations among races and ethnic groups and between the rich and the poor (Riley, 2008, p. 3).

It is possible to fully adopt GE in practice in this country but this requires educational efforts and the promotion of cultural changes. The historical and political background has created conditions to address and perceive GE in terms of equal rights and it may continue doing so. Institutional changes in education and media are essential to eliminate gender-based restrictions that women face while they strive for equal opportunities and results.

It can be appreciated that, although some notable gains have been made, there are still problems when it comes to bringing the gender perspective into the mainstream, adopting genuine policies by the state and ensuring that these processes will not be reversed when political changes take place. In terms of economy, the gaps between men and women appear in the access they have to resources and opportunities, in the control of such resources and opportunities and in the results they obtain. Regarding politics, gender gaps related to participation are really significant.

Is gender equality important? Why? The answer is "yes" because it is an ethical imperative; achieving gender equality and exercising human rights, dignity and capabilities of diverse groups of women is a central requirement for a just and sustainable world (UN Women, 2014). What may ensure or allow progress in terms of gender equality? An important determinant is the opportunity to create changes through which women may expand their ability to make strategic choices about their lives and to participate on equal terms with men in bringing about desired changes in the society they live in. These kinds of processes are multidimensional, encompassing changes in the political, social and economic spheres of life, and these different dimensions are closely interrelated that significant changes in one dimension are likely to generate changes in other ones (Kabeer, 2011).

As it was already mentioned, a society cannot be content with achieving only formal equality. We shall focus on concrete actions and practices as we conclude with a series of guidelines for the eradication of some of the inequalities at the core of gender disadvantage:

1   From a formal point of view it would be important to guarantee GE and improve its formal framework. Thus it would be necessary that the government enact a law to incorporate the definition of discrimination against women according to Article 1 of the CEDAW (Meza Tananta et al., 2016). We must also tackle structural systems that underlie inequality, namely the unequal distribution of time men and women devote to unpaid work. This pattern predominates at the symbolic and practical level in daily life and helps to explain the inequalities women are subject to at work, in a context in which a variety of discrimination structures are superimposed on each other and reciprocally interact. A National Caring System (SNC) provides support and guarantees that women and men are equally able to combine paid and unpaid work, bringing men into unpaid work and women into paid work as well.

2   Overcome the lack of impact assessment of policies and programs in order to know what these policies actually achieve or what design flaws they may have so they can be corrected in subsequent versions. (For example, there should be a proper assessment of the Quota Law to guarantee its correct implementation; rehabilitation programs for male perpetrators should be introduced along with periodical reviews of their outcomes.)

3   Assign more economic and financial resources, e.g., the funds required to strengthen the judicial power, particularly in the areas specialized in guaranteeing women's human rights.

4   Provide training and education about gender to technical and political teams that are social agents responsible for social dialogue. In particular, as it was mentioned above, the state should adopt measures to modify judicial practices affecting women who are victims of violence by providing gender-sensitive training to its judges, particularly those who work in specialized courts. In addition, this training should be included among the credits required for promotion of judges.

5   Full adoption of gender equality requires the strengthening of gender institutionalization in Uruguay as a way of increasing its legitimacy and authority and implementing long-lasting policies that transcend changes of government. It means assigning more economic and financial resources to the National Women's Institute and the Equality Committees set up in the public entities and to introduce these resources in the national budget. Also, it should encourage interaction between the Planning and Budget Office and the National Women's Institute to ensure mainstream gender perspectives in all public policies.

6   A strong national multi-sector plan, coordinating body and formal mechanisms of collaboration and information-sharing.

The importance of political action in terms of promoting a relatively equal society in the international context has been shown by the history of the country. Although significant progress has been made with regard to the situation of women in Uruguay, it is imperative that the commitment to gender equality and compliance with the human rights of women and girls are explicitly included in all policies both at national and local levels. We cannot just expect discrimination and the disadvantages faced by women and girls to eventually disappear over time. In this respect, the collective action of women and their full and equal participation in all aspects of decision-making relating to the development and supervision of policies must be supported by the state, which is essential for achieving positive results.

Notes

1 According to Uruguay's 2011 census, the first one to include race on the questionnaire, 8% of the population is of an African descent (household survey from 2010 indicates 9.9%). In 2013, 25.2% of Afro-Uruguayans lived below the poverty line, compared to 7.8% of the population; 14.5% of Afro-Uruguayans never finished high school, and only 2.7% have university degrees. They are mainly concentrated in Montevideo. They came to Uruguay as Ladino-Hispanic slaves in the 16th century (the group includes people who declare that they have black or "afro" origins, even if they have been identified in another category).

2 Health, measured by female and male life expectancy at birth; education, measured by female and male expected years of schooling for children and mean years for adults aged 25 years and older; command over economic resources, measured by female and male estimated GNI per capita.

3 Latin American average: 54.3% of adult women have reached at least a secondary level of education compared to 55.2% of their male counterparts. For every 100,000 live births, 85 women die from pregnancy-related causes, and the adolescent birth rate is 68.3 births per 1,000 women/girls ages 15–19.

4 Afro-Uruguayan women of 15 years or more reach higher percentages in all levels of education than men and achieve almost twice as many university degrees than men (INE, 2010).

5 57.5% for Afro-Uruguayan women (INE, 2010).

6 In Uruguay the Global Fertility Rate started to decrease early to reach a value of 1.93 (Pellegrino, 2010).

7 José Batlle y Ordóñez served as the President for two terms (1903–07 and 1911–15) in which he defined a reformist economic and social program, later known as *Batllismo*.

8 The Education Reform of 1877 proposed secular, free and compulsory public education both for boys and girls.

9 The export-oriented economic policy took advantage of the growing female labor supply, which was cheaper (owing to gender segregation and gender wage gaps) and more flexible (due to women's lack of experience in trade unions and political organization).

10 Access means having the opportunity to use resources to satisfy specific needs and personal and collective interests. Control means the possibility, in addition to the access, to have power to decide on the use and application of these resources.

11 During this period, information is available from the only two censuses carried out, the first one in 1908 and the second one in 1963.

12 During the stage of promoting non-traditional exports after 1973, there was a growth in the labor-intensive production, such as textiles, garments and footwear. For example, in shoe manufacturing women represented 60.3% of the total employees in 1978, most of whom classified as "unskilled" workers (Prates, 1987).

13 Relevant public policies include severance pay (1914), the eight-hour workday (1915), old-age pensions (1919), retirement pensions for public employees (1919), indemnity for work accidents (1920) and a minimum salary for agricultural workers (1925).

14 Maternity leave for primary schoolteachers (1911); accident prevention forbidding the use of women and children for cleaning or repairing running engines, machinery or other dangerous transmission parts (1914); the so-called "Chair Law," which set out that establishments employing women had to have enough chairs for female employees and workers to be able to sit down whenever their duties allowed (1918); an obligatory weekly day of rest in all occupations (1920) also applicable to domestic service (1920); the reduction of working hours by one-half for all female civil servants during the first six months after childbirth, for the purpose of breastfeeding (1925).

15 There have been some interruptions: from 1968, due to the "freeze in prices and salaries" decreed by the government, and from 1973 to 1985 as a result of the ban on union activities imposed by the dictatorship regime. Since 1985, with the recovery of democracy, Salary Councils were reinstated only to be suspended again in 1992 in order to reduce state intervention in salary negotiations, granting more labor market flexibility. They were restored again in 2005, extending the tripartite collective bargaining process to rural workers and, later, domestic workers as well.

16 Dictatorship lasted from 1973 to 1985.

17 Vertical segregation refers to the "glass ceiling" which indicates the existence of visible or invisible barriers that lead to a rarity of women in power and decision-making positions in public organization or enterprises. This phenomenon is parallel to the concept of the "sticky floor," which describes the forces that tend to maintain women at the lowest levels in the organizational pyramid (Maron & Meulders, 2008).

18 Between 1986 and 1999, the number of skilled workers increased from 10% to 17% of the total employment. For women these figures were 14% and 23% (Amarante & Espino, 2001).

19 The unemployment rate for Afro-Uruguayans is 13.3%.

20 The average wage gap between Afro-Uruguayans and the rest of the Uruguayan population (whose level of education is "primary or less") is 17.7% per hour and 15% per month.

21 In 2011, for individuals aged 25 to 59 the educational gap was 15.8% in favor of women, the female wage was 9.5% lower than male wage.

22 This paragraph, unless otherwise mentioned, is based on Johnson and Josefsson (2015).

23 The Uruguayan government is divided into three levels: (1) National (Executive Power and Parliament); (2) Departmental (the country is divided into 19 departments) and (3) Municipal (local municipalities within each department).

24 The number of women in the Senate was four in 2009.

25 In 2009, without the quota in place, 15 women held seats as titleholders.

26 The Voluntary Interruption of Pregnancy Bill was approved in November 2012 and became Law No. 18.987, which has been in force since January 2013. This law puts an end to the penalty for voluntarily interrupting pregnancy established in the Penal Code, provided that the following requirements are met: (1) first, the woman requests a medical appointment and then meets with an interdisciplinary

team; (2) a five-day refection period is required before taking the final decision; (3) the abortion shall occur within 12 weeks of pregnancy; and (4) it must be performed under the Health National System.

27 These requirements do not apply to victims of rape or incest. The only requirement in these cases is the filing of a criminal complaint.

28 "Conscientious objection" in this case refers to an individual who abstains from adopting certain rules because of moral or religious beliefs. The objector aims to protect their personal principles and values; their morality is the priority. They cannot comply with a specific law because their conscience comes first.

29 For example, the finding of the Second Criminal Court of Appeals in the case of sexual exploitation versus hotel businessman (Corujo Guardia, 2014).

30 Almost seven out of 10 women in Uruguay have gone through situations of gender-based violence at some point in their lives. This figure means about 650,000 women and clearly illustrates that we are facing a serious social problem that directly affects women throughout their lives (UNFPA-MIDES INMUJERES, 2013).

31 The classification levels for Latin America are divided into three: high level is for machinery with Ministerial institutional status or when the head is a Minister with full participation in the Cabinet; intermediate level is for machinery that depends on the presidency and whose head does not participate in the Cabinet; and low level is for machinery depending on a Ministry or a lower-rank authority (CEPAL, n.d.).

32 Gender mainstreaming was established as a global strategy for promoting gender equality in the Platform for Action adopted at the United Nations Fourth World Conference on Women, held in Beijing (China) in 1995.

33 The range of policy actors participating in the policy-making process is widened to include, apart from policy makers and civil servants, gender experts and civil society.

34 Public bodies will have to carry out an Annual Operation Plan specifying human resources and budget needs in order to fulfill the established goals.

35 The National Gender Council was created under Law No. 18.104 (2007) dated March 2007, within the Plan of Equal Opportunities and Rights, for the purpose of defining strategic guidelines for public policies on gender. It is a comprehensive space comprising representatives of the state, academia and civil society at different levels. This Council depends on the Ministry of Social Development and it is headed by the National Institute of Women.

36 As Johnson and Josefsson (2015, p. 17) say in relation to the quota law: "Indeed, the passing of the law can be understood as a politically correct move to avoid further 'shaming' in the international arena."

References

Aguirre, R. (2008). El futuro del cuidado. In I. Arriagada (Ed.), *Futuro de las familias y desafíos para las políticas*, Santiago de Chile: CEPAL—Serie Seminarios y conferencias No 52, pp. 23–34.

Álvarez Rivadulla, M.J. (2014). Tolerancia a la desigualdad en América Latina: Una exploración en Montevideo y Bogotá. *Revista Ensambles*, 1 (1), 99–119. Retrieved from https://www.academia.edu/5375032/Tolerancia_a_la_desigualdad_en_Am%C3%A9rica_Latina (accessed 3 August 2016).

Amarante, V., & Espino, A. (2001). *La evolución de la segregación laboral por sexo en Uruguay (1986–1999): Serie Documentos de Trabajo, DT 3/01: Noviembre de 2001*. Montevideo: Instituto de Economía.

Amarante, V., & Espino, A. (2002). *La segregación ocupacional de género y las diferencias en las remuneraciones de los asalariados privados (1990–2000): Serie Avances de Investigación, DT 05/02, Setiembre 2002.* Montevideo: Instituto de Economía.

Batthyány Dighiero, K. (2015). *Las políticas y el cuidado en América Latina Una mirada a las experiencias regionales.* Santiago de Chile: CEPAL—Serie Asuntos de Género No 124.

Batthyány, K., Espino, A., Fernández Soto, M., Genta, N., Molina, A., Pedetti, G., Sauval, M., Scavino, S., & Villamil, L. (2014). Desigualdades de género en Uruguay: Collection 5. In J.J. Calvo (Ed.), *Atlas sociodemográfico y de la desigualdad del Uruguay,* Montevideo: Programa de Población de la Facultad de Ciencias Sociales, pp. 1–70.

Bianchi, M. (2015). *Políticas Públicas para el Empoderamiento Económico de las Mujeres en Uruguay.* Montevideo: CIEDUR. Retrieved from http://www.ciedur.org.uy/adm/archivos/publicacion_286.pdf (accessed 5 August 2016).

Bjarnegård, E. (2009). *Men in Politics: Revisiting Patterns of Gendered Parliamentary Representation in Thailand and beyond.* Uppsala: Uppsala University.

Calce, C., España, V., Grabino, V., Goñi Mazzitelli, V., Magnone, N., Mesa, S., Meza, F., Pacci, G., Rostagnol, S., & Viera Cherro, M. (2015). *La violencia contra las mujeres en la agenda pública: Aportes en clave interdisciplinar: Colección Artículo 2.* Montevideo: CSIC UDELAR.

Cavallo, S. (2015). *Guarding Abortion Rights Advances in Uruguay.* New York: International women's health coalition. Retrieved from https://iwhc.org/2015/09/guarding-abortion-rights-advances-in-uruguay/ (accessed 20 May 2016).

CEDAW. (2004). General Recommendation No. 25, on article 4, paragraph 1, of the Convention on the Elimination of All Forms of Discrimination against Women, on temporary special measures. Retrieved from http://www.refworld.org/docid/453882a7e0.html (accessed 4 August 2016).

CEDAW/C/URY/CO/7. (2008). Concluding observations of the Committee on the Elimination of Discrimination against Women: Committee on the Elimination of Discrimination against Women. Forty-second session 20 October-7 November 2008.

CEPAL. (n.d.). *Observatorio de Igualdad de Género de América Latina y el Caribe.* Retrieved from http://www.cepal.org/oig/html/niveljerarquico2.html (accessed 4 May 2016).

CEPALSTAT. (2016). *Estadísticas e indicadores sociales.* Santiago de Chile: CEPAL. Retrieved from http://interwp.cepal.org/sisgen/ConsultaIntegrada.asp?IdAplicacion=1&idTema=363&idIndicador=250&idioma=e (accessed 10 May 2016).

Civil Rights of Women Law (Derechos Cívicos de la Mujer). (1932). Normativa y Avisos Legales del Uruguay No. 8927/1932. Montevideo: IMPO. Retrieved from http://www.impo.com.uy/bases/leyes/8927–1932 (accessed 12 August 2016).

Corujo Guardia, W. (2014). Judgement No. 259. Drafted by: Dr. William Corujo Guardia, Montevideo, 10 September 2014.

Divorce Law (Ley de Divorcio). (1907). Normativa y Avisos Legales del Uruguay No. 3245/1907. Montevideo: IMPO. Retrieved from http://www.impo.com.uy/bases/leyes/3245–1907/1 (accessed 12 August 2016).

Domestic Violence Law (Ley de Violencia Doméstica). (2002). Normativa y Avisos Legales del Uruguay No. 17514/2002. Retrieved from https://legislativo.parlamento.gub.uy/temporales/leytemp7788536.htm (accessed 12 August 2016).

Equal Rights and Opportunities among Men and Women in the Republic Law (*Ley de Igualdad de Derechos y Oportunidades de Hombres y Mujeres en la República*). (2007). Normativa y Avisos Legales del Uruguay No. 18104/2007. Retrieved from https://legislativo.parlamento.gub.uy/temporales/leytemp513664.htm (accessed 3 August 2016).

Espino, A. (2012). *Diferencias salariales por género y su vinculación con la segregación ocupacional y los desajustes por calificación: DT 20/12: Documentos de Trabajo*. Montevideo: Instituto de Economía, FCEyA, UDELAR.

Espino, A. (2013). Brechas salariales en Uruguay: Género, segregación y desajustes por calificación. *Problemas del Desarrollo: Revista Latinoamericana de Economía*, 44 (174), 89–117. Retrieved from http://www.iecon.ccee.edu.uy/brechas-salariales-en-uruguay-genero-segregacion-y-desajustes-por-calificacion/publicacion/360/es/ (accessed 8 August 2016).

Espino, A., & Azar, P. (2008). Changes in economics policy regimes in Uruguay from a gender perspective, 1930–2000. In G. Berik, Y. Meulen Rodgers & A. Zammit (Eds), *Social Justice and Gender Equality: Rethinking Development Strategies and Macroeconomics Policies (UNRISD)*, New York: Routledge, pp. 126–152.

Espino, A., & Pedetti, G. (2012). Social dialogue and gender equality in Uruguay. Working Paper No. 15. Industrial and Employment Relations. Department International Labour Office, Geneva ILO DWT for the South Cone of Latin America August 2012.

Espino, A., & Salvador, S. (2013). El sistema nacional de cuidados: una apuesta al bienestar, la igualdad y el desarrollo. *Análisis*, (4), pp. 1–21. Montevideo: Friedrich-Ebert-Stiftung. Retrieved from http://library.fes.de/pdf-files/bueros/uruguay/10362.pdf (accessed 20 July 2016).

Espino, A., Salvador, S., & Azar, P. (2014). *Desigualdades persistentes: Mercado de trabajo, calificación y género: Cuaderno sobre Desarrollo Humano: Serie: El Futuro en Foco*. Montevideo: PNUD. Retrieved from http://www.uy.undp.org/content/uruguay/es/home/library/human_development/cuaderno-sobre-desarrollo-humano-4.html (accessed 15 May 2016).

Filgueira, N. (1990). *La Mujer Uruguaya*. Montevideo: GRECMU.

Gender Quota Law. (2009). "Participación Equitativa de Personas de Ambos Sexos en la Integración de los Órganos Electivos y Dirección de Partidos Políticos". Normativa y Avisos Legales del Uruguay No. 18476/2009. Retrieved from https://legislativo.parlamento.gub.uy/temporales/leytemp7669552.htm (accessed 15 May 2016).

González, M., Calce, C., Magnone, N., & Pacci, G. (2013). *Diagnóstico Sobre las Respuestas del Estado ante la Violencia contra las Mujeres en Uruguay: Programa integral de Lucha contra la violencia de género*. Montevideo: MIDES.

INE. (2010). *Principales Resultados 2010: Encuesta Continua de Hogares*. Montevideo: Instituto Nacional de Estadística. Retrieved from http://www.ine.gub.uy/encuesta-continua-de-hogares (accessed 5 August 2016).

INE. (2013). *Uso del Tiempo y Trabajo No Remunerado en Uruguay*. Retrieved from http://www.ine.gub.uy/documents/10181/340523/Uso+del+Tiempo+y+Trabajo+No+Remunerado+2013/5c21b33e-ddde-41cd-a638-4d73e3f75a8d (accessed 3 August 2016).

INE. (2014). *Principales Resultados 2014: Encuesta Continua de Hogares*. Montevideo: Instituto Nacional de Estadística.

INMUJERES. (n.d.). *Violencia basada en Género*. Retrieved from http://www.inmu jeres.gub.uy/innovaportal/v/15090/6/innova.front/violencia-basada-en-genero (accessed 5 August 2016).

Jackson, R.M. (2006). Opposing forces: How, why, and when will gender inequality disappear? In F.D. Blau, M.C. Brinton & D.B. Grusky (Eds), *Declining Significance of Gender?* New York: Russell Sage Foundation, pp. 215–244. Retrieved from http://www.jstor.org/stable/10.7758/9781610440622.11 (accessed 20 May 2016).

Johnson, N., & Josefsson, C. (2015). The gender quota law vs. male power monop-olies in Uruguay's 2014 elections: A losing battle. Paper prepared for presentation at the European Conference on Politics and Gender, Uppsala University, 11–13 June.

Kabeer, N. (2011). Contextualizing the economic pathways of women's empow-erment: Findings from a multi-country research programme. Pathways Policy Paper, October 2011. Brighton: Pathways of Women's Empowerment RPC.

Katzkowicz, S., & Querejeta, M. (2012). Evolución de la Segregación Ocupacional y su Impacto en las Brechas Salariales de Género. Ph.D. thesis. Montevideo: Uni-versidad de la República, Facultad de Ciencias Económicas y de Administración.

Labor Activity Law (Actividad Laboral). (1989). Registro Nacional de Leyes y Decretos No 16045/1989. Retrieved from https://legislativo.parlamento.gub.uy/ temporales/leytemp2337009.htm (accessed 12 August 2016).

Maron, L., & Meulders, D. (2008). Les effets de la parenté sur la segregation. Work-ing Paper No. 08–21. RS Research Series. Rapport du projet "Public policies towards employment of parents and sociale inclusion". Bruxelles: Département d'Economie Appliquée de l'Université Libre de Bruxelles -DULBEA.

Meza Tananta, F., Lima, A., & Percovich, M. (2016). Alternative report for CEDAW (unpublished). May. Montevideo.

Pellegrino, A. (2010). *La Población Uruguaya: Breve Caracterización Demográfica*. Montevideo: UNFPA.

Pensions and Retirement Benefits Law (Ley de Beneficios de Jubilaciones y Pensio-nes). (1950). Registro Nacional de Leyes y Decretos No 11495/1950. Monte-video: IMPO Retrieved from https://www.impo.com.uy/bases/leyes/11495-1950 (accessed 20 July 2016).

Prates, S. (1987). *Las Trabajadoras Domiciliarias en la Industria del Calzado: Descentralización de la Producción y Domesticidad*. Montevideo: Ediciones de la Banda Oriental—CIESU.

Presidencia. (2014). Uruguay tiene las tasas más bajas de aborto y mortalidad materna de América. Retrieved from https://www.presidencia.gub.uy/comunica-cion/comunicacionnoticias/conferencia-salud-de-la-mujer-en-uruguay (accessed 5 August 2016).

Queirolo, R., & Boidi, M.F. (2013). Cultura Política de la Democracia en Uru-guay y en las Américas, 2012: Hacia la igualdad de oportunidades. USAID. Retrieved from http://www.vanderbilt.edu/lapop/uruguay/Uruguay_Country_ Report_2012_W.pdf.pdf (accessed 3 August 2016).

Riley, M. (2008). *A Feminist Political Economic Framework*. Washington, DC: Cen-ter of Concern. Retrieved from https://www.coc.org/files/Riley%20-%20FPE_0. pdf (accessed 12 August 2016).

Rodríguez Villamil, S., & Sapriza, G. (1984). *Mujer, Estado y Política en el Uruguay del Siglo XX: Serie Temas del Siglo XX, No. 23*. Montevideo: Ediciones de la Banda Oriental and GRECMU.

Salary Councils' Law (Ley de Consejo de Salarios). (1943). Registro Nacional de Leyes y Decretos No. 10449/1943. Montevideo: IMPO. Retrieved from https://www.impo.com.uy/bases/leyes/10449–1943 (accessed 12 August 2016).

Salvador, S. (2010). Hacia un sistema nacional de cuidados en Uruguay. Retrieved from http://www.cepal.org/publicaciones/xml/3/41823/di-uruguay-sistema-cuidado.pdf (accessed 20 May 2016).

UNDP. (2015). Human Development Report 2015: Work for human development. Briefing note for countries on the 2015. Human Development Report Uruguay. Retrieved from http://hdr.undp.org/sites/default/files/2015_human_development_report.pdf (accessed 8 August 2016).

UNFPA-MIDES INMUJERES. (2013). *Estadísticas de Género: Evolución de los indicadores de género: 2009–2013*. Montevideo: UNFPA-MIDES INMUJERES.

UN Women. (2014). Gender equality and sustainable development: World survey on the role of women in development 2014. The Research and Data section of UN Women, United Nations.

UN Women. (2016). Gender Violence Bill presented in Uruguay. UN Women's Regional Office for Latin America and the Caribbean. Retrieved from http://www.unwomen.org/en/news/stories/2016/4/uruguay-gender-based-violence-bill#sthash.e5K7jo5c.dpuf (accessed 12 August 2016).

Voluntary Interruption of Pregnancy Law (Ley de Interrupción Voluntaria del Embarazo). (2012). Registro Nacional de Leyes y Decretos No. 18987/2012. Retrieved from https://legislativo.parlamento.gub.uy/temporales/leytemp6383431.htm (accessed 12 August 2016).

7 Structural and Ideological Gender Equality in Mexico

Sonia M. Frías

Gender inequality is "the departure from parity in the representation of women and men in key dimensions of social life" (Young et al., 1994, p. 57). Its opposite, gender equality, is the measurable equal representation of women and men assuming that men and women, although not the same, have equal value and should be accorded equal treatment. Therefore, in a society with full equality, women and men can enjoy the comprehensive list of political, economic, civil, social and cultural rights, with no one being denied access to these rights, or deprived of them, because of their sex. According to the 2014 United Nations Development Program's (UNDP) Gender Inequality Index,[1] Mexico ranks 74th among the most equal countries of the world (UNDP, 2015).

Mexico, is a federation formed of 32 states that have distinct characteristics based on their history, environment and resources, level of economic development, racial and ethnic composition, and numerous other factors. There are important cross-state and regional differences in terms of education, poverty, development, distribution of basic services and health within Mexico that suggest that the levels of structural gender equality are heterogeneous (Frías, 2008). The origins of gender inequality are traced to social structures that perpetuate men's domination of women in all areas of private and public life. This structural system of domination has existed throughout history and has been labeled *patriarchy*. Legal, political, economic and ideological structures, including the religious system have contributed to its persistence (Dobash et al., 1979; Moghadam, 2004). These structures directly or indirectly maintain and reinforce the ideology and reality of men's authority over women.

There is ample evidence that at the societal level, norms and discourses related to gender roles and equality, as well the structural level of gender inequality influence individual-level behaviors. For example, structural gender inequality is associated with several negative outcomes affecting women, their children and the overall society such as partner violence (Frías, 2009; Smith, 1990; Straus, 1994), rape and sexual violence (Yodanis, 2004), homicides (Brewer & Smith, 1995; DeWees et al., 2003; Titterington, 2006), economic growth (Klasen, 2002) and mortality of children (Brinda et al., 2015).

In this chapter I examine gender (in)equality in Mexico, a developing country where Mexican men are often portrayed as macho, dominant, socialized to be aggressive, fearless and to dominate both women and other men. In contrast, Mexican women are considered to be submissive, obedient and passive (Díaz-Olavarrieta et al., 1996; Guttmann, 1996; Kaufman Kantor et al., 1994; Morash et al., 2000). These differences are rooted in gender inequalities and are a manifestation of patriarchy, which has a structural and ideological component. I review first the nature of gender inequality by describing the complex relationship between patriarchal structures and ideologies, as proposed by Dobash and Dobash (1979). Next, Mexican government's [formal] *commitment* to gender equality is studied by examining Mexican legislation and international agreements and treaties. The third part offers state-level empirical data about structural gender inequality in Mexico, six years after the enactment of the General Law on Women and Men's Equality. It highlights the differences among the 32 states that constitute Mexico by using the Gender Equality Index in Mexican States (Frías, 2008, 2014b). The ideological component of gender inequality is studied in the fourth section by using the 2010 Survey on the Right to Equality between Men and Women, a nationally representative sample conducted by the National Commission on Human Rights. This same survey is used next to study gender inequality in the private sphere. Finally, the conclusions are presented.

Gender Inequality and Patriarchy: Structural and Ideological Components

Dobash and Dobash (1979) suggest that patriarchy is composed of two elements, structure and ideology. The structural aspect becomes manifest in the nature of the gender hierarchical organization of social institutions and social relations in private (household) and public spheres (political, educational and economic). The patriarchal nature of society is also reflected in the state and laws and public policies originated in it (Charles, 2000; Connell, 1990; Kantola et al., 2005; MacKinnon, 1989). Access to socially valuable positions is not based on an individual's achievement, but ascribed status or institutionalized forms of privilege allow certain individuals (mostly males) to reach these privileged positions. The second aspect of patriarchy, the ideological, is related to the acceptance of the inequality between men and women. Patriarchal ideology serves as a legitimate base and a way to reinforce the acceptance of the structural component patriarchy. The ideological component assures that complaints and attempts to transform the patriarchal system will be seen as deviant and immoral. In this way, socialization into an acceptance of the patriarchal hierarchical order allows these inequalities to persist over time as well as to remain unquestioned and unchallenged.

The social patriarchal structure implies a hierarchy in which women are at the bottom of legal, political, educational and economic systems. With women at the lower ranks of these systems, formal inequality is perpetuated, making it almost impossible to challenge patriarchal ideology. In other words, because women do not have the same access as men to influential positions in social institutions, it is impossible or very difficult to change the societal ideology that places women in a subordinated position. At the same time, this ideology prevents women from reaching powerful positions in the social structure. Therefore, ideology and social structure feed on each other and contribute to the production and reproduction of gender inequality. Without women in the ruling positions, their subordination is guaranteed and patriarchal ideology remains unchallenged; the opposite is also true.

The Protection of Gender Equality in Mexico

Since 1936 Mexico has signed an array of binding agreements such as international treaties and conventions aimed at guaranteeing gender equality (see review in CNDH, 2011).[2] In addition, it has subscribed to non-binding international agreements regarding gender equality.[3] At the national level, the Political Constitution of the Mexican United States, first approved in 1917, grants individuals in the Mexican territory all human rights included in the Constitution and binding international treaties signed by Mexico (Article 1). In addition, it bans gender discrimination and installs equality between men and women (Article 4).[4] During the presidency of Vicente Fox (2000–2006), two main laws addressing gender inequality and discrimination were enacted: the Federal Law on Prevention and Eradication of Discrimination (2003) and the General Law on Women and Men's Equality (2006). These laws respond to the compromises reached in the IV World Conference for Women held in Beijing in 1995 (ONU, 1995).

The General Law on Women and Men's Equality has been amended seven times and has two main objectives: first, granting equal treatment and opportunities to women and men; second, defining the guidelines and institutional mechanisms aimed at guaranteeing gender equality in the private and public spheres by promoting women's empowerment. This law, because of its *general* scope, is mandatory for all levels of government: local, state and federal. The 2013 reform entailed the adoption of the Convention on the Elimination of All forms of Discrimination against Women's (CEDAW) (ONU, 1981) definition on discrimination against women in Article 5.3[5] and gender mainstreaming as a strategy for achieving gender equality.[6]

The General Law on Women and Men's Equality set up three governmental mechanisms aimed at guaranteeing gender equality: the National System for Women and Men's Equality, the National Program for Women and Men's Equality and the Monitoring System for Guaranteeing the Observance of the National System and National Program for Women and Men's Equality. The National System stipulates specific responsibilities for public institutions comprising the National System. It also defines structures, methods and procedures aimed at promoting and guaranteeing gender equality. The

National Program for Women and Men's Equality (*Proigualdad* in Spanish) is currently integrated in the National Development Plan[7] and is designed by the National Women's Institute. National, state and local gender equality programs have to be aligned to the National Program for Women and Men's Equality. Finally, the National Commission of Human Rights -equivalent to an Ombudsman office- is responsible of the National System for Guarantee-ing the Observance of the Program, the System and the law in general. It has to oversee, follow up on and evaluate the observance of National Program and to implement information systems that would allow assessing the levels of gender equality in different realms in Mexico.

The General Law on Women and Men's Equality states the specific objec-tives and actions to be included in the national gender equality public policy to eliminate structural and ideological gender inequalities. Table 7.1 sum-marizes these main objectives. At the structural level it aims to tackle gen-der inequality in individuals' relationship with the State, as well as gender inequalities in the political and economic spheres. At the ideological level, it seeks to eliminate gender stereotypes that promote gender discrimina-tion and violence against women. For example, aligned with this law, the General Law on Women's Access to a Life Free of Violence (enacted in 2007, last reformed in 2015) allocates to the Department of State (*Secre-taría de Gobernación*) responsibility for monitoring mass media contents that promote gender stereotypes and violence against women. The National Commission on Prevention and Eradication of Violence against Women (*Comisión Nacional para la Prevención y Erradicación de la Violencia en contra de las Mujeres, CONAVIM*)—dependent on the Department of State—has published and disseminated non-sexist language guides and has organized several global forums on non-sexist language and mass media.

In 2013, under the presidency of Enrique Peña Nieto, the National Pro-gram on Equal Opportunities and Non-Discrimination against Women 2013–2018 (*Programa Nacional para la Igualdad de Oportunidades y no Discriminación contra las Mujeres*) was issued. This Program is part of the National Development Program, and sets the guidelines for designing short-, medium- and long-term public policies aimed at fighting against the historical and structural factors that prevent women and girls' progress because they restrict, discriminate, segregate or exclude women in different spheres.

The implementation of the law by the federal and state governments is heterogeneous. According to the National Commission of Human Rights, the federal government has incorporated a greater number of the provisions of the law into their institutions and public policies than the 32 states that comprise Mexico (CNDH, 2014). The area in which more formal progress has been made is in the enactment of legislation aimed at reducing gender inequality and protection of women's rights. Nevertheless, 26.5% of Mexi-cans have not heard about gender equality laws, and 44% of the population

Table 7.1 Objectives of the General Law on Women and Men's Equality

Structural Inequality

Economic Sphere

- Institutionalization of funds aimed at promoting gender equality in the workplace and production processes.
- Promotion of economic public policies with gender perspective.
- Promotion of gender egalitarian leaderships.
- Establishment of measures aimed at promoting women's access to employment, non-discrimination at the work place, and equal working conditions.

Political Sphere

- Promotion of gender perspective in the parliamentary work.
- Evaluation of gender equality in direct election positions.
- Promote men and women's balanced participation and representation within party structures.
- Encourage equal participation of men and women in administrative positions.
- Develop and update statistical data on decision-making and managerial positions in all levels of public administration, private and non profit sectors by gender.
- Promote balanced non-discriminatory participation of men and women in selection, recruitment and promotion processes in public administration positions.

Individual's relationship with the State (access and protection of rights)

Access to social rights

- Improve current knowledge about legislation on social development and its implementation.
- Supervise incorporation of gender perspective in all phases of public policy making (design, implementation and evaluation), as well as private and social activities.
- Continuous revision of public policies addressing gender-based violence.

Promotion of gender equality in other spheres (civil)

- Evaluation of laws regarding gender equality in different spheres (employment, access to health care, education).
- Promotion of women's rights as universal human rights.
- Eradication of gender violence.

Ideological Inequality

- Promote public actions aimed at eradicating all forms of discrimination based on gender stereotypes.
- Include gender equality in educational contents and raise awareness of the need of eliminating all forms of discrimination.
- Change socio-cultural behavior patterns of both men and women with the goal of putting to an end prejudices and practices based on gender inequality and gender stereotypes.
- Sponsor programs and campaigns addressing gender equality.
- Promote the use of language styles in social relations that incorporate gender equality perspective.
- Monitor closely mass media to offer a diverse, equal and non-stereotyped image of men and women in society, to educate and disseminate gender equality, and to avoid sexist language.

Source: Author on the basis of General Law on Women and Men's Equality.

Note: The objectives have been reorganized for clarity.

have heard about the laws but do not know their contents (CNDH, 2014). This prevents citizens from demanding its observance.

The federal budget for the promotion of gender equality increased 268% from 2008 (7,000 million Mexican pesos) to 2013 (18,760 million pesos)[8] (*Gobierno de la República*, 2013). In 2013, nevertheless, in 53.5% of the 101 programs to be funded with this budget, it was not clear which actions would be implemented with the resources or how these actions will contribute to reducing gender equality (CNDH, 2014). Materially, gender equality is far from being achieved according to the observations made in 2012 by the CEDAW Commission to the Mexican Government (ONU, 2012). The next section assesses the level of gender [in]equality in Mexico six years after the enactment of the General Law on Women and Men's Equality.

Measuring Gender Equality in the Public Sphere by Using the Gender Equality Index in Mexican States[9]

Theoretically, the overall level of structural gender inequality might be traced to inequality in economic resources, political and public power, schooling and legal rights (Di Noia, 2002; Sugarman et al., 1988). The Gender Equality Index in Mexican States (GEIMS) is a measure that combines several variables[10] in these four dimensions to assess the societal or structural level of gender equality (Frías, 2008). As opposed to other measures of gender inequality, this index measures women's position compared to that of men. In other words, the level of economic, political and educational equality in a given state is calculated as a ratio of the percent of gender attainment of women to that of men's in socially valuable positions in the said state. Gender attainment refers "to the absolute degree to which members of a particular gender have achieved socially valued statuses such as education or occupational prestige" (Di Noia, 2002, p. 35). In the case of legal equality, instead of a continuous score, each variable indicates the presence or absence of legislation granting legal rights to women: either protecting previously existing but traditionally ignored rights (i.e., sexual harassment), or statuses that grant new rights (i.e., criminalization of rape within a marriage).

With these four dimensions of equality, the construction of the GEIMS proceeds in two stages. The first one consists of calculating each of the four subindexes (economic, educational, political and legal); and the second combines the four subindexes into a single overall measure. After conducting an internal reliability analysis and selecting the positively associated variables, each of the subindexes is the average of the variables included in that particular dimension (all variables were calculated and created by the author based on available information referenced in Table 7.2). Similarly, the GEIMS is the average of the four dimensions (see Frías, 2008). Theoretically, a score of 100 represents perfect equality between men and women. Scores tending toward zero reflect greater inequality favoring men. This

Table 7.2 Average Equality Across States by Sphere of (In)equality in Mexico in 2012

Economic dimension	49.5%	Educational dimension	81.9%
Labor force	60.2	Average years of education	97.4
Employed	60.2	Literacy	104.3
Civil servants, managers and administrators	47.2	College	92.7
Professional and technicians	75.4	Graduate	80.9
Business owners	24.5	Engineering, agricultural and natural sciences	34.1
Average hourly wage	99.6	Researchers	43.9
Health benefits	63.0		
Above poverty level female-headed households	16.2		
Political dimension	31.7%	Legal dimension	69.2%
Mayors	7.7	Pregnancy interruption	40.6
City councillors	59.1	Forced sterilization (is a felony)	31.3
Aldermen	38.1	Feminicide (is a felony)	28.1
State representatives	31.9	Enforced gender quotas (political representation)	68.8
Federal single-district representatives	31.1	Equal rights legislation	84.4
Magistrates	46.9	Sexual harassment legislation	100.0
State secretaries	13.8	NO: Stealing livestock more punishment than rape	90.6
Federal civil servants	24.2	NO: Rape of a minor is a felony only if she is chaste	90.6
		Obstetrical /reproductive rights violence	15.6
		Family violence (is a felony)	96.9
		Family violence is a cause for divorce	100.0
		Emergency female protection orders	78.1
		Publicly funded shelters	68.8
		NO: Age difference for marriage	68.8
		NO: Time for remarrying	40.6

Source: Author's own calculations based on the National Census (Inegi, 2010); National Survey on Occupation and Employment (*Inegi & Secretaría de Trabajo y Previsión Social*, 2011); Sistema Nacional de Información Municipal (*Instituto Nacional para el Federalismo y el Desarrollo Municipal*, 2005); Hombres y Mujeres en México 2012 (Inegi, 2013); Directorio de Órganos Jurisdiccionales (*Consejo de la Judicatura Federal*, 2012); Statistical Yearbook of Higher Education (*Asociación Nacional de Universidades e Instituciones de Educación Superior*, 2013) and author's revision of state-level legislation and requests of information made to the Federal Institute for Access to Information and Data Protection.

index is a measurement of the relative *social status* men and women enjoy based on four dimensions measured by several indicators per dimension. Therefore, it can provide a more accurate assessment of gender inequality than those based on a single indicator or a limited number of these such as the United Nations Development Program's (UNDP) indexes—Gender Inequality Index and Gender Development Index. These indexes are not perfect since they "can capture only what is measurable and therefore do not cover other important dimensions of gender inequality" (UNDP, 1995, p. 72). The GEIMS, like similar indexes created in the United States and Europe (Bericat, 2012; Bericat et al., 2016; Sugarman et al., 1988; Yllo, 1980), compares the gender gap within any given unit of analysis—country or state—without taking the relative position of women across states into account in the different components of the construct.

Economic Equality

Historically, the most important—and the most achievable—form of power for women has been economic, which has contributed to their overall status in society and which may have set in motion other mutually reinforcing political, economic, cultural and social changes that reduce inequalities. Table 7.2 presents the average across Mexican states (32) for each variable included in the economic dimension. It shows that women are underrepresented in the labor force, having attained only 60% of equality with men. In other words, for every 100 men in the labor force, there are only 60 women. Women's share of executive and public service positions has increased over the last decades, but remains low since women have only attained 47% of public administration and managerial posts and 75% of professional and technical occupations. Despite the fact that women's wages are on average very similar to those of men (99.6%), women are less likely to receive employment-related health benefits than men since women have reached 63% of equality in this aspect. This might be a consequence of women's informal and non-salaried employment. Across states, on average, for every 100 productive establishments owned by males, less than one-fourth (24%) are owned by women. The percentage of female-headed households in Mexico, as in the rest of the world, has increased over time. In 2011, female-headed households above the poverty level represented 16% of male-headed ones (as of 2011, above the poverty level households had an average income of 352 pesos or approximately 24 dollars a month). After calculating the economic subindex, in 2012, Mexican women have attained 49.3% equality in the economic sphere.

Educational Equality

The educational dimension is the second sphere in which structural gender inequality is manifested. Women's access to education is associated with higher rates of participation in the labor market, better working conditions and higher access to decision-making positions. Females' access to higher levels of education has increased gradually, but the gender gap in education still persists among older generations.

Currently, for every 100 literate men, there are 104 women, representing a gap favoring females. In spite of these advances in literacy, however, on average, for every 100 men with a college education, there are 92 women; this figure decreases to 80% for those with graduate degrees (M.A., M.S. and Ph.D.). A closer look at some educational areas traditionally reserved for men, such as agricultural, engineering and natural sciences, reveals that females are largely underrepresented: on average, for every 100 men, there are 34 women.

Women are also underrepresented as researchers: for every 100 male members of the prestigious National System of Researchers (SNI), there are only 44 females. The results of the educational subindex show that Mexican women have achieved 82% equality with men.

The Political Equality Dimension

It has been argued that the unequal access of women to leadership positions is associated with the low status of women in other spheres, such as the economic and educational one (Reynolds, 1999). The consequence of women's better representation in the political sphere tends to be associated with a larger number of public policies and legislation addressing women's issues, which might reduce gender inequality in other spheres (Jones, 1997; Lloren, 2015; Martínez et al., 2013). However, political representation of women's interests and promotion of gender equality is mediated by political ideology. There is ample evidence that the more gender-egalitarian ideologies of left-wing parties are more likely to favor women's election to political offices (Jones, 2008). On the other hand, right-wing parties tend to hold a non-interventionist philosophy; therefore, they tend to have limited involvement in the recruitment process (Saxonberg, 2000). This is the case of Mexico, where before the legal establishment of gender quotas, the Democratic Revolution Party, a left-wing party, introduced a 20% gender quota in its executive directorate in 1990, and in 1992 in the electoral list. In 1993 the quota increased to 30% (Martínez et al., 2013).

In Mexico, the representation of women in certain public offices might depend on the political climate or the nature of the election (Rodríguez, 2003). In addition to the high number of elections taking place every three years and the non-re-election rule, Mexico has experienced a contested democratic transition over recent years. The enactment of mandatory gender quota laws[11] has further contributed to a chaotic pattern of female representation in the political sphere since females tend to occupy substitute positions and it has been documented that they are forced to resign in favor of substitute men (Rodríguez Peñaloza et al., 2013). This occurred, for example after the 2009 federal Congressional elections, when the so-called

"*Juanitas*"[12] congresswomen gave up their seats as elected representatives to substitute men as a result of agreements and political interests of party leaders.

On average, for every 100 municipalities governed by males, there are approximately 8 governed by females; for every 100 male city councillors, there are 59 women and 38 women for every 100 male trustees. The gender gap does not improve in state and federal legislatures: women have around 31% of representation, both as state representatives and as single-district federal representatives.

Women's representation in the judiciary branch is measured by women's representation as magistrates in each State's Supreme Court. The average attainment of women across states is 13.8% (all political data is from 2012). At the executive level, women have attained 23% of the state secretary positions traditionally held by men, and 24% of federal civil servant positions as representatives working as liaisons or commissioners between federal and state governments.

The internal reliability analysis of the variables to be included in the political subindex is not acceptable (Cronbach alpha =.07). This shows that it is not possible to argue for a generalized pattern of female representation in politics within each state since women might score high in some political positions yet very low in others. In spite of this, Mexican women have reached 31.7% equality with men in the political sphere.

Legal Equality Dimension

The legal status of women in a certain society is the fourth sphere in which structural gender equality is measured. It is in the law where the differentiation between men and women tends to be the crudest. According to the Mexican Constitution, men and women are equal before the law. However state-level legislation does not guarantee this equality. Until 1997, it was mandatory for women in Aguascalientes to have written permission from their husbands if they wanted employment. Until 1998, women's employment in Chiapas was conditioned on the husband's permission based on non-interference with household responsibilities.

Gender equality in the legal sphere is assessed by 15 indicators that measure the presence or absence of legislation granting rights, promoting gender equality or protecting already established rights. Interrupting a pregnancy in case of the risk of the mother's death, imprudence, negligence or genetic malformations of the fetus is still considered a crime in 19 states (58.2% of the states). Only in 10 states (31.3%) is forced female sterilization a crime and in nine (28.1%) feminicide typified as a criminal offense. Although most states have enacted laws or statutes that at least formally guarantee gender balance in political representation, only 22 of them have mandatory gender quotas or other affirmative actions (68.8%). All states have enacted specific legislation condemning sexual harassment, but five states lack equal rights legislation (15.6%). Crimes and offenses against females, such as abusing a minor or raping a woman, still receive lesser punishment than stealing livestock in three states (9.4%). The same percentages of states do not consider the rape of a minor a felony if she is not chaste.

The second group of measures determines the presence of legal premises that grant protection to victims of violence. In all states, domestic violence is considered a cause of divorce. All states have enacted legislation guaranteeing women's right to a life without violence in the following areas: family, work, school and community, as well as offering protection from institutional violence resulting from the actions or omissions of public employees. Only five states (15.6%) extended their protection to include obstetrical violence and offenses against women's sexual or reproductive rights. There is still one state in Mexico where domestic violence is not a felony. Only in 25 states (78.1%) can women be granted emergency protection orders in the case of violence. According to the Women's National Institute, as of 2012 there are 66 shelters, 32 of which (48%) are publicly funded, 33 managed by non-governmental organizations, and one has joint management and funding.[13] Only in 68.8% of the states do female victims have a publicly funded shelter to go to.

The third group of legal indicators refers to the institution of marriage. In this sphere, gender inequality still persists. In 22 states (68.8%), the minimum age for marriage is the same for men and women. Women's differential position in the law is also reflected in the fact that in only 13 states (40.6%) women, as opposed to men, do not have to wait for a period that ranges between 180 and 300 days before re-marrying after a divorce.

In sum, legal equality is far from being reached. All states but the Federal District (in February 2016 the name changed to Mexico City) fail in protecting women's rights and the law treats men and women differently. The Federal District is the exception. The existence of laws and statutes, however, does not guarantee their enactment. The legal equality dimension was computed by adding the number of laws and statutes protecting women's rights and granting them rights, and dividing this number by 15 (the total number of indicators). On average, across states, women have reached 69.2% equality with men at the legal sphere.

How Far Have Women Gone in Terms of Gender Equality?

The economic, educational, political and legal spheres are not always correlated. There is a positive small correlation between educational and economic equality (.31, p < .10). However, there is no association between legal equality and economic, educational or political equality. This lack of association suggests the enactment of legislation protecting or granting women's rights is not associated with the level of gender equality in other areas. The final GEIMS index is calculated by computing the average coefficient of gender inequality for the economic, educational and legal dimensions previously presented for each state. The political dimension is not included because of the very low internal consistency of the index. The correlation of the index including and excluding the political dimension is high (.87, p < .0001).

Overall, Mexican women have attained 66.9% equality with men. The results for each state are presented in Table 7.3. The gap between the states ranking highest and lowest in gender equality is 24.5. The Federal District is the state where women have reached the highest level of gender equality, 81%. Its relatively high levels of structural gender equality might be explained by the modernization perspective claiming that high levels of development lead to the reduction of gender inequality. In addition, the left has dominated the legislature and the government for several terms, and the egalitarian ideologies of left-wing parties are more likely to protect women's rights. Campeche, in contrast, has the lowest level of gender equality, 56.5%. There is a relevant gap between the Federal District and Puebla, the state that ranks second in gender equality. The northern states of Nuevo León, Chihuahua, Coahuila and Sonora rank low in gender equality (see Figure 7.1). Some of the poorest states (Puebla, Guerrero or Chiapas) rank among the most egalitarian. It should be remembered that this index does not account for levels of inequality across states, but only measures the gender gap within each state.

Mexican women are still far from reaching gender equality with men in the social structure. Nevertheless, the improvement is remarkable. In 2005, women had barely reached 26% equality with men in the political sphere, and around 42% both in the economic and legal spheres (Frías, 2008). In the educational realm there was a gender gap of 35.2%. Seven years later, the level of gender equality in Mexico has significantly increased from a

Table 7.3 Gender Equality Index in Mexican States (GEIMS 2011)

Ranking	State	Gender Equality	Ranking	State	Gender Equality
1	Federal District	81.0	17	Baja California Sur	66.6
2	Puebla	74.4	18	Baja California	65.5
3	Mexico State	73.5	19	Colima	64.7
4	Guerrero	73.4	20	Sinaloa	64.6
5	Chiapas	73.3	21	Nayarit	64.3
6	Veracruz	72.9	22	Durango	63.8
7	Tamaulipas	72.5	23	Aguascalientes	63.2
8	Hidalgo	72.5	24	Tabasco	62.0
9	San Luis Potosí	72.5	25	Michoacán	61.3
10	Morelos	71.3	26	Sonora	61.1
11	Guanajuato	70.9	27	Querétaro	60.7
12	Yucatán	70.8	28	Coahuila	60.2
13	Zacatecas	69.5	29	Tlaxcala	59.5
14	Jalisco	69.0	30	Chihuahua	57.0
15	Oaxaca	68.0	31	Nuevo León	56.5
16	Quintana Roo	66.7	32	Campeche	56.5

Note: Author's calculation. This index excludes political equality since it is negatively correlated with the economic, educational and legal dimensions.

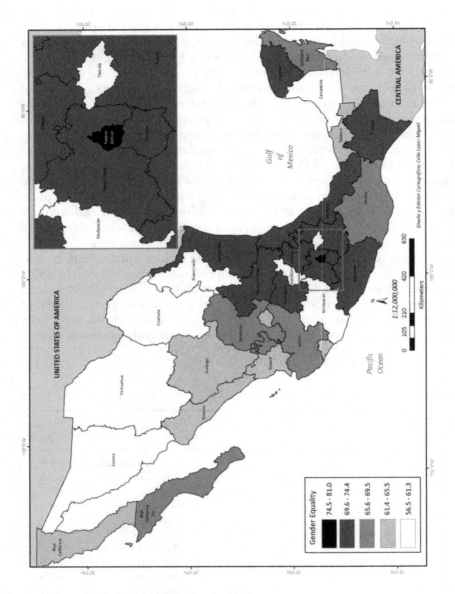

Figure 7.1 Level of Gender Equality in Mexico

state average of 43.9% in 2005 to 66.9% in 2012. The largest improvement in gender equality is taking place in the legal dimension (41.7% in 2005 vs. 69.2% in 2012), followed by the educational one (64.8% vs. 82.2%). In the economic sphere, improvement in gender equality is less noticeable (42.4% vs. 49.5%). Finally, the least improvement has taken place in the political sphere; gender equality has increased 20% (from 26.2% in 2005 to 31.7% in 2012).

The Ideological Component of Gender Inequality

Gender inequality is supported by individuals' gender beliefs and ideologies. These beliefs are often manifested through stereotypes. Stereotypes are generalizations of individuals' social attributes due to their membership in a certain group. Stereotypes are implicit theories and beliefs that a group of individuals share about their own or another social group regarding individuals' knowledge, personality and capacities that are not supported empirically (Loscertales, 2007; Williams et al., 1990).

In 2010, the National Commission of Human Rights, the institution responsible for guaranteeing the observance of the General Law on Women and Men's Equality, sponsored the 2010 Survey on the Right to Equality between Men and Women. It is a nationally representative survey (N=8,500) that had the purpose of analyzing Mexicans' perceptions of and beliefs about gender equality (details in CNDH, 2011). This survey is a valuable resource for examining the ideological component of patriarchy, and is the source of the analyses presented next.

Mexican men and women hold gender beliefs and stereotypes regarding the capability of men and women to perform certain roles both in the private and public spheres. Participants were asked who (men, women or both equally) was more capable of performing certain activities in four social spheres: politics, economics, education and household. In politics the activities and roles were: (a) to govern a country; (b) to be the president of Mexico; (c) to lead a political party; (d) to enforce the law and (e) to administer justice. In the educational sphere: (f) to be an elementary school teacher and (g) to be a secondary school teacher. As for household activities and roles: (h) to take care of children; (i) to raise children and (j) to administer a household. Finally, only one was included in the economic realm: (k) to manage a business. The alpha coefficients for the three first spheres are respectively, .85, .73 and .73.

Figure 7.2 shows that in the educational, economic and political spheres, as well as in the household men and women are not perceived to have the same capacities. The absence of gender stereotypes in these spheres would be represented by a 100, implying that respondents believe that men and women have the same capacity to perform certain activities. Graph 1 highlights two main findings. First, younger generations have more gender-egalitarian ideologies than older generations both in the private sphere (household) and public spheres (politics, education and employment). In the political sphere, on average, 65.3% of the youngest generation (15 to 19 years old) believe that men and women have the same aptitudes; among those between 51 and 54 years old, only six out 10; and among the oldest (81 years and older) only half of them.

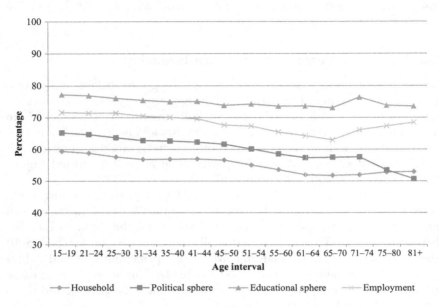

Figure 7.2 Percentage of Individuals that Believe Men and Women Have the Same Competence to Perform Certain Activities in Different Spheres by Age

The second finding shows that the level of ideological gender equality varies by sphere. Gender-egalitarian ideologies are less widespread in the domestic realm than in the political, economic and educational spheres. Regarding this last sphere, it is plausible that if the survey would have included questions regarding the ability to teach in graduate and under-graduate programs, or to be a member of the National Researchers System, the coefficients would have been lower. For example, six of every 10 teens (15 to 19 years old) believe that men and women are equally capable of per-forming certain roles in the household; in the political sphere the percentage is 10% higher (65.3%) and 30% higher in the educational sphere.

The factors associated with ideological gender equality are examined next. Table 7.4 presents the results of two regressions that examine the association of ideological gender equality with sociodemographic characteristics, level of structural gender inequality and inequality experiences (Model 1). The independent variable, ideological gender equality, is an index that measures inequality in the economic, political, educational and household spheres and it includes the 11 variables examined before. It measures the number of roles or activities the respondent believes men and women can perform equally well. It ranges from 0 to 11 and has good internal consistency (Cronbach alpha = .90).

The results of Model 1 show that several sociodemographic variables are associated with more gender-egalitarian ideologies. The generational differences shown previously in Figure 7.2 disappear when other relevant

Table 7.4 Regression Model of Factors Associated with Holding a Gender Egalitarian Ideology

	Model 1	Model 2
Intercept	5.95***	6.44***
Female (male)	.43***	.47***
Age	.003	.004
Place of residence (rural)		
Urban	.46***	.58**
Medium and semi-urban	.28**	.34***
Schooling (no schooling and elementary)		
Secondary	.71***	.74***
High school or equivalent	1.11***	1.04***
University	1.13***	1.26***
Occupation (employed)		
Housewife	−.35**	−0.29**
Student	.30†	.06
Retired	−0.13	.06
Unemployed	−0.09	.05
SES quintile (very low =1)[b]		
2	.28*	.28*
3	.02	−0.07
4	.38*	.34*
5 (high)	.28	.10
Gender inequality experiences		−0.37***
Gender Equality Index in Mexican States (High)		
Medium		.10
Low		−0.43***
Very Low		−0.60***
R^2=	.03	.09

Note: Reference categories are in parentheses.
N=8,303. Weighted percentages. *** $p < .0001$; ** $p < .001$; * $p < .05$; † $p < .10$
a Rural < 2,500 inhabitants; Medium and semi-urban = from 2,500 to 499,999; urban > 500,000
b Variable created according to ECLAC's methodology (ONU, 2007)

variables are included in the model. Females tend to have more egalitarian ideologies than males. Individuals who live in urban areas or semi-urban areas also tend to support more egalitarian ideologies than those who reside in rural settings. Compared to individuals who did not attend school or reached only elementary school, those with higher levels of education also tend to have higher levels of ideological gender equality. Compared to those employed, housewives show lower levels of ideological gender equality, but students tend to hold more gender-egalitarian beliefs. Socioeconomic status is associated with ideological gender equality but not in a linear way. Compared to the most unprivileged individuals (quintile 1), those in the second and fourth quintiles tend to have more egalitarian beliefs regarding the abilities and capacities of men and women in different spheres.

In Model 2, previous experience of gender inequality[14] is included as an explanatory variable. The results show that having been exposed to experiences of gender inequality, after controlling by the other factors in the model, is negatively associated with holding an egalitarian gender ideology. This might suggest that individuals are likely to acquire stereotypical beliefs by socialization—either by direct experience or by being exposed to gender inequality. This model also included the overall level of gender inequality of the state where the respondent lived, as measured by the Gender Equality Index in Mexican States. The analysis did not show any difference between individuals from states with high and medium levels of structural gender equality. However, individuals from states where the level of gender equality is low and very low tend to hold gender-egalitarian ideologies to a lesser extent. This is a relevant finding since it shows the link between individual ideology and social structures. The survey, unfortunately, did not include information about other correlates that might theoretically be associated with gender-egalitarian ideologies such as religion, peers and family of origin information, household structure and marital status.

Some Expressions of Gender Inequality in the Private and Public Spheres

The patriarchal system implies a hierarchy in which women are at the bottom of legal, political, economic and ideological structures. Gender inequality is also manifested in the private sphere and in the public sphere as discrimination against women because of their gender in aspects that men do not experience. This is the case, for example, in pregnancy-based discrimination. This section examines the extent of gender inequality in the private sphere, and the specific case of pregnancy-based discrimination in the public sphere against Mexican women to illustrate other expressions of gender inequality.

Figure 7.3 shows women's and men's experiences of gender inequality in their family of origin according to the data provided by the Survey on the Right to Equality between Men and Women 2010. The experiences of gender inequality seem to be less frequent, although non-negligible, among the youngest generations. For example, one out of four 15- to 19-year-old respondents contend that they have been in a situation in which *somebody* gave preference to male offspring, 28.1% has been in a situation in which only women do household chores, and 7.4% in one where only boys go to school. In contrast, among the oldest generations, such as those who were between 71 and 74 years old when the survey was conducted, these percentages are respectively 64.5%, 47.6% and 108% higher. A similar trend can be observed with other experiences for which the survey collected data: making women look after their brothers, making men look after their sisters and giving less freedom to women. These experiences are shared by men and women and for the majority of age intervals there are no statistically significant differences. Although experiences of gender inequality in the private

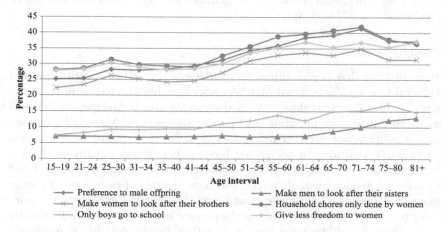

Figure 7.3 Experiences of Gender Inequality in the Private Sphere

sphere seem to have decreased for younger generations, they are still persistent in favoring males over females.

Because of their gender women face certain experiences of discrimination and violence. This is the case, for example, with the pregnancy-based discrimination presented next. According to a study by Frías (2014a) using the 2011 National Survey on Household Dynamics, 14.2% of the women who have ever been employed outside their household have been required to take a pregnancy test, and 3.1% have been fired because they were pregnant. Only during the last twelve months, 7.8% of the employed women were requested to take a pregnancy test. The percentage of women experiencing pregnancy-based discrimination measured as those who where requested to take a pregnancy test during the previous year varies by type of business establishment: 17.1% of those employed in factories; 11% of those working for the federal, state and local government; and 10.7% of those employed in education services. The fact that female public employees are the second group of women facing higher rates of pregnancy-based discrimination suggests that the different levels of the public sector fail to implement the legislation they have enacted.

Men, in contrast, are not required to take a fertility test. Women experience pregnancy and the socially assigned burden of childrearing. In Mexico, women have a 12-week paid parental leave during pregnancy and the birth of a child. However, men are only granted a five-day paternity leave after the birth or adoption of a child. This situation contrasts with that of other countries where parental leave can be shared by men and women or that grant compulsory leave to men such as Chile, Italy or Portugal. The International Labor Organization sustains that granting paternity leave by law "would be a sign of the value that society assigns to men and women's caregiving work, and would foster gender equality" (International Labor Organization, 2014, p. 8).

Conclusions

Formally, Mexico is committed to gender equality. The Constitution and General Law on Women and Men's Gender Equality aim to promote gender equality in different realms of both the private and public spheres, as well as to eradicate discrimination and gender stereotypes. Materially, women and men have not yet reached gender equality in terms of having access to valuable positions in society or having their rights equally protected. Nevertheless, according to the data presented in this chapter, structural and ideological gender inequality seems to have decreased over time. Younger generations tend to hold more gender-egalitarian attitudes toward the roles to be played by men and women in the private and public spheres than older generations. In addition, the level of structural gender equality as measured by GEIMS has increased overall by 52% (from 43.9% in 2005 to 66.9% in 2012, state-level average). This suggests that Mexican men and women are making progress toward a more egalitarian society.

There are large differences among Mexican states, however. In the country's capital, Mexico City, women have attained the greatest levels of structural gender equality (81.0), while, respectively, the northern state of Nuevo León and the southern state of Campeche have attained the lowest (56.5). On the one hand, these differences suggest the need to design public policies aimed at improving women's status in general, and specifically in those regions where gender inequality is greater. On the other, they suggest that states need to closely follow the implementation of existing legislation regarding gender equality.

Theoretically, women's attainments in the economic, political, educational and legal spheres need to be correlated with each other. However, women's political attainment in Mexico has a low association with the other spheres. This might be due to the enactment of legislation promoting mandatory affirmative actions—gender quotas—for women's representation, 40% in 2007 and 50% in 2015 (see Martínez et al., 2013). This suggests that the dynamics of women's gains in the political realm might differ from those of the other spheres.

Structural gender inequality in Mexico is associated with ideological gender inequality. This research has shown that individuals from states where the level of structural gender inequality tends to be higher are more likely to hold gender-unequal ideologies. This finding provides empirical evidence that supports the idea that ideology and social structures feed on themselves and contribute to the inequality between genders. Without women in ruling spheres, their subordination is guaranteed and the patriarchal ideology remains unchallenged; the opposite is also true. Therefore, programs aimed to reduce gender inequality need to address structural inequalities by granting women formal access to positions where they have been histori-cally excluded, as well as to challenge stereotypes and ideologies that dimin-ish women's opportunities to have access to these positions.

The data presented in this chapter suggests that Mexico is making prog-ress toward gender equality. Ideological and structural barriers are being progressively, but slowly, eroded. The General Law on Women and Men's Equality is without any doubt a powerful formal—but broadly defined—tool for fighting gender inequality. However, there are several barriers that have impeded greater progress. Just to mention some, the enactment of such legislation has been not been paralleled with institutional changes that would guarantee its full implementation, nor do institutions have enough resources—institutional capabilities—to promote, monitor and enforce the legislation. At the state level, the enactment of legislation is heterogeneous, and state governments have even fewer resources than the federal govern-ment. States are highly dependent on federal funds to carry out some of the mandates of the General Law such as prevention, assistance and eradication of gender-based violence against women (Ríos, 2014). In addition, in many states institutions responsible for guaranteeing the implementation of the laws are dependent on the government. Therefore, they are not unbiased in their evaluations of progress and do not have the institutional strength to further states' efforts to achieve gender equality.

Some progress has been made, but still more efforts in the private and public spheres are needed to achieve gender equality. I believe that gen-der equality can be achieved when gender ideologies and gender structures become stereotype-free and more inclusive. I do not believe this is impos-sible since the data presented in this chapter suggests a move to higher lev-els of gender equality. The speed at which gender equality will be attained in Mexico, nevertheless, is contingent upon the federal and state resources devoted to promote change and enforce the full implementation of already existing legislation.

Notes

1 The Gender Inequality Index (GII) measures gender inequality in three realms: reproductive health (measured by maternal mortality ratio and adolescent birth rates), empowerment (measured by the proportion of parliamentary seats occu-pied by females and proportion of males and females aged 25 years and over who reached secondary education) and labor market participation as a proxy of economic status (measured by labor force participation rate of females and males 15 years and older). It can be interpreted as a combined loss of achieve-ments in reproductive health, empowerment and labor market participation due to gender inequalities (UNDP, 2015).

2 Convention on the Nationality of Women (entry into force 1936); Charter of the United Nations in 1945, Convention (No. 45) concerning the Employment of Women on Underground Work in Mines of all Kinds in 1939; Convention (No. 100) concerning Equal Remuneration for Men and Women Workers for Work of Equal Value, or Equal Remuneration Convention in 1953; Inter-American Convention on the Granting of Civil Rights to Women in 1954,

Inter-American Convention on the Granting of Political Rights to Women in 1981; Convention and Protocol for the Suppression of the Traffic in Persons and of the Exploitation of the Prostitution of Others in 1956; Discrimination (Employment and Occupation) Convention (No. 111) in 1962; Convention on the Nationality of Married Women in 1979; Inter-American Convention on Human Rights (1981); International Covenant on Civil and Political Rights in 1981; Convention on the Political Rights of Women in 1981; International Covenant on Economic, Social and Cultural Rights in 1981; Convention on the Elimination of All Forms of Discrimination against Women also in 1981; Convention on Consent to Marriage, Minimum Age for Marriage and Registration of Marriages in 1983; Inter-American Convention on the Prevention, Punishment and Eradication of Violence against Women (Convention of Belem do Pará) in 1983; Optional Protocol to the Convention on the Elimination of All Forms of Discrimination against Women in 2002; Protocol to Prevent, Suppress and Punish Trafficking in Persons Especially Women and Children, supplementing the United Nations Convention against Transnational Organized Crime in 2003.

3 The Universal Declaration of Human Rights (1948); Declaration on the Elimination of All Forms of Discrimination against Women (1967); Convention on the Rights of the Child (1989); Declaration on the Elimination of Violence against Women (1993); First (Mexico 1975), Second (Copenhagen 1980), Third (Nairobi 1985) and Fourth (Beijing 1995) World Conferences for Women; International Conference on Population and Development (Cairo 1994); United Nations Summit on Social Development (Copenhagen 1995); First UN International Agencies Meeting on Women and Gender Equality (IAMWGE) (1996).

4 Article 1 was reformed in 2010, and Article 4 was modified in 1974, just before the First World Conference for Women was held in Mexico City in 1975.

5 CEDAW defines gender discrimination as "any distinction, exclusion or restriction made on the basis of sex which has the effect or purpose of impairing or nullifying the recognition, enjoyment or exercise by women, irrespective of their marital status, on a basis of equality of men and women, of human rights and fundamental freedoms in the political, economic, social, cultural, civil or any other field" (Article 1).

6 Gender mainstreaming has been translated into Spanish as *transversalidad* or *transversalización de la perspectiva de género* (Rigat-Pflaum, 2008). In the 2013 reform, *transversalidad* was defined "as the process that allows guaranteeing the adoption of a gender perspective in public and private activities with the goal of evaluating the implications that any legislation, public policy and administrative, economic and cultural activities might have on women and men" (General Law on Women and Men's Equality, Article 5. VII).

7 The National Development Plan contains the guidelines and the basic strategies to be followed by the federal public administration during each presidential period (lasts six years in Mexico). The Planning Law (enacted in 1983, during the presidency of Miguel de la Madrid (1982–1988), mandates public federal programs to be associated with the National Development Plan.

8 About 400 million dollars in 2008 and about 1,072 million dollars as of March 2016.

9 This section was previously published as "Gender equality in Mexico" (Frías, 2014b) (reproduced here with permission of Springer).

10 The use of multiple variables overcomes the limitations of other measures of gender inequality that only include one variable per dimension.

11 Gender quotas are an affirmative action in order to increase women's representation in certain areas of social life. Quotas are considered an exception to the legal norm of gender equality. The first gender quota regulation was introduced in 1993 in the Federal Code of Institutions and Electoral Procedures. Since then,

it was reformed several times in which the quota percentage increased. The General Law on Institutions and Electoral Procedures replaced the Code in 2014 and mandates political parties promote and guarantee gender parity in federal and state congresses.

12 *"Juanita"* is a derogatory term coined to describe and name those female candidates who enter an electoral race leading a ticket where the substitute candidate is a man to comply with quotas established in electoral legislation aimed at closing the gender gap within the political parties and, ultimately, the Mexican Congress (House of Representatives and the Senate). Once elected, the *"Juanita"* candidate, now a member of the congress, steps down so that her male substitute can take her place, which effectively nullifies the original purpose of the electoral rules aimed at closing the gender gap. The name "Juanita" comes after Rafael Acosta (Worker's Party), nicknamed Juanito. "Juanito" won the 2009 election at the district of Iztapalapa in Mexico City and had to resign in favor of Clara Brugada (Revolutionary Democratic Party).

13 Data provided by the Department of Health as a result of a request to the Federal Institute for Access to Information and Data Protection.

14 This variable is an index of exposure of previous gender inequality situations, such as if the individual has been exposed to situation in which: (a) preference is given to male children; (b) preference is given to female children; (c) women are forced to look after their brothers; (d) men are forced to protect their sisters; (e) household chores are exclusively performed by women; (f) household chores are exclusively performed by males; (g) only boys are sent to school; (h) only girls are sent to school; (i) women are given less freedom than men; (j) men are given less freedom than women.

References

Asociación Nacional de Universidades e Instituciones de Educación Superior. (2013). *Anuarios estadísticos de educación superior*. Mexico City: ANUIES. Retrieved from http://www.anuies.mx/informacion-y-servicios/informacion-estadistica-de-educacion-superior/anuario-estadistico-de-educacion-superior (accessed 1 April 2016).

Bericat, E. (2012). The European gender equality index: Conceptual and analytical issues. *Social Indicators Research*, **108** (1), 1–28.

Bericat, E., & Sánchez Bermejo, E. (2016). Structural gender equality in Europe and its evolution over the first decade of the twentyfirst century. *Social Indicators Research*, **127** (1), 1–27.

Brewer, V.E., & Smith, M.D. (1995). Gender inequality and rates of female homicide victimization across U.S. cities. *Journal of Research in Crime and Delinquency*, **32** (2), 175–190.

Brinda, E., Rajkumar, A.P., & Enemark, U. (2015). Association between gender inequality index and child mortality rates: A cross-national study of 138 countries. *BMC Public Health*, **15** (97). DOI: 10.1186/s12889–12015–11449–12883. <http://bmcpublichealth.biomedcentral.com/articles/10.1186/s12889-015-1449-3>

Charles, N. (2000). *Feminism, the State and Social Policy*. New York: St. Martin's Press.

CNDH. (2011). *Cuarto Informe Especial 2010 sobre el Derecho de Igualdad entre Mujeres y Hombres*. México, DF: CNDH. Retrieved from http://www.cndh.org.mx/sites/all/doc/programas/mujer/10_InformesEspeciales/10.4/10.4.pdf (accessed 20 February 2016).

CNDH. (2014). *Séptimo Informe especial 2013 sobre el derecho de igualdad entre mujeres y hombres*. México, DF: CNDH. Retrieved from http://www.cndh. org.mx/sites/all/doc/programas/mujer/10_InformesEspeciales/10.7/10.7.pdf (accessed 1 May 2016).

Connell, R.W. (1990). The state, gender and sexual politics: Theory and appraisal. *Theory and Society*, 19 (5), 507–544.

Consejo de la Judicatura Federal. (2012). *Directorio de Órganos Jurisdiccionales*. México, DF: Consejo de la Judicatura Federal. Retrieved from http://www.cjf. gob.mx/Directorios.htm (accessed 10 April 2012).

DeWees, M.A., & Parker, K.F. (2003). Women, region and types of homicide. *Homicide Studies*, 7 (4), 368–393.

Díaz-Olavarrieta, C., & Sotelo, J. (1996). Domestic violence in Mexico. *Journal of the American Medical Association*, 275 (24), 1937–1941.

Di Noia, J. (2002). Indicators of gender equality for American states and regions: An update. *Social Indicators Research*, 59 (1), 35–77.

Dobash, R.E., & Dobash, R.P. (1979). *Violence against Wives: A Case against the Patriarchy*. New York: Free Press.

Federal Law on Prevention and Eradication of Discrimination (*Ley Federal para Prevenir y Eliminar la Discriminación*). (2003). Diario Oficial No. 2003. Retrieved from http://www.diputados.gob.mx/LeyesBiblio/pdf/262.pdf (accessed 10 March 2016).

Frías, S.M. (2008). Measuring structural gender inequality: Toward the construction of a gender equality index in Mexican states. *Social Indicators Research*, 88 (2), 215–246.

Frías, S.M. (2009). *Gender, the State and Patriarchy: Partner Violence in Mexico*. Saarbrücken, Germany: VDM.

Frías, S.M. (2014a). Acoso, hostigamiento y violencia sexual en el trabajo y en el ámbito público. In I. Casique & R. Castro (Eds), *Expresiones y Contextos de la Violencia contra las Mujeres en México*, Cuernavaca, Mexico: INMUJERES & CRIM, pp. 313–365.

Frías, S.M. (2014b). Gender equality in Mexico. In A. Michalos (Ed.), *Encylopedia of Quality of Live and Well-Being Research*, Dordrecht, Netherlands: Springer, pp. 2430–2436.

General Law on Women and Men's Equality (*Ley General para la Igualdad entre Mujeres y Hombres*). (2006). Diario Oficial No. 2006. Retrieved from http:// www.diputados.gob.mx/LeyesBiblio/pdf/LGIMH_240316.pdf (accessed 8 July 2016).

General Law on Women's Access to a Life Free of Violence (*Ley General de Acceso de las Mujeres a una Vida Libre de Violencia*). (2007). Diario Oficial No. 2006. Retrieved from http://www.diputados.gob.mx/LeyesBiblio/pdf/LGAMVLV_1712 15.pdf (accesed 10 February 2016).

Gobierno de la República. (2013). *Programa Nacional para la Igualdad de Oportunidades y No Discriminación Contra las Mujeres*. México, DF: Presidencia. Retrieved from http://cedoc.inmujeres.gob.mx/documentos_download/101222. pdf (accessed 21 January 2016).

Guttmann, M.C. (1996). *The Meanings of Macho: Being a Man in Mexico City*. Berkeley, CA: University of California Press.

Inegi. (2010). *Censo de Población y Vivienda 2010*. Aguascalientes, Mexico: Inegi. Retrieved from http://www.inegi.org.mx/est/lista_cubos/consulta.aspx?p=pob&c=1 (accessed 10 March 2012).

Inegi. (2013). *Hombres y Mujeres en México 2012*. Aguascalientes, Mexico: Inegi. Retrieved from http://cedoc.inmujeres.gob.mx/documentos_download/101215. pdf (accessed 28 April 2012).

Inegi & Secretaría de Trabajo y Previsión Social. (2011). *National Survey on Occupation and Employment*. Aguascalientes, Mexico: Inegi. Retrieved from http://www.inegi. org.mx/est/lista_cubos/consulta.aspx?p=encue&c=3 (accessed 20 March 2012).

Instituto Nacional para el Federalismo y el Desarrollo Municipal. (2005). Sistema Nacional de Información Municipal. Retrieved from http://www.inafed.gob.mx (accessed 18 September 2012).

International Labour Organization. (2014). La Maternidad y la Paternidad en el Trabajo. Retrieved from http://www.ilo.org/wcmsp5/groups/public/—-dgreports/—-dcomm/documents/publication/wcms_242618.pdf (accessed 1 March 2016).

Jones, M.P. (1997). Legislator gender and legislator policy priorities in the Argentine chamber of deputies and the United States house of representatives. *Policy Studies Journal*, 25 (3), 613–629.

Jones, M.P. (2008). Gender quotas, electoral laws and the election of women: Evidence from the Latin American vanguard. *Comparative Political Studies*, 42 (1), 56–81.

Kantola, J., & Dahl, H.M. (2005). Gender and the state: From differences between to differenes within. *International Feminist Journal of Politics*, 7 (1), 49–70.

Kaufman Kantor, G., Jasinski, J.J., & Aldarondo, E. (1994). Sociocultural status and incidence of marital violence in Hispanic families. *Violence and Victims*, 9 (3), 207–222.

Klasen, S. (2002). Low schooling for girls, slower growth for all? Cross-country evidence on the effect of gender inequality in education on economic development. *The World Bank Economic Review*, 16 (3), 345–373.

Lloren, A. (2015). Women's substantive representation: Defending feminist interests or women's electoral preferences. *The Journal of Legislative Studies*, 21 (2), 144–167.

Loscertales, F. (2007). Las mujeres y los medios de comunicación: Interacciones y consecuencias. In F. Loscertales & T. Núñez (Eds), *La Mirada de las Mujeres en la Sociedad de la Información*, Madrid: Siranda Editorial, pp. 71–88.

MacKinnon, C.A. (1989). *Toward a Feminist Theory of the State*. Cambridge, MA: Harvard University Press.

Martínez, M.A., & Garrido, A. (2013). Representación descriptiva y sustantiva: La doble brecha de género en América Latina. *Revista Mexicana de Sociología*, 75 (3), 407–438.

Moghadam, V.M. (2004). Patriarchy in transition: Women and the changing family in the Middle East. *Journal of Comparative Family Studies*, 35 (2), 137–162.

Morash, M., Bui, H.N., & Santiago, A.M. (2000). Cultural-specific gender ideology and wife abuse in Mexican-descent families. *Domestic Violence: Global Responses*, 67 (7), 67–91.

ONU. (1981). Convention on the Elimination of All Forms of Discrimination against Women. Retrieved from http://www.un.org/womenwatch/daw/cedaw/index.html (accesed 29 December 2007).

ONU. (1995). Declaración y Plataforma de Acción de Beijing. Retrieved from http://www.un.org/womenwatch/daw/beijing/pdf/BDPfA%20S.pdf (accesed 1 May 2016).

ONU. (2007). *Potencialidades y Aplicaciones de los Datos Censales: Una Contribución a la Explotación del Censo de Población y Vivienda en Nicaragua*. Santiago de Chile: CEPAL.

ONU. (2012). *México ante la CEDAW*. México City: UN. Retrieved from http://www.hchr.org.mx/index.php?option=com_content&view=article&id=173:conoce-todas-las-recomendaciones-que-este-comite-le-ha-hecho-al-estado-mexicano&catid=17&Itemid=278 (accessed 2 May 2016).

Political Constitution of the Mexican United States. (Constitución Política de los Estados Unidos Mexicanos). (1917). Diario Oficial No. 1917. Retrieved from http://www.diputados.gob.mx/LeyesBiblio/ref/cpeum.htm (accessed 13 August 2016).

Reynolds, A. (1999). Women in the legislatures and executives of the world: Knocking at the highest glass ceiling. *World Politics*, 51 (4), 547–572.

Rigat-Pflaum, M. (2008). Gender Mainstreaming: Un enfoque para la igualdad de género. *Nueva Sociedad*, 218, 40–56.

Ríos, A. (2014). Los Institutos estatales de la mujer: Diagnóstico, retos y perspectivas. In UNPD (Ed.), *Indicadores de Desarrollo Humano y Género en México: Nueva Metodología: Identificar las Barreras para Lograr la Igualdad*, México: UNDP, pp. 23–47.

Rodríguez, V.E. (2003). *Women in Contemporary Mexican Politics*. Austin, TX: University of Texas Press.

Rodríguez Peñaloza, M., Arriaga Álvarez, E.G., & Ángeles Constantino, M.I. (2013). Cultura democrática de género: Discriminación, cuotas de género y simulación. *Espacios Públicos*, 16 (38), 41–63.

Saxonberg, S. (2000). Women in East European parliaments. *Journal of Democracy*, 11 (2), 145–158.

Smith, M.D. (1990). Patriarchal ideology and wife beating: A test of feminist hypothesis. *Violence and Victims*, 5 (4), 257–273.

Straus, M.A. (1994). State-to-state differences in social inequality and social bonds in relation to assaults on wives in the United States. *Journal of Comparative Family Studies*, 25 (1), 7–24.

Sugarman, D.B., & Straus, M.A. (1988). Indicators of gender equality for American states and regions. *Social Indicators Research*, 20 (3), 229–270.

Titterington, V.B. (2006). A retrospective investigation of gender inequality and female homicide victimization. *Sociological Spectrum*, 26 (2), 205–236.

UNDP. (1995). *Human Development Report 1995*. New York: Oxford University Press.

UNDP. (2015). *2015 Human Development Report*. New York: UNDP. Retrieved from http://hdr.undp.org/sites/default/files/2015_human_development_report.pdf (accessed 29 February 2016).

Williams, J.E., & Best, D.L. (1990). *Measuring Sex Stereotypes: A Multination Study*. Thousand Oaks, CA: Sage.

Yllo, K. (1980). The status of women and wife-beating in the U.S.: A multi-level analysis. Paper presented at the National Council of Family Relations, Portland, Oregon.

Yodanis, C. L. (2004). Gender Inequality, Violence against Women, and Fear: A Cross-National Test of Feminist Theory of Violence against Women. *Journal of Interpersonal Violence*, 19 (6), 655–675.

Young, G., Fort, L., & Danner, M. (1994). Moving from "the status of women" to "gender inequality": Conceptualisation, social indicators and an empirical application. *International Sociology*, 9 (1), 55–85.

8   Gender Equality in the United States

Colleen E. Arendt and Patrice M. Buzzanell

Gender equality in the United States has, at times, been an activist movement in and of itself and, more recently, has been subsumed within diversity and inclusion as well as human rights initiatives. As an activist movement, gender equality has shaped and been shaped by three distinct major "waves." The first wave focused on women's suffrage, or the right of women to vote, which appealed to the ways women differently and necessarily shaped the moral character of the nation and culminated in the passing of the 19th amendment to the US Constitution in 1920. In the 1960s and 1970s and concurrent with social change (e.g., widespread political unrest, demographic shifts including large-scale entry of white women into the US labor force, and other activist agendas such as civil rights), the second wave fostered the reexamination of legal, institutional, socialization, cultural, psychic, biological and other forces that contribute to differential treatment of women and men (for overview, see Buzzanell, 1994). These forces, while noting difference, were also harnessed for sameness arguments for women's rights to equal pay and distribution of marital properties upon marital dissolution, amongst other arguments, legislation, policies and practices in institutions across sectors.

Beginning in the 1990s and early 2000s, the third wave and, some would argue, subsequent waves, fostered more complicated considerations and correctives or expansions of gender equality agendas. Third-wave agendas sought to transcend the difference-versus-sameness (either-or) dialectics and foster more dialogic (both-and) arguments useful in domestically diverse, global, technologically sophisticated and virtual transnational organizing world. In addition to recognizing the need to incorporate women and men of color, class, sexual orientations and other differences that sustained deeply embedded power dynamics, more recent movements also admitted that moral, demographic and business cases for equality were necessary but insufficient to promote sustainable change. Indeed, gender equality and, more broadly, diversity and inclusion agendas are considered worthy causes in and of themselves, in addition to being consistent with labor force profiles and essential for harnessing talent and innovative capacities (Pauly & Buzzanell, 2016). Moreover, these initiatives promote institutional reputations within the US population at large.

Even so, some contend that the United States is in a post-feminist era where equality is achieved legally, politically and in practice (Faludi, 2006). Popular media contend "choice" now distinguishes what, how and why women and men conduct their work and personal lives differently (McRobbie, 2004) and "microaggressions" or covert and benign sexisms (i.e., everyday talk and interactions that exclude women, and beliefs against sexism that contradict behavior) often unintentionally maintain the status quo (Sue, 2010). Moreover, neoliberal political economic agendas within the United States not only promote such choice rhetorics and beliefs undermining gender equality but also consider gender disparities to be the results of individual efforts and meritocracy, rather than systemic differences and advantages in upbringing, majority membership and access to financial and other resources (Edgell et al., 2016; Hayden & O'Brien Hallstein, 2010).

Gender equality often is subsumed within widespread diversity (promoting representation) and inclusion (constructing climates of participation and belongingness) initiatives that attempt to strategically manage difference as leverage for beneficial institutional and corporate outcomes (for critique of global diversity management, see Pauly & Buzzanell, 2016). Gender equality is also incorporated within global human rights agendas, although more recent human rights campaigns situate women and gender initiatives within large-scale projects aimed at the promotion of democratic, economic and food security, clean water and non-violence campaigns (for overview, see Naples & Gurr, 2016). As a result, there remains much work to do regarding gender as a category in and of itself and in regarding men as benefiting from gender equality efforts. Given this broad historical, social, political and cultural backdrop for situating gender equality in the United States, this chapter aims to chart the landscape of contemporary gender equality focusing on particular contexts and current discussions. The second part of this chapter describes where contradictions offer opportunities for further change. Our closing offers some recommendations for change.

Part I. US Landscape of Gender Equality

Long considered a forerunner in diversity management and a country against which other nations benchmark their efforts (see Klarsfeld, 2010; Klarsfeld et al., 2014), the United States in many ways both exemplifies and challenges understandings of how gender equality can be promoted ideologically and accomplished in practice. In this section, we document specific contexts in which laws and practices advance gender equality. These contexts include: (a) education, (b) workforce, (c) healthcare and (d) politics and law.

Gender Equality in Education

Education has long been regarded as a means to promote gender equality for a politically astute citizenry, economic advantage and needed skills for national development. In the United States, all boys and girls are educated by law through secondary education (although there are differences at the state level in terms of the age at which students are allowed to drop out of school voluntarily (National Center for Education Statistics, 2015). Furthermore, more women than men are now earning college, master's and Ph.D. degrees (National Center for Education Statistics, 2016a; National Science Foundation, 2016), and the White House called for the entry and retention of more women in STEM disciplines (science, technology, engineering and math) in February 2013 (United States Office of Science and Technology Policy, 2016).

Despite these policies and national agendas, the United States as a whole ranks poorly in education (#40 according to the Global Gender Gap Index [World Economic Forum, 2016). One of the highlights of gender equality regarding education is the fact that, by law, both boys are girls must attend schooling, usually at least until age 16. Additionally, 95.1% of women in the United States have at least some secondary education, slightly more than US men, at 94.8% (United Nations Human Rights, 2015). Women also have more higher education than men: 37.1% of women hold at least a bachelor's degree, which is slightly higher than men in the United States at 34.9% (United States Department of Labor, 2011). According to the Council of Economic Advisers (2014b), women are more likely to attend and complete graduate school and as of 2013, 25–34-year-old women are 21% more likely to be college graduates and 48% more likely to have completed graduate school than men. Overall, women earn almost 60% of all undergraduate degrees awarded, 60% of all master's degrees (Warner, 2014) and 52% of all doctoral degrees (National Center for Education Statistics, 2016a).

This acceleration of higher education attainment by women has led some to argue that *all* men are being left behind at the expense of women's equality. However, there remains a great disparity in who is and is not earning these degrees. Broken down by race, the data show that 18–24-year-old white men and women continue to earn college degrees in near percentages at 40.2% and 44.2%, respectively, while only 28.5% of black men and 30.3% of Hispanic men aged 18–24 are earning bachelor's degrees. Meanwhile, at 44.2%, white women may earn more college degrees than black women (36.6%) and Hispanic women (39.4%) (National Center for Education Statistics, 2016c), but the disparity between races is greater for men than for women. Conversely, white men are earning 70% of bachelor's degrees awarded to men, while black men are earning only 9% and Hispanic men are earning 11%. Once again, the disparity between white men and women is small, with white women earning 66% of all bachelor's degrees awarded to women, while black and Hispanic women each earn 12% of the bachelor's degrees awarded to women (National Center for Education Statistics, 2016b).

Additionally, although women may be entering and completing higher education in greater numbers, the fields they are entering are not uniform.

Though occupational segregation has decreased to such an extent that young college-educated women are just as likely to be doctors, dentists and attorneys as they are teachers, nurses or administrative assistants (secretaries) (Council of Economic Advisers, 2014b), their participation in certain STEM disciplines remains low. Women earn 50.4% of bachelor's degrees in science and engineering, but far fewer degrees in certain subfields, such as computer sciences (18.2%), engineering (19.2%) and physics (19.1%). This dearth of participation has important consequences for women's employment. Specifically, this disparity matters because STEM degrees have lower unemployment rates, with greater job growth in future decades, and pay more than non-STEM degrees (Bureau of Labor Statistics, 2014; Jones, 2014; The White House, 2016). These and other consequences will be addressed more thoroughly in the next section.

Many scholars have examined the roots of this discrepancy. Research findings suggest that the pathways or barriers to entry begin early in children's education as they figure out the meanings of work, gender politics and power and prestige issues as young as 2–4 years old (Buzzanell et al., 2011).

In summary, women have made exceptional gains, broadly speaking, in education. Despite being underrepresented in the highly prestigious, well-compensated and high-employment STEM disciplines, the overall picture of women's education is a positive one, and has been for at least a generation. Unfortunately, despite the fact that women have been earning more post-secondary diplomas than men for *decades* (since 1982 for bachelors, 1987 for master's and 2006 for doctorates) (Catalyst, 2014), the next section will discuss many continuing workforce barriers to gender equality.

Gender Equality in the Workforce

Gender equality in the workforce has been making slow progress since women's mass entry into the workforce in the 1950s. We acknowledge that poor women and women of color have always been in the labor force but demographers took note when white women, even with young children, left homes in large numbers to engage in paid work (e.g., see Medved, 2015). This section breaks down the struggles for gender equality into three sections: women's representation, pay inequality and paid and unpaid leave.

Women's Representation

First, women represent 47% of the labor force in the US and 59% of the college-educated, entry-level workforce (Council of Economic Advisers, 2015; Warner, 2014). However, despite earning a majority of college degrees, and representing 47% of the labor force in the US and 59% of the college-educated, entry-level workforce (Warner, 2014), women's representation begins to narrow with every ascending level of the workforce, much like a pyramid. According to Catalyst (2016), women comprise 45% of the workforce in S&P[1] 500 companies, yet only 37% of first- and mid-level managers, and only 25% of executive or senior managers, 19% of board members, and represent only 4% of Chief Executive Officers. Despite research and company analyses demonstrating that both women CEOs and companies with women board members outperform other companies (Adams, 2014; Catalyst, 2007; Fairchild, 2014), too few companies include women at the highest levels.

Pay Inequality

According the Council of Economic Advisers (2014b), "on average, full-time, year-round women workers make 78 percent of what men earn" (p. 12). The pay gap is even greater for women of color: compared to non-Hispanic white men, non-Hispanic black women earned 64 cents and Hispanic women earned 56 cents for every dollar earned for full-time, year-round, employment by non-Hispanic white men in 2013 (Council of Economic Advisers, 2014b). The wage gap persists across a variety of sectors, across income distributions and within occupations, when men and women work side-by-side completing similar tasks, and is particularly high even among workers with professional degrees, where men earn nearly 50% more than women by their late thirties, despite women's earnings being slightly higher than men's in their twenties (Council of Economic Advisers, 2014b). Women are also more likely to work in minimum wage jobs and work in lower-paying occupations (Council of Economic Advisers, 2014b, 2015).

The first bill President Obama signed in office was the Lilly Ledbetter Fair Pay Act of 2009, which stipulates that employees have a 180-day statute of limitations to file an equal pay lawsuit that resets after *each* distributed paycheck to the employee, which overturned an earlier law giving employees only 180 days from the initial unequal paycheck, i.e., only 180 days into his or her job, to file a lawsuit (United States Equal Employment Opportunity Commission [EEOC], 2016). That earlier law was upheld by a 5–4 Supreme Court decision in *Ledbetter v. Goodyear Tire & Rubber Co.* Of the decision, dissenting justice Ruth Bader Ginsburg wrote: "In our view, the court does not comprehend, or is indifferent to, the insidious way in which women can be victims of pay discrimination" (Barnes, 2007, para. 5).

Paid and Unpaid Leave

The United States is one of only two countries—the other being Papua New Guinea—who offer no paid maternity leave, according to the International Labor Organization's (2015) study of 188 countries, not all of whom are considered developed or industrialized.

Considered groundbreaking legislation at the time it was passed in 1993, the Family Medical Leave Act protects employees' jobs for up to 12 weeks if they need to take family leave for qualifying medical or family reasons, such as for a new birth, adoption or elder care. However, this protected leave is *unpaid*, meaning that many employees cannot afford to take advantage of it. In addition, the act provides a number of exemptions for employers. In order to be covered, an employee must work for a location with 50 or more employees, and must have worked there for at least a year and at least 1,250 hours over the prior year. As a result of these exemptions, only 60% of workers, and not even one-fifth of new mothers, are even covered by the act (Council of Economic Advisers, 2014a).

Some companies offer paid maternity leave for some workers in varying industries, usually stipulating that a woman must work for a particular number of years before being eligible, but for many women that paid leave is often only six weeks. Large disparities exist in who has access to paid leave. The gap in this access is particularly high for Hispanics, less educated workers and low-wage workers. According the Council of Economic Advisers (2014a), college-educated workers are more than twice as likely to have access to paid leave than workers without a high school degree and workers in the top income quartile are 1.7 times as likely to have access to paid leave than workers in the bottom quartile of income. Considering our earlier figures demonstrating the discrepancy between who are earning college degrees, clearly the ability to earn a college degree has large implications not only for future earnings, but for access to paid leave later in life—as well as access to employment that offers some scheduling flexibility (Council of Economic Advisers, 2014a).

Finally, considerations regarding gender equality in the workplace may be stifled because of the prominence of sex difference language and policies rather than considerations of organizations and organizing as gendered (Ashcraft & Mumby, 2004). In other words, language, imagery and policy content may prompt gender disparities about which many are unaware, especially because they assume that organizing is neutral. For instance, prominent imagery of organizations and organizing maintain that the institutional contexts are genderless, with the best rising to the top through competitive career systems, the ideal worker being unhindered by family and other non-organizational aspects, and the war imagery predominating and promoting rational, strategic, linear and objectively based thinking and action is primary (see Buzzanell, 1994, 2000; Kemp, 2016). In this regard, gender equality persists in the workplace, a claim recently supported by 40 years of research on gender stereotypes in science but also applicable to other domains (Miller et al., 2015).

Gender Equality in Health Care

Kreps (2004) noted several characteristics of health care that reinforce gender inequalities particularly for US health care systems and members. These issues include: dysfunction in modern health care (e.g., bureaucratization leading to inefficiencies, injustices and constraints for those needing services) and marginalization of women consumers of health care (i.e., "widespread evidence of profound discrimination and gender bias in the provision of health care for women who are often denied equal access to competent care and treatment" and who are not the standard for clinical research and health care policy (p. 171).

The Patient Protection and Affordable Care Act of 2010 (upheld by Supreme Court in 2012), frequently called "Obamacare," marked a significant improvement in healthcare for women. The Act, first signed into law in 2010 and upheld by the Supreme Court in 2012,[2] gives 47 million women access to guaranteed preventive women's health services and no-cost birth control (low-cost birth control was a major barrier to many women prior to the ACA; many women's insurance companies would not cover women's contraceptives). In addition, the ACA gave nearly nine million women new access to guaranteed maternity care (*Obamacare Facts*, 2016). As of 2014, the new law also prevents insurance companies from charging women more for identical health plans; prior to the law women were charged $1 billion dollars more per year for the same health plans on the individual market (i.e., not through one's employers).[3]

Unfortunately, despite the progress achieved thanks to ACA's legislation, women's access to reproductive health is under threat or already diminishing at an alarming rate across many areas of the country. Reasons include legislation designed to force the closure of abortion clinics in certain states, a policy in many states of teaching abstinence-only sex education in schools instead of comprehensive sex education, and concerted attacks to defund Planned Parenthood, one of the nation's largest providers of low-cost women's healthcare. Planned Parenthood is often under attack because one of the services they provide is abortion. As will be discussed shortly, abortion remains a highly contentious topic in the United States with some states fighting to outlaw it.

Gender Equality in Politics

Arguably, one of the reasons why gender equality has not progressed further is the lack of gender diversity (and overall diversity) in our political system. Before he was elected president, Barack Obama was only the fifth African American ever elected to the US Senate, one of the two chambers of Congress that comprises our legislative branch, and only one African American woman has ever been elected to the Senate (United States Senate, 2016). Currently women comprise 19.4% of Congress (Center for American Women in Politics [CAWP], 2016). Additionally, 24 states (out of 50) have never elected a woman governor, 22 states have never elected a woman to the US Senate, and four states have never elected a woman to either the Senate or the House of Representatives (American Association of University Women [AAUW], 2014). Nationwide, the proportion of women in state legislatures is 24.5% and currently only six states have women governors (CAWP, 2016).

At the executive level, Obama was the first African American to be elected president, and to date, no woman has ever been elected president or vice president of the United States. In 2016, former Senator from New York and Secretary of State Hillary Clinton ran unsuccessfully for president for the Democratic Party. Prior to Clinton's historic candidacy, only two women have ever been on the presidential ballot as Vice Presidential running mates of a major political party, Geraldine Ferraro in 1984 for the Democrats and Sarah Palin in 2008 for the Republicans.

Part II: Contradictions and Opportunities for Gender Equality

In this second part of our chapter, we ask why the landscape of gender equality indicates advances in, but also tensions that complicate, the achievement of gender equality in the United States. We begin with (a) global comparisons, then discuss the (b) legal structure of the United States, and conclude with (c) some reasons why the United States has such a contradictory gender equality profile.

Global Comparisons

First, despite many significant advances in gender equality, the United States still falls behind many other countries in a variety of important markers. According to the 2015 Global Gender Gap Index (World Economic Forum, 2016), the United States ranks #40 in education, #60 in women's empowerment, #64 in health and survival and #72 in politics. The United Nations sent a working group to the United States in December 2015 to research the issue of discrimination against women in law and in practice in the United States. The working group noted that despite promises in 2010 and 2015 to ratify the Convention on the Elimination of All of Forms of Discrimination Against Women, CEDAW, the United States remains one of only seven countries that have not signed the convention because of differing political goals and opinions.[4] The working group recommends the United States not only sign the CEDAW but also pass the Equal Rights Amendment, which was first introduced in the 1920s and never passed, so that women's status as equal citizens protected from discrimination becomes codified in the United States Constitution.

Describing the state of gender equality and discrimination in the United States, the United Nations Human Rights working group (2015) wrote in their final report:

> . . . in global context, US women do not take their rightful place as citizens of the world's leading economy, which has one of the highest rates of per capita income. In the US, women fall behind international

standards as regards their public and political representation, their economic and social rights and their health and safety protections. . . . Our visit is particularly timely at a moment when the political rhetoric of some of the candidates for the Presidency in the upcoming elections has included unprecedented hostile stereotyping of women; when there are increasingly restrictive legislative measures in some states and violent attacks to prevent women's access to exercise of their reproductive rights; and when there is an increase in the rate of women living in poverty, a persistent wage gap and increasingly precarious employment.

(para. 3 & 7)

US Legal Structure

Complicating the question of gender equality of the United States is the governing structure of the country, specifically, the divide and tension between the federal government's ultimate jurisdiction with each state's own laws, many of which reflect their own culture, demographics and history. Before moving into issues concerning states and gender equality, we first discuss how the country's complicated governing structure and its tensions are perhaps best exemplified in two court battles regarding same-sex marriage and women's access to abortion.

In June 2015 the Supreme Court ruled 5–4 in *Obergefell v. Hodges* that state bans on same-sex marriage are unconstitutional and states must allow and recognize same-sex marriage. Prior to this landmark ruling, which immediately made same-sex marriage legal nationwide, states were allowed to decide on the legality of gay marriage (other states would not be forced to recognize same-sex marriages performed in other states). Previously, individual states had been following two paths: some states legalized gay marriage while others passed marriage amendments banning same-sex marriage, with the idea that an amendment to a state's constitution would make it much harder for future legislatures (and generations) to overturn and legalize. At the time of the *Obergefell v. Hodges* ruling, when same-sex marriage became the "law of the land," 36 states and Washington, DC had already legalized it and the remaining 14 states had passed constitutional amendments banning it (Garvin, 2016).[5]

Without that Supreme Court decision, the remaining 14 states might not have legalized same-sex marriage for decades, if ever. This is because of regional and state-by-state differences in the acceptance of LGBTQ individuals. In addition, even if some states have citizens who might be more accepting of same-sex marriage, their state officials might fight adamantly against legalizing it due to religious beliefs, or pressure from donors. Also, severe gerrymandering in some states would make electing officials who more accurately represent a state's population difficult, if not impossible. Although the case of LGBTQ differs somewhat from the overall treatment of gender equality in this chapter, it provides a recent and highly controversial case of how difference, including sexual orientation and gender, moves through and can be stymied in the US political system.

Now that gay marriage is legalized nationwide, some states are still fighting the decision in other ways. For example, some state legislatures have passed, or are trying to pass, dozens of "religious freedom" laws allowing businesses, like wedding vendors, from helping gay marriage, such as bakeries making cakes for gay weddings. As just two examples, Indiana passed their "Religious Freedom Restoration Act" and Georgia has their "Religious Liberty Bill," which was passed by legislators but vetoed by Governor Deal after immense pressure from businesses including Coca-Cola, Delta Airlines, the National Football League, and film and media companies like Disney and Marvel, as a number of television shows and movies are filmed in Georgia.

In addition, legalizing same-sex marriage has not protected LGBTQ couples from discrimination at the state level. For example, employers being asked to now provide spousal benefits to a newly-married gay employee could fire him or her, and depending on the state, employers would be acting within their rights. That is because 28 states do not protect LGBTQ individuals from discrimination, including housing, employment and interactional discrimination, as in the case of wedding vendors mentioned above, or gay teachers who teach in private, religious schools. Of the states that do outlaw gender discrimination, three states—New York, New Hampshire and Wisconsin—do not protect its transgender citizens (Green, 2016). Clearly, though same-sex marriage may be legalized and recognized nationwide, states are utilizing their individual authority to chip away at same-sex rights that may or may not be related to marriage. In July 2015, the Equality Act was introduced to Congress. This proposed legislation would update existing federal civil rights laws such as the Civil Rights Act (1964) and the Fair Housing Act (1968) to include protections for LGBTQ persons, including outlawing discrimination in public spaces and services as well as federally funded programs on the basis of sex (Human Rights Campaign, 2016).

The second example of federal versus state legislation regards women's access to abortion, which became legalized at the federal level in the famous and still-controversial 1973 *Roe v. Wade* decision. As with gay marriage, because of the design of the United States' legal system, the fight for abortion rights did not end with a federal decision in *Roe v. Wade*. Rather, each state can create its own laws, which can be challenged in either state court or federal court. If the case involves a federal law or the US Constitution, a losing party could appeal all the way to the Supreme Court of the United States (SCOTUS), regardless of whether the case started in state court or federal court. If SCOTUS decides to hear a case, it determines whether a law violates federal law or the US Constitution.

Because of this legal system, ever since the *Roe v. Wade* decision legalized abortion more than 40 years ago, abortion remains a key topic in elections across the country. Candidates and voters identify as "pro-choice" or "pro-life." Many states fight the ruling at the state level, proposing and passing more and more restrictive laws when able. Arguably, more important than the *Roe v. Wade* decision is the 1992 *Planned Parenthood v. Casey* decision, which, while upholding the *Roe v. Wade* decision, allowed states to set their own restrictions to a woman's access to abortion, provided that these restrictions, like mandatory waiting periods or parental consent, do not create an "undue burden" to the women seeking abortions. The *Planned Parenthood v. Casey* decision, while overturning spousal consent laws, chipped away at the *Roe* decision by ruling that some restrictions were acceptable; a woman's access to abortion was not unfettered. Abortion opponents in the years since *Casey* shifted strategy and instead focused on restrictions involving clinics under TRAP, or Targeted Regulation of Abortion Providers, laws. This strategy has proven so successful that it has taken abortion rights advocates by surprise (Biskupic, 2016).

At the time this chapter was being written, the Supreme Court of the United States was hearing arguments in the case of *Whole Women's Health v. Hellerstedt*, regarding Texas' House Bill 2, a TRAP law that created such extreme requirements for abortion clinics, including requiring that they follow the same building standards as surgical centers (like eight-foot-wide hallways so two gurneys can pass at a time) and that doctors providing abortions must have admitting privileges at nearby hospitals, who in turn will not grant them. These bills, often passed in the name of protecting women's health, resulted in the overnight closure of nearly all the abortion clinics in Texas. Abortion rights attorneys argued that the law and subsequent clinic closings are directly related and thus have created undue burdens on women, particularly low-income women, who have neither the paid leave nor money for such extensive travel to find remaining abortion providers located hundreds of miles away. The 1992 *Casey v. Planned Parenthood* decision, they argued, had already deemed these burdens illegal. In a surprising 5–3 decision, SCOTUS overturned the law, ruling Texas cannot place restrictions on abortion services that create an undue burden on women.[6]

As evidenced by just two important gender and women's issues, the legal state of gender equality is complicated. Despite federal oversight and authority, the state of gay and abortion rights vary widely by state. Even within the same geographical region two adjoining states can have opposing cultures and laws that reflect and/or support it.

Reasons for Contradictory Gender Equality Profile in the United States

In the United States, the active promotion of legislation, policy and practice becomes confounded by the issue of *needs interpretation*, which manifests itself in struggles over who defines needs for particular populations and how they do so (Ferguson, 1984; Fraser, 1989), and neoliberalism, which manifests itself in hypercompetitiveness, individualism, promotion of entrepreneurialism, elevation of risk as desirable, and denigration of human vulnerability in different life spheres (Collins, 2016; Edgell et al., 2016). The US Congress, entrusted with the creation of laws on behalf of US citizenry and global positioning, can become ineffective in gender equality and related efforts because needs interpretation is highly politicized in the development, passage and revision of bills and policies. Moreover, as documented repeatedly in empirical studies and ideological critiques (with a Google Scholar™ search on November 10 2016, on "US neoliberalism and gender equality" resulting in 50,600 entries), neoliberal assumptions underscore thinking and action that result in material consequences of such everyday and cultural discourses. These consequences include making women and children susceptible to food and housing insecurity, poverty, crime, fewer health care and educational options, and sexual politics from sexual harassment and unequal pay in the workplace to discourses of difference that affect educational experiences and career and employment trajectories across the lifespan. We argue that gender equality has not progressed further because of two dominant narratives and rhetorics, specifically: a narrative and culture of extreme individualism and American exceptionalism, and a framing of gender issues, like equality, as matters of choice instead of rights.

Individualism and Exceptionalism

This rhetoric maintains that success results from individual efforts, from the exceptional qualities that individuals bring to their different activities and interests, and from underlying beliefs in meritocracy. Positioning the exceptional individual within meritocratic systems means that advantages accrued through access to different kinds of capital and inheritances of privilege are discounted as reasons for success. Differential treatment of and resources available to people are ignored by the US mentality captured in the "American Dream" that anyone from any circumstances who has the drive to pursue excellence and associated material benefits can do so. Those who are unsuccessful are perceived as "undeserving" of assistance. Differential treatment and resources are noted in linguistic choices recommending women and men for employment positions (e.g., Trix & Psenka, 2003), in evaluation processes that excuse men for missing criteria because of "potential" but that do not do the same for women (e.g., van den Brink & Benschop, 2012), and in numerous everyday instances that interlock to contribute to inequality regimes (see Acker, 2009).

This rhetoric also results from *American exceptionalism*, namely the idea that the United States has uniquely superior qualities that lead (or should lead) other countries to admire and emulate it (see Ceaser, 2012; Restad, 2015; Stone, 2015). While many non-Americans might be surprised reading here that gender equality is not more advanced in the United States, the mentality of American exceptionalism means that a large contingent of Americans would be *shocked* that other countries might have it better, or upon hearing, for example, that every other country except the United States and Papua New Guinea has some form of paid maternity leave. Because of American exceptionalism the reaction to this cognitive dissonance is not an attempt to improve one's position but rather emphasis on the belief that "we are the exception" because "we are too different," "our circumstances and demographics too unique to implement similar policies in the United States." In other words, American exceptionalism maintains the beliefs that other countries' policies "could never work in the United States."[7] The rhetoric thus resulting from exceptionalism prevents meaningful searches for and subsequent discussions about gender relations in other parts of the country or wider world.

Choice vs. Rights

We argue that one of the reasons gender equality has not advanced further in the United States is due to the framing of many issues as matters of choice, and, the previous section discussed, as a hyperindividualistic society, one's choices are one's own and not the responsibility of others. This rhetoric of choice often stalls any reasonable discussion of many issues central to gender equality such as increasing minimum wage ("choose another, higher-paying job"), legalizing paid family leave ("don't choose to have children"). This notion of choice also remains at the heart of some anti-gay bias among those who believe that being gay is a choice.

Of course, any discussion of gender equality in the United States that mentions the word *choice* immediately connotes the pro-choice/pro-life abortion debate. Relatedly, the previous examples of this rhetoric of telling people to live with their choices is used to help frame the abortion debate. Abortion opponents, in part, want women to live with the consequences of their choice to have sex, and of course abortion supporters frame the debate as bodily autonomy in the form of choices: to choose the end the pregnancy, to carry to term, to keep the baby, to use adoption. In a country that frames much of our gender problems as one of choices, the idea that a woman has *choices* of her own to make has not advanced access to abortion services in some areas of the country. In fact, as reviewed previously, anti-abortion laws around the country are making it very difficult for women to access abortion services, thereby limiting their choices.

Interestingly, this use of the term pro-choice is a unique strategy, as the original *Roe v. Wade* decision that legalized abortion was framed as a woman's (or rather, *everyone's*) right to privacy. We argue that shifting the debate from choice to rights might be a compelling strategy to consider and note that this focus on *rights* helped gay marriage become the "law of the land" in roughly the same time span since the 1973 *Roe v. Wade* decision. In other words, one would not merely be "pro-choice" but "pro-rights."

Just three years before the 1973 *Roe* decision, two men in Minnesota applied for a marriage license. Upon being denied one, they sued the state of Minnesota. The Minnesota Supreme Court dismissed the case, *Baker v. Nelson*, "for want of a substantial federal question" (Condon, 2012). This is considered by many to be the start of the movement for gay marriage (Garvin, 2016).[8] During the same approximately 45-year period, gay marriage rights have exploded while abortion rights have contracted. One of the reasons why gay rights have advanced so quickly, we argue, is that enough people began to recognize that being gay is not a *choice* with consequences one should be forced to live with. Rather, being gay is an inherent, immutable trait for some Americans. If we accept this as true, then gay Americans are still Americans who are entitled to certain *rights*.

Indeed, much of the arguments to legalize gay marriage in the United States focused on this idea of one's *rights* as an American. To deny someone a marriage because of an immutable quality is to discriminate.

Ironically, those still fighting gay marriage also frame the issue as one of rights—and choice—arguing that people have the right to refuse employment, housing, and business services to someone if they feel it interferes with their religion. In other words, anti-gay proponents focus on wanting to have a choice in whether to acknowledge another's rights. The idea of collective rights has been a problem in the US legal context because of pervasive individualism. This tension between collective and individual rights dates back to the country's origins and persists today through the (various and intersecting) fights for equality. This deeply-rooted tension also mirrors states' rights versus federal oversight, which not only is exemplified by the abortion and gay rights issues addressed in this chapter but recently has also crossed over into transgender individuals' right to use restrooms that correspond to their gender identity instead of their biological sex. The federal government and the state of North Carolina are currently suing each other over North Carolina's "Bathroom Bill." Shortly after those lawsuits were filed, on May 13, 2016, the Justice and Education Departments of the Obama Administration issued a federal directive guiding public schools across the country to allow students to use restrooms and other facilities that correspond with their gender identity. Eleven states responded by suing the Obama Administration in response (Alabama, Arizona, Georgia, Louisiana, Maine, Oklahoma, Tennessee, Texas, Utah, West Virginia and Wisconsin).

Discussion

In the United States, strides toward and resistance against gender equality offer a contradictory historical and contemporary landscape filled with opportunities for greater reform in laws, policies, language and practices. Consistent with transformation efforts on individual through societal levels, gender equality is not a singular "problem" to be fixed but an ongoing and situated process that requires continuous advocacy and analyses. In this section, we build upon our discussion of global comparisons, US legal structures, and rhetorics of individualism-exceptionalism and choice-rights couched within meritocracy to develop specific recommendations for change on behalf of greater gender equality in the United States.

First, we encourage engaged scholarship that not only makes explicit how the neoliberal context undermines women's equality in every domain, but also takes a processual rather than a problem focus. To encourage long-term commitment to gender equality, initiatives must be questioned, supported and institutionalized in homes, organizations, institutions and society as a whole. For instance, Cohen (2015) notes how education overall has displayed support for gender equality, but that there continues to be vertical and horizontal sex segregation insofar as women still have not ascended to the highest ranks of their professions and organizations and women still tend toward more women-dominated and communal majors and occupations (just as men orient toward and work in more male-dominated areas). Furthermore, work-life policies and reward systems remain inconsistent with family patterns, biological and lifespan considerations, and career trajectories.

Second, these initiatives must demonstrate how men, families and communities benefit from gender equality as a "right" as well as, rather than versus, a "choice." If gender equality was situated in the United States as a right or non-negotiable aspect of everyday quality of life then, in theory, women would have equal access to education, work-life policies, objective evaluations and treatment, health care, property and other aspects of everyday life. On the one hand, rights were and continue to be a major part of feminist waves for advocacy on behalf of and with women. Yet, the issue of rights is complicated by neoliberal discourses that, within these rights, women also have choices. And those choices result in taken-for-granted assumptions about what women can and should do (e.g., women should have children, relocate for men's careers, not be overly assertive in salary negotiations, consider family needs more than individual interests). Even when women acknowledge societal and familial pressures to conform to gendered expectations, their decisions are couched as choices that can be framed as selfish and inconsistent with others', including organizational, needs. Thus, using the language of rights with choice joins what should be equally available to women and men with what should be considered viable variations in what individuals elect to do.

Third, meritocracy needs to be dismantled and exposed for its unrealistic nature. Sliwa and Johansson (2014) outline the main arguments in meritocracy critiques, such as its conceptualization of merit as objective/absolute and solely due to individual efforts without contributions of networks, and its absence of power, gendered character and multiple bases for inequality. Even faced with personal experience and statistical proofs, people tend to support meritocracy. Meritocracy is an ideal to which US members aspire, but also as a deterrent to the availability of interventions and resources needed to enable meritocracy to function.

Rather than meritocracy, perhaps ideologies of justice and agency would promote gender equality. Kemp (2016) argues that reframing thinking, language and interactions from prominent imagery and associated policies and practices away into conscious calls toward organizing for justice and against direct harms toward women can stimulate a foundation on which gender equality can be achieved. Kreps (2004) advocates that women become active rather than passive participants in their health care, resisting traditional systems that do not suit their interests and needs, via informed care through Internet, face-to-face information and opinion-seeking as well as positioning of patients as central within health care provider collaborations.

Finally, US citizenry may encounter discouragement and disillusionment in gender equality. We note that social transformation is never linear or resistance-free. Social change and movements for equality always involve struggle. Despite contestations and efforts to reverse laws through political dynamics and despite difficulties in putting policies into practice (e.g., Affordable Care Act; Family and Medical Leave Act, *Roe v. Wade*, gay rights), there is noticeable movement toward greater gender equality in the United States. Gender equality has required and continues to need the legal and policy changes that legitimate movement in this direction, plus interrogation of and reworking of the macro or societal discourses, everyday framings and talk, and practices surrounding and reinscribing gender in ordinary activities. These efforts are ongoing and mandate multidisciplinary efforts. As noted in this chapter, gender equality practices are the result of multilevel changes that require different strategies for creating awareness and transforming systems. However, unless there are champions, mass understanding about how inequalities harm men as well as women, and how correction of one "problem" cannot solve gender inequality as a whole (because of its multiple and deeply intertwined roots and manifestations), then ongoing efforts to challenge and correct gender inequalities will make small efforts but not transform the underlying political-economic and related ideologies and practices that sustain inequality. Given the examples above, US history tells us that change happens when there are mass efforts and rhetoric that appeal to contemporary audiences (first-wave vote, second-wave legal measures), and when there is a human face to suffering that affects majority and minority members (publicized civil rights violence and injustices in media from the 1960s civil rights push to today's Black Lives Matter activism) and champions (presidents and members of Congress, other policymakers and top corporate officials). What is left unstated in this chapter because of its focus on gender is that legacies of racism and classism coupled with ongoing debates about religion, immigration and other differences mean that gender equality in the United States is not, nor has it ever been, solely about gender.

Notes

1 Standard and Poor's 500, or the S&P 500, is an American stock market index based on 500 large companies.
2 The Affordable Care Act was upheld in a 5–4 decision in the case *National Federation of Independent Business v. Sebelius*.
3 Gender rating in employer-sponsored plans has been illegal for decades but was still legal in many states in the individual market until the Affordable Care Act

passed. The steep price differential between men and women's plans on the individual market pre-ACA was not due to maternity care on women's plans. One study found that only 3% of the best-selling individual plans that used gender rating even offered maternity care (Kahn, 2016).

4 Ratifying CEDAW remains a contentious (yet rarely mentioned) issue in the United States. A Google search of both "why the U.S. should (and should not) ratify CEDAW" reveals strong opinions for and against the convention.

5 Previously, in 2013, the Supreme Court struck down the Defense of Marriage Act, DOMA, ending a federal ban on same-sex marriage. This 2013 decision, *United States v. Windsor*, mandated federal recognition of same-sex marriages.

6 The 5–3 decision surprised many because of wide speculation that SCOTUS would uphold the law due to the rules of a "tie" given the open ninth seat on the bench as a result of Justice Scalia's February 2016 death. In the event of a tie, the lower court ruling's stands, which in this case would have upheld Texas HB 2. Instead, the law was overturned, signaling a major victory for abortion rights advocates. Kennedy joined the four liberal judges in the ruling.

7 We note that this exceptionalism applies both to the country as a whole and to certain regions that consider themselves superior to other US regions (e.g., the East and West Coasts' superiority over the Midwest and South) and stems from the premise that if a country can be superior than another, then certainly a region or area is superior than others, especially in a country as diverse and large as the United States.

8 This one-sentence dismissal was used by other states to dismiss same-sex marriage for decades. The *Obergefell v. Hodges* decision explicitly overturned the *Baker v. Nelson* decision.

References

Acker, J. (2009). From glass ceiling to inequality regimes. *Sociologie du travail*, 51 (2), 199–217. DOI: 10.1016/j.soctra.2009.03.004.

Adams, S. (2014). Companies do better with women leaders but women need more confidence to lead, study says. Retrieved from http://www.forbes.com/sites/susan adams/2014/08/05/companies-do-better-with- women-leaders-but-women-need-more-confidence-to-lead-study- says/#36e989382840 (accessed 10 March 2016).

American Association of University Women. (2014). *Leadership*. Retrieved from http://www.aauw.org/2014/10/16/elect-her-new-sites/ (accessed 10 March 2016).

Ashcraft, K., & Mumby, D. (2004). *Reworking Gender: A Feminist Communicology of Organization*. Thousand Oaks, CA: Sage.

Barnes, R. (2007). Over Ginsburg's dissent, court limits bias suits. Retrieved from http://www.washingtonpost.com/wpdyn/content/article/2007/05/29/AR2007 0529 00740.html (accessed 10 March 2016).

Biskupic, J. (2016, February 28). U.S. court test on abortion reflects success of strategy shift. *Reuters*. Retrieved from http://www.reuters.com/article/us-usa-court-abortion- strategy-idUSKCN0W10HY (accessed 10 March 2016).

Bureau of Labor Statistics. (2014). STEM 101: Intro to tomorrow's jobs. Retrieved from http://www.bls.gov/careeroutlook/2014/spring/art01.pdf (accessed 10 March 2016).

Buzzanell, P.M. (1994). Gaining a voice: Feminist organizational communication theorizing. *Management Communication Quarterly*, 7 (4), 339–383. DOI: 10.1177/0893318994007004001.

Buzzanell, P.M. (ed.) (2000). *Rethinking Organizational and Managerial Communication from Feminist Perspectives*. Thousand Oaks, CA: Sage.

Buzzanell, P.M., Berkelaar, B., & Kisselburgh, L. (2011). From the mouths of babes: Exploring families' career socialization of young children in China, Lebanon, Belgium, and the United States. *Journal of Family Communication*, **11** (2), 148–164. DOI: 10.1080/15267431.2011.554494.

Catalyst. (2007). The bottom line: Corporate performance and women's representation on boards. Retrieved from http://www.catalyst.org/system/files/The_Bot tom_Line_Corporate_Performance_and_Womens_Representation_on_Boards. pdf (accessed 10 March 2016).

Catalyst. (2014). Women in the United States. Retrieved from http://www.catalyst. org/knowledge/women-united-states (accessed 10 March 2016).

Catalyst. (2016). Pyramid: Women in S&P 500 companies. Retrieved from http://www. catalyst.org/knowledge/women-sp-500-companies (accessed 10 March 2016).

Ceaser, J.W. (2012). The origins and character of American exceptionalism. *American Political Thought*, **1** (1), 3–28. DOI: 10.1086/664595

Center for American Women in Politics. (2016). *Women in Elective Office 2016*. Retrieved from http://www.cawp.rutgers.edu/women-elective-office-2016 (accessed 10 March 2016).

Civil Rights Act. (1964). 42 U.S.C. § 2000d. Washington, DC: United States Government Publishing Office.

Cohen, P.N. (2015). *The Family: Diversity, Inequality, and Social Change*. New York: Norton.

Collins, J. (2016). One big labor market: The new imperialism and worker vulnerability. In J. Maskovsky & I. Susser (Eds), *Rethinking America: The Imperial Homeland in the 21st Century*, New York: Routledge, pp. 280–299.

Condon, P. (2012). Minneapolis gay couple in '71 marriage case still joined. Retrieved from http://www.mprnews.org/story/2012/12/10/news/jack-baker-michael-mcconnell-same-sex-marriage (accessed 15 May 2016).

Council of Economic Advisers. (2014a). The economics of paid and unpaid leave. Retrieved from https://www.whitehouse.gov/sites/default/files/docs/leave_report_final.pdf (accessed 10 March 2016).

Council of Economic Advisers. (2014b). Women's participation in education and the workforce. Retrieved from https://s3.amazonaws.com/s3.documentcloud.org/documents/1350163/women_education_workforce.pdf (accessed 10 March 2016).

Council of Economic Advisers. (2015). Gender pay gap: Recent trends and explanations. Retrieved from https://www.whitehouse.gov/sites/default/files/docs/equal_pay_issue_brief_final.pdf (accessed 17 May 2016).

Edgell, S., Gottfried, H., & Granter, E. (eds) (2016). *The Sage Handbook of the Sociology of Work and Employment*. Los Angeles: Sage.

Fairchild, C. (2014). Women CEOs in the Fortune 1000: By the numbers. Retrieved from http://fortune.com/2014/07/08/women-ceos-fortune-500–1000/ (accessed 10 March 2016).

Fair Housing Act. (1968). 42 U.S.C. § 3601. Washington, DC: United States Government Publishing Office.

Faludi, S. (2006). *Backlash: The Undeclared War against American Women* (2nd edition). New York: Three Rivers Press.

Ferguson, K.E. (1984). *The Feminist Case against Bureaucracy*. Philadelphia, PA: Temple University Press.

Fraser, N. (1989). *Unruly Practices: Power, Discourse, and Gender in Contemporary Social Theory*. Minneapolis, MN: University of Minnesota Press.

Garvin, P. (2016). A time-line of same-sex marriage in the U.S. Retrieved from https://www.bostonglobe.com/2016/01/09/same-sex-marriage-over-time/mbVFMQPyxZCp M2eSQMUsZK/story.html (accessed 10 March 2016).

Green, E. (2016, January). Can states protect LGBT rights without compromising religious freedom? Retrieved from http://www.theatlantic.com/politics/archive/2016/01/lgbt-discrimination- protection-states-religion/422730/ (accessed 10 March 2016).

Hayden, S., & O'Brien Hallstein, L. (eds) (2010). *Contemplating Maternity in the Era of Choice: Explorations into Discourses of Reproduction*. Lanham, MD: Lexington Press.

Human Rights Campaign. (2016). *The Equality Act*. Retrieved from http://www.hrc.org/resources/the-equality-act (accessed 25 May 2016).

Jones, J.I. (2014). An overview of employment and wages in science, technology, engineering, and math (STEM) groups. Retrieved from http://www.bls.gov/opub/btn/volume-3/an-overview-of-employment.htm (accessed 10 March 2016).

Kahn, S. (2016). The end of gender rating: Women's insurance under the ACA. Retrieved from http://publicpolicy.wharton.upenn.edu/live/news/819-the-end-of-gender-rating-womens-insurance-under (accessed 25 May 2016).

Kemp, L. (2016). "Trapped" by metaphors for organizations: Thinking and seeing women's equality and inequality. *Human Relations*, 69 (4), 975–1000. DOI: 10.1177/0018726715621612

Klarsfeld, A. (ed.) (2010). *International Handbook on Diversity Management at Work: Country Perspectives on Diversity and Equal Treatment*. Cheltenham, UK and Northampton, MA, USA: Edward Elgar.

Klarsfeld, A., Booysen, A., Ng, E., Roper, I., & Tatli, A. (eds) (2014). *International Handbook on Diversity Management at Work: Country Comparisons on Diversity and Equal Treatment* (2nd edition). Cheltenham, UK and Northampton, MA, USA: Edward Elgar.

Kreps, G. (2004). Commentary: Communication and women's health. In P.M. Buzzanell (Ed.), *Rethinking Organizational and Managerial Communication from Feminist Perspective*, Thousand Oaks, CA: Sage, pp. 169–175.

McRobbie, A. (2004). Post-feminism and popular culture. *Feminist media studies*, 4 (3), 255–264.

Medved, C.E. (2015). Work and family communication research: Contemplating possibilities of undoing gender. *Electronic Journal of Communication*, 25.

Miller, D.I., Eagly, A.H., & Linn, M.C. (2015). Women's representation in science predicts national gender-science stereotypes: Evidence from 66 nations. *Journal of Educational Psychology*, 107 (3), 631–644. DOI: doi.org/10.1037/edu0000005.

Naples, N., & Gurr, B. (2016). Human rights and gender. In N. Naples, R.C. Hoogland, M. Wickramasinghe & W.C.A. Wong (Eds), *The Wiley Blackwell Encyclopedia of Gender and Sexuality Studies*. Published Online: 10.1002/9781118663219.wbegss724.

National Center for Education Statistics. (2015). Table 5.1 Compulsory school attendance laws, minimum and maximum age limits for required free education, by State: 2015. Retrieved from https://nces.ed.gov/programs/statereform/tab5_1.asp (accessed 10 March 2016).

National Center for Education Statistics. (2016a). Table 318.30: Bachelor's, Master's, and Doctor's degrees conferred by postsecondary institutions, by sex of student and discipline division: 2013–14. Retrieved from https://nces.ed.gov/programs/digest/d15/tables/dt15_318.30.asp?current=yes (accessed 10 March 2016).

National Center for Education Statistics. (2016b). Table 322.20: Bachelor's degrees conferred by postsecondary institutions, by race/ethnicity and sex of student: Selected years, 1976–77 through 2013–14. Retrieved from https://nces.ed.gov/programs/digest/d15/tables/dt15_322.20.asp (accessed 10 March 2016).

National Center for Education Statistics. (2016c). Table 302.60: Percentage of 18- to 24-year-olds enrolled in degree-granting postsecondary institutions, by level of institution and sex and race/ethnicity of student: 1970 through 2014. Retrieved from https://nces.ed.gov/programs/digest/d15/tables/dt15_302.60.asp (accessed10 March 2016).

National Science Foundation. (2016). Science and engineering doctorates. Retrieved from http://www.nsf.gov/statistics/2016/nsf16300/report.cfm (accessed 10 March 2016).

Obamacare Facts. (2016). ObamaCare and women: ObamaCare women's health services. Retrieved from http://obamacarefacts.com/obamacare-womens-health-services/ (accessed 10 March 2016).

Patient Protection and Affordable Care Act. (2010). 42 U.S.C. § 18001. Washington, DC: United States Government Publishing Office.

Pauly, J., & Buzzanell, P.M. (2016). Considering difference in diversity management: A critical take on practices and policies around the world: Book Review Essay: "International Handbook on Diversity Management at Work: Country Perspectives on Diversity and Equal Treatment". (2 volumes; editors: A. Karsfeld, L. Booysen, E. Ng, I. Roper, & A Tatli; Cheltenham, UK: Edward Elgar.). *Scandinavian Journal of Management*, 32 (2), 114–118. DOI: http://dx.doi.org/10.1016/j.scaman.2016.03.001.

Restad, H.E. (2015). *American Exceptionalism: An Idea that Made a Nation and Remade the World*. New York: Routledge.

Sliwa, M., & Johansson, M. (2014). The discourse of meritocracy contested/reproduced: Foreign women academics in UK business schools. *Organization*, 21 (6), 821–843. DOI: 10.1177/1350508413486850.

Stone, J. (2015). American exceptionalism. *The Wiley Blackwell Encyclopedia of Race, Ethnicity, and Nationalism*, 1–5. DOI: 10.1002/9781118663202.wberen684.

Sue, D. (2010). *Microaggressions in Everyday Life: Race, Gender, and Sexual Orientation*. Hoboken, NJ: Wiley.

Trix, F., & Psenka, C. (2003). Exploring the color of glass: Letters of recommendation for female and male medical faculty. *Discourse & Society*, 14 (2), 191–220. DOI: 10.1177/0957926503014002277.

United Nations Human Rights. (2015). UN working group on the issue of discrimination against women in law and in practice finalizes country mission to the United States. Retrieved from http://www.ohchr.org/EN/NewsEvents/Pages/DisplayNews.aspx?NewsID=16872&LangID=E (accessed 10 March 2016).

United States Department of Labor. (2011). Women's employment during the recovery. Washington, DC. Retrieved from http://www.dol.gov/_sec/media/reports/FemaleLaborForce/FemaleLaborForce.pdf (accessed 10 March 2016).

United States Equal Employment Opportunity Commission. (2016). *Equal Pay Act of 1963 and Lilly Ledbetter Fair Pay Act of 2009*. Retrieved from http://www.eeoc.gov/eeoc/publications/brochure-equal_pay_and_ledbetter_act.cfm (accessed 10 March 2016).

United States Office of Science and Technology Policy. (2016). Women in STEM. Retrieved from https://www.whitehouse.gov/administration/eop/ostp/women (accessed 10 March 2016).

United States Senate. (2016). Breaking New Ground: African American Senators. Retrieved from http://www.senate.gov/pagelayout/history/h_multi_sec tions_and_teasers/Photo_Exhibit_African_American_Senators.htm (accessed 10 March 2016).

van den Brink, M., & Benschop, Y. (2012). Gender practices in the construction of academic excellence: Sheep with five legs. *Organization*, **19** (4), 507–524. DOI: 10.1177/1350508411414293.

Warner, J. (2014). Fact sheet: The women's leadership gap. Retrieved from https://www.americanprogress.org/issues/women/report/2014/03/07/85457/fact-sheet-the-womens-leadership-gap/ (accessed 26 May 2016).

The White House. (2016). Women in STEM. Retrieved from https://www.white house.gov/administration/eop/ostp/women (accessed 10 March 2016).

World Economic Forum. (2016). Economies. Retrieved from http://reports.wefo rum.org/global-gender-gap-report-2015/economies/#economy=USA (accessed 10 March 2016).

9 Gender Equality in Serbia

Suzana Ignjatović and Aleksandar Bošković

Introduction

On December 6, 2015, Serbian Minister of Defense Mr. Bratislav Gašić visited a town in his local constituency. When a journalist in front of him ducked so that her colleagues could film the minister, he remarked jokingly that "he loved these female journalists who so easily get on their knees" (*Tanjug*, 2015). The comment, with its overt vulgar sexist message, paradoxically put in a gender-sensitive form ("female journalist"), provoked an outrage among Serbian journalists and the wider public. However, it took quite a while, many debates in the media and many journalists' protests throughout Serbia for Mr. Gašić to suffer the consequences for his remark, and he was formally removed from his office only on February 5, 2016 (*Blic*, 2016).

This incident illustrates the complexity of gender equality in Serbia: it is assumed that it exists, but only when a high-ranking member of the ruling party and the government minister, steps out of bounds do people begin asking questions about it. Is it present and what does it actually mean in everyday life? Serbia was ranked 45th out of 145 countries according to the 2015 Gender Gap Index (World Economic Forum, 2015). The 2014 Gender Equality Index shows that Serbia has accomplished 40.6% gender equality, compared to the average of 52.9% in the European Union (Babović, 2016). Yet, the official statistics reflect only the formal side of gender equality. According to statistics, Serbia has already achieved gender equality in many areas, although violence against women is definitely not among them. The concluding observations from the Committee on the Elimination of Discrimination against Women suggest that violence against women should be addressed in a more comprehensive way, and revisions of the Criminal Code and the Family Code were suggested (Committee on the Elimination of Discrimination against Women, 2016).

In this chapter, we look at the issue of gender equality in Serbia. On the one hand, it cannot be seen in isolation from the country's turbulent history, as well as its most recent past. On the other hand, it also presents a case study of a country where large segments of the population hold views that are comparable to the ones by the citizens of the member states of the EU, for example (Ignjatović et al., 2011). Our main reference point is the Convention on the Elimination of All Forms of Discrimination against Women (CEDAW). Before we focus on Serbia as a special case, some critical observations should be made about the most comprehensive international instrument for gender equality policy.

Assessing the achieved level of CEDAW standards in any country raises many practical questions. First, there is a conceptual problem of the *goals* definition. What is the scope of gender equality in each of the 16 CEDAW areas? What does it mean to fully adopt gender equality in marital and family relations? Does it include equality before the law, household labor or intimacy issues? How should we assess gender equality if certain countries opt for "reservations" to some CEDAW standards by stating that they "will adhere to only those parts of the treaty that are consistent with their internal laws, religion, or culture" (Keller, 2014, p. 316)? Obviously, gender equality comprehensiveness as stated in the Convention has already been subject to compromises. Another question concerns the *instruments* and their efficacy, sustainability and ethics. Are quotas the best method to substantially improve political participation of women? What if certain policy measures lead to unintended consequences?

Finally, the main question boils down to: who "owns" the gender equality concept in practice? Gender equality policy is developed by different *actors/agents*. In real-life politics, gender equality is operationalized through a complex process in which differences may arise among policy makers, the non-governmental sector and citizens. There may be diverging perspectives regarding the achieved level of gender equality in a particular country, as we can see from the CEDAW "shadow reports" prepared by non-governmental actors (ASTRA et al., 2013). In a situation when different paradigms coexist, which one has more legitimacy? Who has the ultimate right to change the dominant concept and impose it on others?

Between the Legacy of Socialism and EU Accession

Modern history of gender equality in Serbia started after the Second World War.[1] In socialist Yugoslavia, equality of women was incorporated in the official ideology and it was high on the political agenda in almost all "public" and "private" domains. Women were able to vote following the 1946 Federal Constitution.[2] Women's equality in marital and family relations, property rights and inheritance, and the right to abortion were all introduced during the 1950s and 1960s (Gudac-Dodić, 2006). The country employed a very progressive concept of women's emancipation for that time.

Whether positive transformations during socialism had a sustainable impact on contemporary status of gender equality is an open question. Political participation had a formal character, or what Pitkin has termed "descriptive representation" (Schwindt-Bayer & Mishler, 2005). Relatively high proportions of women in the political domain disappeared immediately after the first multi-party elections in 1990. Unlike the fragile changes in political participation, there have been more sustainable improvements in the education and labor markets. Domestic violence, gender stereotypes in the media and textbooks, and division of household labor were not systematically addressed as gender equality issues.

In recent history, the public policy of gender equality in Serbia has been guided mostly by the EU accession process. Relevant international standards have been incorporated into policies of gender equality—like the CEDAW and other UN resolutions and conventions,[3] as well as the Council of Europe's Convention on preventing and combating violence against women and domestic violence. The history of CEDAW (hereafter: the Convention) in Serbia is inseparable from the history of socialist Yugoslavia. The Convention was signed in 1979, and the Socialist Federal Republic of Yugoslavia (SFRY) prepared two reports. The third report submitted by the Federal Republic of Yugoslavia (FRY, a successor of SFRY) was not considered.[4] The first Initial CEDAW Report (period 1992–2003) for Serbia was submitted in 2006.[5] The Second and Third Reports were submitted in 2011. The next report is scheduled for 2017.

The focus and priorities have changed between the two reporting periods (2003–2013). In the Initial Report, some issues were context-specific (the status of refugees). Domestic violence was introduced as a new issue (recognized as a criminal act in the Criminal Code in 2002). However, the Initial Report was very formalistic, sometimes purely technical in its description of regulations. Except for the sections about health and education, not much attention was given to statistics and facts related to implementation issues. For example, work regulations were presented through the law provisions, and it was mentioned only that "there exist restrictions" for application of non-discriminatory regulations (Committee on the Elimination of Discrimination against Women, 2006).

Another interesting topic from the perspective of gender equality policy creation is the relation between the state and non-governmental sector. The state perception of the role of non-governmental sector has changed in 10 years. In the Initial Report, the role of NGOs was recognized in certain areas (for example, violence against women) and different programs organized with donor financial support were described in detail in the Report (Committee on the Elimination of Discrimination against Women, 2006). The first Shadow Report was prepared by NGOs and was very critical of the Initial Report: although it was admitted that the role of NGOs was recognized after 2000, but also that a "systematic marginalization" of NGOs occurred during the conservative government (2003) and the Draft Law on Gender Equality was withdrawn from Parliament in 2006 (Voice of Difference from Serbia, 2007). In the Shadow Report from 2013 (based on the Second and Third Reports), among many critical remarks, it has been acknowledged that "The issue of gender equality became more present and visible in the previous period . . ." (ASTRA et al., 2013, p. 8).

The process of accession to the EU has become the major driving force for the recent reforms (Ignjatović & Bošković, 2013).[6] Harmonization with EU regulations, norms and standards includes gender equality, which is monitored through Progress Reports. In the 2015 Progress Report, the issue of violence against women (especially domestic violence) is emphasized as an issue to be addressed, but also the low participation of women in politics and in the private sector, gender pay gap, discrimination of pregnant women and sexual harassment. Certain improvements have been recognized, like the increased proportion of women as members of parliament (34%) (European Commission, 2015).

During the country's democratic transition (after 2000), the institutionalization of gender equality has become intensive. Two strategic documents were implemented, the first one in 2009, and the second one for the period 2016–2020 (*Vlada Republike Srbije*, 2009, 2016). Gender equality, in terms of equal opportunities, is guaranteed by the Serbian Constitution (2006), the Law on Gender Equality (2009) and the set of laws on discrimination, education and employment: the Labor Law, the Law on the Prohibition of Discrimination (2009) and the Law on Fundamentals of Education (*Zakon o osnovama sistema obrazovanja i vaspitanja*, 2009; *Zakon o radu*, 2005; *Zakon o zabrani diskriminacije*, 2009). The Law on the Prohibition of Discrimination established the institution of Commissioner for Protection of Equality, which enabled institutional mechanisms for complaints on the basis of gender of discrimination and other forms of discrimination. It is difficult to assess the level of implementation of the abovementioned law's provisions. The Law on the Prohibition of Discrimination has brought about an increasing number of complaints based on gender discrimination. Discrimination based on pregnancy is explicitly prohibited by the Labor Law, yet pregnant women are at a higher risk of losing their job (Sekulić, 2012).

National gender equality strategic policies have been guided consecutively by the following institutions, before the Law on Gender Equality was adopted (2008): Council for Gender Equality (2004), Sector for Gender Equality within the Ministry for Labor and Social Policy (2007) and Directorate for Gender Equality (2008) (Committee on the Elimination of Discrimination against Women, 2011). Recently (2014), the Coordinating Body for Gender Equality took over the strategic role in gender equality policy. It is difficult to estimate the capacities of the newly established Coordinating body, as an inter-ministerial body consisting of the appointed members, but without operative capacities. Responsibilities and capacities of the abovementioned bodies have changed, from advisory (the Council), strategic and operative (the Directorate), to primarily strategic (the Coordinating Body).

There are another two relevant institutions for gender equality. Ombudsperson was established according to the Law on the Protector of Citizens (2005), which is compatible with the Law on Gender Equality. Ombudsperson is established "as an independent body that shall protect the rights of citizens and control the work of government agencies . . . bodies and organisations, enterprises and institutions which have been delegated public authority (hereinafter: administrative authorities)" (Article 1), and gender equality is mentioned explicitly in Article 6 (Law on the Protector of Citizens, 2005). Another institution is the already mentioned Commissioner for Protection of Equality (it monitors legal acts and regulations and initiates legal proceedings in the area of discrimination) (Ignjatović & Bošković, 2013; *Ministarstvo rada, zapošljavanja i socijalne politike*, 2014). Their role seems to be recognized by gender equality activists; for example, NGOs have claimed that they have had better cooperation with the Ombudsman than with the Gender Equality Directorate (ASTRA et al., 2013). Although there has been an increasing number of complaints filed to the Commissioner on grounds of gender discrimination, most of them were unsustainable (*Ministarstvo rada, zapošljavanja i socijalne politike*, 2014).

Gender equality monitoring has been improved with new methods of data collection and disaggregation used by the National Statistical Office (which participated in the preparation of Gender Equality Index). In this process, there is a strong influence of EU accession reporting, because the mechanisms for monitoring gender equality are contained in the EU Progress Reports. Of course, there has always been a discrepancy between formal reforms and actual changes, between the ideology and practice, between the ideal and reality. This is another shared "negative legacy" with socialism. In the next section we are looking at the long-duration processes and changing patterns of gender policy making and gender equality achievements in four areas: education, employment, health and politics.

Education Between the "Modern Dowry" and "Biological Trap"

Education was a very important component of post-WWII Marxist humanism. The new policy of democratization of education was beneficial to women, because the majority of women were illiterate (Gudac-Dodić, 2006).[7] The whole transformation was a slow process, from the resistance to girls' education in the 1950s, to the full acceptance of education as a part of girls' upbringing in later decades (Gudac-Dodić, 2006, p. 49; Ignjatović et al., 2011). A study of women in rural areas from 1991 found that, during the socialist period, education became a kind of a substitute for a dowry, and paradoxically, girls were encouraged to get educated more than boys (Milić, cited in Korać, 1991, p. 87). However, there have always been some obstacles to girls' education within certain social groups, mostly based on cultural and religious values. For example, parental support of education of Roma girls is still an issue (Kočić-Rakočević & Miljević, 2003). Recent re-traditionalization of Muslim women has influenced education, too. For example, one of the Muslim organizations in Serbia has recommended that girls should choose university/school based on the demands of their religion—they should not attend schools that do not support their covering (*Mešihat islamske zajednice u Srbiji*, 2016).[8]

In the general population, education has remained the strongest legacy of socialism, even during difficult times of social transition. A recent public opinion survey (2010) shows that women's education is still highly valued by both genders. The assertion: "A university education is less important for a girl than for a boy" (taken from the World Value Survey) was rejected by the majority (85%) of men and women (Ignjatović et al., 2011). The results from the World Values Survey (wave 2000–2004) show similar patterns of deep-rooted gender equality as a value orientation in education and employment (World Values Survey, 2004).[9]

The attitudes towards education are associated with agency—actual women's participation in education. Probably the highest standard of gender equality in Serbia has been achieved in education. Of course, there are still illiterate women and women with no education. However, in education, we should differentiate between systemic obstacles and the achieved education level in the majority population and minority groups. As for the system, women participate at all levels of education. There are equal proportions of boys and girls at all levels of the education system, with similar drop-out rates (*Republički zavod za statistiku*, 2014).[10] Only the categories of Roma women and older women have much higher illiteracy rates and lower levels of education compared to the general population (Committee on the Elimination of Discrimination against Women, 2013; *Republički zavod za statistiku*, 2014). In order to improve the education status of the Roma in general, affirmative measures have been introduced (scholarships, enrollment quotas) (*Ministarstvo rada, zapošljavanja i socijalne politike*, 2014). However, illiteracy is a long-duration issue for some categories of women, even in the 21st century.[11]

In the general population, proportions are equal for tertiary education. Women make up the majority of the student population (over 50%), with an increasing proportion among the university graduates in favor of the female population (currently the gap is 2.5%) (Babović, 2016). At lower levels of education, women tend to have fewer years of education, but these differences may not be significant if age (life expectancy) and other variables are taken into account. Just like in the case of gender pay gap, a more thorough analysis should be performed to understand the real differences, before labeling them "discrimination."

Women make up 40% of researchers in science (*Committee on the Elimination of Discrimination against Women, 2011*; Ignjatović, 2006). However, the high proportion of women in education and academia is not followed by women's equal participation in high-ranking positions in academic institutions (Ignjatović & Bošković, 2013). The best example is Serbian Academy of Sciences and Arts, with 90% men (*Republički zavod za statistiku*, 2014). The underlying issue of life-work balance is the key determinant of women's status in this domain. Women are trying to harmonize their key life events in their private and professional lives (Ignjatović, 2006). They face difficulties in meeting the standards for the highest positions at universities and research institutes. This is not so much the result of discrimination ("old boy network"), but rather the consequence of a "biological trap." It is more an issue of "unfair competition" due to the juggling of family life and career (Ignjatović, 2006). Life trajectories also depend on individual choices based mostly on education level, especially starting a family (Tomanović & Ignjatovic, 2010).

Today, other issues are prioritized in gender equality policy in education: textbooks and language. Sexist use of language is still the norm in Serbian society. Even though the words for different professions can be in both male and female gender, the male gender is usually used for women as well. It is very common to see in the subtitles of foreign movies or series words translated in male gender only—even though they obviously refer to women (Bošković, 2010, p. 79). Gender stereotypes are addressed in the last CEDAW Report (Committee on the Elimination of Discrimination against Women, 2011, 2013). The NGO Report claims that primary education school textbooks have improved and contain more gender-sensitive material, compared to the secondary education textbooks (ASTRA et al., 2013). However, "all textbooks analyzed share the same deficiencies: absence of themes important for the understanding of gender equality, uneven number of male and female characters and uneven number of quotations of female and male authors" (ASTRA et al., 2013, p. 20).

Employment Between "Working Heroes" and Early Retirement

Employment was promoted as the key instrument of women's emancipation during socialism, and it has remained valued in recent decades after the end of socialism. After the Second World War, employment of women was strongly encouraged, for ideological and practical reasons, even though working conditions were usually very poor. There was a great need for labor force, so the biggest national women's organization, Women's Antifascist Front, promoted women's participation in the labor force. The media were celebrating "female working heroes" and job desegregation through articles about women engaged in male-dominated professions, like tractor drivers (Gudac-Dodić, 2006).

However, during the 1950s, there was a different trend, similar to the one in Western countries. In many developed democracies during the war (the United States or the UK), women were employed to replace the male workforce. Immediately after the war, a discussion arose whether woman's place should be at home, because there was no more need for their participation in the labor market. Similarly, during the 1950s, in the former Yugoslavia, the similar rationale was used, because the after-war reconstruction was finished. The change was evident in the media, which started promoting "classical feminine values" (Gudac-Dodić, 2006, p. 65). Pregnant women were discriminated against in employment, and women were more likely to lose their jobs than men, especially if they had children (Gudac-Dodić, 2006). For a good reason, in socialist sociology, the status of women was explained within the feminist Marxist paradigm, using the concepts of alienation and exploitation (Blagojević, 1991).[12]

The status of employed women today is much more difficult to assess due to macro-economic factors. There has been a strong confounding influence of transitional factors on the economic status of women in recent decades. For example, women are employed in low-investment businesses with an uncertain future (like wire and cable manufacturing). These low-paid, low-skilled jobs are compared to the socialist textile industry (Petrović, 2016).

The employment gap of 15 percentage points on average is a result of women's higher economic inactivity (Avlijaš et al., 2013, p. 165). This has changed during the economic crisis. Since women are more employed in public sector, their employment was more resistant to the crisis (Avlijaš et al., 2013).[13] The official unemployment figures do not include women working in the "informal economy." In 2009, the employment rate for women was 44%, and according to 2014 GEI, the gender gap increased, as the employment rate was 28.4% for women and 41.3% for men (Babović, 2016; *Vlada Republike Srbije*, 2009).

The retirement age gap is another legacy of socialism. Women make up the majority of the so-called "inactive population", that is, people not officially included in the workforce(around 60% at ages 15–74, and 75% at ages 55–74) (Arandarenko et al., 2012). On average, men work five years longer than women, and the gap will decrease with the new legislation (Babović, 2016; *Vlada Republike Srbije*, 2009). A public opinion survey shows that 67% of women and 57% of men were opposed to introducing equality in this area (Ignjatović et al., 2011). Also, the trade unions were opposed to it.[14] The division is evident among women based on the socioeconomic status of women. Working-class women prefer to retire earlier, while different kinds of professionals (doctors, professors) would rather work longer.[15] There was a recent protest against "early" retirement of women pediatricians, before the age of 65, as part of the rationalization process.[16] Working-class women may consider this "early retirement" as a privilege.

Gender disproportion is evident in high-ranking positions in the economy: there are low proportions of women among the owners of private property, farms and among entrepreneurs (*Republički zavod za statistiku*, 2014).[17] The unfavorable status of rural women as "helping members" (working on family-owned farms) is an example of the lack of adequate policies that would properly target certain discriminated populations. In the Strategy 2009, the status of rural women was only mentioned together with other "multiple discrimination" groups (Roma women). Among the measures to address the very difficult status of rural women, it was suggested that their information and communications technology or ICT literacy should be improved, and that awareness-raising campaigns be organized to "support transition to new values from traditional patriarchal values" (*Vlada Republike Srbije*, 2009). A much better understanding of the problem can be found in the new Strategy (2016–2020): improving access to health insurance and pensions are the goals that correspond better with the real problem (*Vlada Republike Srbije*, 2016).

The gender poverty gap seems to be increasing with age, but not consistently in all cohorts. In 2013, the risk-of-poverty rate among women aged 55–64 was 18%, compared to 26% for men; among women aged 65 and older, 23% were at risk of poverty, compared to the men of the same age (15%) (*Republički zavod za statistiku*, 2014). Older women are also a majority in the informal economy (*Republički zavod za statistiku*, 2014).

However, explanation of the gender pay gap is more complicated. A recent study shows that a common belief about discrimination against women of the same education and qualifications is not grounded. The unadjusted pay gap was 3% and the adjusted pay gap was 11%, when differences between the genders in characteristics like education are taken into account (Avlijaš et al., 2013). According to Avlijaš et al.: "Usually, in developed economies, one part of the gender pay gap can be explained by objective differences in personal labour market characteristics between men and women (such as different levels of education, work experience or choice of occupation) due to the historical female disadvantage in access to education and economic opportunities." This means that in developed/Western countries, lower education of women usually explains the difference, so the adjusted gap is lower than the unadjusted one. In Serbia, the adjusted pay gap is higher than the unadjusted one, which raises some methodological issues. When adequate econometric models are applied, it shows that women are not paid less for the same observed characteristics (they are not paid less for additional years of education). How is this difference then explained? According to Avlijaš and colleagues, the gap "exists due to the different returns between men and women on unobserved characteristics. . . . These could include differences in female and male labour market behaviour which employers reward or punish within the same occupations and sectors of the economy, e.g., that women may be less flexible in terms of working hours or business trips, due to home and reproductive responsibilities; other non-measurable effort- and ability-related variables, as well as labour market frictions" (Avlijaš et al., 2013, p. 10). Contrary to common belief, this means that discrimination is even more pronounced in the public sector, where the adjusted gap widens from 1.6% to 7.5%, (Avlijaš et al., 2013, p. 88.). Since the public sector is supposed to be more flexible regarding the above-mentioned unobservable characteristics, it seems that the greater gender gap is a result of greater discrimination in the public sector. Avlijaš and colleagues explain that employers in the public sector can "afford" discriminatory behavior because they are less exposed to competition demands (Avlijaš et al., 2013, p. 175). These results have important policy implications because they show that the idea of discrimination against women based on education and competencies is not supported. However, the data about sources of differences raises the work-family balance issue.

The work-family balance for women of reproductive age reflects two different time points. First, starting a family brings many difficulties for women at work. Pregnant women are at a higher risk of losing their job in spite of their formally guaranteed rights (Sekulić, 2012). Work-family balance has another component, which in turn affects women's professional life. The division of household labor still follows the patriarchal model. Women ("mothers") shouldered the biggest burden of housework 10 years ago, and the situation seems to have remained similar today (*Republički zavod za statistiku*, 2014; Tomanović & Ignjatović, 2004; 2006). On the one hand, Serbian parental leave policies are supportive—mothers are entitled to the full salary for 365 days after the first and second child, and two years for the third child. In the recent Strategy on Gender Equality, the goals and measures are set to encourage fathers to use their right to parental leave more (*Vlada Republike Srbije*, 2016).[18] Sharing other family responsibilities is also emphasized, which confirms that the official policy turns towards "private domain" in the next period. The question is whether these measures will be popular and embraced, from the cost-benefit perspective of the family.

Nevertheless, the persisting gender inequalities in economy and work-family domain have not influenced women's attitudes towards employment negatively. The long-term effects of gender equality policies from socialism are still evident in positive attitudes towards the employment of women (Ignjatović & Bošković, 2013). In our survey from 2010, a huge majority of the respondents (90% of men and 74% of women) agreed with the statement that "Being employed is the best instrument for women's independence." Also, the statement "When jobs are scarce, men should have more right to a job than women" was rejected by two-thirds of the interviewed respondents (Ignjatović et al., 2011). These attitudes may be the result of the labor market reality—low wages, job insecurity and poor working conditions. Women are forced to get a job out of necessity to provide resources for the family.

Health of Women Between Poor Health Culture and Partial Discrimination

As stated in the last CEDAW Report (2013), there are few categories of women lacking access to health care due to the limited implementation of regulations: Roma women, disabled women and victims of rape (Committee on the Elimination of Discrimination against Women, 2013). However, the access to health care has improved for Roma women after certain measures were introduced: health mediators for Roma settlements, legal regulation of access to health care for the Roma without health insurance, many workshops for health care providers, etc. (*Ministarstvo zdravlja*, 2014).

Except for these special categories of women, there is generally no discrimination against women in access to health care. Poor health culture, unhealthy lifestyles (smoking and nutrition) and inadequate health care service are not gender-specific issues. The indicators of life expectancy and healthy life expectancy are more favorable for women (Babović, 2016).[19] Health problems may arise as a consequence of psychological and physical domestic violence. Especially, psychological well-being is compromised in those women suffering long-term violence. There are improvements regarding the psychological aspects of partnership violence in ongoing changes of the Criminal Code.

The only specifically female health problems are related to reproductive health. There is a general problem of poor health culture and low awareness of health prevention. Women's reproductive rights are guaranteed by the Constitution and legislation, but the category of women with fertility issues is not monolithic. Exercising reproductive rights depends on a type of infertility. For the "socially infertile" women (single women, lesbians), there are no options to exercise their reproductive rights. Discrimination is evident in the programs for medically assisted reproduction financed by the state health fund, because only heterosexual couples are eligible for State Health Fund's financial support, and the law refers only to couples married and unmarried couples, and only "exceptionally," a single woman has the right to assisted reproduction, with a minister's approval (*Zakon o lečenju neplodnosti postupcima biomedicinski potpomognutog oplodjenja*, 2009). However, this option is technically not possible with no available reproductive cell donation. This is a "partial discrimination," excluding one group of woman for certain health services.

Another group of women is also denied their reproductive rights. The issue of gestational surrogacy has recently spurred a debate within the feminist camp. The question is whether to introduce legal regulation of surrogacy as a method of assisted reproduction. The opposition to surrogacy is strong among radical feminists, not only in Serbia. They see surrogacy as an instrument of patriarchal exploitation of both groups of women: surrogates and women who need surrogacy (McElroy, 2008). The opponents are embracing surrogacy as a manifestation of women's reproductive rights.[20] Not allowing this type of medical assistance can be viewed as discrimination based on the type of infertility, excluding one group of women from their rights.

Abortion is another issue, though not in terms of unfulfilled CEDAW norms, but as a social issue. According to the current legislation, abortion is legal on request up to 10 weeks of pregnancy (Rašević & Sedlecki, 2011). However, there is a strong "abortion culture" in Serbia, which results in high abortion rates (Rašević & Sedlecki, 2011). Although the abortion rates have officially decreased since the 1990s, it is difficult to make proper estimates due to unregistered procedures in private health institutions (Rašević, 2008). According to the 2014 UNICEF survey, 15% of women aged 15–49 have had an abortion, as well as 32% of women aged 45–49 (UNICEF, 2014).[21] Abortion is most common among women who already have two children (*Institut za javno zdravlje Srbije*, 2015). Permissive norms towards abortion are rooted in Serbian culture. An anthropological study from the 1930s indicated a long tradition of this method of contraception in Serbia, compared to the other parts of former Yugoslavia (Erlich, 1971). The reason may be a more permissive attitude of the Orthodox Church towards the abortion compared to the Catholic and Muslim religious affiliations (Erlich, 1971).

Women in Politics Between the Male Political Culture and Quotas

For the last 60 years, the trajectory of formal political participation of women has been close to a parabolic shape. Between the 1960s and 1980s the proportion of women in the representative bodies was between one-sixth and one-fifth (Markov, 2001). Compared to the developed democracies of that time, Yugoslavia (Serbia) and other socialist countries were officially more committed to gender equality (Kolin & Čičkarić, 2010).[22] However, these achievements turned out to be fragile within the new multi-party political system in the 1990s. In order to improve participation of women, quotas were re-introduced within a different context of the post-2000 democratic transition.

During the socialist period, there were around 20% women in the Federal Parliament, and around 15% in the parliaments of federal republics. The percentage was much lower in local parliaments. Quotas were used for the young people, workers and women, with the aim to create formal representation of the relevant social categories with a precondition of their loyalty to the Communist Party (Markov, 2001). Women did not have influence on political decisions and political hierarchy (Blagojević, 1991; Gudac-Dodić, 2006; Markov, 2001).[23] Just like in other socialist countries, "male-dominated 'nomenclature'" had the real power (UNICEF, 1999). It was a two-layer system: patriarchy was intertwined with socialist ideology. This is the reason why participation of women in legislative bodies suddenly decreased in the post-socialist multi-party systems (Čičkarić, 2009; *UNICEF*, 1999).

The proportions of women in positions of power decreased radically during the "blocked" transition (1990–2000). There were 1.6% of women among members of parliament in 1990 (Markov, 2001). The third phase of women's participation in politics started after 2000. The issue of unequal representation of women has been addressed systematically at the national and local level. The rationale for the new gender equality policy is based on legitimacy (the fact that women represent around 51% of the population), development (under-use of human resources), and self-representation (women should have influence on public policy according to their own interests) (Baćanović, 2012).

This change is in line with global change of gender equality paradigm. According to Inglehart and Norris, during the 1980s and 1990s, there was a shift in the international women's movement "from focusing on the problems facing women's well-being toward emphasizing the active role of women's agency and voice" (Inglehart & Norris, 2003, p. 6). In that process, the role of the state has been emphasized to enable women's agency through legislation. This is another similarity with the socialist period: the reforms were imposed "from above."

The number of women in politics has slowly increased, primarily due to the same system that was used in socialism: quotas. The Law on Election of National Deputies stipulates that "an election list must include a candidate of the less represented sex in the list among every four candidates in sequence of the list (the first four seats, the second four seats and on to the end of the list), and the total number of candidates in the list must be at least 30 percent of candidates of the less represented sex in the list" (Committee on the Elimination of Discrimination against Women, 2011, p. 30). In order to tackle a very low representation of women in local politics, the Law on Local Elections introduced obligation that "an election list must have at least 30 percent of candidates in total belonging to the less represented sex in the list" (Committee on the Elimination of Discrimination against Women, 2011, p. 30). This is based on the Law on Gender Equality stipulation that if (any) gender is represented by less than 30% in governing positions and the public sector, it has to be addressed by public authorities (*Zakon o ravnopravnosti polova*, 2009, p. 5).

The quota system had an immediate effect on the formal aspect of women's participation. Both during socialism and in the current gender regime, the improvements are evident, but their sustainability and effectiveness are debatable. In 2010, there were 12.5% of female members in the national parliament of Serbia, and in 2014 the number of women increased to 34% (European Commission, 2015; Ignjatović & Bošković, 2013; *Vlada Republike Srbije*, 2009). Women are underrepresented in local legislative and executive institutions and public sector companies (Baćanović, 2012). Only in the judiciary sector are women represented equally to men—again, two-thirds of men are presidents of the court (Mitrović, 2012). Today, women's participation in politics has become the issue of democratic legitimacy. Women's participation is compatible with the EU accession process (Rajačić-Čapaković & Pajvančić, 2005). However, women are a small minority in executive power (the number of women ministers has been between two and four since 2001), and women are also a minority among parliament boards and governing boards (*Vlada Republike Srbije*, 2016). Interestingly, most of the political parties in Serbia have introduced quotas within the party organization by themselves in the early days of post-2000 democracy. They also have "women's forums" (Rajačić-Čapaković & Pajvančić, 2005). These inconsistencies confirm the limitations of the quota system.

The findings from a relatively recent study show that Serbian citizens are aware of the low level of women's participation in decision-making, but political participation is the least important among the six priorities of gender equality (Ignjatović & Bošković, 2013).[24] At the same time, they have negative attitude towards quotas (Ignjatović et al., 2011). The reason for this position is that citizens equate the goal (political participation of women) with the instrument (quotas). Citizens believe that quotas interfere with voters' preference or party activities, and they fear corruption and nepotism (Ignjatović & Bošković, 2013). These anticipated unintended consequences related to the quota principle have been discussed in the literature. Franceschet has called this phenomenon a "label effect": "While not necessarily factually accurate, these beliefs nonetheless generate stereotypes about 'quota women' that negatively affect how female legislators are received and regarded by their colleagues" (Franceschet, 2008, p. 402).

The slow improvement of women's equal political representation has its roots in values and beliefs within the dominant political culture. The reason is a strong patriarchal political culture, represented in public opinion attitudes. For example, the citizens are divided about the statement that men are better political leaders than women: 42% of men agree (and 36% disagree) and 28% of women agree with the statement (54% disagree) (Ignjatović et al., 2011). Earlier evidence from the World Values Survey (2004) in Serbia shows higher level of mistrust about women's capacities for political leadership: 52% of men and 32% of women agreed that "men make better political leaders" (World Values Survey, 2004). According to Inglehart and Norris, inclusion of women in politics may lead to even more polarized attitudes about women as leaders (Inglehart & Norris, 2003).

Formalism, Conceptual Disputes and the Invisible Issues

Gender equality policy in Serbia has always been partly guided by formalism and ambivalence. As previously mentioned, during socialism, there was a gap between ideology and practice. After the war, a new model of the "strong woman" was celebrated and women's participation in the labor force was encouraged. At the same time, there was an underlying turn towards re-traditionalization and conservatism, in the promotion of "classical feminine values" (Gudac-Dodić, 2006, p. 65). Recently, we have seen the government showing a commitment to creating strategies and legislation for gender equality, and at the same time, a member of the government is showing his disrespect for women and misogyny in public.

There is evident a discrepancy between the legislation and implementation, and imbalance between different domains of intervention. In the evaluation of the previous Action Plan (2010–2015) it was stated that the focus was much more on political participation and participation in the economy, and much less on the media, education and health, and violence against women was not addressed in coordination with the Strategy for Elimination of Violence Against Women (Pajvančić et al., 2015). For example, the legislation on domestic and gender-based violence has been criticized for this (Ignjatović et al., 2014).

Another issue is the implementation of the introduced rights and legal provisions. There are legislative sanctions against gender-based discrimination in the labor market, education and other domains. However, "Shadow over Serbia" (2013) claims that the Gender Equality Law has no real effects on gender equality: the sanctions are not being enforced and the law's provisions are implemented only as recommendations (ASTRA et al., 2013). Other measures should be evaluated from a long-term perspective. For example, in gender-related strategies and laws, the quota system (or simple equalization of gender proportions) is favored as a policy instrument in all areas: the media, school textbooks, companies' management and political participation. There is a danger of quota formalism, and its effectiveness is yet to be confirmed.

Another important question is: what is the dominant gender equality paradigm in Serbia? It seems that a comprehensive "gender perspective" and "gender mainstreaming" have been a consensus. In strategic documents, the official policy is committed to gender equality in all areas of life, including beliefs and lifestyle, gender stereotypes in textbooks, in the media and generally in public discourse. For example, "the public information media are obliged to raise awareness of gender-based equality in their programs, as well as to undertake adequate measures to change social and cultural patterns, customs and any other practice. . . ." (Committee on the Elimination of Discrimination against Women, 2011, p. 23). The official statistics have started to register "time budget" and household labor broken down by gender, which was until recently addressed only in sociological studies (*Republički zavod za statistiku*, 2014; Tomanović & Ignjatović, 2006). However, it is debatable whether gender mainstreaming is always a good approach. As Booth and Bennet say, ". . . mainstreaming can appear to be a diluted version of positive action strategies and may appear irrelevant to women's lives" (Booth & Bennett, 2002, p. 441).

There are some disagreements among the public policy officials and women's rights organizations as to whether they are purely conceptual or interest-based. In the Shadow Report, NGOs have criticized the Gender Equality Directorate for their decision to support (financially and otherwise) local government bodies instead of NGOs; NGOs have also accused the Directorate of inadequate participatory process and marginalization in decision-making (ASTRA et al., 2013). A new draft law on gender equality is another example of the many dissonant voices in this process. The new draft law has been presented recently to the public. It has immediately received a critical response. The strongest criticism came from the representatives of the women's rights movement. The key issue was that the concept of gender equality from the 2009 law was replaced with a formulation: "equality between men and women." The key point was that this change was basically reducing the concept of gender, as social category, to sex as biological category.[25] Finally, the law was withdrawn due to the harsh criticism by women's rights groups, Ombudsperson, Commissioner for Equality. On the more general level, the dominant paradigm of gender equality policy seems to be very dependent on foreign aid and strategic steering, not only by the EU. This orientation has also been criticized by NGOs: the introduced mechanisms for gender equality are based on donor funding (ASTRA et al., 2013). It should be noted that not only financial support, but also the general concept and dominant paradigm has been influenced by donors' agendas.

Another line of dispute is among the gender equality activists, mostly based on different theoretical/ideological positions, as we saw in the case of surrogacy. A third source of disputes is related to different positions of the official gender equality policy and the majority of the population (including women). Not many citizens recognize the importance of gender equality as a political issue, and do not even consider gender equality when making voting decisions (Ignjatović & Bošković, 2013). Also, not all the areas are equally important to people, unlike the promoted comprehensiveness of the CEDAW convention. The citizens' disapproval of certain goals and policy instruments is found in a recent public opinion study. There is a consensus about the importance of dealing with violence against women, but not so much about women's political participation (Ignjatović & Bošković, 2013). The policy goals targeting the media, textbooks, political participation and participation of women have low support from the citizens. Content regulation and quotas are among lowest-ranked policy measures (Ignjatović & Bošković, 2013). Quotas are not acceptable in politics, even though the citizens acknowledge the low participation rate of women in politics. This should be taken into consideration, because the lack of consensus may cause problems in policy implementation. Another rarely discussed issue is gender equality as a political topic and its place in the political spectrum (Ignjatović & Bošković, 2013). Evidently, promotion of the political participation of women does not occur in a social vacuum, so right-wing orientation among women is a source of ambivalence for women's rights groups.[26]

In addressing the gender equality issues, there is always a risk of biased perspective, so we propose a more differentiated model of gender discrimination in Serbia based on "intersectionality."[27] We propose a provisory typology of five different types of discrimination of women in Serbia, some of which are not recognized by legislation: "*general discrimination*" that potentially has influence on all women, and usually this kind of discrimination is grounded in widely accepted social norms and stereotypes about gender roles (for example, job segregation in labor market or implicit exclusion of women from certain professions, or women's participation in politics);[28] "*multiple discrimination*," already recognized as a special case of discrimination in CEDAW reporting and national strategies, based on combination of gender and other characteristics (Roma women, rural elderly women,

IDP women with personal documents issues); *"partial discrimination"* that excludes only some women from exercising certain right (medical assisted reproductive rights are available only for married women, but not for women in same-sex partnerships or single women); *"contradictory discrimination"* that contains ambivalence because it can be understood as discrimination or advantage, depending on a woman's position (for example, early retirement is considered discrimination only by women in highly paid professions); and *"tacit discrimination,"* defined by non-recognition due to its political or other sensitivity (discrimination within certain religious groups).

Many forms of "general" and "multiple" discrimination have been addressed in strategies and legislation. However, many cases of partial, contradictory or tacit discrimination are either not recognized as such or remain torn between conflicting positions (even in the women's rights movement). The retirement issue is a good example of contradictory discrimination. As it was mentioned before, there has been a lot of resistance to the equalization of the retirement age for men and women. However, there was a division among women, because their "economic interest" is dominant over "gender interest." There is no unique solution to this problem, hence it can be considered "contradictory discrimination." "Tacit discrimination" is related to the reasons for the official CEDAW "reservations" that are usually based on religious norms (Brandt & Kaplan, 1995). Even though Serbia has not declared reservations to any of the CEDAW standards, there are tacit "reservations" when gender-based issues have a strong cultural/religious dimension. For example, child marriages are still common in Roma population, but policy actors are reluctant to address these issues. Nevertheless, this issue was addressed in the Initial Report as "negative customs" found in Roma and Vlach communities (Committee on the Elimination of Discrimination against Women, 2006). The Committee on the Elimination of Discrimination recommended focusing on the issue of early marriages (Committee on the Elimination of Discrimination against Women, 2007). Similarly, in the Shadow Report from 2007, it was only mentioned in one paragraph that the state does not impose sanctions on the "negative traditional customs," like child marriages in Roma population and bigamy (Muslim population) (Voice of Difference from Serbia, 2007). Social workers are still reluctant to deal with these issues. In addition to this, there is a fragmentation within the women's rights movement that impedes further actions. The arranged marriages and child marriages within the Roma community are not addressed as a general problem—they are perceived as a "niche" granted to Roma NGOs. The mainstream "violence against women" paradigm focuses on "general" violence in families and intimate relations, but it does not include culture-specific forms of violence against girls. Even Roma NGOs have only recently started to deal with this sensitive issue systematically (*Bibija*, 2016).

Another "taboo" for policy actors is religion. A recent survey shows an increasing level of domestic violence, marital rape and rape of under-age girls in the Muslim-dominant city of Novi Pazar in southwest Serbia (*Helsinški odbor za ljudska prava u Srbiji,* 2010). Another study shows that acts of violence in public space against women are common in this city (Mršević & Spasić, 2015). However, the ongoing process of re-traditionalization and its effects on certain categories of women have not been addressed in CEDAW reporting.

Conclusions

Some general conclusions can be made for the recent CEDAW history in Serbia, between the Initial Report, and just one year before the next report (2017). Formalism combined with gender mainstreaming has been the dominant orientation. The focus was mostly on new regulations, gender equality mechanisms and comprehensive gender equality perspective (from politics to family life). In less than 10 years, Serbia has seen two legislative frameworks for gender equality (the second one failed); two strategies for gender equality; introduction of mechanisms for gender equality at the national, regional and local levels (most of them being donor-based, project-type limited endeavors); and many different administration modalities for gender equality policy coordination (the last one, currently, being more political than operative body).

Another prominent issue is related to different actors involved in policy of gender equality. The ambivalence of the NGO sector towards the state has been prominent since the Initial Report. Non-governmental actors have constantly complained of their marginalization (both substantial and financial) and yet, many of the introduced policies are directly shaped by the most influential among them. Also, they have rightfully drawn attention to the fact that most of the programs are based on foreign donations rather than on the state budget. However, most of these programs are implemented by NGOs. The myth of division "NGO-versus-state" has permeated all reports, and yet, many activists have taken the responsibilities as policy makers. Further research is needed to understand the dialectics between the state and non-state part of gender equality policy making. Some of these questions have been raised by Ignjatović and Bošković (2013).

In order to understand the status of women from the perspective of CEDAW, much more is needed than a combination of "regulations plus statistics" approach. Relying on the official statistics and biased research may be misleading. Gender differences should not be automatically equalized with gender discrimination. In order to estimate the models of reality, more methodologically sound research is needed to gain insight into women's status, especially when some hidden factors reflect the wrong picture.

Here we come to the most difficult issue of all: what is the picture that we would like to see? Differences among gender equality concepts are now obvious, not only between the state and non-governmental activists, but between the official policy and the general public, and within the women's rights movement. This means that policies and methods are never consensual and without doubt: if citizens do not support quotas, should we look for other options as more legitimate? If the gender wage gap is not the result of direct gender discrimination, should we abandon this common belief in further evaluations? Should we continue focusing on the "gap approach" or move our attention to the "basic rights approach" if there are more striking examples of child marriages and illiteracy in the 21st century? In the light of these issues, the question "Is it possible to fully adopt gender equality in Serbia?" should be probably rephrased to: "Is it possible to be fully certain about gender equality?"

Notes

1 After 1918, Serbia formed part of the Kingdom of Serbs, Croats and Slovenes, renamed the Kingdom of Yugoslavia in 1929. After the Second World War, Serbia became part of Socialist Yugoslavia that was in 1963 renamed the Socialist Federal Republic of Yugoslavia (SFRY). The country dissolved through a series of wars from 1991, but Serbia remained in the union with Montenegro, first as the Federal Republic of Yugoslavia (FRY) and then as the State Union. In 2006 Montenegro declared its independence. The Republic of Serbia has been independent since then. CEDAW reporting has been influenced by these historical transformations.

2 Actually, women were granted the right to vote before the War, but there were no elections in Serbia before 1946.

3 The National Action Plan (2010–2015) was adopted for the implementation of the UN Resolution 1325.

4 Socialist Federal Republic of Yugoslavia was the official name of Yugoslavia between 1963 and 1992. In 1992, following the break up of the country, a new political entity, Federal Republic of Yugoslavia, was established. It lasted until early 2003.

5 The Initial Report was submitted on behalf of Serbia and Montenegro, as separate reports for Serbia and Montenegro (Committee on the Elimination of Discrimination against Women, 2006). The report had been submitted just before Montenegro declared independence.

6 The Stabilization and Association Process for the Western Balkans started in 1999, and Serbia joined the process in 2000. Serbia was granted a candidacy status in 2012, and the accession negotiations were formally opened in 2014 (European Commission, 2015).

7 In 1931, 62.8% of women were illiterate (in some areas over 90%), and in 1991, there were still 10% of illiterate women in Serbia (Gudac-Dodić, 2006).

8 The trend of veiling (hijab) has been increasingly popular in Muslim-dominant parts of southwest Serbia. "Revitalization" of covering among Muslim women started in the former Yugoslavia during the 1990s (Đurović, 2015).

9 Several items were used in both surveys. The results indicate that the respondents expressed a more positive attitude towards gender equality in the recent survey (Ignjatović et al., 2011; World Values Survey, 2004).

10 In 2013, drop-out rates were 0.3% (girls) and 0.2% (boys) in primary education, and 1.3% and 1.8% in secondary education for girls and boys, respectively.

11 Ignjatović's professional experience with Roma IDP women (mostly Muslims) from Kosovo in Novi Pazar (southwest Serbia) confirms that around 90% of young underage girls were illiterate because they were not encouraged (or allowed) to go to school. WHO organized literacy classes for those girls in 2014.

The Human Security Program was supported by the Japanese government, and implemented by WHO, UNDP, UNOPS and UNFPA (UN Country Team, 2012).

12 Since women were more likely to be employed in manual, non-creative jobs, they were more affected by alienation (Blagojević, 1991, p. 19). Also, exploitation was understood as a twofold phenomenon. In the labor market women were "reserve labor force." Another domain of exploitation was a non-economic exploitation of woman's emotional resources within the family (Blagojević, 1991, p. 20).

13 Gender employment gap is identified at primary and secondary levels of education, but not at tertiary level of education (Avlijaš et al., 2013).

14 The age of retirement for women has been raised gradually, with the aim of setting the age limit at 65 for both genders in 2032.

15 Actually, there is a combination of age (65) and minimum paid insurance contribution (15 years). Another option is 45 years of paid insurance contribution, regardless of age.

16 One of the women doctors said sarcastically that she would go through a sex change if that was necessary to keep her job. The Constitutional Court has ordered a delay of the retirement decision (Nikitović, 2015).

17 The number of women entrepreneurs has increased from 2003 to 2014 from 64,000 to 83,000, but women still make up approximately half of the men entrepreneurs (*Republički zavod za statistiku*, 2014).

18 Parental leave consists of three months of leave after childbirth and the rest of the leave until a child turns one year. Fathers are entitled to use the second part of the leave freely, but they rarely do that. The first part of the leave is limited to special cases (if mother dies or leaves a child) (*Zakon o radu*, 2005).

19 In 2014, life expectancy was 77.7 for women and 72.6 for men. Healthy life expectancy was 67.3 for women and 64.8 for men (Babović, 2016).

20 Informal debate within a closed mailing list. The Serbian case is part of the wider debate. At the global level, there is a question about the rationale for intervention at the EU level, because surrogacy is predominantly regulated by member states (family domain) (Brunet et al., 2013). The European Parliament has condemned surrogacy as a method of exploitation of women, which confirms the ambivalence inherent in this issue. Interestingly, this position is supported by both sides on the political spectrum, only for different reasons. Both the conservatives and radical-left groups are against it (ECPM, 2015; European Parliament, 2015; McElroy, 2008).

21 Abortion rates are even higher for Roma women: 31% and 56% for women aged 15–49 and 45–49, respectively (UNICEF, 2014).

22 For example, the proportion of women among members of parliament was 34% during Ceausescu's regime in Romania (UNICEF, 1999). In 2015, the proportion of women in the Cuban parliament was 49% (Inter-Parliamentary Union, 2015).

23 Political power was concentrated in the Communist Party, and participation of women was low within the Party's governing structures.

24 This is similar in the Eurobarometer survey of EU citizens' attitudes (Ignjatović & Bošković, 2013).

25 The new terminology has been criticized by the Ombudsman because of the legal inconsistencies (Ombudsman, 2015). The Commissioner for Protection of Equality has criticized different aspects of the new law: a lack of measures to encourage fathers to opt for the shared parental leave, missing provisions on stalking as gender violence, etc. (*Poverenik za zaštitu ravnopravnosti*, 2015).

26 In Western democracies, women's political preferences have started to move towards center-left parties. Unlike developed democracies, in the post-socialist countries, only the youngest and oldest generations of women opted

for center-left parties, but the majority of mid-generations moved towards right-wing options (Inglehart & Norris, 2000).
27 Intersectionality means that "the individual's social identities profoundly influence one's beliefs about and experience of gender" (Shields, 2008, p. 301).
28 Even though women were not explicitly forbidden from participation in professional military service (except as employed civilians), the conditions for student enrollment practically excluded them, and discrimination was implicitly socially acceptable. Women are now allowed to enroll in the Military Academy (since 2007) and Police Academy (since the school year 2002/2003) (Committee on the Elimination of Discrimination against Women, 2006; Committee on the Elimination of Discrimination against Women, 2011).

References

Arandarenko, M., Žarković-Rakić, J., & Vladisavljević, M. (2012). *Od Neaktivnosti do Zaposlenosti*. Beograd: Tim za socijalno uključivanje i smanjenje siromaštva, Kabinet potpredsednice Vlade za evropske integracije. Retrieved from http://socijalnoukljucivanje.gov.rs/wp-content/uploads/2014/05/Od-neaktivnosti-do-zaposlenosti-FINAL.pdf (accessed 14 April 2016).

ASTRA, Voice of Difference, Women in Black, & Labris and Autonomous Women's Center. (2013). *Shadow over Serbia: NGO Report for the 55th CEDAW Committee Session 2013*. Beograd: Autonomni ženski centar. Retrieved from http://www.astra.org.rs/wp-content/uploads/2008/07/Senka-nad-Srbijom.pdf (accessed 14 April 2016).

Avlijaš, S., Ivanović, N., Vladisavljević, M., & Vujić, S. (2013). *Gender Pay Gap in the Western Balkan Countries: Evidence from Serbia, Montenegro and Macedonia*. Belgrade: FREN. Retrieved from http://www.fren.org.rs/sites/default/files/Gender%20pay%20gap%20in%20the%20Western%20balkan%20countries.pdf (accessed 24 April 2016).

B92. (2015). Gašić će biti smenjen sa funkcije. Retrieved from http://www.b92.net/info/vesti/index.php?yyyy=2015&mm=12&dd=07&nav_category=11&nav_id=1071640 (accessed 2 May 2016).

Babović, M. (2016). Indeks rodne ravnopravnosti Koordinaciono telo za rodnu ravnopravnost/Tim za socijalno uključivanje i smanjenje siromaštva (2016). Retrieved from http://socijalnoukljucivanje.gov.rs/wp-content/uploads/2016/02/Izvestaj_Indeks_rodne_ravnopravnosti_2016_SRP.pdf (accessed 14 April 2016).

Baćanović, V. (2012). *Žene i Odlučivanje na Lokalnom Nivou sa Predlogom Metodologije za Praćenje*. Beograd: Uprava za rodnu ravnopravnost. Retrieved from http://www.gendernet.rs/files/Publikacije/Publikacije/Zene_i_odlucivanje_lokal.pdf. (accessed 13 April 2016).

Bibija. (2016). *(Pre)rani brakovi*. Beograd: Bibija. Retrieved from http://www.bibija.org.rs/publikacije/87-pre-rani-brakovi-zivotne-price-romkinja (accessed 2 May 2016).

Blagojević, M. (1991). *Žene izvan kruga*. Beograd: Institut za sociološka istraživanja Filozofskog fakulteta.

Blic. (2016). GAŠIĆ KONAČNO SMENJEN *Poslanici jednoglasno za razrešenje ministra odbrane*. Retrieved from http://www.blic.rs/vesti/politika/gasic-konacno-smenjen-poslanici-jednoglasno-za-razresenje-ministra-odbrane/v6ncq98 (accessed 25 September 2016)

Booth, C., & Bennett, C. (2002). Gender mainstreaming in the European Union: Towards a new conception and practice of equal opportunities? *European Journal of Women's Studies*, 9 (4), 430–446.

Bošković, A. (2010). Jezik, razlike, politike. In J. Filipović, A. Bošković, N. Mićunović, Z. Mršević, Lj. Rajić, D. Todorov, D. Stanojević, M. Trkulja, S. Vuković, A. Begović, J. Stefanović & S. Savić (Eds), *Okrugli sto na temu rodno osetljivih jezičkih politika*, Beograd: UNDP, pp. 75–81.

Brandt, M., & Kaplan, J.A. (1995). The tension between women's rights and religious rights: Reservations to CEDAW by Egypt, Bangladesh and Tunisia. *Journal of Law and Religion*, 12 (1), 105–142.

Brunet, L., Carruthers, J., Davaki, K., King, D., Marzo, C., & Mccandless, J. (2013). *A Comparative Study on the Regime of Surrogacy in EU Member States*. Brussels: European Parliament. Retrieved from http://www.europarl.europa.eu/Reg Data/etudes/etudes/join/2013/474403/IPOL-JURI_ET(2013)474403_EN.pdf (accessed 14 April 2016).

Čičkarić, L. (2009). Žene u političkoj areni: insajderke ili autsajderke? *Sociologija*, 51 (4), 423–436.

Committee on the Elimination of Discrimination against Women. (2006). Consideration of reports submitted by states parties under article 18 of the convention on the elimination of all forms of discrimination against women initial report of states parties—Serbia. Retrieved from http://tbinternet.ohchr.org/_layouts/treatybodyexternal/Download.aspx?symbolno=CEDAW%2fC%2fSCG%2f1&Lang=en (accessed 20 April 2016).

Committee on the Elimination of Discrimination against Women. (2007). Concluding Comments of the Committee on the Elimination of Discrimination against Women: Serbia. Retrieved from http://tbinternet.ohchr.org/_layouts/TreatyBodyExternal/Countries.aspx?CountryCode=SRB&Lang=EN (accessed 14 April 2016).

Committee on the Elimination of Discrimination against Women. (2011). Consideration of reports submitted by states parties under article 18 of the convention on the elimination of all forms of discrimination against women. Combined second and third periodic reports of States parties. Serbia. Retrieved from http://tbinternet.ohchr.org/_layouts/treatybodyexternal/Download.aspx?symbolno=CEDAW%2fC%2fSRB%2f2-3&Lang=en (accessed 14 April 2016).

Committee on the Elimination of Discrimination against Women. (2013). Concluding observations on the combined second and third periodic reports of Serbia. Retrieved from http://tbinternet.ohchr.org/_layouts/TreatyBodyExternal/Countries.aspx?CountryCode=SRB&Lang=EN (accessed 14 April 2016).

Committee on the Elimination of Discrimination against Women. (2016). Concluding observations on the combined second and third periodic reports of Serbia. Addendum. Retrieved from http://tbinternet.ohchr.org/Treaties/CEDAW/Shared%20Documents/SRB/CEDAW_C_SRB_CO_2-3_Add-1_15052_E.pdf (accessed 18 April 2016).

Criminal Code. (2002). Official Gazette of the Republic of Serbia No. 26/77. Beograd: Službeni glasnik. Retrieved from: http://www.legislationline.org/documents/section/criminal-codes/country/5 (accessed 18 April (2016).

Đurović, M. (2015). Hidžab kao fenomen konstruisanja i osporavanja identiteta: primjer savremenog Novog Pazara. *Etnoantropološki problemi*, 10 (4), 821–838.

ECPM. (2015). European Parliament condemns surrogacy. Retrieved from http://ecpm. info/news/european-parliament-condemns-surrogacy (accessed 14 April 2016).

Erlich, St. V. (1971). *Jugoslavenska Porodica u Transformaciji.* Zagreb: Liber.

European Commission. (2015). Serbia 2015 report accompanying the document communication from the commission to the European parliament, the council, the European economic and social committee and the committee of the regions. Retrieved from http://ec.europa.eu/enlargement/pdf/key_docu ments/2015/20151110_report_serbia.pdf (accessed 14 April 2016).

European Parliament. (2015). Report on the annual report on human rights and democracy in the World 2014 and the European Union's policy on the matter. 2015/2229(INI). Retrieved from http://www.europarl.europa.eu/sides/getDoc. do?pubRef=-//EP//NONSGML+REPORT+A8-2015-0344+0+DOC+PDF+V0// EN (accessed 17 June 2016).

Franceschet, S. (2008). Gender quotas and women's substantive representation: Lessons from Argentina. *Politics and Gender,* 4 (3), 393–425.

Gudac-Dodić, V. (2006). Položaj žene u Srbiji (1945–2000). In L. Perović (Ed.), *Srbija u modernizacijskim procesima: žene i deca,* Belgrade: Helsinki Committee for Human Rights in Serbia, pp. 33–130.

Helsinški odbor za ljudska prava u Srbiji. (2010). Položaj žena u Sandžaku. In S.Biserko (Ed.), *Sandžak i evropska perspektiva,* Belgrade: Helsinki Committee for Human Rights in Serbia, pp. 91–95.

Ignjatović, S. (2006). Engendering education/science policy analysis: Women scientists in Serbia. In M.F. Gajdusek, A.C. Mayr & M. Polzer (Eds), *Science Policy and Human Resources Development in South-Eastern Europe in the Context of European Integration,* Vienna: Austrian Federal Ministry for Education, Science and Culture, pp. 197–206.

Ignjatović, S., & Bošković, A. (2013). "Are we there yet?" Citizens of Serbia and public policy on gender equality within the EU accession context. *European Journal of Womens's Studies,* 20 (4), 425–440.

Ignjatović, S., Pantić, D., Bošković, A., & Pavlović, Z. (2011). *Građanke i građani Srbije o rodnoj ravnopravnosti.* Beograd: Uprava za rodnu ravnopravnost, Institut društvenih nauka.

Ignjatović, T., Drobnjak, T., Sekulović, I., Lukić, M., Jelačić, M., Anđelković, M., Macanović, M., & Pešić, D. (2014). *Analiza usklađenosti zakonodavnog i strateškog okvira Republike Srbije sa Konvencijom Saveta Evrope o sprečavanju i borbi protiv nasilja nad ženama i nasilja u porodici—osnovna studija.* Beograd: Autonomni ženski centar. Retrieved from http://www.womenngo.org.rs/images/ vesti-14/Studija.pdf (accessed 14 April 2016).

Inglehart, R., & Norris, P. (2000). The developmental theory of the gender gap: Women's and men's voting behavior in global perspective. *International Political Science Review,* 21 (4), 441–463.

Inglehart, R., & Norris, P. (2003). *Rising Tide.* Cambridge, MA: Cambridge University Press.

Institut za javno zdravlje Srbije. (2015). *Zdravstveno-statistički godišnjak Republike Srbije 2014.* Beograd: Institut za javno zdravlje Srbije. Retrieved from http:// www.batut.org.rs/download/publikacije/pub2014.pdf (accessed 13 April 2016).

Inter-Parliamentary Union. (2015). Women in national parliaments. Retrieved from http://www.ipu.org/wmn-e/classif.htm (accessed 13 April 2016).

Keller, L. (2014). The impact of states parties' reservations to the convention on the elimination of all forms of discrimination against women. *Michigan State Law Review*, 309 (2), 309–326.

Kočić-Rakočević, N., & Miljević, A. (2003). *Romi i obrazovanje između potreba, želja i mogućnosti/The Roma Education between Needs, Wishes and Possibilities.* Beograd: Romski dečji centar.

Kolin, M., & Čičkarić, L. (2010). *Ekonomska i politička participacija žena u Srbiji u kontekstu evropskih integracija.* Beograd: Institut društvenih nauka.

Korać, M. (1991). *Zatočenice pola.* Beograd: Institut za sociološka istraživanja Filozofskog fakulteta.

Law on the Protector of Citizens. (2005). Official Gazette of the Republic of Serbia No. 79/2005 and 54/2007. Beograd: Službeni glasnik. Retrieved from: http://www.zastitnik.rs/index.php/o-nama/normativni-okvir-za-rad/643–2009–10–27–16–01–21 (accessed 4 August 2016).

Markov, S. (2001). *Pravo glasa žena.* Beograd: CESID.

McElroy, W. (2008). Feminists against women: The new reproductive technologies. Retrieved from http://www.wendymcelroy.com/reason2.htm (accessed 13 April 2016).

Mešihat islamske zajednice u Srbiji. (2016). Hidžab i obrazovanje. Retrieved from http://mesihat.org/2016/02/06/hidzab-i-obrazovanje/ (accessed 13 April 2016).

Ministarstvo rada, zapošljavanja i socijalne politike. (2014). *Izveštaj o prvom intervalu (od 25.jula 2013. godine do 25. marta 2014. godine) praćenja sprovođenja preporuka Komiteta Ujedinjenih nacija o eliminaciji diskriminacije žena (CEDAW).* Beograd: Ministarstvo rada, zapošljavanja i socijalne politike/Uprava za rodnu ravnopravnost. Retrieved from http://www.gendernet.rs/files/doku menta/Izvestaji_Uprave/CEDAW_-_Prvi_ciklus.pdf (accessed 24 April 2016).

Ministarstvo zdravlja. (2014). Rezultati rada zdravstvenih medijatorki u naseljima od 01.01.2009.—31.05.2014. Retrieved from http://www.zdravlje.gov.rs/show-page.php?id=73 (accessed 13 April 2016).

Mitrović, B. (2012). *Rodna nejednakost na pozicijama odlučivanja u Srbiji.* Beograd: Uprava za rodnu ravnopravnost. Retrieved from http://www.slideshare.net/BranimirMitrovic/urrnejednakostlr-49801387 (accessed 13 April 2016).

Mršević, Z., & Spasić, D. (2015). Nasilje nad ženama u islamskoj kulturi i uloga policije u zaštiti žrtava. In J. Ćirić, V. Džomić & M. Jeftić (Eds), *Religija, Politika Pravo*, Beograd: Institut za uporedno pravo, Mitropolija Crnogorsko-primorska, Centar za proučavanje Religiji i versku toleranciju, pp. 541–570.

Nikitović, V. (2015). Ustavni sud odlaže penzije, doktorka ostaje pri promeni pola. *Radio Slobodna Evropa.* Retrieved from http://www.slobodnaevropa.org/con tent/ustavni-sud-odlaze-penzije-doktorka-ostaje-pri-promeni-pola/27296844. html (accessed 17 June 2016).

Ombudsman. (2015). Mišljenje o Nacrtu zakona o ravnopravnosti žena i muškaraca. Retrieved from http://www.ombudsman.rs/index.php/lang-sr/2011–12–11–11–34–45/4515–2015–12–31–11–07–36 (accessed 14 April 2016).

Pajvančić, M., Babović, M., Jarić, I., Dimitrijević, B., Mršević, Z., Milivojević, S., & Vuković, O. (2015). Evaluacija Nacionalnog akcionog plana za primenu Nacionalne strategije za unapređenje položaja žena i unapređenje rodne ravnopravnosti u Republici Srbiji 2010–2015—(sažetak). Report. Retrieved from http://www. gendernet.rs/rrpage.php?chapter=24 (accessed 28 April 2016).

Petrović, B. (2016). *Субвенције страним „инвеститорима"—јефтини политички поени који нас скупо коштају.* Retrieved from https://bogdanpetrovicblog.wordpress.com/2016/04/03/субвенције-сТраним-инвесТиТорима/ (accessed 2 May 2016).

Poverenik za zaštitu ravnopravnosti. (2015). Mišljenje o pojedinim odredbama nacrta Zakona o ravnopravnosti žena i muškaraca. Retrieved from http://www.ravnopravnost.gov.rs/rs/законодавне-иницијаТиве-и-мишљење-о-прописима/мишљење-о-појединим-одредбама-нацрТа-закона-о-равноправносТи-жена-и-мушкараца (accessed 13 April 2016).

Rajačić-Čapaković, J., & Pajvančić, M. (2005). Žene u političkim strankama. In Z. Lutovac (Ed.), *Političke stranke u Srbiji: struktura i funkcionisanje*, Beograd: Friedrich Ebert Stiftung, pp. 75–91.

Rašević, M. (2008). Da li je evidentirani broj abortusa u Srbiji realan? *Stanovništvo*, 46 (2), 7–21.

Rašević, M., & Sedlecki, K. (2011). Pitanje postojanja abortusne kulture u Srbiji. *Stanovništvo*, 49 (1), 1–13.

Republički zavod za statistiku. (2014). *Žene i muškarci u Republici Srbiji.* Beograd: Republički zavod za statistiku. Retrieved from http://pod2.stat.gov.rs/ObjavljenePublikacije/G2014/pdf/G20146008.pdf (accessed 14 April 2016).

Schwindt-Bayer, L.A., & Mishler, W. (2005). An integrated model of women's representation. *The Journal of Politics*, 67 (2), 407–428.

Sekulić, J. (2012). *Usklađivanje privatnog i profesionalnog života.* Beograd: Uprava za rodnu ravnopravnost. Retrieved from http://www.gendernet.rs/files/Publikacije/Publikacije/URR-Studija-SRB_LR.pdf. (accessed 13 April 2016).

Shields, S.A. (2008). Gender: An intersectionality perspective. *Sex Roles*, 59 (5–6), 301–311.

Tanjug. (2015). Gašić: Volim novinarke koje ovako lako kleknu. N1. Retrieved from http://rs.n1info.com/a115681/Vesti/Gasic-Volim-novinarke-koje-ovako-lako-kleknu.html (accessed 17 June 2016).

Tomanović, S., & Ignjatović, S. (2004). Mladi u tranziciji: Između porodice porekla i porodice opredeljenja. In: M. Nikolić & Srećko Mihailović (Eds), *Mladi zagubljeni u tranziciji*, Beograd: Centar za proučavanje alternativa, pp. 39–64.

Tomanović, S., & Ignjatović, S. (2006). The transition of young people in a transitional society. *Journal of Youth Studies*, 9 (3), 269–285.

Tomanović, S., & Ignjatovic, S. (2010). The significance and meaning of family transitions for young people: The case of Serbia in comparative perspective. *ANNALES: Annals for Istrian and Mediterranean Studies*, 20 (1), 27–40.

UN Country Team. (2012). Improving human security for vulnerable communities in Southwest Serbia. Retrieved from http://www.rs.undp.org/content/dam/serbia/docs/Our%20Projects/UNDP_SRB_Improving_Human_Security_for_Vulnerable_Communities_in_Southwest_Serbia.pdf (accessed 29 April 2016).

UNICEF. (1999). Women in transition: The MONEE project CEE/CIS/Baltics regional monitoring report—No. 6. 1999. Retrieved from https://www.unicef-irc.org/publications/pdf/monee6/cover.pdf (accessed 13 April 2016).

UNICEF. (2014). Serbia multiple indicator cluster survey. UNICEF Belgrade. Retrieved from http://www.unicef.org/serbia/Serbia2014MICS_NationalandRomaSettlements_Eng_2015FINAL.pdf (accessed 23 April 2016).

Vlada Republike Srbije. (2009). Nacionalna strategija za poboljšanje položaja žena i unapređivanje rodne ravnopravnosti. Retrieved from http://www.gendernet.rs/files/dokumenta/Domaci/Nacionalna_strategija_cir.pdf (accessed 28 April 2016).

Vlada Republike Srbije. (2016). Nacionalna strategija za rodnu ravnopravnost za period od 2016. do 2020. godine sa akcionim planom za period od 2016. do 2018. godine. Retrieved from http://www.gendernet.rs/rrpage.php?chapter=24 (accessed 28 April 2016).

Voice of Difference from Serbia. (2007). Alternative report to the CEDAW committee. Retrieved from http://www.astra.org.rs/wp-content/uploads/2008/07/CEDAW.pdf (accessed 17 June 2016).

World Economic Forum. (2015). The global gender gap index results in 2015. Retrieved from http://reports.weforum.org/global-gender-gap-report-2015/the-global-gender-gap-index-results-in-2015/ (accessed 13 April 2016).

World Values Survey. (2004). Online data analysis, world values survey wave 4: 2000–2004. Retrieved from http://www.worldvaluessurvey.org (accessed 13 April 2016).

Zakon o lečenju neplodnosti postupcima biomedicinski potpomognutog oplođenja. (2009). Službeni glasnik Republike Srbije No. 72/2009. Beograd: Službeni glasnik. Retrieved from http://www.rfzo.rs/download/zakoni/Zakon_vto.pdf (accessed 19 June 2016).

Zakon o osnovama sistema obrazovanja i vaspitanja. (2009). Službeni glasnik Republike Srbije No. 72/2009, 52/2011, 55/2013, 35/2015, 68/2015. Beograd: Službeni glasnik. Retrieved from http://www.paragraf.rs/propisi/zakon_o_osno vama_sistema_obrazovanja_i_vaspitanja.html (accessed 16 April 2016).

Zakon o radu. (2005). Službeni glasnik Republike Srbije No. 24/2005, 61/2005, 54/2009, 32/2013, 75/2014. Beograd: Službeni glasnik. Retrieved from http://paragraf.rs/propisi/zakon_o_radu.html (accessed 16 April 2016).

Zakon o ravnopravnosti polova. (2009). Službeni glasnik Republike Srbije No. 104/09. Beograd: Službeni Glasnik. Retrieved from http://www.parlament. gov.rs/народна-скупшТина.115.html (accessed 13 April 2016).

Zakon o zabrani diskriminacije. (2009). Službeni glasnik Republike Srbije No 22/09. Beograd: Službeni glasnik. Retrieved from http://www.paragraf.rs/pro pisi/zakon_o_zabrani_diskriminacije.html (accessed 16 April 2016).

10 Gender Equality in Croatia

Snježana Vasiljević

Introduction

The gender equality concept in the Republic of Croatia has been developed in a comprehensive legal framework. Since the adoption of the first Gender Equality Act (GEA) in 2003, Croatia has significantly changed the legal and policy framework in terms of gender mainstreaming. Croatia ratified CEDAW in 1992, and its Optional Protocol in 2001. However, the most relevant legal changes happened after Croatia signed the Stabilization and Association Agreement with the EU, which entered into force in February 2005 (it was signed in October 2001). Croatian equality legislation is in accordance with the EU legal framework and gender equality standards are recognized on paper. However, deep understanding of the implementation of the gender equality concept is missing.

The first section of this paper will explore the Croatian historical background of gender equality protection and how women were protected before the break-up of the former Yugoslavia. The second section will introduce the legal and policy framework concerning gender equality. While the transformation of gender equality policies can be considered from different perspectives, for the purpose of this paper a view will be taken from a select number of them. I will consider changes in Croatian law and their applicability to women's lives. I will discuss how Croatian equality legislation has changed under the influence of the EU, whether the new laws are sufficient, and to what extent the international gender equality concept is applied. While changes in the law are the most important ways in which the EU has impacted on gender equality in Croatia, the effects of these changes are most visible in the government actions and activities that are directed at women. This chapter will explore how the concept of gender equality is mainstreamed through the most relevant documents and how it is understood by relevant stakeholders and practitioners. The third section will reveal the deficiencies in the existing legal and policy framework and how they might be overcome. This also means that there is a need for precise recommendations in order to fully implement certain concepts imported from the EU legal and policy framework. The following question in particular will be analyzed: how is equality understood and in what areas is equality implemented? Finally, I will consider the impact of the EU on the Croatian public sphere, and explore what trends in EU debates on women and gender equality are most visible in Croatia, and also ask how debates conducted in the EU impact on Croatian social policies. The fourth section will analyze the practice of the national equality body and national courts in cases of gender discrimination. This will show that although relevant gender discrimination cases are sometimes treated as such, on other occasions gender discrimination is hidden behind other forms of harassment or other forms of legally recognized concepts. The fourth section is dedicated to critical considerations of whether international and European gender equality concepts are different from those existing in Croatia.

The key findings presented in the conclusion are that in the regulation of equality between men and women, Croatia is not essentially behind the current member states of the EU, but there is still room for the improvement.

Historical Background

Croatia is a country located in southern Europe with a total population of 4,284,889 inhabitants, 2,218,554 (51.8%) of whom are women (Croatian Bureau of Statistics, 2011). According to the 2011 census, in the ethnic structure of the Republic of Croatia, there are 90.42% Croats, 4.36% Serbs, 0.73% Bosnians, 0.42% Italians, 0.41% Albanians and 0.40% Roma, while the share of other national minorities is lower than 0.40% each. According to religious affiliation, there are 86.28% Catholics, 4.44% Orthodox and 1.47% Muslims, while the share of other religious affiliations is lower than 1.00% each (Croatian Bureau of Statistics, 2013). Croatia passed through the transition period where war raged until 16 years ago, and left behind a devastated country with many problems, ranging from economic ones to problems associated with high tolerance to all forms of violence, including violence against women.

Western democratic systems, characterized by the gradual entry of women into the public sphere and an increase in their political participation, were founded on reform within the political system. At the same time, politics in Central and Eastern European (CEE) countries produced only formal equality (Tomšić, 1981, p. 67). Since 1988, the proportion of women in parliaments in all CEE countries has declined following national elections. "One of the reasons could be the rising importance of parliament, in that it might more accurately reflect the real power in society, in contrast to previous occupational and social group representation" (UN, 1992, pp. 15–16). The Croatian case has been no exception (Deželan et al., 2013, p. 23).

In Croatia, which was part of the Federal People's Republic of Yugoslavia (from 1963, the Socialist Federal Republic of Yugoslavia), women obtained the right to vote on August 11, 1945. In socialist Yugoslavia, the emancipation of women was primarily fueled by a general focus on the accelerated development of the country. It was necessary to overcome patriarchal patterns by taking special measures. Despite industrialization, women were considered primarily responsible for childcare, cooking and tending to the home. During socialism some of the rights in the public sphere, especially those related to the labor market (e.g., the right to work, equal treatment and equal pay, protective provisions for pregnancy and maternity, the working conditions of women) were imposed by the state and benefited gender equality. However, some other issues, especially those seen as part of the private sphere (e.g., domestic violence, marital rape, abortion, the gendered division of labor, LGTB rights) were never addressed by policy measures, thus negatively affecting women's status and the gender equality agenda in general (Havelková, 2010). Some authors claim that "although socialism introduced the principle of gender equality and parity that legally granted women rights equal to those of men, gender equality legislation in socialist countries did not create possibilities for women to achieve their career goals, especially in highly paid jobs" (Bliss & Garratt, 2001, p. 4). The situation in former socialist countries has changed slightly since the 1970s.

The role of women in politics changed with the institutional development of the socialist one-party system. The *Constitution of the Socialist Republic of Croatia* (1974) guaranteed equality before the law on the grounds of sex (Article 229). The Constitution, statues or social agreements introduced women's quotas, and there was a kind of positive action regarding improving women's political representation which was expressed through pragmatic guidelines in resolutions and other legally non-binding documents (Deželan et al., 2013, p. 14). The inclusion of women's issues in Croatian politics fostered women's participation in education, employment and political decision-making.

The breakdown of socialism revealed that political control and social interventionism led to faster solutions, but their quality remains questionable. The period of transition was a very difficult time for the development of the principle of equality between men and women. "During the early transformation period, a gender equality agenda was not among the priority policy areas in post-communist countries" (Dobrotić et al., 2013, p. 221). The established political order, after the first multiparty elections, is most commonly defined as an authoritarian regime (Kasapović, 2001, p. 17) or as a frozen democracy (Fink-Hafner & Hafner-Fink, 2009, p. 16). Some authors divide the forms of the Croatian state since independence (1991) as follows: 10 years of nationalist rule, divided into the period of war (1991–1995), the time of reinforced authoritarianism searching for the enemy within (1996–1998), and the beginnings of democratic transformation (1998–2000), culminating in the elections in January 2000 (Stubbs, 2006, p. 165).

As religion and ethnicity became integrated into Croatia's identity in the 1990s, the traditional role of women emerged as increasingly dominant. "The valorization of Croatian women's role as mothers and the expectation that they will stay in the home to care for children has contributed to the unfavorable position of women in the Croatian labor markets" (Irvine & Sutlović, 2015, p. 74). This process was highly supported by the Catholic Church and the national government, which has created strong pressures and incentives for women to stay home and have more children. This ideology prevented women from entering the labor force, becoming entrepreneurs, or rising to positions of economic leadership and decision-making. Hence, it is no surprise that women participated in such disappointing proportions in the Croatian Parliament. Until the elections in 2000, these proportions were among the lowest in comparable countries (1990–4.6%, 1992–5.1%, 1995–7.1%).

Tomić-Koludrović and Kunac argues that economic transition and crisis have resulted in the "triple burden" for women, i.e., economic necessity forced them to take on, besides their regular work, additional women's work or to work in the black economy (Tomić-Koludrović & Kunac, 2000, pp. 5–20). Women performed a range of agricultural tasks and were often largely responsible for the livestock and gardening and nowadays they participate in part-time work as well as paid and unpaid work in the grey economy, which is often less secure and lower paid (Irvine & Sutlović, 2015, p. 73).

In 2000, the winning reformist center-left coalition began constitutional changes, establishing Croatia as a parliamentary democracy and bringing to an end the political monopoly of the Croatian Democratic Union (a right-wing party). "A significant improvement was made as 21.9% of women won parliamentary seats. Although not exclusively, electoral system reforms from 1999, which established a proportional electoral system, have positively affected women's representation—the proportion of elected women in the parliament tripled compared to 1995. The majority of elected seats went to the center-left political parties. The Social Democratic Party (SDP) took the lead, resulting in a drastic increase of women in parliament" (Deželan et al., 2013, p. 20).

Following the democratic reforms started in 2000 by the center-left coalition, the process of Europeanization also became one of the most important processes to mark post-communist transformation in Europe. The Europeanization process covered a wide range of policy areas in post-communist countries, including the gender equality agenda. However, some problems remain, such as a segregated labor market, income inequalities, lack of women in decision-making bodies, imbalance between family and work responsibilities, etc.

The institutionalization of gender equality systems in Croatia is the result of a threefold process: the obligations that were put before Croatia as an EU candidate country, the demands and initiatives of women's organizations with respect to state administration, and, finally, the victory of the social-democrat coalition in the 2000 parliamentary election, an option traditionally more inclined to gender equality (Deželan et al., 2013, p. 20). A review of gender equality literature emphasizes the failure to implement the EU agenda and domestic resistance to implementing and discussing gender equality. Although recent literature gives more weight to domestic factors, it still seems that the EU agenda is pictured in an ambiguous way (Dobrotić et al., 2013, p. 235). The changes have not had a radical and systemic impact on women's issues. I would rather call them "soft changes." Soft changes came through "translation" and "transplantation" of various international concepts which impact on government projects, producing a variety of outcomes. There was no consistent interpretation of internationally adopted standards, which resulted in the non-implementation of policy measures scattered throughout different policy documents. In my opinion, multiple norms and overlapping policy measures led to legal uncertainty.

Croatia joined the EU on July 1, 2013. Since then, Croatia has aligned its national legislation with EU law and policies, including the gender equality framework. However, the parliamentary elections held in Croatia in November 2015 mirrored the conservative background of the Croatian population and growing nationalism, expressed through the public speech of leading politicians. The leading political parties (the Croatian Democratic Union and MOST—Bridge of independent representatives) declared publicly that Croatia should follow its traditional routes. This can be seen in public initiatives to forbid abortion and in proactive demographic policy through "pro-life" initiatives, which put a huge burden on women, who are considered to be responsible for negative demographic trends. Discussions in the media predominately occupied by male politicians, philosophers, sociologists and lawyers are limited to *"pro-choice"* and *"pro-life"* debates. No one has invoked the issue of women's rights, except for a small percentage of women invited to say something about this topic. Abortion is not characterized as a question of rights, but as a controversial hot political issue. Unsuccessful movements and conservative ideology of the new government led to the political crisis and new elections in September 2016.

Despite the fact that Croatia, according to the Croatian Constitution, is a secular state, it is a predominately Catholic country (86.28%) and the Catholic Church seeks to shape public opinion in all "controversial" issues, such as abortion and same-sex marriage. This attitude has deepened the nationalistic drive to suppress debate on the freedom of choice. This caused a chain reaction and the left-leaning intellectual elite is warning citizens of the serious consequences of leading the country into a nationalistic cave. Most women's organizations have supported left-wing parties in their struggle to challenge growing nationalism. In 2016, the left-leaning intellectual elite, including women's organizations, have held several demonstrations against the current nationalistic political mainstream.[1]

The disruption of advances in gender equality is closely related to the ongoing economic crisis. Unfortunately, there is no political will to take steps in terms of economic development. Instead, public debates continue to be related to history and the communist regime, which is declared evil. Croatia needs an efficient, clean and reform-minded government, reform of public administration, a modern educational system, efforts to lower the level of corruption and more women in politics. In recent years, due to the economic crisis in Croatia, the status of women has fallen. In the parliamentary elections held in November 2015, women gained only 15% of the seats in the Parliament, which was dominated by conservative parties. This problem can be seen across the EU member states (Freedom House, 2015). In the early parliamentary elections held in September 2016, women gained 12.6% of the seats in the Parliament which is the lowest representation of women in the Croatian parliament in the last fifteen years.

For comparison, after the elections in Croatia in 2011, 19.8% of the newly elected representatives were women in a parliament dominated by social democrats, which is fewer than in the previous parliamentary term that began in 2007 (22.5%). However, although women are still not equal to men in political and public decision-making, there has still been visible progress in this area. According to the Report by the Republic of Croatia on the application of the Beijing Declaration and Platform for Action (1995) and the outcomes of the 23rd Special Session of the UN General Assembly (2000)—Beijing + 20, published by the Gender Equality Office of the Government of the Republic of Croatia in May 2014, "in 1995, only 7.1% of Members of Parliament were women, but in 2000 the proportion rose to 21.9%. After the elections in 2003, 2007 and 2011, the share of women remained at roughly the same level. In 2007, female parliamentary representation in the Parliament dominated by the right-wing party (Croatian Democratic Union) reached a promising 25.5%, whereas in 2011, when the Parliament was dominated by social democrats, the percentage of female MPs dropped to 19.8% in 2011. For comparison, in 1995, 9.5% of ministers were female, and in 2011 this rose to 20.0%. The Republic of Croatia also had a woman in the position of Prime Minister from 2009 to 2011."[2] On the basis of the quantitative evidence currently available, it seems fair to suggest that the percentage of 25% seems to represent a glass ceiling in the political representation of women. In this paper, I claim that women in the Croatian political arena and society in general are hidden behind traditional curtains. Even though Croatia elected its first woman president in January 2015, women are generally underrepresented in political office.

Legal and Policy Framework—The Current State of Affairs

This section introduces the legal and policy framework concerning gender equality in Croatia. It will explore how the concept of gender equality is mainstreamed through the most relevant documents and how it is understood by relevant stakeholders and practitioners in an attempt to address the issue of the diminishing role of women in all spheres of life.

Firstly, the analysis is based on official government documents and reports on gender equality—mainly the *National Policy on Gender Equality 2011–2015* (published in 2011), which describes the goals and strategies of antidiscrimination policy, and the Croatian *IV and V Report to the CEDAW Committee* (submitted in 2013). Secondly, I analyze national equality legislation, including the Antidiscrimination Act and the Gender Equality Act and other legislative acts which implement the concept of equality. Thirdly, I discuss the annual reports of the Ombudsperson for Gender Equality and their role in the suppression of gender discrimination. Finally, I report on interviews with representatives of antidiscrimination and women's organizations to share their knowledge and experiences of the last 13 years.

The *Constitution of the Republic of Croatia* (2010) recognizes gender equality as one of the highest values. Croatia has had a comprehensive antidiscrimination legal framework since the adoption of the Antidiscrimination Act in 2008, which entered into force on January 1, 2009.[3] In Croatia, equal treatment is currently guaranteed under many legislative acts, of which the Antidiscrimination Act (hereinafter: ADA) is considered as the most important.[4] As regards the enforcement of equal treatment legislation, the Ombudsperson for Human Rights (established in 1990), the Ombudsperson for Gender Equality (established in 2003), the Ombudsperson for People with Disabilities (established in 2008) and the Ombudsperson for Children (established in 2003) play a significant role. Several NGOs are also very active in promoting equality.

The first gender equality concept was adopted in 2003, when the first Gender Equality Act (hereinafter: GEA) and the Same-Sex Relationships Act entered into force, but in January 2008 the Constitutional Court decided to revoke the GEA because of an infringement in Parliament of the constitutional procedures required for its entry into force.[5] Under national and international pressure, a new version of the Act was formulated. In February 2008 the Ministry of Veterans, Family Affairs and Inter-generational Solidarity created a working group to bring the new Gender Equality Act in line with relevant EU directives. The new Gender Equality Act entered into force in July 2008 and it defines gender equality in line with the definition in the UN Convention on the Elimination of all Forms of Discrimination against Women (hereinafter: CEDAW) and with European Union directives on gender equality, direct and indirect discrimination, sexual harassment and other special measures. Its scope of application lies in areas such as employment and work, education, political parties, the media and official statistics.

The new Gender Equality Act (2008) introduces sanctions for the discriminatory conduct of the employer. It also defines separately the provisions on misdemeanors with a view to sanctioning every legal and physical entity not respecting the provisions contained in the GEA. As opposed to the 2003 Gender Equality Act, the new Act provides for fines for natural and legal persons. In addition to protection in the civil procedure, victims of discrimination may seek court protection in misdemeanor proceedings as well, which is an important addition to the previous Act (*CEDAW Report for Croatia*, 2013).

Article 4 GEA states that "its provisions may not be interpreted or applied in a manner that would restrict or reduce the content of the guarantees on gender equality arising from the general rules of international law, the EU acquis, CEDAW, agreements of the United Nations (hereinafter: UN) on civil and political rights, as well as economic, social and cultural rights, and the European Convention on the Protection of Human Rights and Fundamental Freedoms" (*Croatian Report on the Application of the Beijing Declaration and the Platform for Action*, 2014).

All forms of gender discrimination are also prohibited by the Antidiscrimination Act, including multiple discrimination. However, since the ADA entered into force (2009), no case of multiple discrimination has been brought to the national courts. There is no awareness of its definition or meaning. Courts are also reluctant to interpret discrimination cases using a teleological method and prefer to interpret discrimination in a formal manner. Citizens and equality bodies recognize multiple discrimination but their action in this field is limited because of a collision of competences. The Ombudsperson for Human Rights collects complaints on grounds of multiple discrimination. There has been a decline in reporting multiple discrimination in last three years (2015–15.9%, 2014–18.6%, 2013–24.19%). Despite the tendency of prohibiting all discrimination through a single act, legislative gender equality measures just do not work in cases of multiple discrimination.

Antidiscrimination provisions have also been included in many other acts. The first Act for Protection against Violence in the Family was adopted in 2003 and amended in 2009. The definition of domestic violence includes physical abuse, psychological abuse, intimidation, sexual harassment and the restriction of freedom of movement or communication. The National Strategy on Protection from Family Violence 2011–2016 (Government of the Republic of Croatia, 2011b) was adopted in February 2011. In 2003, the Croatian Parliament adopted the first Gender Equality Act and the first Act on Same-Sex Partnership. The principle of prohibition of discrimination is scattered throughout different pieces of legislation (e.g., the Civil Servants Act, the Media Act, the Criminal Code, etc.). In July 2014, the Croatian Parliament adopted the Act on Life Partnership, giving same-sex unions most of the rights that married couples enjoy, except in the field of adoption. The initiative for the law came from the center-left government. The Act on Life Partnership was adopted after the first Croatian referendum on gay marriage in December 2013, whose results will be discussed later in the text.

The Croatian Constitution contains a non-exhaustive list of protected characteristics. However, some equality norms are not adjusted with the constitutional principle of equality.[6] Furthermore, the constitutional prohibition of discrimination does not independently constitute a basis for a constitutional lawsuit.[7] Gender equality is declared by the Croatian Constitutional Court as one of the highest values of the Croatian constitutional order.[8] In its decision of 2007, the Croatian Constitutional Court also implemented the EU general principle of equality between men and women as a fundamental right and ruled that men and women have to retire at the same age (65).

Besides a comprehensive legal equality framework, the Croatian government has adopted numerous policy documents in the field of gender equality. The first-established equality mechanism was the Commission for Equality Issues (1996–2004), which was merged in 2000 with the Government Office for Human Rights and is responsible, as a government advisory body, for promoting gender equality and empowering women (Paliković & Paliković, 2013, p. 6). "The Commission for Equality Issues" ("gender" was omitted in the title) produced the first National Policy for the Promotion of Equality (1997–2000) by taking as a starting point the Beijing Platform for Action. It was oriented at translating *de jure* equality into *de facto* equality and was written in a declarative and uncritical matter. Throughout its existence, the Commission for Equality Issues has avoided identifying women as a social group whose equality it is supposed to promote and has also failed to make any significant connection to, at the time, a very vibrant and dynamic women's scene, which has in turn denied its support to the institution. Finally, it was clear at the time that the politics of gender equality were treated as an issue imposed by the international community rather than a real social issue that needed to be dealt with. The office, i.e., Commission, was founded to meet the Beijing demands (Deželan et al., 2013, p. 21).

This policy was followed by the second National Policy for the Promotion of Gender Equality (2001–2005), which aimed to promote women's rights in all spheres of activities and to raise awareness. It signified a symbolic starting point since it was the first time that state officials and women NGO representatives had cooperated. After November 2003, the social-democrat coalition was replaced in government by the Croatian Democratic Union (HDZ) and the Democratic Centre coalition. The new government, without explanation, closed the Commission for Gender Equality (Deželan et al., 2013, p. 24). The move created a void in the gender equality system at the executive level until the foundation of the Government Office for Gender Equality (Kesić, 2007, p. 20). After the first Gender Equality Act entered into force in 2003, the Gender Equality Office was established the same year and the Government's Gender Equality Office was established in February 2004. The establishment of the Office can be regarded as the institutionalization of gender equality. The Gender Equality Office delivered the Third (2006–2010) and Fourth National Policy on Gender Equality (2010–2015). The core idea of the national gender equality policies was very well shaped but with a lack of emphasis on reproductive rights due to political incentives under the influence of a conservative block of different associations and right-wing political parties. The Parliamentary Committee for Gender Equality (established in 2001) consists of members of the largest political parties and is responsible for monitoring policy and law implementation. Since its establishment in 2001, the Parliamentary Committee for Gender Equality has been quite active. However, it mostly consists of women politicians who in most cases follow the opinions of their male counterparts in their political parties. It is interesting that in the Parliament after the elections held in November 2015, the Parliamentary Committee for Gender

Equality consisted only of women. Women activists criticized this decision, claiming that women are ghettoized in politics. After the early elections in September 2016, the president of the newly established Parliamentary Committee for Gender Equality is a man.

The last adopted National Policy introduced three novelties in "implementing international cooperation, enhancing the mechanisms for the implementation of gender equality on the national and local level and the enforcement of their activities."[9] However, achieving greater gender equality remains a big challenge despite the good legal and policy instruments.

Deficiencies in Making Equality Effective

This section reveals the deficiencies of the existing legal and policy framework and how these might be overcome. "Gender equality is overall a rather new subject in Croatia which has been addressed seriously only in the last ten years" (Zrinšćak, 2011, p. 3).

In 2015, Croatia was ranked 59th out of 145 countries according to the 2015 Gender Gap Index (World Economic Forum, 2015). According to the *Annual Report 2014 of the Ombudsperson for Gender Equality*, "women represent 51.7% of the population in the Republic of Croatia, make up 45.4% *of the labor active population* and 58% of them are not participating in the labor market. The extremely low labor activity rate of women—39.1%—points towards the unfavorable status of women in the Croatian labor market. At the same time, the labor activity rate among men is 52.2%, although the labor activity rate among young and middle-age women is considerably lower (10%) than the labor activity rate of their male peers."[10]

In Croatia there is discrepancy between official statistics and the real situation in practice. "However, the economy is not doing well at all, companies struggle to survive, many workers do not receive salaries for their work, the grey economy is flourishing and due to the political scandals, an anomic feeling is widespread—these are the social circumstances which are unlikely to create preconditions for dealing with the issue of the gender pay gap, at least in the near future" (Zrinšćak, 2011, p. 6).

After the global economic crisis in 2008, the position of Croatian women in the labor market follows the negative economic trends in Europe. Due to the economic crisis, women are economically less active and the unemployment rate for women is slightly higher than for men.[11] Women in Croatia earn on average considerably less than men, despite the fact that the Labor Act (2014) guarantees equal pay for equal work or for work of equal value. The Ombudsperson for Gender Equality in her last Annual Report for 2015 reveals that the gender pay gap in Croatia is 10.2%. Compared to the other member states, Croatia has the lowest employment rate of women and the lowest employment rate of men. Croatia is the country with by far the lowest part-time work rate for both men and women in the EU. When looking at the difference in the employment rates of men and women, Croatia takes second place after Estonia, with the difference being 8% which is 2.6% lower than the EU-28 average (Broz & Levačić, 2015, p. 1).

The gender pay gap in substance results in lower retirement pay for women. In the market areas with the highest personal incomes, there is an increased number of men and a decreased number of women.[12] Despite lower gender pay gap official statistics, the Ombudsperson for Gender Equality in her Annual Report for 2014 claims that "the status of women in the Croatian labor market was significantly unfavorable." This is supported by the fact that the majority of single parents are women and there is a lack of daycare centers for dependents, and women (because of their lower earnings) sometimes leave their jobs in order to take care of their families (Ombudsperson for Gender Equality, 2015). According to the national labor legislation, the compulsory maternity leave includes the period from day 28 before the expected date of delivery for a period of 70 days after birth. After that period expires, a working or self-employed mother is entitled to an additional maternity leave that lasts until the child turns six months of age and that she may transfer to the father of the child by a written statement.

The proportion of those taking parental leave slightly increased, in line with the expansion of provisions in the early 2000s, but only among mothers (Dobrotić et al., 2013, p. 234). Therefore, women are more likely to take leave, to work part time, or to stop working. These discrepancies between official statistics and the situation explained in the annual reports of the Ombudsperson for Gender Equality show that gender equality in Croatia remains formal, not substantive (Ombudsperson for Gender Equality, 2015).

Domestic violence continues to be a serious problem in Croatian society, with growing numbers of reported cases and victims, despite the comprehensive legislative framework.[13] Some women's activists believe that traditional patriarchal relations in society are the root causes of the problem: "The main reasons, of course, lie in the patriarchal relations in the society and the relationships of power among genders. Domestic violence is not just social, but also a major political problem. Difficult social situations, alcohol and drugs are triggers for new waves of violence against women, but they cannot be seen as the actual causes" (Tolle & Vukmanić, 2011). However, Tolle and Vukmanić (2011, p. 2) claim that "in spite of the solid legislative framework, the implementation of laws and other legal provisions (platforms, strategies, action plans, etc.) often still ends up being at the expense of the victims and in favor of the perpetrators. Women reporting violence are often not taken seriously, their experiences and fears are doubted, leading to additional structural victimization of women by a system designed to assist and protect them." As a result, Tolle and Vukmanić (2011, p. 3) add "Croatia's murder rate of women who decided to leave violent partners, by the latter, is very high."

The available research shows the problem of hidden figures and that victims often do not report violence (Mamula, 2012, p. 3). The National

Strategy on Protection from Family Violence 2011–2016 (Government of the Republic of Croatia, 2011b) is supposed to implement the Act on Protection against Domestic Violence. The main objection to the new strategy is that it is not gender-based and it is not clear who will be performing certain activities, the ministries or local communities (Paliković & Paliković, 2013, p. 13). One important addition is that in 2015, the Croatian Parliament adopted the Act on the Rights of Victims of Sexual Violence in the Homeland War. Victims of sexual violence during the war were granted the status of war victim. Other forms of violence against women are not receiving adequate public attention because of a lack of institutional mechanisms and a lack of awareness. Therefore, at the end of 2010 the initiative of the Women's Court for the Region of Former Yugoslavia working on rape as a war crime was acknowledged. The specificity of the initiative of the Women's Court is that it gathers women from all successor states of the former Yugoslavia: Bosnia and Herzegovina, Montenegro, Croatia, Kosovo, Macedonia, Slovenia and Serbia (Zajović, 2015, p. 11).

One of the serious deficiencies in the implementation of the new GEA is the non-application of the gender quota system. "While women's share in Parliament increased in the second decade of the transition period, it is just slightly higher than during the socialist period and is reaching parity level very slowly" (Dobrotić et al., 2013, p. 235). The Gender Equality Act obliges political parties to make candidate lists with at least 40% of men and women each. Even though the Gender Equality Act of 2008 stipulated sanctions (in the amount of a maximum EUR 6,000) for the violation of the "quota" representation of 40% of women on the candidates' list, no sanction was imposed during the last local elections. The reason for the "silent" discrimination is the different interpretation of the quota definition incorporated in the GEA 2008.[14] Non-implementation of this mechanism could be sanctioned by non-acceptance of the candidate lists by the State Election Commission. The majority of actors perceive a need to introduce more effective sanctions against the violation of gender quota provisions (Vasiljević, 2013, p. 129).

One of the reasons why quotas are not implemented is the lack of public pressure because of the relatively conservative values still dominant in the population. This was obvious in the recent referendum held on December1, 2013 for the insertion into the Croatian Constitution of the definition of marriage as a living union between a woman and a man, which showed that Croatian society still walks on the side of traditional values. The referendum was initiated by the conservative group In the Name of the Family (supported by the Catholic Church), which gathered 750,000 signatures in its support after Croatia's center-left government drafted a law to allow gay couples to register as "life partners."[15] The majority of citizens (65.87%) voted for the insertion of the definition of marriage into the Croatian Constitution, whereas 33.51% voted against. After the referendum, the Croatian constitution was amended to ban same-sex marriage.

In July 2013, the County Court in Varaždin rendered a final judgment in a case of harassment based on sexual orientation. This is the first final judgment in a case of discrimination on grounds of sexual orientation in Croatia.[16]

Since 2003, there has been a lack of reported cases of sex discrimination as well as final judgments before courts. The main issue in the Croatian justice system is that it is impossible to track all judgments in cases of gender discrimination. Even though there is a national register of judgments, the register is not conducive to research by gender as a protected characteristic. The other problem is that court practice is not uniform and transparent. There is an urgent need to publish national case law on the web in order to make it more transparent and accessible to researchers and other members of the interested public.

Existing Practice of the National Equality Body and National Courts

The Gender Equality Act defines institutional mechanisms for achieving gender equality, the establishment and competences of an authority responsible for its implementation at the national and local level, and establishes an independent body for eliminating discrimination based on gender. It introduced improvements in the area of judicial protection against discrimination by means of procedures such as a joint claim, the determination of the issue of the burden of proof, the compensation of damage to the victim and the principle of urgency in judicial proceedings. Sex discrimination claims directed to the Ombudsperson for Gender Equality mostly refer to sex discrimination in the labor market.[17]

In Croatia, there are several bodies that deal with different grounds of discrimination. As a National Equality Body, the Ombudsperson for Human Rights (established in 1992) is responsible for the promotion of equality and reporting to the Parliament on 17 grounds (the Anti-Discrimination Act) and for handling complaints on all of these grounds, except gender, gender identity and expression and sexual orientation (Ombudsperson for Gender Equality), disability (Ombudsperson for Persons with Disabilities) and discrimination complaints which concern children (Ombudsperson for Children). The Ombudsperson's institution became the Central Equality Body with the entry into force of the Anti-Discrimination Act on January 1, 2009. Unfortunately, there is a lack of a clear division of competence among the equality bodies in cases of multiple discrimination. Women are mostly affected by sex discrimination (sexual harassment claims dominate). According to the Ombudsperson for Gender Equality, all the complaints related to harassment and sex-based harassment were brought by women, but the greatest number of sex-based harassment is still not reported.

How does the situation look in other spheres of life? Research and annual reports of the Ombudsperson for Gender Equality show that women are underrepresented in management positions.[18]

Equality bodies are potentially highly effective actors in terms of combating discrimination and promoting equal opportunities. However, the weak institutional grounding of gender equality policies, the lack of financial resources and the narrow understanding of gender equality, which sees it limited to the labor market and the economy, mean that the impact of the European Union on gender equality within Croatian politics has not been as profound as many people expected. Equality bodies can be better used, for example, as alternative dispute resolution mechanisms that can resolve potential disputes without going to court. If we aim to have time-saving solutions, saving money (attorneys' fees, court costs and fees, fees for expert witnesses and other expenses), and more control over the case and outcome (use of the third party in court proceedings or joint claims), then we have to provide equality bodies with more concrete competences (I would call it an "equality body's action model"). This equality body's action model, which includes individual and collective complaints, including third-party intervention (equality bodies, NGOs and other relevant institutions), can deal with a larger number of complaints than judicial procedures. However, the Ombudsperson for Gender Equality statistics show that this model is still not widely used. This was explained in various ways in the annual reports.

Some Critical Thoughts

After almost two decades of equality policy, men still earn more, dominate in the media and wield the most power in politics. In the regulation of equality between men and women, Croatia is not essentially behind the current member states of the EU, but there is still room to improve the current state of affairs. By taking over existing solutions, a point of departure is created for further regulation of the question of gender equality. The implementation of policies aimed at the enhancement of gender equality in Croatia still requires improvement.

National legislation seems to be fully harmonized with EU law, and people who feel discriminated against have all the legal instruments at their disposal to defend themselves (Vasiljević, 2011, p. 250). In the last 13 years, Croatia has done a tremendous amount of work in transposing EU equality standards into national law. Numerous policy instruments have been built and legal changes have taken place, introducing serious mechanisms to combat inequality, such as the Government Office for Gender Equality, the Gender Equality Ombudsperson and the Parliamentary Committee for Gender Equality. Moreover, every county government has similar branches/offices for gender equality. However, little progress has been made up to 2016 to achieve substantive gender equality, and all these measures have had hardly any impact on the status of women in Croatia. I support current research which seems to hold the view that the main document regarding women's rights, the National Policy for Gender Equality issued by the Government Office for Gender Equality (Government of the Republic of Croatia, 2011a), "is vague and mostly non-operative, simply because no instruments and mechanisms are included which could assure that the problems supposedly addressed in this document would be effectively dealt with, let alone resolved" (Knežević, 2013, p. 3).

Specialized bodies created for that specific purpose have neither been consistent and effective in implementing measures defined by existing legislation nor have they proven to be coherent with the recently adopted European standards. Legislative gender equality measures alone do not work in Croatia. Equality cannot be realized without positive duties and proactive strategies implemented with the assistance of institutional and political support. Fredman clearly articulates this view:

> the initiative should start with policy makers and implementers, service providers, employers and trade unions in order to relieve individual victims of the burden and expense of litigation. There is also a need for systematic change at the institutional level. In recognition of the institutional basis of discrimination, there is no need to prove discrimination or find a named perpetrator. Instead, the duty to bring about change lies with those with the power and capacity to do so. Rather than determining a breach of the law, the focus is on identifying systemic discrimination and creating institutional mechanisms for its elimination. Finally, proactive models broaden the participatory role of civil society, both in norm setting and in norm enforcing. In this sense, the citizen is characterized not as a passive recipient but an active participant.
>
> (Fredman, 2009, p. 3)

In Croatia, the gender equality concept is transferred from CEDAW and different forms of discrimination from EU secondary law. A brief look into domestic equality legislation shows that some EU definitions are adopted literally (lost in translation). However, the implementation has not been understood in the sense of adjusting national equality standards with EU legislation and policy. Implementation is understood simply as a "cut and paste" job. One of the reasons for the "negative" implementation of EU law is a misunderstanding of the recently adopted concepts and standards, the lack of political will to support the implementation of these legal norms, and the lack of comprehensive and reliable statistics and case law in the field of discrimination. Although Croatian legislation has become richer because of the new equality standards, certain consequences of rapid technical harmonization (actually the speed of written laws) still remain. After 2008, when the new GEA entered into force, there have been a small number of final court judgments which prove their effectiveness and which show that the newly adopted standards have been completely implemented (*Decision of the County Court*, 2013). Furthermore, the case law often refers to discrimination without sufficient explanation (*Decisions of the Supreme Court*, 2007) or there is no evidence suggesting the existence of discrimination (*Decisions of the Supreme Court*, 2008a). In practice, there is an increasingly common problem of not recognizing what gender discrimination is and what it is not, and some prosecutors have often subsumed under discrimination every form of different treatment, ignoring the existence of protected characteristics (*Decisions of the Supreme Court*, 2008b).

The experience of implementation of equality standards shows that "the current equality legislation is ineffective, because the tools for implementation are too vague or complicated to be applied simply" (Knežević, 2013, p. 3). Consequently, the Croatian case shows three obstacles in the implementation of gender equality concepts: a lack of understanding definitions; a lack of raising awareness, which has resulted in a low percentage of reporting of sex discrimination; and a lack of political will to implement legal and policy measures. The governmental mechanisms are not efficient in monitoring the implementation of gender equality policies or in suggesting innovative and comprehensive equality approaches. Gender equality and women's rights are not often seen as a priority in the political decision-making process. In terms of legal measures, national courts have not shown great enthusiasm in taking part in a teleological interpretation of European gender equality norms. Gender equality policies have not been used as an efficient tool for the suppression of discrimination and for raising awareness of the issue.

Following its obligation as a new EU member state, Croatia should work further on the implementation of EU legal standards and norms in the field of gender equality. The Republic of Croatia bound itself to respect the norms of international law (e.g., the European Convention on Human Rights, CEDAW, etc.), and this obligation derives from the constitutional provision according to which international laws that have been ratified and published are ipso facto a part of the internal legal system.

One of the problems in the comprehensive implementation of gender equality is the issue that the concept of gender equality in the EU is narrowed down to gender equality in the labor market. Unfortunately, even in the EU there is no debate on the origins of discrimination, such as sexism and patriarchy. Despite the numerous gender equality rules that have been put into place in Croatia over the past decades, the realization of gender equality in everyday life still remains highly problematic. The analyzes of national solutions regarding labor law in the field of gender equality and equal treatment raises a dilemma about whether modifications made in the harmonization process are sufficient and of good quality, and whether the harmonization process can be regarded as completed (Vinković, 2005, p. 210). The overall picture which emerges from this chapter is that, in many fields, Croatia is still far from reaching satisfactory results, due to deeply rooted gender stereotypes and a lack of courage to bring cases before the courts. Despite all laws and mechanisms, the problem is still underreporting and the underuse of complaint mechanisms. This is partially because there is a lack of knowledge of the existence of legislation and because of stereotypes which are present even in the justice system. Stereotypical thinking about women's professional and family roles continues to be a very relevant cause of sex discrimination and gender inequality and, as such, a matter of huge concern that needs to be appropriately addressed. This issue comes clearly to the fore in an article by Ivana Radačić (2012, pp. 13–22). Her discussion of gender equality cases that have been brought before the European Court of Human Rights shows that national governments as defendants may still rely on outdated perceptions of women's roles to justify their discriminatory behavior.

Finally, due to the lack of gender mainstreaming at all levels of education, awareness-raising campaigns and the promotion of gender equality in all policy and legal instruments, achieving de facto equality looks like mission impossible. Further, it is hard to compare Croatia with all countries included in this research on the global effects of gender equality due to the Croatian historical and cultural background. However, it is possible to compare Croatia with Central and Eastern European countries because they share the heritage of a socialist regime and values. The traditional role of women in a patriarchal social structure is still present, like a ghost from the past that prevents countries in democratic transitions from moving forward. The present nationalist discourse takes us back to the past, and traditional discourse prevents us from looking forward. Still, the Gender Equality Act is the strongest tool in the hands of party activists, feminists and women in Croatia in general (Šinko, 2009, p. 20).

Notes

1 Campaign "Croatia Can Do Better."
2 Report by the Republic of Croatia on the application of the Beijing Declaration and Platform for Action (1995) and the results of the 23rd Special Session of the UN General Assembly (2000)—Beijing + 20, Gender Equality Office of the Government of the Republic of Croatia, May 2014: "the proportion of women amongst officials and high-ranking state and civil services increased from 20% in 2000 to 32.1% in 2013. Since 1995, women have held the position of deputy prime minister and have run departments/ministries, which were traditionally allocated to men, such as the ministries of defense, foreign affairs, finance and construction" p. 7.
3 The concept of discrimination is defined in such a manner that the existence of discrimination requires certain actions related to the grounds for discrimination referred to in the previous Article. The Act elaborates in detail procedural provisions which envisage the filing of several types of complaints (complaints for establishing discrimination, complaints to prohibit or eliminate discrimination and a claim for damages) for the purpose of the judicial protection of victims of discrimination. The Act introduces certain novelties such as the intervener on the side of the plaintiff (Article 21) and the possibility of a joint claim for protection against discrimination (Article 24), thus clearing the way for the better protection of collective rights of those groups of citizens that are at a higher risk of discrimination. The Act has particularly elaborate misdemeanor provisions aimed at sanctioning any legal or natural person acting contrary to the provisions of this Act.
4 The Anti-Discrimination Act prohibits discrimination based on race or ethnicity or color, gender, language, religion, political or some other conviction, national

or social origin, wealth, membership in a union, education, social position, marital or family income, age, health, disability, genetic heritage, sexual identity, expression or sexual orientation (Article 1).

5 In January 2008, the Constitutional Court of the Republic of Croatia declared the 2003 Act unconstitutional because, as an organic act concerning fundamental human rights, it should have been passed by a two-thirds majority in Parliament, which was not the case. The first Gender Equality Act had 75 votes in favor, while the two-thirds majority rule required 76 votes.

6 For instance, the Constitution prohibits discrimination on the basis of education, while the Labor Act does not explicitly mention it. However, since the Constitution has a higher legal power, it can be concluded that discrimination on the basis of education is prohibited in labor relations as well. "The Constitution itself prohibits discrimination on the basis of education in Article 14, paragraph 1, which effectively includes the prohibition of such discrimination in the field of labor relations as well" (*Decision of the Constitutional Court*, 2001).

7 In a decision of 2003, the Constitutional Court states that "Article 24, paragraph 1 of the Constitution contains the constitutional guarantee of non-discrimination. Discrimination as defined by Article 14, paragraph 1 is not an independent legal basis for a constitutional lawsuit, but needs to be put forward together with another (material) constitutional right guaranteed by the Constitution" (*Decision of the Constitutional Court*, 2003). "In her lawsuit, the plaintiff failed to state the reasons on the basis of which the Court could assess whether the discrimination obstructed her from realizing another right guaranteed to her by the Constitution, and the Court could not identify them either in its procedure. Therefore, the Court assesses the plaintiff's referral to the constitutional prohibition of discrimination as unfounded."

8 "With the goal of attaining Gender Equality in the political realm, Article 15 of the Act stipulates that political parties registered in the registry of national political parties need to adopt an action plan on issues of equal representation of men and women in their parties every four years, and, in line with that, define methods for the promotion of equal representation in party bodies, on party slates for parliamentary and local elections. Article 15, paragraph 3 of the Act stipulates that, when drafting the party slate for elections, the party needs to take into consideration the principle of Gender Equality. This stipulation, according to the Constitutional Court, does not contain a measure according to which it could be assessed whether it has been violated. This means that the implementation of the principle of Gender Equality will depend on the concrete circumstances of each specific party slate" (*Decision of the Constitutional Court*, 2005).

9 The Policy includes seven particular activities and obliges the Republic of Croatia to incorporate the gender dimension into every field of politics through: (1) promoting the human rights of women and gender equality; (2) generating equal opportunities on the labor market; (3) enhancing the functioning of gender sensitive education and training; (4) balancing the involvement of men and women in the process of political and public decision making; (5) eliminating all forms of violence against women; (6) promoting international cooperation and gender equality outside Croatia; (7) further enhancing institutional mechanisms and methods of implementation (Paliković & Paliković, 2013, p. 9).

10 The National Employment Promotion Plan for 2011, 2012 and 2013 incorporates measures to increase the employment rate of vulnerable groups of people (Ombudsperson for Gender Equality, 2015).

11 The employment rate of men in 2014 was 58% in comparison with 56.6% for the same period in 2013. The employment rate of women in 2014 was 50.1% in comparison with 48.4% for the same period in 2013. The unemployment rate among men in Croatia was 16%, and among women 18.1%.

12 In 2014 the average gross wage in Croatia was HRK 7,863 (Croation kunas), while the proportion of the average wage of women (HRK 7,424) to the average wage of men was 90.2%. Further, on average, a man in Croatia earns HRK 9,708, which is more than women earn (e.g., for every 10 average gross wages earned by a woman, a man earns 12).

13 According to the Annual Report 2014 of the Ombudsperson for Gender Equality (2015), in 2014 there was a total of 1,107 criminal acts with elements of domestic violence with 1,155 victims out of whom 328 were men (28%), and 827 women (72%). There is an increasing trend of criminal acts with elements of domestic violence, as well as an increasing number of victims. The total number of victims of these criminal acts increased in 2014 by 276 persons (23.9% in comparison to 2013), out of whom 135 were women (an increase of 17.7% in comparison with 2013) and 91 were men (an increase of 27.7% in comparison with 2013).

14 The official interpretation of the Croatian government is that the third election cycle started in 2019 for parliamentary elections, considering that local and parliamentary elections constitute two separate electoral institutes, whereas women's NGOs and the Ombudsperson for Gender Equality provided the opposite interpretation, claiming that the first electoral cycle started in 2009, with local elections in 2011 and the third cycle is considered to be the local elections in 2013 (Broz & Majnarić, 2013, pp. 1–8).

15 "Marriage is the only union enabling procreation," Croatian cardinal Josip Bozanić said in his message to followers. "This is the key difference between a marriage and other unions."

16 The County Court in Varaždin delivered the first final judgment regarding discrimination on grounds of sexual orientation on July 9, 2013.

17 In 2014, the complaints were mostly related to discrimination on the ground of sex; the majority of complainants were women (72.6%). The biggest number of complaints was related to social security (39.3%) and labor rights (30.3%). These two areas make up 69.6% of all the complaints submitted to the Ombudsperson and in percentages are followed by complaints in areas related to the media—6.1%, health care—2.8%, etc.

18 In 2014, the Ombudsperson conducted two studies on the representation of women and men in management positions—one on a sample of 500 and the other on a sample of 100 of the most successful companies in Croatia. Both Progress studies clearly indicate the inequality of opportunities: (1) on average in governing bodies of Croatian companies there is fewer than one female member; (2) for every female member in governing or supervisory boards in Croatian companies, there are three male members; (3) in governing and supervisory boards, there are male members with only primary school education, while there is not one female member with only this educational level; (4) the probability of women older than 55 participating in governing bodies is more than 100% less than the probability of men of the same age participating; (5) the probability that a woman will not be a member of a supervisory board when she is between 60–65 years of age is two times greater than for the men of the same age group.

Literature

Act on Life Partnership (Zakon o životnom partnerstvu). (2014). Narodne novine No. 92/14. Zagreb: Narodne novine.

Act on Protection against Domestic Violence (Zakon o zaštiti od nasilja u obitelji). (2003). Narodne novine No. 116/03. Zagreb: Narodne novine.

Act on the Rights of Victims of Sexual Violence in the Homeland War (*Zakon o pravima žrtava seksualnog nasilja u Domovinskom ratu*). (2015). Narodne novine No. 64/15. Zagreb: Narodne novine.

Bliss, R., & Garratt, N. (2001). Supporting women entrepreneurs in transitioning economies. *Journal of Small Business Management*, 39 (4), 336–345.

Broz, T., & Levačić, D. (2015). Some facts about the gender pay gap in Croatia. Retrieved from http://genderpaygap.eu/documents/Factsheet_Croatia.pdf (accessed 17 March 2016).

Broz, T., & Majnarić M. (2013). *Sudjelovanje žena u lokalnim izborima 2013. godine na regionalnoj i županijskoj razini*. Zagreb: CESI, 2013. Retrieved from http://www.cesi.hr/attach/_s/sudjelovanje_zena_u_lokalnim_izborima_2013_godine_na_regionalnojzupanijskoj_razini.pdf (accessed 17 May 2016).

CEDAW Report for Croatia. (2013). *Croatian Fourth and Fifth Periodic Reports to the CEDAW Committee in 2013*. New York: UN General Assembly. Retrieved from http://www.un.org/womenwatch/daw/cedaw/reports/18report.pdf (accessed 5 June 2016).

Constitution of the Republic of Croatia (*Ustav Republike Hrvatske*). (2010). Narodne novine No. 85/10. Zagreb: Narodne novine.

Constitution of the Socialist Republic of Croatia (*Ustav Socijalističke Republike Jugoslavije*). (1974). Narodne novine Socijalističke Republike Hrvatske No. 8/1974. Zagreb: Narodne novine.

Croatian Bureau of Statistics. (2011). *Woman and Men in Croatia 2011*. Zagreb: Croatian Bureau of Statistics.

Croatian Bureau of Statistics. (2013). *Census of Population, Households and Dwellings 2011, Population by Citizenship, Ethnicity, Religion & Mother Tongue: Statistical Report*. Zagreb: Croatian Bureau of Statistic. Retrieved from http://www.dzs.hr/Hrv_Eng/publication/2012/SI-1469.pdf (accessed 26 June 2016).

Decision of the Constitutional Court. (2003). Decision No. U-III/3192/2003. Zagreb: Constitutional Court of Croatia.

Decision of the Constitutional Court. (2005). Decision No. U-VIIA/1895/2005. Zagreb: Constitutional Court of Croatia.

Decision of the Constitutional Court. (2011). Decision No. U-I/2273/2001. Zagreb: Constitutional Court of Croatia.

Decision of the County Court. (2013). Decision of 9 July 2013 No. Žs Zg Gž-5048/12–2. Varaždin: County Court.

Decisions of the Supreme Court. (2007). Decision of 3 October 2007 No. VS RH REVR 554/07–2; Decision of 11 January 2007 No. VS RH REVR 617/06–2. Zagreb: Supreme Court.

Decisions of the Supreme Court. (2008a). Decision of 14 May 2008 No. VS RH REVR 829/07–2; Decision of 31 January 2008 No. VS RH REVR 850/07–2. Zagreb: Supreme Court.

Decisions of the Supreme Court. (2008b). Decision of 23 January 2008 No. VS RH REVR 787/07; Decision of 4 April 2008 VS RH REVR 22/07–2. Zagreb: Supreme Court.

Deželan, T., Pešut, J., Siročić, Z., Fink-Hafner, D., Sutlović, L., Krašovec, A., Krupljan, S., Velić, A., & Vasiljević, S. (eds) (2013). *Levelling the Playing Field: Monitoring Croatian Policies to Promote Gender Equality in Politics*. Ljubljana: Fakultet za družbene vede.

Dobrotić, I., Matković, T., & Zrinšćak, S. (2013). Gender equality policies and practices in Croatia: The interplay of transition and late Europeanization. *Social Policy & Administration*, 47 (2), 218–240.

Fink-Hafner, D., & Hafner-Fink, M. (2009). The determinates of success of transitions to democracy. *Europe-Asia studies*, 6 (9), 1603–1625.

Fredman, S. (2009). *Making Equality Effective: The Role of Proactive Measures*. Brussels: European Commission.

Freedom House. (2015). Nations in transit 2015—Croatia. Retrieved from https://freedomhouse.org/report/nations-transit/2015/croatia (accessed 19 June 2016).

Gender Equality Act (Zakon o ravnopravnosti spolova). (2003). Official Gazette No. 116/03. Zagreb: Narodne novine.

Gender Equality Act (Zakon o ravnopravnosti spolova). (2008). Narodne novine No. 82/08. Zagreb: Narodne novine.

Gender Equality Office of the Government of the Republic of Croatia. (2014). Report by the Republic of Croatia on the application of the Beijing Declaration and Platform for Action (1995) and the outcomes of the 23rd Special Session of the UN General Assembly (2000)—Beijing + 20. Retrieved from https://ravnopravnost.gov.hr/UserDocsImages/arhiva/images/pdf/Izvješće%20Republike%20Hrvatske%20o%20primjeni%20Pekinške%20deklaracije%20i%20Platforme%20za%20djelovanje–%20Peking%2020_ENG.pdf (accessed 28 May 2016).

Government of the Republic of Croatia. (2011a). National policy for gender equality 2011–2015 (Nacionalna politika za ravnopravnost spolova 2011–2015). Narodne novine No. 88/2011. Zagreb: Government of the Republic of Croatia.

Government of the Republic of Croatia. (2011b). National strategy on protection from family violence 2011–2016 (Nacionalna strategija za zaštitu od nasilja u obitelji 2011–2016). Narodne novine No. 88/2011. Zagreb: Government of the Republic of Croatia.

Havelková, B. (2010). The legal notion of gender equality in the Czech Republic. *Women's Studies International Forum*, 33 (1), 21–29.

Irvine, J.A., & Sutlović, L. (2015). Gender equality in Croatia: Closing the compliance gap. In C.M. Hassenstab & S.P. Ramet (Eds), *Gender (in) Equality and Gender Politics in Southeastern Europe: A Question of Justice*, New York: Palgrave & Macmillan, pp. 62–87.

Kesić, V. (2007). *Feminizam i Država*. Zagreb: Centar za edukaciju, savjetovanje i istraživanje.

Knežević, Đ. (2013). *Are Good Laws Enough? The Situation of Women in Croatia*. Brussels: EU Heinrich Boll Stiftung. Retrieved from https://eu.boell.org/sites/default/files/uploads/2013/12/knezevic.are_good_laws_enough.pdf (accessed 7 May 2016).

Labor Act (Zakon o radu). (2014). Narodne novine No. 93/2014. Zagreb: Narodne novine.

Mamula, M. (2012). *Awareness raising Activities to Fight Violence against Women and Girls*. Brussels: European Commission, UK, 7–8 February. Retrieved from http://ec.europa.eu/justice/gender-equality/files/exchange_of_good_practice_uk/hr_comments_paper_uk_2012_en.pdf (accessed 27 March 2016).

Ombudsperson for Gender Equality. (2015). Annual report. Retrieved from http://www.prs.hr/attachments/article/1555/01_IZVJESCE_2014_CJELOVITO.pdf (accessed 12 March 2016).

Ombudsperson for Gender Equality. (2016). Annual report. Retrieved from http://www.prs.hr/attachments/article/1923/Izvješće%20o%20radu%20Pravobran-iteljice%20za%20ravnopravnost%20spolova%20za%202015.pdf (accessed 22 March 2016).

Paliković, M., & Paliković, A. (2013). The policy on gender equality in Croatia: DG for Internal Policies, Policy Department C: Citizens Rights and Constitutional Affairs. Retrieved from http://www.europarl.europa.eu/RegData/etudes/note/join/2013/493016/IPOL-FEMM_NT(2013)493016_EN.pdf (accessed 17 March 2016).

Radačić, I. (2012). The European court of human rights' approach to sex discrimination. *European Gender Equality Law Review*, 1 (1), 13–22.

Same-Sex Relationships Act (Zakon o istospolnim zajednicama). (2003). Narodne novine No. 116/03. Zagreb: Narodne novine.

Šinko, M. (2009). Women in Croatian parliament: Have they reached their glass ceiling? Paper presented at the European Consortium for Political Research Standing Group on Gender and Politics conference First European Conference on Politics and Gender, Queen's University, Belfast, UK, 21–23 January.

Stubbs, P. (2006). Aspects of community development in contemporary Croatia: Globalisation, neo-liberalisation and NGO-isation. In L. Dominelli (Ed.), *Revitalising Communities in a Globalising World*, Aldershot: Ashgate.

Tolle, N., & Vukmanić, M. (2011). *Domestic Violence: Slow Progress in Croatia.* Retrieved from http://www.balcanicaucaso.org/eng/Regions-and-countries/Croatia/Domestic-violence-slow-progress-in-Croatia-100240 (accessed 25 February 2016).

Tomić-Koludrović, I., & Kunac, S. (eds) (2000). *Rizici modernizacije: Žene u Hrvatskoj devedesetih.* Split: Udruga građana Stope nade.

Tomšić, T. (1981). *Žena u Razvoju Socijalističke, Samoupravne Jugoslavije.* Beograd: Novinsko/izdavačka radna organizacija.

Vasiljević, S. (2011). *Slično i različito: Diskriminacija u Europskoj uniji i Republici Hrvatskoj.* Zagreb: Tim Press.

Vasiljević, S. (2013). Discrimination unveiled: The intersection between gender and ethnicity in the Croatian political arena: The case of minority women. In S. Vasiljević, T. Deželan, J. Pešut, Z. Siročić, D. Fink-Hafner, L. Sutlović, A. Krašovec, S. Krupljan & A. Velić (Eds), *Levelling the Playing Field: Monitoring Croatian Policies to Promote Gender Equality in Politics*, Ljubljana: Faculty of Social Sciences, pp. 101–121.

Vinković, M. (2005). Gender equality and the process of harmonisation of the Croatian labour law. In T. Ćapeta (Ed.), *Croatian Yearbook of European Law and Policy (CYELP)*, 1 (1), 203–211.

World Economic Forum. (2015). *The Global Gender Gap Report 2015.* WEF: Geneva. Retrieved from http://www3.weforum.org/docs/GGGR2015/cover.pdf (accessed 28 June 2016).

Zajović, S. (2015). The women's court—A feminist approach to justice: Review of the process of organizing the women's court. In S. Zajović (Ed.), *Women's Court: About the Process*, Novi Sad, Serbia: Art Print, pp. 6–68.

Zrinšćak, S. (2011). *Gender Pay Gap: A Non-Existent Topic in Croatia? Exchange of Good Practices on Gender Equality: Reducing the Gender Pay Gap.* Berlin: European Commission.

11 Gender Equality in Estonia[1]

Raili Marling

Introduction

Estonia is in many ways a model example of post-socialist transition. Separation from the Soviet Union, its economic system and ideology, was decisive and quick. It was accompanied by a 30% decline in industrial production and a 45% fall in real wages, to which the then-government responded with radical economic reform to reorient the economy from the East to the West (Laar, 2007). The shock therapy was anything but easy, but it was nevertheless embraced by the population of the country allergic to anything suggestive of the Soviet period. The sacrifice seemed necessary and also worth it as before the recent recession Estonia seemed like an economic miracle and widely celebrated for its economic freedom and swift economic growth. Estonia is today a member of the EU (2004) and the Eurozone (2011). The successive governments of the past 25 years have prioritized the economic sphere and neoliberal laissez-faire economic agenda has been pursued through all these years. The policies that have benefitted relatively few members of society have been embraced by the population at large (Annist, 2011, p. 86) and there has been no major social unrest despite the dramatic changes of the past 25 years.

However, there is increasing social science literature (e.g., annual Human Development Reports) to suggest that the economic success of Estonia was achieved partly through increased social inequality, including gender inequality. Estonia continues to be prominent in international indices of economic freedom—for example, it holds the ninth position in the world in the 2016 Index of Economic Freedom (compiled by the Heritage Foundation and the *Wall Street Journal*) (Heritage Foundation, 2016). However, when we turn to international indices of gender equality, the picture is somewhat different: Estonia ranks 30th in the United Nations Development Program's Gender Inequality Index (United Nations Development Program, 2015, p. 224) and 21st in the Word Economic Forum's Global Gender Gap Index (World Economic Forum, 2015). It is also below the EU average on the EU Gender Equality Index for 2012 (Estonia 49.8, EU average 52.9, Finland 72.7) (European Institute for Gender Equality, 2015). In Estonia's case the position in the rankings seems to be dropping instead of improving. How do we explain this discrepancy?

Traditionally, gender equality has been associated with a high level of economic development and postmaterialist values (see e.g., Inglehart & Norris, 2003), yet in Estonia economic development has not meant advances in gender equality. Rather, the opposite seems to be the case, despite the adoption of international documents, the creation of local institutions and regulations. Estonia signed the CEDAW in 1991 and, as a member nation of the UN, it has committed itself to the Beijing Platform for Action from 1995. As a member nation of the EU, it has to adhere to the Amsterdam Treaty, which declares the equal opportunities of men and women a fundamental aim of the EU. To comply with the EU norms, the Estonian Gender Equality Act was adopted in 2004 *(Gender Equality Act, 2004)* and the institution of the Gender Equality Commissioner was set up in 2005 to oversee gender equality policies (since 2009 called Gender Equality and Equal Treatment Commissioner with a portfolio that now also includes ethnicity, disability, sexuality and other intersectional differences). However, quite tellingly, the national Gender Equality Council, an advisory body consisting of politicians as well as representatives of the civil society that was prescribed by the Gender Equality Act took eight years and six ministers to convene (it first met in 2013). After the initial accession period, political establishment's commitment to gender equality provisions has been waning. Whether the election of the first woman president in October 2016 will make any difference remains to be seen. Although Estonia has aspired to become a boring Nordic country, as once suggested by President Toomas Henrik Ilves (cited in Rajasalu, 2006, p. 10), its path of development in the context of gender equality is very far from the goal.

The present chapter argues that the causes of Estonia's mixed reaction to gender equality can be found in the country's recent history and socioeconomic development. Gender equality as a social and political problem emerged as a topical issue in Estonian political scene only after the country regained its independence in 1991. Not surprisingly, the Soviet period's legacy strongly shaped the perception of and reactions to gender equality. It helped to create a misperception of gender equality that persists to this day and has rendered the adoption of international standards a formalistic exercise rather than a substantive effort to move towards a type of democracy that grants men and women equal rights and opportunities in the public and private sphere. Therefore the present chapter will first discuss the historical background of gender equality in Estonia, before proceeding to the current legal framework and its shortcomings in order to show how Estonia does and does not meet the CEDAW definition of gender equality.

Historical Background

According to the Soviet ideology, gender equality was irrelevant in the Soviet Union as the equality of men and women had supposedly been achieved with the overthrow of capitalism. Women were engaged in waged labor outside of the home, childcare services and free health care were made available, token women were members of the central political committees. The fact that the reality men and women lived in was anything but gender-equal did nothing to alter the ideological slogans. As different historians (e.g., Goldman, 1993; Wood, 1997) have shown, the Soviet regime did not dismantle the patriarchal family but may have strengthened it. Rochelle Ruthchild (2010) has demonstrated in her study of the Russian revolution that even women's leading roles in revolutionary activities were downplayed. The woman question was seen as a distraction from class struggle and feminism was declared an ideologically suspicious bourgeois relic, because of its focus on individual rights (e.g., Miroiu, 2007, p. 199).

These Soviet ideological rules were transferred to the Estonian context when the country was occupied by the Soviet Union in 1940 (and re-occupied in 1944). Estonia's feminist movements of the pre-Soviet period had been relatively sedate, as most of the local activists energies were channeled either into the national or socialist movements in the late 19th century and early 20th century (see e.g., Biin & Albi, 2012, p. 113; Hallik, 2001, p. 24). The issue of women's rights did not get the attention it received in countries where women were exclusively barred from voting. Like elsewhere, the Estonian national movement was ambivalent about women's rights in the public sphere (Hallik, 2001, p. 25; Põldsaar, 2009, pp. 71–72). In socialist circles women's rights were seen as secondary to workers' rights. Both men and women were granted the right to vote and run for political office by the newly independent Republic of Estonia in 1918. Women's political participation was not very high in that period (e.g., the first parliament had 5.8% women members, the last before WWII had 8.8% [Biin & Albi, 2012, p. 121]), but this is not unexpected and similar patterns can be found in other countries after women got the vote (perhaps the exception here is Finland; see Blanc, 2017).

In the process of Sovetization pre-Soviet feminism was labeled bourgeois and was forcefully silenced. Many prominent women activists, including socialist women activists, were persecuted. Women were elected to representative bodies by a set quota (e.g., 24% in the second Supreme Soviet), but this was not meaningful political participation (Biin & Albi, 2012, p. 122). The woman question was likely to be related to the purging of bourgeois influences, rather than a serious discussion of gender equality. The effectiveness of this erasure is reflected in the fact that the Estonian Encyclopedia from 1987 defines feminism as a medical term, "the existence of feminine physical features or characteristics in a man" (Marling, 2011, p. 157). Gender discourses, as Annuk has recently shown, were more diverse, but overall they reflected the sexual puritanism of the Soviet regime and its unwillingness to address domestic patriarchy (Annuk, 2015). If anything, the Soviet regime deepened the burden on women: in addition to the compulsory work outside of the home, women still shouldered the majority of domestic duties, the latter made onerous by constant shortages. They also lived in the world of double standards.

This hypocritical vision of gender equality where public slogans hid deep inequalities is one of the reasons why Soviet-style equality policies were deeply discredited and Estonia, like other countries in the region, exhibited a deep allergy against feminist and gender equality initiatives in the immediate post-Soviet period (Snitow, 2006, p. 288). It seemed to many that equality had been achieved: women's labor force participation rates were higher than in many Western countries, women's numbers in higher education exceeded those of men, reproductive rights had been granted long ago. Because Estonia is marked by its religious tepidness (only 29% of the population profess any faith, according to the 2011 census), reproductive rights have not been politicized or come under pressure. In the 1990s, Estonia sought to turn its back to all that was assumed to be Soviet and this also included the Soviet ideology of gender equality. Instead of asking how we could make the vacuous equality slogans of the past meaningful, they were thrown out completely, replaced by neoliberalist economic policies and Western consumer culture, neither of which was interested in investigating the politics of gender. Instead, Estonian women were exhorted to bear more children for the nation and congratulated on their ability to ignore the supposedly misguided feminist ideologies of their Western sisters (Marling, 2011, p. 157).

Gender in Different Social Indicators

Public opinions and statistical data, however, are not necessarily in harmony. Below I will review certain key indicators of men's and women's positions in Estonian society: education, labor force participation, pay, parental leave and life expectancy.

In 2014 91% of Estonians ages 25–64 had received secondary education (the EU average for this age group is 76% and Estonia holds third place in the EU in the 2014 figures) (*Eesti Statistika*, 2016, p. 16). The balance of boys and girls is even in basic and middle schools, but in secondary schools a gender gap appears and in a perhaps unexpected direction. Girls make up 56% of the secondary school graduates, boys 44% (*Eesti Statistika*, 2016, p. 18). Boys constitute 62.9% of school drop-outs (Kuurme, 2010, p. 128). A similar gender disparity can also be seen in higher education. Women were able to enter universities for the first time in early 20th century but today they make up 66% of university graduates, men 34%. The discrepancy has decreased somewhat but it has held relatively steady for the past 10 years (although the female advantage disappears when we come to full professors and leaders of research teams, of whom women form around 18%) (Lõhkivi, 2010, p. 132); in 2015 only two of the 79 members of the Academy of Sciences were women). Women predominate among the graduates of vocational schools (*Eesti Statistika*, 2016, pp. 18–19). More women also participate in in-service training throughout their careers (Kuurme, 2010, p. 129). Education seems to be a woman's task in Estonia and, not surprisingly, the ratio of women is the highest among the graduates in the field of education (94%). There are more men than women graduates only in the fields of science, engineering and technology (Kuurme, 2010, p. 129).

Thus, in the context of gender and education, Estonian social debate has focused on the troubling lack of boys and men in secondary and especially higher education. Indeed, the question of why men do not complete their educations is important. However, the statistics cited above also lead to an equally troubling question of why education is not valued by men and why it is not giving more social rewards to women. It appears that women need to gather educational credentials to enter the labor market and to advance at all on the career ladder. Credentials and constant self-improvement are essential for women's careers, something that does not seem necessary for men (see e.g., Roots, 2011).

Estonia may have very high secondary and tertiary educational attainment among women, but the better level of education does not yield benefits for Estonian women in the labor market. Labor force participation for men in the age group 15–74 is 69.3% for men, 61.3% for women in 2015 (*Eesti Statistika*, 2016, p. 23). Most Estonian women work full time (only 13% of women and 5% of men work part time (*Eesti Statistika*, 2016, p. 52). Estonian women's labor force involvement rate has been above the EU average and the gap between male and female labor force participation the lowest (Masso, 2010, p. 27). Despite this, Estonia has the widest gendered income gap in the EU, 29.9% (EU average is 16.4%), according to 2013 figures (the gap increases to the striking 44.9% in the financial sector) (Osila, 2015). The lower pay will in turn result in lower retirement pensions and thus perpetuates inequality across the whole life span. Thus, poverty has a woman's face in Estonia, especially the face of an older woman (Karu, 2010, pp. 58–59).

As could be seen above, women value education, but persistent gender stereotypes in education and socialization also lead to women opting for careers in fields traditionally considered feminine (and underpaid). Estonia is characterized by notable horizontal discrimination, among the highest in the EU (Masso, 2010). There is also vertical discrimination: occupation-based segregation index was 38% (*Eesti Statistika*, 2015, p. 39). Only 8% of women work in managerial positions, while 32% of women work in the lowest-paid positions. Even among managers, women earn 17% less than their male counterparts. Education, a field dominated by women, also has a wide wage discrepancy: women teachers earn 29% less than their male colleagues (2010 figures, cited in Paats & Lunev, 2015, p. 2). In other words, the gender wage gap is not just due to the segregated labor market and women and men choosing different occupations.

Discrepancies in male and female wages are also caused by women shouldering most of the childcare and the resultant challenges of balancing work and family,[2] despite Estonia's generous parental leave policies. For the first 70 days of the child's life, the parental benefit is paid only to the mother; after that, either parent can stay home with the child. The length of parental leave is 435 days, during which time the parent who stays at home with the child receives 100% of the average monthly pay of the previous year unless it exceeds a certain sum (the maximum for 2017 is 2,907 EUR, according to the Estonian Social Insurance Board (2016)). In other words, the state has attempted to reduce the costs of opting out of the labor force for the highly paid as well, including men (the average pay in the first quarter of 2016 was 1,091 EUR in Estonia).

However, the majority of parental benefit recipients still continue to be women, although the percentage of men has been growing steadily since 2006 (until 2007, the percentage was around 2%, it has remained around 6% since then (*Eesti Statistika*, 2015, p. 58). This percentage has remained low, although the benefits claimed by men exceed those paid to women (in 2013, the average parental benefit for women was 653 EUR, for men 1,081 EUR, in other words, around 40% higher) (*Eesti Statistika*, 2015, p. 60). What keeps men from using this opportunity is the values prevalent in society: because a work-centered vision of masculinity is culturally preferred, men do not feel they have a real choice to step out of the labor force and care for their children (Pajumets, 2010).

This, in turn, perpetuates the belief that women are and should be the primary caregivers of children, which affects women's position in the labor market and their incomes both while working and in retirement. This is also borne out in statistics: gender pay gap is the lowest in the case of men and women who do not have pre-school-age children (18%). It is the highest for women who have at least two pre-school-age children (40%) (2013 figures) (*Eesti Statistika*, 2015, p. 35). Having children continues to deepen gender inequality for women, despite egalitarian and generous parental leave policies because of the strength of ingrained gender norms.

Estonian women's education outpaces that of Estonian men; women are actively involved in the labor force, mostly as full-time workers, but underpaid compared to men. Men's and women's time use statistics are also telling: according to a Statistics Estonia time use survey, men spent 30 minutes a day more than women in the paid labor force in 2010, but they contributed much less to the unpaid domestic labor, leaving them with approximately one hour more of leisure time a day than women (*Eesti Statistika*, 2015, p. 56). In other words, the domestic sphere continues to be considered the place where women do most of the unremunerated work.

However, despite these continued inequalities women outlive men in Estonia. In 2014 the expected life expectancy at the moment of birth was 81.5 years for women and 72.3 for men. Men's life expectancy has increased by 4.7 years in the last decade, faster than in the case of women (3.3 years for the same period), largely thanks to the reduction in the number of accidents and cases of cardiovascular disease. However, the gap is still larger than for EU on average (82.9 years for men and 86.3 years for women) (*Eesti Statistika*, 2016, p. 12). Men might have a favored position in Estonian society, but the traditional masculinity also is taking its toll, as can be seen in the average life expectancy of Estonian men.

Thus, although Estonian opinion leaders have long claimed that Estonia has all the gender equality it needs, a closer look at statistics in the field of education, pay, parental leave and life expectancy shows that the picture is anything but balanced. It is women who bear the brunt of this continued inequality, but men's educational and life expectancy statistics show costs for them as well. What has been done on the legislative level, then, to deal with the fact of gender inequality?

Post-Soviet Legal and Social Developments

The early-post-Soviet years saw an almost instinctive recoiling from the word "equality" because of its associations with the Soviet period and its ideological pressures. Since the superficial measures of gender equality such as labor force participation were high, feminist activism did not find a receptive audience in Estonia, similar to the situation in other post-socialist countries. It was met with not just indifference, but even hostility—there was a backlash against feminism before any could organically develop in newly independent Estonia (Marling, 2010, p. 8). Competition and meritocracy were the dominant values; equality evoked fears of government intervention in business and private life.

Estonia was forced to confront gender equality as a serious issue in the EU accession process. It was also an issue on which Estonia's progress was slow as the public discourse presented gender equality legislation as something imported, not as something needed by Estonian society. However, the team tasked with the preparation of the law decided to create a legal text that would not be a minimalist formality, but would take into account the decades of development in thinking about gender equality in the West (Albi et al., 2010, p. 12). EU accession was accepted as a desired aim by all major political parties, but despite this the reading of the Gender Equality Act (GEA) was long and laborious (the process lasted from 2000 to 2004; the preparation of the law began already in 1999 at the Ministry of Social Affairs). When the GEA was first discussed by the government, six ministers voted for and five against it (Albi et al., 2010, p. 11). The process did not, most regrettably, produce a meaningful public debate, but instead descended into essentialist reiteration of male and female biological differences, echoing the internationally widely recorded confusion of the binary pairs of sameness-difference and equality-inequality. Eventually, the goal of EU accession overcame the resistance. The law entered into force on the same day that Estonia entered the EU (May 1, 2004).

The GEA established a legal definition of gender equality, defined as equal rights, duties, opportunities and responsibilities of men and women. It is to promote "gender equality as a fundamental human right and general good in all areas of social life" (Open Society Institute, 2005, p. 67). The GEA covers all areas of social life, not just employment (e.g., also access to goods and services). It excepts religious organizations and private life from its purview. Both direct and indirect discrimination are banned. Not only does the law prohibit discrimination; it also mandates that state and local governments should promote gender equality and engage in gender mainstreaming. Yet, the law also stipulates that an individual who has experienced discrimination may lodge an individual complaint and present relevant evidence, including references to a comparable person of the opposite sex to demonstrate discrimination. In the context where the full meaning of gender inequality and discrimination is not fully understood by the general public, this has limited the number of cases.

Intersectionality is another challenge. Discrimination is addressed in Estonia by the Gender Equality Act (2004) as well as the Equal Treatment Act (2008). The latter covers discrimination on the basis of ethnic origin, race, skin color, religious and other beliefs, age, disability and sexual orientation. The Equal Treatment Act was adopted to conform to EU directives and thus it follows the minimum requirements set in the directives (Albi & Sepper, 2010, p. 104). While gender equality is protected in all areas of life (with the exception of religious organizations and family life), other intersectional aspects of identity are covered with greater limitations: discrimination on the basis of religion, age, disability or sexual orientation is banned only in the context of employment, while discrimination on the basis of ethnicity, race and skin color is also banned in social welfare, health and social insurance, education, provision of goods and services (Albi & Sepper, 2010, p. 105). This discrepancy makes it harder to handle cases of multiple or intersectional discrimination, especially in contexts other than the workplace. Multiple and intersectional discrimination has not yet been defined in the Estonian legal system (Albi & Sepper, 2010, p. 106) and this may lead to such cases being overlooked.

However, although intersectional discrimination is covered in two laws (without having been explicitly identified as such) (the Gender Equality Act and the Equal Treatment Act), oversight for both is given to the Gender Equality and Equal Treatment Commissioner and this should facilitate attention to intersectionality in the handling of cases. What hampers the work of the Commissioner is the limitation of funds available to her/him, a fact pointed out also by the CEDAW committee in 2007 (Albi & Sepper, 2010, p. 109). Intersectional approaches are important as statistics as well as qualitative studies (e.g., Aavik, 2013, 2015) show that minority and immigrant women of all ages face discrimination in the labor market, compared both to minority/immigrant men and Estonian women, as do younger women of childbearing age. These are cases of multiple discrimination where the intertwined causes cannot be untangled and hence an intersectional approach would be necessary. There is hope that attention to this factor will increase, as a 2016 study commissioned by the Office of the Gender Equality and Equal Treatment Commissioner considered not just gender, but also ethnicity, age, disability and sexuality in its gender equality model (*Soolise võrdõiguslikkuse ja võrdse kohtlemise voliniku kantselei*, 2016).

The GEA, thus, is not just a formalistic document but sets up a framework for addressing discrimination on the basis of gender but also for gender mainstreaming. It also has the potential of being used in the cases of intersectional discrimination, in combination with the Equal Treatment Act. Gender equality is also mentioned in other laws: for example the Employment Contracts Act and Administrative Procedure Act stipulate the need to observe principles of equal treatment. The Penal Code (2001) has a section (in Chapter 10 that covers offenses against political and civil rights, amendment from 2006) on offenses against equality (incitement of hatred, violation of equality on the basis of nationality, race, color, sex, language, origin, religion, sexual orientation, political opinion, financial or social status). However, the content and significance of the laws protecting gender equality have not and are still not being widely understood.

As already suggested above, the GEA's provisions have been filled very slowly: the Gender Equality Council it mandates took eight years to establish. The first time the Estonian Supreme court cited the GEA in one of its cases was 2009 (Albi et al., 2010, p. 11). Some 192 complaints were submitted to the Gender Equality and Equal Treatment Commissioner's office in 2014 (65% more than in 2013), 90 of which were about unequal treatment on the ground of gender; 114 were related to the workplace. The Commissioner's office took seven cases to the court (*Soolise võrdõiguslikkuse ja võrdse kohtlemise voliniku kantselei*, 2015, p. 26). The number of complaints and also requests for information from the Commissioner's office has increased steadily. For example, 2005 saw only 10 complaints. After equal treatment more broadly was added to the Commissioner's portfolio, the majority of complaints are still about gender discrimination (Sepper, 2010).

The GEA is being used by members of the public, but the cases are still relatively few, considering the widespread gender stereotypes and differential treatment of women and men. According to the 2013 gender equality monitoring, 58% of women have been asked about their marital status and 57% about whether they have children in job interviews. The same study demonstrates differential goals set in the education of boys and girls (*Sotsiaalministeerium*, 2014). The former Gender Equality and Equal Treatment Commissioner Mari-Liis Sepper (2010) attributes the passivity in the context of gender equality to cultural norms, fear of stigmatization and lack of information about and trust in the effectiveness of such complaints. More troublingly, one study showed that almost half of men under the age of 30 believe that just being male should have a positive impact on their salaries (Vöörmann & Plotnik, 2008).

Awareness of gender equality as a serious social issue has emerged only gradually as the income gap between men and women has increased and as the toll of hegemonic masculinity on Estonian men has become more and more evident. Estonia has had the widest gendered income gap in the EU for years, with no significant attempts to alleviate the situation, despite the lobbying of different women's organizations and NGOs (for example, the Estonian Association of Business and Professional Women has organized an

Equal Pay Day campaign every year starting from 2010). The government did develop an action plan to reduce the gender pay gap in 2012, stressing the need to implement the existing gender equality laws better, ensure the balancing of work and family life, reduce gender segregation and analyze pay structures in different fields (Osila, 2015). The calls by the then–Gender Equality and Equal Treatment Commissioner to initiate a new four-year action plan in 2015 have not been met.

As could be seen from the statistics given in the previous section, despite the 12 years of the existence of the gender equality legislation in Estonia, statistics show that gender equality is certainly not achieved—and perhaps not even seriously striven for, despite obvious disadvantages that the current system has created for both women and men. The laws that have been adopted have been of enormous significance in defining gender inequality and discrimination, and the steady increase in the number of cases taken to court also shows the public's increasing awareness of gender inequality. However, the change in public perceptions and value judgments has been slow.

Discussion and Conclusions

On the one hand, the answer to the question posed in the book is yes: Estonia has formally accepted all international standards of gender equality, including the CEDAW and hence its definition of gender equality is compatible with and incorporated into Estonian legal system. The equality of men and women is stated in the Constitution of the country, as well as a special Gender Equality Act (2004), which not only protects women and men from discrimination but also stipulates the promotion of gender equality. On the other hand, the answer is no, as when we look at government policies and public attitudes, it is clear that the obligations taken in the context of international gender equality regulations have not been met beyond the formal level. The most important factor contributing to the effectiveness of gender equality policies is the existence of clear political will to reduce gender inequality (Papp, 2010, p. 182). This political will has been lacking in the Estonia, especially in the past few years. Gender equality is increasingly incorporated into and vanishes into general questions of welfare. A telling example is the current national plan of action on welfare where gender equality is the first of its five aims, but it is hidden under a general vague title, distracting attention away from gender equality specifically as a social good.

As can be seen from above, the Estonian legal system is in full accordance with the international legal standards on gender equality, but this has not meant the change of women's disadvantaged position in Estonian society or the public acceptance of gender equality. Estonia may have passed from the preschooler level in the EU, as Ülle-Marike Papp (2010, p. 181) notes, but Estonian support for gender equality is not in harmony with the norms of the Union. The fact that even the greatest gender wage gap in the EU has not generated public pressure on the political establishment is striking.

A recent study by policy analysis firm Praxis reveals that after 12 years of the Gender Equality Act, employers are largely ignorant of the duties the law places on them and also have a poor understanding of what constitutes gender discrimination (Praxis, 2015). There is a similar lack of understanding among public servants, as has been shown by the analysis commissioned by the Office of the Gender Equality and Equal Treatment Commissioner. They, too, do not perceive gender inequality because of firmly rooted cultural norms, even when the latter have ceased to correspond to reality. Because the gendered division of social roles is considered natural, it is not believed that it can be changed. This means that gendered impacts of laws and other policies remain unanalyzed and actual gender equality does not appear as a policy aim. Lack of prosecuted cases of discrimination does not yet constitute gender equality in the context where women are not encouraged to report discrimination. The only conclusion that we can draw from this fact is that neither employers nor public servants have been forced to acquaint themselves with EU-level gender equality policies and terminology behind them. At the moment of writing, there are also doubts about the ability of the Commissioner to fulfill her duties because of the limitations of her budget and staffing. There is an increasing number of Estonian studies and analyses on different aspects of gender equality and they have the potential of compensating for some of the limitations of minimalist state, but this will not be enough for meaningful change on a state level.

It is naïve to expect changes fast, but 12 years of EU membership and the Gender Equality Act have not generated the supportive public environment that would demand greater gender equality and pressure the government to take the issues more seriously. A 2009 Eurobarometer study showed that only 35% of Estonian women were concerned about equal pay and inequality in the workplace; only 10% believed that more women were needed in positions of power (Eurobarometer, 2009). The Ministry of Social Affairs and academic institutions have produced numerous studies and analyses testifying to gaps and problems, but there has been little movement towards more serious political action. Today it is impossible to hide behind the claim of ignorance. Rather, we need to look for causes in the general socio-political climate and how this promotes or at least condones the lack of political interest in gender equality. Estonian attitudes towards and policies on gender equality are strongly influenced by the country's embrace of neoliberal policies that has been intertwined with nationalism. These dominant ideologies that have been supported across society are in a direct tension with the ideal of gender equality. Saarts and Kalev (2009) see the problem in Estonian political culture, its focus on instrumental thinking, individualism, fear of the strong state and weak civil society groups.

Kuhl (2009, p. 58) elucidates the paradoxes of Estonian society by three normative fundamental structures: anti-Soviet attitudes, continuity with the first Estonian republic and what she calls "turbomodernism." As a result of strong anti-Soviet attitudes everything deriving from the Soviet period is uncritically considered negative and irrelevant to today's Estonia. Kuhl (2009, p. 59) suggests that this attitude helps to explain Estonian skepticism about the word "social" that was considered too redolent of the Soviet era (for example Estonian Social Democrats called themselves Moderates in 1996–2003). Gender equality itself was one of the terms tainted by Soviet associations and it dealt with social issues, thus evoking two taboos. The anti-Soviet stance is paralleled by an equally uncritical celebration of the first Estonian republic and attempts to recreate it. This is evident also in the context of gender equality. The dominant discourses of gender of the 1920s–1930s were constructed around gender difference and they are being revived in changed social and gender reality (Kuhl, 2009, p. 60). In the Estonian context turbomodernism means the embrace of everything that is modern, innovative and progressive. Estonia perceives itself to be more nimble than (Old) Europe and able to overcome the restrictive European rules in the name of innovation—especially market innovation colored by neoliberalist principles. Kuhl (2009, p. 61) sees the influence of turbomodernism in the redefinition of "equality," which in Estonia is viewed from a neoliberal perspective. In other words, inequality just reveals people's different levels of achievement or effort and this is how things should be. This definition, however, is in direct conflict with the normative EU definition of equality according to which all people should be guaranteed the same opportunities. This redefinition also helps to explain why gender equality initiatives have failed to gain wide public support and why people engaged in gender equality issues have often ended up stigmatized.

Estonia has filled all the formal requirements on gender equality at the level of legislation and the CEDAW definition has never caused any public outcries or protest. However, when it comes to the everyday implementation of gender equality as a practice that is mainstreamed on the national and local level, we see a significant gap. Successive gender equality monitorings (2005, 2009, 2013) have shown relatively stable attitudes in the context of gender. The last, 2013 monitoring, however, did reveal some changes towards the acceptance of gender equality and also greater tolerance for sexual minorities. Regrettably men's attitudes have not changed as much as women's. 35% of men surveyed believe women and men have an equal position in Estonian society and thus no further work is needed on gender equality, while only 15% of women think so (*Sotsiaalministeerium*, 2014, p. 67).

In the context where economic growth and national security are prioritized in politics, social issues will continue to receive insufficient attention. In an aging society with a limited labor pool, gender inequality has the potential to become a hindrance to economic growth. Laws alone, however, cannot change public perception, as the Estonian experience of the past 12 years has shown, to create pressure on the political establishment to implement meaningful change.

Notes

1 This study was supported by the Estonian Research Council (PUT192), and by the European Union through the European Regional Development Fund (Centre of Excellence in Estonian Studies).
2 The effect of children on women's wages has not been systematically studied, but a 2010 comparison of women with and without children showed that the addition of each child results in a 1.2% loss in wages (Anspal & Rõõm, 2011, p. 41).

References

Aavik, K. (2013). Strategies for managing difficulties related to employment: Narratives of Russian-speaking women in the Estonian labour market. In A.A. Allaste (Ed.), *"Back in the West": Changing Lifestyles in Transforming Societies*, Frankfurt: P. Lang, pp. 203–224.
Aavik, K. (2015). "The most important decisions are made in the sauna": The role of social capital in creating intersectional privilege in the career narratives of Estonian male managers. *NORMA: International Journal for Masculinity Studies*, 10 (1), 39–54.
Albi, K., Laidvee, J., Papp, Ü.-M., & Sepper, M.-L. (2010). *Soolise võrdõiguslikkuse seadus: Kommenteeritud väljaanne*. Tallinn: Juura.
Albi, K., & Sepper, M.-L. (2010). Mitmene diskrimineerimine: Mõistest õigusliku raamistiku ja õiguskaitse küsimusteni. In R. Marling, L. Järviste & K. Sander (Eds), *Teel tasakaalustatud ühiskonda: Naised ja mehed Eestis II*, Tallinn: Sotsiaalministeerium, pp. 97–111.
Annist, A. (2011). *Otsides kogukonda sotsialismijärgses keskuskülas: Arenguantropoloogiline uurimus*. Tallinn: TLÜ Kirjastus.
Annuk, E. (2015). Soodiskursustest Eestis nõukogude perioodil. *Ariadne Lõng*, 15 (1-2), 70–89.
Anspal, S., & Rõõm, T. (2011). Sooline palgalõhe Eestis: empiiriline analüüs. *Sooline palgalõhe Eestis: Sotsiaalministeeriumi toimetised*, (2), 27–66.
Biin, H., & Albi, A. (2012). Suffrage and the nation: Women's vote in Estonia. In B. Rodríguez-Ruiz & R. Rubio-Marín (Eds), *The Struggle for Female Suffrage in Europe: Voting to Become Citizens*, Leiden and Boston: Brill, pp. 111–125.
Blanc, E. (2017). "Comrades in battle": Women workers and the 1906 Finnish suffrage victory. *Aspasia: The International Yearbook of Central, Eastern and Southeastern European Women's History*, 11.
Eesti Statistika. (2015). *Soolise võrdõiguslikkuse näitajad / Indicators of Gender Equality*. Tallinn: Eesti Statistika.
Eesti Statistika. (2016). *Eesti. Arve ja fakte 2016*. Tallinn: Eesti Statistika.
Equal Treatment Act. (2008). Riigi Teataja No. 315/2008. Retrieved from https://www.riigiteataja.ee/en/eli/530102013066/consolide (accessed 8 March 2016).
Estonian Social Insurance Board. (2016). Parental benefit. Retrieved from http://www.sotsiaalkindlustusamet.ee/parental-benefit/ (accessed 19 June 2016).
Eurobarometer. (2009). Attitudes and opinions of European women prior to the 2009 EP elections. Retrieved from http://www.europarl.europa.eu/pdf/euro barometre/european_women/socio_demo/sociodemo_report_en.pdf (accessed 13 March 2016).
European Institute for Gender Equality. (2015). *Gender Equality Index 2015: Measuring Gender Equality in the European Union 2005–2012*. Vilnius, Lithuania: European Institute for Gender Equality.

Gender Equality Act. (2004). Riigi Teataja No. 181/2004. Retrieved from https:// www.riigiteataja.ee/en/tolge/pdf/511042014004 (accessed 8 March 2016).

Goldman, W.Z. (1993). *Women, the State and Revolution: Soviet Family Policy and Social Life, 1917–1936.* Cambridge, UK: Cambridge University Press.

Hallik, T. (2001). Eesti naine poliitikas enne iseseisvusaega: Hääleõigus ja poliitika. In K. Johanson, K. Karelson, I. Laidna, A. Lätt & C. Ojango (Eds), *Eesti naine sillakohtust võrdõiguslikkuseni,* Tartu, Estonia: Filiae Patriae, pp. 21–31.

Heritage Foundation. (2016). 2016 index of economic freedom. Retrieved from http://www.heritage.org/index/ (accessed 9 March 2016).

Inglehart, R., & Norris, P. (2003). *Rising Tide: Gender Equality and Cultural Change around the World.* New York: Cambridge University Press.

Karu, M. (2010). Vaesus kui soolistunud nähtus. In R. Marling, L. Järviste & K. Sander (Eds), *Teel tasakaalustatud ühiskonda: Naised ja mehed Eestis II,* Tallinn: Sotsiaalministeerium, pp. 52–65.

Kuhl, M. (2009). Siirdeloogika juured. *Acta Politica Estica,* (3), 56–64.

Kuurme, T. (2010). Pilguheit soolisele tegelikkusele Eesti haridussüsteemis. In R. Marling, L. Järviste & K. Sander (Eds), *Teel tasakaalustatud ühiskonda: Naised ja mehed Eestis II,* Tallinn: Sotsiaalministeerium, pp. 127–137.

Laar, M. (2007). The Estonian economic miracle. Retrieved from http://www.heritage. org/research/reports/2007/08/the-estonian-economic-miracle (accessed 9 March 2016).

Lõhkivi, E. (2010). Naised teaduses. In R. Marling, L. Järviste & K. Sander (Eds), *Teel tasakaalustatud ühiskonda: Naised ja mehed Eestis II,* Tallinn: Sotsiaalministeerium, pp. 132–133.

Marling, R. (2010). The intimidating other: Feminist critical discourse analysis of the representation of feminism in Estonian print media. *NORA—Nordic Journal of Feminist and Gender Research,* 18 (1), 7–19.

Marling, R. (2011). Out of the room of one's own? Gender studies in Estonia. *Aspasia: The International Yearbook of Central, Eastern and Southeastern European Women's History,* 5, 157–165.

Masso, M. (2010). Mehed ja naised tööelus. In R. Marling, L. Järviste & K. Sander (Eds), *Teel tasakaalustatud ühiskonda: Naised ja mehed Eestis II,* Tallinn: Sotsiaalministeerium, pp. 26–39.

Miroiu, M. (2007). Communism was a state patriarchy, not state feminism. *Aspasia: The International Yearbook of Central, Eastern and Southeastern European Women's History,* 1, 197–201.

Open Society Institute. (2005). *Equal Opportunities for Women and Men: Monitoring Law and Practice in New Member States and Accession Countries of the European Union.* Budapest: Open Society Institute.

Osila, L. (2015). Some facts about the gender pay gap in Estonia. Retrieved from http://genderpaygap.eu/documents/Factsheet_Estonia.pdf (accessed 16 June 2016).

Paats, M., & Lunev, M. (2015). *Sooline palgalõhe pole kasulik kellelegi, ka meestele.* Retrieved from http://www.vordoigusvolinik.ee/wp-content/uploads/2015/01/ Sooline-palgalohe-pole-kasulik-kellelegi-ka-meestele-Paats-Lunev.pdf (accessed 16 July 2016).

Pajumets, M. (2010). Estonian couples' rationalizations for fathers' rejection of parental leave. *Fathering,* 8 (2), 226–243.

Papp, Ü.-M. (2010). Eesti võrdõiguslikkuse teel: Kokkuvõte. In R. Marling, L. Järviste & K. Sander (Eds), *Teel tasakaalustatud ühiskonda: Naised ja mehed Eestis II,* Tallinn: Sotsiaalministeerium, pp. 180–194.

Penal Code. (2001). Riigi Teataja No. 364/2001. Retrieved from https://www.riigite-ataja.ee/en/eli/522012015002/consolide (accessed 16 June 2016).

Põldsaar, R. (2009). Isamaa ja mehemeel: mehelikkuse ideoloogiad ja rahvuslik identiteet. *Ariadne Lõng,* **9** (1-2), 63–75.

Praxis. (2015). *Uuring Soolise võrdõiguslikkus seaduse rakendamisest tööandjate seas ja indikaatorite väljatöötamineseaduse mõjude hindamiseks: Uuringuaru-anne.* Retrieved from http://www.praxis.ee/wp-content/uploads/2015/09/SVS-rakendamine.pdf (accessed 8 March 2016).

Rajasalu, T. (2006). Eesti—vaikne ja igav Põhjala riik? (Estonia—a quiet and boring Nordic country). Retrieved from http://vm.ee/sites/default/files/content-editors/web-static/246/triinu_rajasalu.pdf (accessed 16 June 2016).

Roots, A. (2011). Enesetäiendamise viisi ja kõrgema ametipositsiooni seos meeste ja naiste puhul. *Ariadne Lõng,* **11** (1/2), 48–57.

Ruthchild, R.G. (2010). *Equality & Revolution: Women's Rights in the Russian Empire, 1905–1917.* Pittsburgh, PA: University of Pittsburgh Press.

Saarts, T., & Kalev, L. (2009). *Poliitiline kultuur ja Eesti ühiskonna uuen-emine.* Retrieved from http://www.vikerkaar.ee/archives/11842 (accessed 13 March 2016).

Sepper, M.-L. (2010). Naiste ja meeste võrdõiguslikkus Eestis: Probleemid, eesmär-gid ja lahendused. Presentation at the 90th anniversary of the Estonian Women's Union, 3 December.

Snitow, A. (2006). Cautionary tales. In J. Lukíc, J. Regulska & D. Zaviršek (Eds), *Women and Citizenship in Central and Eastern Europe,* Aldershot, UK: Ashgate, pp. 287–297.

Soolise võrdõiguslikkuse ja võrdse kohtlemise voliniku kantselei. (2015). *Soolise võrdõiguslikkuse ja võrdse kohtlemise voliniku 2014.aasta tegevuse aruanne.* Tallinn: Soolise võrdõiguslikkuse ja võrdse kohtlemise voliniku kantselei.

Soolise võrdõiguslikkuse ja võrdse kohtlemise voliniku kantselei. (2016). *Kellel on Eestis hea, kellel parem? Võrdõiguslikkuse mõõtmise mudel.* Tallinn: Soolise võrdõiguslikkuse ja võrdse kohtlemise voliniku kantselei. Retrieved from http://www.vordoigusvolinik.ee/wp-content/uploads/2016/03/mudel_final.pdf (accessed 12 July 2016).

Sotsiaalministeerium. (2006). *Soolise võrdõiguslikkuse monitooring 2005.* Tallinn: Sotsiaalministeerium.

Sotsiaalministeerium. (2010). *Soolise võrdõiguslikkuse monitooring 2009.* Tallinn: Sotsiaalministeerium.

Sotsiaalministeerium. (2014). *Soolise võrdõiguslikkuse monitooring 2013.* Tallinn: Sotsiaalministeerium.

United Nations Development Programme. (2015). *Human Development Report 2015.* New York: United Nations Development Programme.

Vöörmann, R., & Plotnik, H. (2008). Sostiaalne õiglus ja sugu. In H. Plotnik (Ed.), *Sotsiaalse õigluse arusaamad Eesti ühiskonnas,* Tartu, Estonia: Tartu Üikooli Kir-jastus, pp. 107–121.

Wood, E.A. (1997). *The Baba and the Comrade: Gender and Politics in Revolution-ary Russia.* Bloomington, IN: Indiana University Press.

World Economic Forum. (2015). The global gender gap report 2015. Retrieved from http://reports.weforum.org/global-gender-gap-report-2015/ (accessed 1 July 2016).

Part III
Comments and Conclusions

12 Commentary
The Nature and Impact of Gender Equality Initiatives Around the Globe—Tensions and Paradoxes

Patrice M. Buzzanell

The impetus for this edited collection, *Gender Equality in a Global Perspective*, is an intriguing and urgent question that presents opportunities for empirical research and reflection; namely, what is gender equality and, more specifically, what is gender equality in different national contexts around the globe? By definition, the answer should be relatively straightforward given policies and statistical evidence for equal representation, treatment, expectations, inclusion and benefits for women and men in different life realms. Yet, the introductory comments and chapters about gender equality in specific countries indicate that the answer is much more complicated than the numbers and standards of compliance to global directives such as the UN Convention on the Elimination of all Forms of Discrimination Against Women (CEDAW) would indicate. Considerations of societal norms and values, as well as policies and consequences for noncompliance, and the way people do gender equality and inequality on an everyday basis are the bases on which we, as readers, learn how and why gender equality has not progressed as far as we might imagine and hope.

As the title of this commentary suggests, there are different ways to address gender equality in theory and in practice. Certainly, one way is to analyze the development of policies and metrics within countries. Chapter authors provide historical bases, often but not always starting with the 20th century, with listings of and explanations for pivotal points in these socio-political and economic contexts. For instance, Serbia exhibits gender equality in ideology and in practice for the educational realm, as aligned with its recent political past: "In the general population, education has remained the strongest legacy of socialism, even during difficult times of social transition. A recent public opinion survey (2010) shows that women's education is still highly valued by both genders." (Ignjatović & Bošković, Chapter 9 in this volume). Similarly, the Soviet legacy in Estonia (Marling, Chapter 11 in this volume) has contributed to misperceptions of gender equality accomplishment with paradoxes that women are highly educated, even more so than men. However, such credentials are needed by women for labor force entry and advancement, but unnecessary for men. Moreover, while gender equality is protected, the legal system makes it difficult to deal with cases of multiple or intersectional discrimination.

In remarkably condensed and highly lucid writing, the authors explain how policies were formed and where they have had more or less impact. They rely upon empirical evidence, using statistics and findings from qualitative inquiry, but they also provide ideological analyses tracing systems of thought from their earliest glimmers through current manifestations. For Nigeria (Para-Mallam, Chapter 2 in this volume), the main story begins with a return to democratic governance in 1999, but for China (Zhao, Chapter 4 in this volume), gender equality began at the end of 19th century and had different iterations depending on political upheavals and governmental programs (e.g., political and economic turbulence affecting gender equality in Egypt). The China's one-child policy—which recently has been amended—prompted urban parents with female children to invest in these girls whereas rural parents paid penalties for having multiple children and did not invest in daughters' education. In Australia (Voola, Beavis & Mundukur, Chapter 5 in this volume), early efforts toward gender equality have been stalled by racism, sexism and the persistent belief in meritocracy (a "fair go") that erases the visibility of deep structural barriers toward equality.

Throughout *Gender Equality in a Global Perspective*, chapter authors uniformly produce coherent accounts of gender equality in the nations of which they are members. They not only interpret the meanings of different policies and events but also frame these policies and events according to their meaningfulness for women. Authors often take an intersectionalities lens to address difference and where policies and practices have and have not changed for particular groups of women. In China (Zhao, Chapter 4 in this volume), gender equality is complicated by age, rural-urban divides, (see also Espino, Chapter 6 in this volume) household residencies, locations in regions marked for influx of funding (or not) for advancement and economic gain, and minority-majority ethnic group status. In other countries, differences in religion (e.g.,, Para-Mallam, Chapter 2 in this volume) and retirement age gaps segmented by occupational and class differences (e.g., Ignjatović & Bošković, Chapter 9 in this volume) pose challenges. In still other countries, there are particular groups of women who have limited access to benefits. As one case in point, Roma women, disabled women and victims of rape in Serbia have limited access to health care with little implementation of regulations to rectify such injustices.

In this first way of approaching gender equality through documentation and evidence of impact, the editors have insured that chapters are consistent with well-supported claims and enough detail for readers to understand what may actually be happening in the countries. For instance, the chapter on Egypt (Arafa & El-Ashry, Chapter 3 in this volume) describes inheritance in Islamic Law so that the nature of gendered familial obligations and practices is not misperceived or confused with what happens in other countries. Besides this very appropriate and useful way of approaching gender equality, there is yet another way of addressing gender equality. This way requires that we take a tensional approach whereby readers can consider the different tensions, meanings and meaningfulness of gender equality in specific countries and worldwide. The rest of my commentary discusses how a tension-centered lens underlies the chapters in *Gender Equality in a Global Perspective* and highlights other ways of reading these chapters.

A tensional approach encourages contestation of language, time and place, and struggles to achieve desired outcomes. In the contestation of the phrase "gender equality," the language, interactions and artifacts, such as workplace and governmental policies, religious and cultural underpinnings, and statistical reports about shifts in different life realms are interrogated. Although in many chapters, "gender equality" is used and framed conceptually and operationally for the particular national context, some chapter authors note explicitly that "gender justice" (Arafa & El-Ashry, Chapter 3 in this volume) and "gender equity" (Para-Malla, Chapter 2 in this volume) are more appropriate. A tensional approach encourages transformation over time and place because contradiction, irony and paradox expose spaces in which current endeavors are not working and need to be changed and where and/or how what works at one site might be replicated with modifications in another. A tension-centered approach calls attention to the emotions, struggles, ongoing policy making and revising and political implications of human action. Through these processes, gender equality as a phrase and as lived experience are destabilized so that the different realities can be exposed and addressed. This approach highlights the ongoing assessment of gender equality, such as where having policies on the books or having increased numbers of women in public office means that people believe that the problems have been resolved. For instance, in my own scholarship, I have learned that policy is essential for its legitimization of causes and for the baseline character of gender equality but that once policy is formed, it is taken as "fixed" or invariant by those very people for whom accommodation, policy revision and choice are most needed (e.g., Buzzanell & Liu, 2005; Buzzanell & Lucas, 2013).

In short, tensions, contradiction and paradox are key to productive organizing (Trethewey & Ashcraft, 2004). A tensional approach moves gender inequality from a problem to be solved to the ongoing organizing of human activity. In its overarching tensional approach, the editors and chapter authors contributing to *Gender Equality in a Global Perspective* have done a remarkable job of exposing the "cracks" in gender equality narratives and systems. They also advocate for particular changes but admit that such interventions are complicated. Through their ongoing and iterative questioning of gender equality, they offer points of resistance and solidarity.

Finally, a tensional approach shifts attention to the spaces between equality and inequality. This approach interrogates the space between genders, asking how gender equality changes women's and men's lives in different ways and to greater and lesser extents for particular subpopulations and different ideas of well-being. A tensional approach examines the contradictions found in social welfare state and other national or regional systems that offer benefits for parenthood but that also may inadvertently result in less gender equality in the workplace and in long-term inequities such as labor-force participation length and resources for retirement (e.g., Boeckmann et al., 2015; Budig et al., 2016). A recurring focus in most gender equality scholarship and programs has been on the elimination of gender inequalities, but perhaps the question is not about elimination but about how to utilize the tensions between equality and inequality productively and with movement toward sustainable solutions. This edited collection moves us along this direction.

Within *Gender Equality in a Global Perspective*, several tensions emerge throughout this edited collection: (a) sameness-difference, (b) past-present, (c) formal-substantive frames, (d) discouragement-hope and (e) assessment-advocacy.

First, regarding sameness-difference, co-editors Anders Örtenblad, Raili Marling and Snježana Vasiljević note that they took transnational and inter-sectional feminisms as key to avoiding dichotomization of Western and non-Western societies and to avoiding essentializating all women. They encouraged authors to elaborate on regional and national notions of gender equality and grapple with how gender and gendered practices are situated amidst other differences. For instance, the chapter on Egypt (Arafa & El-Ashry, Chapter 3 in this volume) discusses female genital mutilation (FGM also is mentioned in Para-Mallam, Chapter 2 in this volume). They directed chapter authors to distinguish among issues, indicate why and how different points of view are advantageous and/or detrimental, and propose pathways between extremes such that readers know authors' opinions as well as practical strategies. For instance, well-educated Chinese women (see Zhao, Chapter 4 in this volume) over the age of 45 are subject to layoffs but these same women in their 30s who are married with a child have work-life balance because of their parents' caregiving activities. Moreover, in their introductory chapter, the co-editors clearly specified their decision criteria for inclusion of countries, especially those in post-socialist transitions, and to offer different perspectives than those typically provided, such as in Nordic countries.

Second, most chapters move within and extend past-present tensions. Chapter authors typically provide an overview of national and international history with nuanced explanations so that readers can see how gender equality initiatives began and coincide with other changes. They also comment about how different events redirected gender equality activities and often lengthened the time tables for equality agendas. Given chapter authors' research plus their deep personal experiences in the countries about which they write, we really get a sense of how diverse initiatives are and how difficult it is to move a gender equality agenda while also accommodating cultural and religious differences. For instance, marriageable ages for girls are highly controversial in Nigeria (Para-Mallam, Chapter 2 in this volume), with Muslim practices and national policy language differing. Moreover, there are three aspects to the Nigerian legal system that complicates gender equality policy and renders formal mechanisms necessary but insufficient in the systems of culture and religion, socioeconomics and politics that, in turn, affect women's everyday lives. Finally, readers might think that the question "Do Nigerian women really want equality?" would not be asked in a book devoted to gender equality, but the answer is telling in its frank response about the high costs to women of fighting for equality, especially the loss of income, community recognition and marital status.

Third, formal-substantive frames surface where, as the Australian case (Voola, Beavis & Mundukur, Chapter 5 in this volume) demonstrates, the formal equality moves over the last three decades have not resulted in the substantive and sustained equalities that one would expect. Education seemed to be a success story, but statistics, when broken down, tell a different story. In all, Australia's pioneering efforts in gender equality pale in comparison to the very vivid cases of violence against women, particularly Aboriginal women, throughout the country. Coupling violence with poverty, low educational attainment and prior political and societal changes indicates that the formal-substantive tensions also surface in idealism and reality, discourse and materialities, and a legal infrastructure supporting gender equality and a socio-political mechanism that curtails progress. In Uruguay (Espino, Chapter 6 in this volume), abortion is presumably legalized, but legal procedures make it very difficult for women to avail themselves of these rights. Abortion is listed as a crime under Uruguay's criminal code but penalties are waived. Furthermore, women need to inform doctors about the circumstances surrounding and hardships incurred by pregnancy and birth. Finally, teams of professionals review their cases and pose alternatives to and risks of the procedure, followed by five-day reflection periods before the women can exercise their "choice," hoping that they can locate gynecologists, given their legal recourse to refuse performance of abortions citing conscientious objection. These measures contrast with Serbian practices where abortion is viewed as a form of contraception and is common among women with two children. Serbians' (Ignjatović & Bošković, Chapter 9 in this volume) more permissive Orthodox religious background on issues such as abortion contrasts with Croatia's (Vasiljević, Chapter 10 in this volume) predominately Catholic population with its controversies over abortion as well as same-sex marriage. Rounding out this section and as a final example, in Croatia "women are more likely to take [parental] leave, to work part time, or to stop working. These discrepancies between official statistics and the situation explained in the annual reports of the Ombudsperson for Gender Equality show that gender equality in Croatia remains formal, not substantive" (Vasiljević, Chapter 10 in this volume).

Fourth, discouragement-hope tensions operate within and across chapters. These tensions surface in language and arguments, in the framing of stances and questions, and in authors' comments on infrastructure and logistical issues regarding discouragement-hope. With respect to language and arguments, the chapter on Mexico (Frías, Chapter 7 in this volume) comments on the "remarkable" improvements in gender equality in legal and educational realms but points out that economic improvements for women are "less noticeable" with the area of least improvement being political. Despite these changes and trends indicating that younger generations hold more gender egalitarian views, particularly in political, economic and educational realms, "Mexican women are still far from reaching gender equality with men in the social structure" (Frías, Chapter 7 in this volume). Similarly, "women have made exceptional gains, broadly speaking, in education" in the United States yet there are clear struggles for gender equality in the workforce (i.e., concerning women's representation, pay inequality and unpaid parental leave), health care and politics (Arendt & Buzzanell, Chapter 8 in this volume). This chapter explicitly discusses contradictions that emerge when contrasting formal policies against dominant cultural narratives and ideologies, such as extreme individualism and American exceptionalism, and a framing of gender issues as "choice" rather than "rights."

To manage discouragement-hope tensions, authors frame their vantage points. They provide their own insights and means of adjudicating claims. For Serbia (Ignjatović & Bošković, Chapter 9 in this volume), questions about gender equality become reframed for somewhat different considerations: "the question 'Is it possible to fully adopt gender equality in Serbia?' should be probably rephrased to: 'Is it possible to be fully certain about gender equality?'" For Croatia (Vasiljević, Chapter 10 in this volume), disentangling church and state are essential for gender and related forms of equality, such as the connection between the Catholic Church and political issues including the definition of marriage in the Croatian Constitution and its amendments that ban same-sex marriage.

As authors remark, the infrastructures for gender equality are in place and may still need to be refined, updated, reworked or developed in the same and other areas—but the main issue is that we must remain vigilant and mindful for the discouragement-hope tensions to be sustained sufficiently to prompt change. Using a tensional approach, our obligation is to juxtapose different aspects, countries and regional patterns for gender, and tease out where women are similar and different depending on race, class, religion, immigrant or indigenous status, marital status, employment variations and so on.

In addition, logistical issues contribute to discouragement-hope tensions. As noted in the chapter on Croatia, the "main issue . . . is that it is impossible to track all judgments in cases of sex discrimination. . . . The other problem is that court practice is not uniform and transparent. There is an urgent need to publish national case law on the web in order to make it more transparent and accessible to researchers and other members of the interested public." (Vasiljević, Chapter 10 in this volume) Moreover, in Croatia, there are several bodies that deal with different grounds of discrimination, accounting for the assessment that "little progress has been made."

Fifth, assessment-advocacy tensions prevail throughout this edited collection. A common theme here is "why so slow?" Policies often have taken years to develop and even longer to implement, if they are implemented at all. In some cases the authors conclude that there simply is not "political will" to make changes. This political will and/or lack thereof may have many different sources. For instance, gender equality may not be taken seriously. It may be too different from societal norms and cultural values. When subsumed within other social initiatives, such as civil rights or diversity and inclusion programs, the need to focus on gender as the most prominent inequality may be diminished. Furthermore, gender equality may be perceived as having been achieved in principle, if not in practice. As some chapter authors phrase it, they discuss "to what degree the nature of Egyptian society would accommodate gender equality" (Egypt), the "lack of political will" (Nigeria, Croatia, Estonia and Uruguay), and enforcement of gender equality policies and principle "contingent upon political will and civil society support" with little progress (Australia).

Continuing with assessment-advocacy dynamics, all authors consider political will or interest in gender equality, as well as assessments about transformational initiatives along with the efforts and resources needed to accomplish even small changes. All take a stand regarding the state of gender equality in their nations. Chapters close with final reflections and policy recommendations. To work toward greater gender equality in Uruguay, for example, chapter authors urge a focus on concrete actions and practices, such as "tackle[ing] structural systems" and examining and rectifying the "design flaws" in policies (Espino, Chapter 6 in this volume). For China, a major shortcoming in gender equality policies and practices is that gender equality practices have been subordinated to economic development since the 1980s (Zhao, Chapter 4 in this volume). Similarly, "gender equality and women's rights are not often seen as a priority in political decision-making" with a real need to implement gender equality legal standards and norms in Croatia (Vasiljević, Chapter 10 in this volume). These reflections are essential for understanding the complicated state and ironies surrounding gender equality and transformational policies and programs designed to engage in social justice (e.g., Morimoto & Zajicek, 2014).

In summary, tensional approaches underlying *Gender Equality in a Global Perspective* provide readers with insights that do not lead to simple root causes or easy answers for inequalities (for processes to constitute ongoing and sustainable change, see Buzzanell, in press). Yet we, as readers, find satisfying mixes of different tensions. These tensions emerge from authors' accounts of historical contexts, ideological critiques, empirical analyses, nuanced interpretations and practical recommendations that encourage aspirations of gender equality tempered by realism. Furthermore, it would be easy to be disillusioned by the lack of timely progress toward gender equality. Yet the chapter authors manage these and other tensions in straightforward and thoughtful ways. As put in the chapter on Egypt (Arafa & El-Ashry, Chapter 3 in this volume):

> Endorsing gender equality in the legal framework and committing the state to its enforcement is a must. More interest to boost the quality of education and awareness campaigns on gender issues will help eliminate the deep-rooted social obstruction. The Egyptian society after recent developments in the political sphere is more ready to embrace values of social justice including gender equality. Thus, there has never been a better time to continue the struggle.

Undoubtedly there has never been a better time for this edited collection. For this reason and many others, we can thank co-editors Anders Örtenblad, Raili Marling and Snježana Vasiljević and all the chapter authors. They have produced an exceptionally well written and documented set of cases that can help us work toward fulfilling gender equality aspirations in individual countries as well as globally.

References

Boeckmann, I., Misra, J., & Budig, M. (2015). Cultural and institutional factors shaping mothers' employment and working hours in postindustrial countries. *Social Forces*, **93** (4), 1301–1333.

Budig, M., Misra, J., & Boeckmann, I. (2016). Work: Family policy trade-offs for mothers? Unpacking the cross-national variation in motherhood earnings penalties. *Work and Occupations*, **43** (2), 119–177.

Budig, M., Misra, J., & Boeckmann, I. (2016). Work: Family policy trade-offs for mothers? Unpacking the cross-national variation in motherhood earnings penalties. *Work and Occupations*, **43** (2), 119–177.

Buzzanell, P. M. (in press). Constituting intercultural harmony by design thinking: Conflict management in, for, and about diversity and inclusion work. In X. Dai & G.-M. Chen (Eds), *Conflict Management and Intercultural Harmony*. New York, NY: Routledge.

Buzzanell, P.M., & Lucas, K. (2013). Constrained and constructed choice in career: An examination of communication pathways to dignity. In E. Cohen (Ed.), *Communication Yearbook 37*, New York, NY: Routledge, pp. 3–31.

Morimoto, S., & Zajicek, A. (2014). Dismantling the "master's house": Feminist reflections on institutional transformation. *Critical Sociology*, **40** (1), 135–150.

Trethewey, A., & Ashcraft, K.L. (2004). Practicing disorganization: The development of applied perspectives on living with tension. *Journal of Applied Communication Research*, **32** (2), 81–88.

13 Conclusion

Raili Marling, Snježana Vasiljević
and Anders Örtenblad

Patrice Buzzanell's preceding comment (Chapter 12 in this volume) has demonstrated the complexities revealed in the chapters collected in this volume when it comes both to the interpretation and implementation of gender equality across the globe and invites us to think tensionally in analyzing gender equality comparatively. In the present conclusion we want to take a step back from the specific case studies and return to the aims we set in the introduction. We will reflect on the possible answers to the questions that we posed to our authors and also attempt to arrive at some practical suggestions both for researchers and policy makers or activists.

As we suggested in our introduction, our aim has been to interrogate how gender equality, a universal value promulgated in many international and national laws, is actually interpreted and applied in a variety of geographical locations. Despite globalization and increased international mobility, cultural differences continue to be central in interpreting international norms, especially when it comes to gender. It is because of this awareness of culture that we sought analyses written by experts from the different countries we covered to arrive at a nuanced understanding of the tension between the universal and the local. The diversity of viewpoints also informs our concluding comments here. Chapters 2–11 above show that even when gender equality (GE) is accepted in public rhetoric and enshrined in national legislation, there continue to be great obstacles to the actual realization of gender equality in daily practice and in the value systems of different countries.

Universality of Gender Equality

Nine of the ten countries covered in the book are signatories of CEDAW (the only exception is the US [Arendt & Buzzanell, Chapter 8 in this volume], the only democracy that has not ratified CEDAW because of the opposition of conservative and religious groups), but this has not meant that the convention is universally understood and applied in different national contexts. The signatories of CEDAW are very differently placed in global GE indices (e.g., on the World Economic Forum's Gender Gap Index for 2015 that ranks countries from the most to least gender-equal Estonia ranked 21st and

Australia 36th, but Nigeria 125th and Egypt 136th among the 145 countries covered) (World Economic Forum, 2015).

The full equality of women and men is declared a fundamental right in the constitutions of seven of the countries analyzed (Nigeria, Egypt, China, Mexico, Serbia, Croatia, Estonia); four (Mexico, Serbia, Croatia, Estonia) have a specific GE law; and all countries ban discrimination against women in some form of legislation. However, when we look at the statistics on political and labor force participation, we see that women are still under-represented in politics, paid lower wages than men and are greatly under-represented in the higher levels of economic and political power in all of the countries analyzed. Women increasingly work outside of the home, but are paid less than men while still shouldering the majority of household chores and childcare responsibilities as well as the care of the elderly. Women's public sphere roles have changed considerably since the mid-20th century, but this has not been accompanied by a comparable change in their domestic duties. There continue to be serious challenges to GE in the context of reproductive health, especially the continued erosion of the right to abortion in several of the countries analyzed (e.g., strikingly in the case of Uruguay [Espino, Chapter 6 in this volume] where abortion is legal but access to it is curtailed). In many of the countries covered, domestic violence is a pervasive problem that has not been necessarily recognized as a form of gender discrimination. Sexual harassment of women has been used in Egypt (Arafa & El-Ashry, Chapter 3 in this volume) as a political tool to discourage women's participation in public protests. In poor nations, the low level of human development and pervasive poverty set obstacles for the development of women's rights, as is persuasively presented in the case of Nigeria (Para-Mallam, Chapter 2 in this volume) and Egypt (Arafa & El-Ashry, Chapter 3 in this volume).

The one area where we see major progress in most of the countries studied is education. Women's education rates equal and even exceed those of men in post-secondary education in the European and American countries discussed. Yet, women's educational attainment continues to be a problem in China (Zhao, Chapter 4 in this volume) and the African countries. Continued attention to the quality of education will be crucial in ensuring the continued progress in the field of gender equality. Unfortunately, the impressive improvements of women's levels of education have not translated into comparable gains in the labor market, both in terms of positions and pay levels. However, the change itself shows that gender indicators can be changed and do change.

Thus, we can give a positive answer to the first question set in the introduction of the book, "To what degree is there GE already in the country you study?" Yes, all countries analyzed have some legal provisions on gender equality in place. Nine of the ten countries have ratified CEDAW (the only exception being the US [Arendt & Buzzanell, Chapter 8 in this volume]); three European countries have also harmonized their legal systems with EU gender equality provisions. Four of the nations have national gender equality laws and seven of the countries also declare the equality of men and women in the constitutions of the country, as mentioned above. Those countries that lack specific GE laws express the ban on discrimination against women in different other legal acts (anti-discrimination laws, penal code, etc.). The legal developments have followed different paths, depending on the history and geopolitical location of the country. The need for international aid has helped to keep GE on the political agenda in Egypt; the goal of EU accession helped GE legislation to succeed in Serbia (Ignjatović & Bošković, Chapter 9 in this volume), Croatia (Vasiljević, Chapter 10 in this volume) and Estonia (Marling, Chapter 11 in this volume). Political will has been crucial for the legal development in the context of GE. Legally, most countries, with possibly the exception of Nigeria (Para-Mallam, Chapter 2 in this volume) and Egypt (Arafa & El-Ashry, Chapter 3 in this volume), guarantee women and men equality in law and at least formally guarantee women comparable, if not exactly the same rights and opportunities as men.

Gender Equality in Reality

However, as persisting inequalities show, this legislative progress has not resulted in substantive equality. That is, although laws exist, they are not always enforceable and enforced. In many countries, the challenge is a lack of institutions that would have the right to enforce GE laws and the burden of litigation is placed on people who have suffered discrimination and who are often ill-informed about GE legislation. These comments are repeated from chapter to chapter. In the three European countries, for example, there are specific state and independent institutions that are set up to oversee GE, but they are underfunded, at the mercy of changing political priorities of different governing coalitions and lack the right to enforce laws. In other countries, for example Mexico (Frías, Chapter 7 in this volume), great regional differences make the enforcement of laws very difficult. In other countries like Nigeria (Para-Mallam, Chapter 2 in this volume), it is the structure of the legal system itself that makes international standards unenforceable. Widespread misinterpretations of religious principles reduce gender justice in Egypt (Arafa & El-Ashry, Chapter 3 in this volume). Market forces and the process of neoliberalization have impacted countries in all regions of the world, from China (Zhao, Chapter 4 in this volume) to the US (Arendt & Buzzanell, Chapter 8 in this volume).

This information leads us to answer our second question, "Is GE only formally guaranteed in legislation or also embraced in everyday social life?," that only partly. Largely, GE is formally covered in legislation but the wide-ranging mainstreaming of GE in everyday life has lagged behind legal changes. There are countries where GE is widely embraced (US (Arendt & Buzzanell, Chapter 8 in this volume), Australia (Voola, Beavis & Mundkur, Chapter 5 in this volume)). In the market socialist China (Zhao, Chapter 4 in this volume) GE is publicly declared and practiced, but a closer look at statistics shows that de facto GE is not a reality and women are disadvantaged in the labor market. In the post-socialist countries of Central and Eastern Europe GE was enforced under socialism and thus, after the fall of socialism the countries cooled to GE because of its supposed association with an oppressive past. GE is a fact in many areas of life, but increasing conservative tendencies also threaten GE gains in Eastern Europe, South America and Africa. Conservative backlashes can even be seen in the US and Australia. The gap between the de jure and de facto GE continues to be large everywhere.

The gap between de jure and de facto GE is partially produced by the lack of precise and comprehensive legislation and enforcement. In terms of legislation, the biggest problem is the vague definitions of GE and gender-based discrimination. Usually, laws are unclear in defining what behaviors constitute gender discrimination. Furthermore, despite the increasing number of legal provisions to protect GE, the laws do not provide concrete instructions on how to implement these provisions.

The obstacle for the enforcement of laws is that the legal systems lack targeted and valid punishments. In most of the cases the usual punishments for discriminating against women include administrative penalties and fines in a form of economic compensations. On the labor market, many employers remain unpunished or, when punished, the financial sanctions are so minor as to be ineffective. This problem is even more evident in cases of multiple discrimination because there is no unique standard for the calculation of economic loss caused by gender discrimination. A similar problem exists in legal sanctions against domestic violence. In some countries, these problems are partially solved by independent specialized bodies that are faster in finding settlements, but they are still inefficient in terms of lack of competences in imposing effective, dissuasive and proportionate sanctions. Consequently, victims of gender discrimination remain unprotected and legal systems are ill trained to deal with the issue. The overall picture which emerges from the chapters is that GE in many countries is still far from reaching satisfactory results, due to deeply rooted gender stereotypes and a lack of courage to bring cases before the courts. This is partially because there is a lack of knowledge of the existence of legislation, and because of stereotypes which are present even in the justice system.

Even in countries where GE is widely embraced by the public, we see that internal political divisions and great intersectional differences have made the achievement of substantive equality for all of the population problematic. Intersectionality is a challenge for all of the countries studied. Ethnic and racial minorities, older and poor women, women from peripheral regions, women with disabilities continue to confront greater inequality than white middle-class women from the metropolitan areas. Moreover, multiple discrimination has only recently started to make its way to the national legal systems and is anything but widely recognized.

A major obstacle is a very narrow interpretation of GE as applying only to the labor market or the public sphere that leaves the private sphere underscrutinized. This, in turn, feeds female disadvantage in the public sphere as women continue to be responsible for the majority of household duties because of entrenched gender norms. Pregnancy and childbirth still disadvantage women in the labor force in most, if not all of the societies analyzed in the present volume. Even when laws make it possible for men to stay at home with children without losing financially, as the Estonian case has shown (Marling, Chapter 11 in this volume), cultural norms discourage this practice.

Is Substantive Gender Equality Possible?

Cultural norms have been the greatest deterrent of progress of GE. Cultural norms are rooted in the history (e.g., the history of socialism or colonialism), religious background (i.e., the strengths of traditional religious denominations) and demographic situations of the countries (e.g., countries with low birth rates have argued for traditional interpretations of gender roles). In countries with strong patriarchal cultural values supported by religion, GE has faced an uphill struggle, as the Nigerian case dramatically shows. The inclusion of Islamic law in the Egyptian constitution creates persistent tensions with GE initiatives. Continued patriarchal thinking has prevented women's advancement in Latin America. Re-traditionalization has been a challenge also in Central and Eastern Europe where nationalism also encourages traditionalist thinking on gender. Women's right to reproductive freedom is anything but guaranteed in this day and age in a range of societies in this context.

All chapters show that, next to cultural values that change slowly, perhaps the biggest obstacle to the creation of the substantive equality of men and women is the political one, because inequality is deeply rooted not just in cultural traditions but also in the political and legal establishment. Feminism has this far failed to provide a clear and unified vision of a post-patriarchal world. Without such a vision we do not have clear guidelines as to how to act in the future. Women still confront male dominance in law, even though the profession is becoming more and more feminized. Women lawyers have remained passive in part out of the fear of the consequences of critiquing the jurisprudence dominated by white men. Women have also remained politically weak and therefore they have not been able to confront internal partisan structures of the political establishments. However, it also has to be noted that women often remain passive in order to keep even the smallest fraction of advances made and political power gained. Many women have strategically chosen to speak in the language of male power (e.g., famously Margaret Thatcher, described during her time in office as the best man in the cabinet). There are too few women politicians who identify with GE. Women's careers also continue to be challenged by the double burden of domestic and family obligations and fear of a patriarchal backlash against women who violate cultural norms. When observing the share of women in politics and decision-making bodies in the countries that are the focus of this study, it is clear that there is not yet the critical number of women that could create meaningful change in political power. For instance, public debates on whether to ban or legalize abortion are dominated by men who adopt the patriarchal pattern of making decisions on the female body.

Another problem is the relative weakness of civil society and NGOs that could pressure the conservative and passive political establishment towards making changes in the countries analyzed. In countries like Egypt (Arafa & El-Ashry, Chapter 3 in this volume), civil society organizations are, in fact, actively suppressed. Most of the countries lack vocal and powerful feminist movements that could mobilize widespread grassroots support. Where feminist movements exist, they are confronted by powerful, well-organized and often well-funded conservative movements. There has also been no public pressure on the political and legal establishment with regard to GE in the past decade because of the widespread false impression that GE has largely been achieved because it is now enshrined in the legal systems of the countries.

Thus we have to answer our third question, "Would it be possible to fully (everywhere, always) adopt GE in practice in your country?", that today GE cannot be fully implemented in practice in the countries studied because of cultural norms and historical circumstances. Legal changes are quicker than culture change. Culture change, however, does happen and thus the situation might be quite different if we returned to our case studies 10 years from now. Also, as the Egyptian (Arafa & El-Ashry, Chapter 3 in this volume) and Nigerian chapter (Para-Mallam, Chapter 2 in this volume) show, GE defined as "sameness of rights" does not today fit societies where religion plays a central role. This, however, does not mean that discrimination against women is being tolerated. Rather, Egyptian society applies the concept of gender justice compatible with Islamic law and Nigeria has chosen the concept of gender equity. The international community needs to analyze these local adaptations not just as compromises, but as necessary steps towards a more equitable treatment of women and men.

Thus, we leave our fourth question, "Which parts of GE would be impossible to adopt in practice?", unanswered. No chapter indicated any areas in which GE would be impossible to implement. The fact that women's education levels have improved in most of the countries studied, including Egypt, gives us hope, as does the increasing legal attention to support to balancing working outside of home with family life. In countries where such statistics were available (e.g., Mexico), we could also see an increasing acceptance of GE by the younger generations. The speed of change in attitudes can be very fast, as was shown in the case of the speedy and widespread embrace of same-sex marriage in the US. What is needed for improvement in GE is the erosion of traditional values, but also increasing local and international political pressure on the political and legal establishments that have been slow to support substantive change.

Conclusions and Recommendations

Although the case studies in the collection testify to great cultural differences, they also show a surprising number of similar challenges. All countries covered are confronting the twin forces of globalization and neoliberalism that have prioritized market logic and made gender equality initiatives lose urgency in the eyes of the political elites. All countries have struggled with the aftermath of the recent global recession and different austerity policies that have negatively affected GE enforcement. All countries need to attend to ethnic minorities, differences between different regions of the country, marginalization of the elderly and all the other aspects that intersectional theory has brought to the fore. Many countries face re-traditionalization of social life. In other words, there are important differences but also thought-provoking similarities between the countries studied.

We conclude with four main proposals:

- First, GE scholarship and practice should move from mere ranking of the world's diverse countries in league tables on the basis of statistics and the formal existence of legislation. The rankings and government reports do not reveal the reality on the ground as they tend to be formalistic. Formal frameworks are crucial for GE, but our efforts should not end with them. Different state actors, international organizations and local NGOs should maintain pressure on the often reluctant political establishment to ensure that formalistic interpretation of equality becomes substantive. It is not important whether we use the term of "equality," "equity" or "justice," but that we ensure that women and men get fair chances in different societies, regardless of their ethnic origin, race, sexuality, disability and other intersectional differences.
- Second, in the context of GE it is important to consider not just the labor market and the public sphere, but the complex web of domestic duties and cultural traditions that prevent women from achieving a greater degree of equality with men. This has been often stated in feminist literature, but international rankings have still prioritized the public sphere. Greater awareness of and attention to intersectionality should be central to this multi-pronged approach to GE.
- Third, as the chapters of this book testify, the discovery of differences between women and men cannot be interpreted identically across the globe. Differences need to be interpreted in the local socio-cultural context. GE is not an imported product that arrives ready-made. We need to continue to be attentive to the processes of translation, interpretation and adaptation that is necessary in the domestication of any international norm. This does not mean that we give up on the universality of human rights and gender equality, but that we approach it with cultural sensitivity.
- Fourth, as scholars, we invite more comparative work on gender equality. The past decades have seen numerous case studies or analyses of

individual countries. Those are an important first step, but it is only in comparison that differences are revealed and explained. A better understanding of why gender inequality persists in different countries will enable us to move towards more substantive equality.

Universalist language of human rights continues to be important in the international arena to ensure that the dignity of both men and women are being respected and their access to the public sphere is not prevented by hiding behind tradition. Yet, this universalist language needs to be combined with sensitivity to cultural differences, to ensure that human rights, among them GE, do not become an instance of Western imperialism. Western feminism, as postcolonial writers (Mohanty, 1984; Spivak, 1988) have shown, has not always been aware of its privilege. Attention to and respect for local histories and traditions is vital for successful implementation of GE. The politics of location, to use the much cited phrase from Adrienne Rich (1986), has never been more important than today. GE norms can be adapted to the local circumstances without compromising with the core aims of GE: participation of women in public life outside of the home, their bodily integrity and freedom to choose to realize themselves in different spheres of life. Culture cannot be used as an excuse for violations against basic human rights.

We need more comparative localized analyses like the present one for the universalist international language of human rights to be combined successfully with local sensitivity, without allowing the entrenched traditions to hinder women's rights (as they all too often do now). The tensional analysis proposed by Patrice Buzzanell (Chapter 12 in this volume) should lead scholars to a more nuanced understanding of GE policies and practices and guide activists as well as politicians in more informed and more effective decision-making.

References

Mohanty, C.T. (1984). Under Western eyes: Feminist scholarship and colonial discourses. *Boundary 2*, **12** (3), 333–358.

Rich, A. (1986). *Blood Bread and Poetry, Selected Prose, 1979–1985*. New York: Norton & Co.

Spivak, G.C. (1988). Can the subaltern speak? In C. Nelson & L. Grossberg (Eds), *Marxism and the Interpretation of Culture*, London: Macmillan, pp. 271–313.

World Economic Forum. (2015). The global gender gap report 2015. Retrieved from http://reports.weforum.org/global-gender-gap-report-2015/ (accessed 13 August 2016).

Index

Page numbers in *italics* refer to figures and tables.

Printed in the United States
by Baker & Taylor Publisher Services